THE IMPACT OF IDEAS ON LEGAL DEVELOPMENT

This book explores the intellectual contexts in which the development of tort law took place in Europe. With contributions from legal theorists, social and intellectual historians and comparative lawyers, it examines how conceptions of community and responsibility have changed over time, providing a context both for new notions of the role of the state in protecting its citizens and for new interpretations of older private law concepts. The book also examines how the law of tort was shaped and applied by judges in the codified and uncodified systems, comparing the common law system of England with the systems in France and Germany, whose codes were created in very different contexts. The book includes chapters that look at the role of experts in shaping the law's response to workplace hazards and concludes with a discussion of the role of academic networks in developing the notion of a European private law.

MICHAEL LOBBAN is Professor of Legal History at Queen Mary, University of London, where his research interests lie in the fields of English legal history and the history of jurisprudence.

JULIA MOSES is a Lecturer in Modern History at the University of Sheffield, where her research focuses on the intersection of social policy, the law and transnational connections in nineteenth- and early twentieth-century Britain and Europe.

COMPARATIVE STUDIES IN THE DEVELOPMENT OF THE LAW OF TORTS IN EUROPE

Series editors
John Bell and David Ibbetson

THE IMPACT OF IDEAS ON LEGAL DEVELOPMENT

Edited by

MICHAEL LOBBAN

and

JULIA MOSES

Comparative Studies in the Development of the Law of Torts in Europe

VOLUME 7

CAMBRIDGE
UNIVERSITY PRESS

CAMBRIDGE
UNIVERSITY PRESS

University Printing House, Cambridge CB2 8BS, United Kingdom

Cambridge University Press is part of the University of Cambridge.

It furthers the University's mission by disseminating knowledge in the pursuit of education, learning and research at the highest international levels of excellence.

www.cambridge.org
Information on this title: www.cambridge.org/9781107023116

First published 2012
First paperback edition 2014

A catalogue record for this publication is available from the British Library

Library of Congress Cataloguing in Publication data
Lobban, Michael.
The impact of ideas on legal development / Michael Lobban, Julia Moses.
p. cm. – (Comparative studies in the development of the law of torts in Europe ; 7)
Includes index.
ISBN 978-1-107-02711-4 (hardback)
1. Law – Philosophy – Europe. 2. Law – Europe – History.
I. Moses, Julia, 1979– II. Title.
KJC450.L63 2012
340′.1094–dc23 2012007316

ISBN 978-1-107-02711-4 Hardback
ISBN 978-1-107-47560-1 Paperback

Hardback only available as
ISBN 978-1-107-02311-6 3-volume set

CONTENTS

SERIES EDITORS' PREFACE

The European Legal Development series has arisen from a project funded by the Arts and Humanities Research Council from January 2005 until February 2008.

The aim of the project as a whole was to examine the nature of legal development in western Europe since 1850, focusing sharply on liability for fault. Behind this there is a more abstract purpose: to attempt to cast some light on the factors that have influenced the way in which the law has changed over this period. Legal historians have looked at the general question, usually focusing on the rather facile distinction between the English common law and continental European legal systems. Though rooted in the sources, these works have been marred by a somewhat unsophisticated methodology and an inevitably selective use of evidence. Comparative lawyers have developed far more sophisticated methodologies, but their theoretical perspectives have too often borne little relation to empirical data. Over the last twenty years, tort lawyers have looked at the same types of question; but their analysis has invariably been at a high level of generality and has rarely looked at the historical component. By bringing together experts with different disciplinary backgrounds – comparative lawyers and legal historians, all with an understanding of modern tort law in their own systems – and getting them to work collaboratively, we have aimed to produce a more nuanced comparative legal history, and one that is theoretically better informed.

The topic of legal development is broad, so, to make it manageable, we have undertaken a programme of work that has built up from a number of case studies and has moved towards a more general analysis and conclusions. Although we have been concerned with the development of the law, and although many of those involved in the project have been lawyers, we have also been concerned to include and benefit from the insights of historians and scholars in other disciplines.

Liability for fault between 1850 to 2000 has been our major area of study. Around 1850 there were many similarities in approaches to liability for fault across the legal systems of western Europe. Since then, however, there has been significant divergence. Our method has been first to chart the changes and then to seek the explanations for what happened. Although there have been many changes in tort and delict laws over the period, the idea of liability for fault remains central to private law approaches to the compensation of victims of harms caused by the actions of others.

As a first stage, the project worked on six case studies, which illustrate the general theme of liability for fault and its development within the period:

- product liability
- legal doctrine
- medical liability
- relations between neighbours
- technological change
- traffic and railways

Each of the topics gave rise to a volume published by Cambridge University Press in 2010. This research involved scholars from a range of countries, in particular England and Scotland, Spain, the Netherlands, Germany, France, Sweden, Austria and Italy. Each working group drew on the expertise of scholars, both senior and more junior, familiar with different European legal systems, and contained a mixture of comparative lawyers and legal historians.

A second stage has involved further groups examining a number of salient factors in legal development. The topics covered in this stage are:

- social and political ideas
- institutions and professions
- the economy (including the impact of insurance)

A final strand to the work is an overview book.

This book, edited by Michael Lobban and Julia Moses, is the first of the second stage reviews of factors that influence legal development. In the study of the impact of ideas, we begin to see how far the law is influenced by the general intellectual and social climate within which the law operates. We are grateful to them and to their multinational team for reflecting deeply on the issues involved in this relationship.

John Bell
David Ibbetson

1

Introduction

MICHAEL LOBBAN AND JULIA MOSES

This volume is concerned with the influence of ideas on the development of the law of torts in Europe between 1850 and 2000. It seeks to provide an intellectual context in which the developments described in the earlier volumes in this series took place. Like the other contributions to this series, this volume focuses on a number of illustrative national case studies, including England, France and Germany, in order to illuminate the factors that have influenced the way in which law develops in modern legal systems. It also stresses, however, the international connections, between social theorists, jurists and states, as well as within empires, that have characterised the development of tort law during this period.

Tort was not a particularly significant area of law in most jurisdictions at the start of the nineteenth century. Its importance grew during that century, as urbanisation and industrialisation created an ever-expanding range of risks of accidental damage. In this context, tort lawyers needed to adapt their law to new social problems. In doing so, they often moulded existing doctrine in a creative way in order to offer new remedies for new situations, adapting old legal ideas to new contexts. *Internal* doctrinal developments were, therefore, a vital motor of legal change. At the same time, even if judges and jurists in many jurisdictions seemed to speak only the language of doctrine, they were often strongly influenced by influences *external* to the law. Such influences could include wider social and political views about where liability should lie, as well as more practical considerations, such as the presence of insurance.

While legal doctrine developed, so other bodies of law began to evolve beyond the sphere of private law. The prevailing ideological mood in the middle of the nineteenth century, which was so closely associated with leaving social interaction to be regulated primarily by private law – individualism and laissez-faire – came under increasing attack later in the century from a variety of forces, including the growth of new collectivist ideas and pressure from organised working-class movements. In this context, politicians on both the left and the right turned to greater state intervention. The state now began to pass legislation to promote social welfare, creating special regimes of regulations and rules that would operate outside the sphere of traditional tort law. The growth of the state also saw the growth of experts, within and without government, who could identify or define new social problems, and suggest solutions. These new forms of regulation operated alongside, and, at times, in conjunction with, tort law. They also emerged at a time when tort was increasingly becoming a matter for international emulation, cooperation and standardisation.

1.1 Starting points

Let us begin with the question of how tort law was defined. In this volume, we focus in particular on three systems: France, Germany and England. At first glance, there are significant differences in the manner in which they came to define their law. France enacted a *Code civil* in 1804 while it was still a predominantly agrarian, and pre-industrial, country. Germany's *Bürgerliches Gesetzbuch* – which was much longer in the making than the French code – came into force in 1900, at a time when that country had already become a leading industrial power. By contrast, England never codified its law of tort. Although it was the earliest to industrialise and urbanise, it was not until the later nineteenth century that private treatise writers began to develop coherent theories of the law of tort, and not until the early twentieth century that the courts adopted the kind of generalised fault principle that lay behind much Continental thought. Three of our contributions, by Jean-Louis Halpérin, Nils Jansen and Alexandra Braun (Chapters 8, 9 and 10, respectively), consider the issues of the creation (or non-creation) of codes, and how judges reasoned within the code.

The *Code civil* was the final achievement of the French Revolution. It was the product of a political philosophy (embodied in the Declaration of the Rights of Man) that all individuals were free and equal and that legislative power belonged to the nation, united by a form of social contract into a single entity. Although this was a philosophy that allowed the state to recast the law, it was nevertheless not one of a strong interventionist state. The drafters did not seek to create all law from scratch but, rather, used the learning of the natural lawyers to draw together much of existing French law into a coherent whole.[1]

[1] On the making of the code, see J.-L. Halpérin, *L'impossible Code civil* (Paris: Presses universitaires de France, 1992). See also J.-É.-M. Portalis, 'Discours préliminaire prononcé

The natural lawyers of the seventeenth and eighteenth centuries had reformulated the Roman law of delict around the concept of fault. For Samuel von Pufendorf, harms were to be imputed only to those who had acted intentionally or negligently, since moral actions could be attributed only to those with the power and ability to perform them.[2] In his view, there was no reason to hold a man liable for an accident he had physically caused, if he had not been the moral cause of it.[3] Pufendorf's approach was taken up by the French jurist Jean Domat:

> All the losses, and all the damages which may happen by the act of any Person, whether out of Imprudence, Rashness, Ignorance of what one ought to know, or other Faults of the like Nature, however trivial they may be, ought to be repaired by him whose Imprudence, or other Fault, has given Occasion to it.[4]

Robert-Joseph Pothier distinguished between delicts ('when a person by fraud or malignity causes any damage or wrong to another') and quasi-delicts (when 'a person causes damages to another, without malignity, but by some inexcusable imprudence'),[5] but also left no conceptual space for strict liabilities.

Domat's formulation was particularly influential on the formulation of the first two general provisions of the *Code civil* dealing with delicts – articles 1382 and 1383.[6] Although this seemed to put fault at the heart

lors de la présentation du Projet de la Commission du Gouvernement,' in P.-A. Fenet (ed.), *Recueil complet des travaux préparatoires du Code civil* (15 vols.), vol. I (Paris: Ducessois, 1827), p. 467, quoted by J. Gordley, 'Myths of the French civil code' (1994) 42 *Am. J. Comp. L.* 459 ff., 460.

2 S. von Pufendorf, *Of the Law of Nature and Nations*, trans. B. Kennett, 2nd edn (Oxford: A. & J. Churchill *et al.*, 1710), book 1, pp. 37–8 (ch. 5, sect. 5). For Pufendorf's role, see N. Jansen, 'Duties and rights in negligence: a comparative and historical perspective on the European law of extracontractual liability' (2004) 24 *Oxford Journal of Legal Studies* 443 ff., 458–60; and D. Ibbetson, 'Harmonisation of the law of tort and delict: a comparative and historical perspective', in R. Zimmermann (ed.), *Grundstrukturen des Europäischen Deliktsrechts* (Baden-Baden: Nomos, 2003), pp. 83 ff.

3 Contrast C. Thomasius, *Larva Legis Aquiliae: The Mask of the Lex Aquilia Torn Off, the Action for Damage Done: A Legal Treatise*, trans. M. Hewett (Oxford: Hart, 2000).

4 J. Domat, *The Civil Law in Its Natural Order*, trans. W. Strahan (2 vols.), vol. I (London: E. Bell *et al.*, 1722), book 2, p. 326 (ch. 8, sect. 4, para. 1). According to E. Descheemaeker, *The Division of Wrongs: A Historical Comparative Study* (Oxford University Press, 2009), p. 143, Domat was the first noteworthy French writer to use the word *faute*.

5 R.-J. Pothier, *A Treatise on the Law of Obligations or Contracts*, trans. W. D. Evans (2 vols.), vol. I (London: J. Butterworth, 1806), pp. 70–1 (sect. 116).

6 Article 1382: 'Every act which causes damage to another obliges him, by whose fault it happened, to make reparation.' Article 1383: 'Everyone is liable for the damage he has caused, not only by his act, but also by his negligence or imprudence.'

of the conception of delict, the code itself was not unambiguous, for the three following clauses (which completed the treatment of delictual liability) did not mention fault: article 1384 was on vicarious liability, article 1385 on liability for animals and article 1386 on liability for buildings. Moreover, the *travaux préparatoires* reveal that the makers of the *Code civil* had been far from having a settled view of how to formulate the principle of liability; indeed, the early draft by Jean-Jacques-Régis de Cambacérès made no mention of fault, stating only: 'He who causes loss is bound to repair it, whatever the event which caused it.'[7] When the draft of the code was presented to the *corps législatif*, however, it had become clear that all the provisions were to be interpreted in light of the fault-based principle of articles 1382–3, derived from Domat and Pothier. Early nineteenth-century commentators duly took this approach.[8]

In the French system, the code was supposed to be the definitive statement of the law, which the judges were strictly bound to apply. Applying the early principles of the Revolution, the *Code civil* in effect adopted the view of Montesquieu, that judges should be 'the mouth that pronounces the words of the law, mere passive beings incapable of moderating either its force or rigour'.[9] In taking this view, the revolutionary legislators reacted against the powerful eighteenth-century *parlements*, which were perceived to have too much discretionary power to make rules. To curb the power of the judiciary, the judges were to follow the code, and to refer any question of doubt to the legislature. They were not to bind themselves to precedents or rules of their own making; only legislation could determine the outcome of a case.[10]

7 See, further, Descheemaeker, *The Division of Wrongs*, ch. 5.

8 Thus, Charles-Bonaventure-Marie Toullier said that a person was to be held liable for harms caused by things under his care, because the law presumed negligence or a failure to control on his part. An owner was liable for the harms done by his animals, since he who had the property had the power to control it. In his view, others' actions were to be imputed to us when we concurred in them, or when we could and should have prevented them or directed them. C.-B.-M. Toullier, *Le Droit civil français suivant l'ordre du Code* (13 vols.), 4th edn, vol. XI (Paris: Warée, 1828), p. 138 (sect. 115), pp. 415–16 (sect. 306), pp. 322–3 (sect. 230).

9 C. de Secondat, Baron de Montesquieu, *The Spirit of Laws*, trans. T. Nugent (2 vols.), 3rd edn, vol. I (London: J. Nourse and P. Vaillant, 1758), book 11, p. 226 (ch. 6). The Law on Judicial Organisation of 1790 had declared that courts were not permitted directly or indirectly to take any part in the exercise of legislative power. Article 5 of the code added that 'it is forbidden for judges to pronounce by way of general and regulatory provisions on the cases which are submitted to them'. At the same time, article 4 stated that the judge who refused to judge, under a pretext of the silence, obscurity or insufficiency of the law, should be prosecuted for denial of justice.

10 See E. A. Tomlinson, 'Tort liability in France for the act of things: a study in judicial law-making' (1988) 48 *Louisiana Law Review* 1299 ff., 1303.

Consequently, for much of the nineteenth century, judges and treatise writers both regarded the code as a complete system, which should be elaborated in a syllogistic way. The dominant form of treatise literature – practised by the 'exegetical school' – was formalist. The writers who produced commentaries on the code regarded it as complete. Any case could be resolved by a correct interpretation of the code. If a case could not be resolved by a simple grammatical interpretation of the text, then the interpreter was to make a 'logical' interpretation, by drawing analogies from other parts of the code, or make a 'historical' interpretation, looking at the purposes behind the text.[11]

In interpreting the *Code civil*, the early writers of the exegetical school referred back to the natural lawyers whose works had so informed the code, and also discussed Roman law doctrines. Nevertheless, they did not make reference to social or political matters, nor did they seek to look outside the words of the code. They did develop a highly individualistic view, however, seeing property in terms of the will of the proprietor, seeing contractual obligations as products of the united wills of the parties and seeing tort as reflecting liability for fault. If the code was an enactment of the state, so that all law was related to this positive root, French writers of the early nineteenth century regarded private law as largely autonomous: the rules that governed interactions in civil society, as opposed to the public law concerned with the state.[12] Reflecting its natural law heritage, the code saw private law not as a matter of social engineering but as a means to empower individuals to conduct their own affairs.

The notion that private law was a sphere autonomous of the state was held even more powerfully in Germany. As in France, the legacy of the French Revolution was to undermine a society of estates and allow the growth of a modern civil society, based on equality of citizenship. But the Napoleonic and post-Napoleonic eras did not see the birth of a single code across the German states. At the end of the Napoleonic Wars a number of different legal systems existed in Germany. Besides the four codes – the *Allgemeines Bürgerliches Gesetzbuch* (ABGB) in Austrian lands, the *Allgemeines Landrecht* (ALR) in Prussia, the *Codex Maximilianus Bavaricus* (CMB) in Bavaria and the *Code civil* in the Rhineland – there was also the German 'common law', based on Roman law. In this context, Anton Friedrich Justus Thibaut argued in favour of

[11] See Tomlinson, 'Tort liability in France', 1305–7.

[12] See H. S. Jones, *The French State in Question: Public Law and Political Argument in the Third Republic* (Cambridge University Press, 1993), p. 19.

a new code for Germany, in the style of the French code. Thibaut felt that German private law was in a state of chaos, and that it needed reform. It should be simple, it should be easily accessible and it should be the sole point of reference for judges, who would use only logical or grammatical interpretations. Thibaut's call famously elicited a sharp response from Friedrich Carl von Savigny, who denied that Germany was ready for a code.

Savigny's vision would prove highly influential on subsequent German legal scholarship. Like his mentor, Gustav Hugo, he rejected the deductivism of eighteenth-century German natural lawyers, such as Gottfried Leibniz and Christian Wolff, who had looked at private law as a manifestation of abstract reason. For Savigny, the subject of study was not to be an abstract or ideal form of law; rather, it was to be the existing positive law. As Savigny saw it, the law in Germany did not reflect a universal natural law. Instead, the source of law lay in the spirit of the people, in its *Volksgeist*. In his view, positive law originated in the custom of the people, and lived in the general consciousness of the people. Over time, however, it became the special preserve of jurists, whose expertise allowed them to understand and develop it.[13] By imparting a new scientific form on the material, jurists could both describe the law that existed and develop it. In this vision, private law was the preserve of the scientific jurist: it was taught in scientific universities, in which the core curriculum was to be the *ius commune*, rather than the local law. Scientific judges educated in these schools would then become the guardians of private law. Savigny was highly sceptical of the ability of legislators to understand these complexities, and he felt that, in the divided Germany in which he lived, the development of private law should not be left to the arbitrary lawmaking of different states. Although Savigny's school stressed the need to look at the positive law as developed in history, his was not a sociological approach. Rather, the historical law that he and other 'Pandectists'[14] examined was Roman law, which Savigny argued had a continuous history that needed to be recovered by the jurist.

By the middle of the nineteenth century hostility to the notion of codification had begun to wane in Germany. There were increasing calls

[13] F. C. von Savigny, *System des heutigen Römischen Rechts* (8 vols.), vol. I [1840] (Berlin: Veit, 1940), pp. 13–18 (sect. 7), pp. 45–9 (sect. 14).

[14] The aims of the nineteenth-century German legal scholars known as the Pandectists were to distil concepts from the Digest (or 'Pandects') of Justinian, to put them into a systematic form and to use these concepts to build a modern system of law. See M. Reimann, 'Nineteenth-century German legal science' (1990) 31 *Boston College Law Review* 842 ff.

for the law to be put into a code, albeit one that would be premised on the original theory of the historical school and that would build on that school's work. The proposal for codification now obtained support from conservatives who had previously been sceptical. They dropped Savigny's hostility to codification,[15] perceiving that a code that had been thoroughly prepared and that reflected existing legal science would head off radical demands for a transformation of the German state system. By the 1850s the only obstacle to the creation of a national code came from Prussia, which sought to forestall any moves that might weaken its own influence in the movement towards unification.[16] Until 1867 the debate over codification was complicated by the wider political debates over the nature of German unification; but once the question of German unification had been resolved, and Prussian dominance had been secured, the way was open for a code. Codification of the law would contribute to the creation of a nation state, with a national identity. It also represented the cementing of a notion that all law derived from the legislator, expressing the national will.

The code was not, however, seen to be the instrument of social legislation or reform. By 1873 it had been settled that the code would be a systematic compilation of the law of the German states, using the method of the Pandectist scholars, and following the settled doctrines and principles found in common law and juristic works. Savigny's student Bernhard Windscheid may have resigned from the first commission in 1883, but his was perhaps the most decisive influence in shaping the code, seeking formal precision and systematic rigour. The codifying commission was dominated by lawyers who felt that new law was developed by jurists through the study of existing legal concepts, which suggested that law developed independently of social changes. The code would be a coherent statement of juridical science. Legislation addressing particular social concerns would proceed outside the code.

[15] Although he was hostile to the project of codification, Savigny played a major role in the Prussian legislation of 1838, which established a no-fault liability for railway accidents. See S. Lohsse, 'The development of traffic liability in Germany', in W. Ernst (ed.), *The Development of Traffic Liability* (Cambridge University Press, 2010), pp. 75 ff., pp. 82–92; and J. Scherpe, 'Technological change and the development of liability for fault in Germany', in M. Martin-Casals (ed.), *The Development of Liability in Relation to Technological Change* (Cambridge University Press, 2010), pp. 134 ff., pp. 160–70.

[16] M. John, *Politics and the Law in Late Nineteenth-Century Germany* (Oxford: Clarendon Press, 1989), pp. 23–41. See also A. J. Kanning, 'The emergence of a European private law: lessons from nineteenth-century Germany' (2007) 27 *Oxford Journal of Legal Studies* 193 ff.

The vision of law produced by the Pandectists, and reflected in the code, was an individualistic one. As Georg Friedrich Puchta put it, private law was concerned with 'the individual's full and unconditional sovereignty'.[17] For Windscheid, '[t]he law creates for every will an arena within which it is dominant and from which alien wills recoil. Law is, in the first place, not a restriction but a recognition of human freedom. The restrictive element is merely the other side of freedom thus guaranteed.'[18] Private law was seen to be the framework set up and enforced by the state, within which private individuals exercised their autonomy. The Pandectist vision was therefore wedded to a strong notion of freedom of contract and private property rights. It was the unimpeded freedom of individual wills that was seen to lie at the root of the law of obligations. In the area of tort, fault became central to the notion of liability.

The unified German code, the *Bürgerliches Gesetzbuch* (BGB), may not have been enacted until 1900, but it owed its character to decisions taken in the 1870s, and to a legal science developed earlier. By the time the first draft appeared, in 1888, the German Chancellor, Otto von Bismarck, had already commenced his programme of social reform, which was created, in part, to draw the potential sting from socialism. The draft code came in for strong criticism, notably from Otto von Gierke. Rather than being a neutral expression of principles, he saw the draft as pro-capitalist and hostile to the community – and wholly out of step with the German legal tradition as well as with recent social legislation. Gierke sought to uncover the historical roots of German law and criticised the draft code for overemphasising Roman law, which he saw embodied in the draft's individualism and its strong division between public and private law. It was the association, he said, rather than the individual that was the key form of modern life. For Gierke, there were social obligations that could limit the exercise of individual rights. He attacked the idea that there could be a pure, abstract, individualistic private law, which ignored the social needs of the people. He therefore criticised the exclusivity of the fault principle (given classic formulation by Rudolf von Jhering in his Pandectist mood), since it disregarded the social function of private law. Social justice, in Gierke's view, demanded strict liability for employers or for dangerous activities.[19]

[17] Quoted by H.-P. Haferkamp, 'The science of private law and the state in nineteenth-century Germany' (2008) 56 *Am. J. Comp. L.* 667 ff., 670.

[18] Quoted by John, *Politics and the Law*, p. 86.

[19] I. Englard, 'Victor Mataja's *Liability for Damages from an Economic Viewpoint*: a centennial to an ignored economic analysis of tort' (1990) 10 *International Review of Law and Economics* 173 ff., 177.

Although the 1888 draft generated enormous debate in Germany, the subsequent discussions had very little effect on the final shape of the BGB. Men such as Gierke wanted the code to be an articulation of a set of ideological values reflecting Christian traditions that they believed were inherent to German culture. However, the codifiers had a less all-encompassing vision. The code would not be a statement of the whole legal order; it would be a statement of the basic rules of private law. Special interests would be dealt with separately. Given the wealth of private law scholarship that had grown up in the nineteenth century, the commissioners were able to consider in more detail the kinds of liability that should be included and those that should not. The BGB was, accordingly, much fuller than the *Code civil*, containing thirty-one articles on tort. Moreover, although the first draft had contained a general clause analogous to article 1382, the final version was more casuistic, setting out three general clauses and a number of more detailed ones, each of which could be applied to different cases.

In contrast to the German and French systems, England never codified its law of tort. As Alexandra Braun shows (Chapter 10), there were many debates in nineteenth-century England over codification, notably of the criminal law, with reformers seeking to create an accessible, simple and complete code. The movement failed, though there were some areas of commercial law that were codified in the later nineteenth and early twentieth centuries. These reforms were not the result of a wholesale recasting of the common law (such as was desired by Jeremy Bentham) but were, rather, the result of private initiatives by treatise writers who put the rules of the common law into a coherent, digested form. Moreover, these were areas in which the law was relatively settled, making it easier to digest the rules. By contrast, the law of torts remained very unsettled in the second half of the nineteenth century, which made projects to codify this area of law all the more difficult.[20] English thinking about tort was dominated, at least into the middle of the nineteenth century, by the structures imposed by the forms of action used in common law procedure. It was only in the aftermath of the mid-century reforms of procedure that writers such as Sir Frederick Pollock (in England) and Oliver Wendell Holmes (in the United States) began to look for broader principles around which to organise the law of tort. Even then, the English law of tort continued to be driven by the courts rather than by academic jurists, who had far less influence than

[20] Frederick Pollock did draft a code of tort law for India, while writing the first edition of his textbook on torts, but it was never enacted.

their German counterparts.[21] The common law was, and remained, the custom of the judges of the superior courts: it developed in a casuistic way, through their case law reasoning.

Treatise writers such as Pollock aimed to order the material found in these decisions in a coherent and systematic way, which would reveal the true foundational principles of the common law. At a time of increasing legislative intervention in social policy, they therefore turned away from writing textbooks designed to cover both the statutory and common law rules regulating particular activities to write general books focused on the common law. In some ways, their ambition reflected that of the German Pandectists: to create a formal, logical system of rules, teased out of the historical material of the common law – a law that reflected the culture and history of the English people, and that would not be infected by legislation.

The common lawyers' suspicion of legislation helps explain the considerable resistance put up by judges and jurists to projects of codification in the late nineteenth century. Those who were hostile to codification did not tire of pointing out that the common law was a developing body, which progressed with the growth of the nation. It was feared that, once these principles of common law had been cast in the form of a statute, emanating from a sovereign parliament, they would ossify. Moreover, as soon as private law became statutory in form, it would have to be treated simply as another form of legislation. Keeping the law uncodified was one way of keeping it private. This attitude contrasted with the Continental understanding of codification. Although French and German codifiers undoubtedly saw their codes as positive law emanating from the will of the state, they also regarded them essentially as statements of private law – the area that was not a matter for state interference or regulation.

Nonetheless, they struggled to find a coherent set of principles to explain English case law. Whereas the ordering of private law in France and Germany (and its codification) could build on an extensive academic literature, which was the product of a marriage of Roman law learning and medieval and early modern philosophy, English academic legal

[21] In the era of Savigny, law professors were expected to develop doctrine that would be applied by the judges (who until the middle of the nineteenth century desisted from publishing the reasons for their decisions). In the later nineteenth century, however, although the legal texts were shaped by academics, the operation of the law, particularly in tort, was often driven by professional reaction to circumstances and especially to litigation. German academics did not write much about tort law in serious journals in the period up to 1920, but there was a great deal of case law; and it was this case law, rather than academic work, that was most cited in the Reichsgericht and Oberlandesgerichte.

writing was far less philosophical. Moreover, the impact of Roman law learning on English tort law was far more limited.[22] Although Pollock enthusiastically applied Savigny's will theory to contract law,[23] his views on the law of tort were influenced far more by the work of Oliver Wendell Holmes, whose admiration of German Pandectism was limited.[24] Like their Continental counterparts, nineteenth-century English lawyers placed increasing emphasis on the notion of fault, in part because of the development of the action on the case for negligence,[25] but they could not ignore the large space left within the common law for strict liabilities. The variety of torts bequeathed by English legal history meant that English jurists would continue to puzzle over whether there was a law of tort.

1.2 The turn to theory and the rise of welfarism

The codified private law of France and Germany, and the uncodified law of tort in nineteenth-century England, were all premised on individualism. Some critics, including Gierke, regarded this as 'pure Manchester doctrine'[26] – an ideology that favoured industrialism and financial gain at the expense of the working class. Some historians (particularly in the Anglo-American context) have also linked the nineteenth-century individualist approach to private law, with its association with will theory and concepts of fault, to the rise of industrialism.[27] We need to be cautious

[22] It was only in very rare cases that treatise writers resorted explicitly to the language of Roman law to analyse their own law of tort. The prime example is Sir William Jones: see D. Ibbetson (ed.), *Sir William Jones: An Essay on the Law of Bailments* (Bangor: Welsh Legal History Society, 2007). For an argument suggesting a greater civilian influence, see D. Ibbetson, 'The law of business Rome: foundations of the Anglo-American tort of negligence' (1999) 52 *Current Legal Problems* 74 ff.

[23] F. Pollock, *Principles of Contract at Law and in Equity* (London: Stevens & Sons, 1876), pp. 1–2.

[24] See W. Cornish, J. S. Anderson, R. Cocks, M. Lobban, P. Polden and K. Smith, *The Oxford History of the Laws of England*, vol. XII (Oxford University Press, 2010), pt. 4, chs. 1–2.

[25] Note, however, that the notion that there was a simple shift from an earlier strict liability to liability based on fault has been challenged by those who have shown that notions of fault had always been present in English tort law. See G. T. Schwartz, 'Tort law and the economy in nineteenth-century America: a reinterpretation' (1981) 90 *Yale Law Journal* 1717 ff.; R. J. Kaczorowski, 'The common-law background of nineteenth-century tort law' (1990) 51 *Ohio State Law Journal* 1127 ff.; and, more generally, D. Ibbetson, *Historical Introduction to the Law of Obligations* (Oxford University Press, 1999).

[26] Quoted by John, *Politics and the Law*, p. 110.

[27] See, especially, P. S. Atiyah, *The Rise and Fall of Freedom of Contract* (Oxford: Clarendon Press, 1979); and M. J. Horwitz, *The Transformation of American Law, 1780–1860* (Cambridge, MA: Harvard University Press, 1977).

in attributing to private lawyers an overtly instrumentalist view of their subject, however, particularly in countries such as France and Germany, whose private law doctrines developed largely before the impact of heavy industrialisation was felt.[28] The individualism of the codes may be attributed more easily to their philosophical backgrounds and to the Roman law jurisprudence on which they built. Nonetheless, once the social effects of industrialism had become felt throughout western Europe, by the last third of the nineteenth century, the individualist premises on which these systems of private law were based were beginning to be challenged by policy and ideas alike.

The first steps away from the mid-century individualism took the form of legislation responding in a pragmatic way to problems associated with industrialism and urbanism. Regulatory legislation served to diminish the autonomous working of private law in a number of ways. First, regulatory legislation was passed to prevent harms occurring in the first place. For instance, Britain saw a series of Factory Acts regulating both health and safety at work and employment conditions for women and children.[29] Public transport, and especially the railways, were subject to regulations to reduce the risk of accidents.[30] Questions of pollution were also increasingly addressed through statute.[31] Regulatory legislation was often long in coming, however, and relatively ineffective when it arrived.[32] Second, special statutory regimes were created imposing strict liabilities. In Germany, a series of statutes, dating back to the 1838 Railway Act in Prussia, imposed a strict liability for harms caused by railways, by automobiles (in 1909) and by aircraft (in 1936). Strict liabilities were also imposed on employers to provide compensation for workers injured

[28] See J. Gordley, 'Disturbances among neighbours: an introduction', in J. Gordley (ed.), *The Development of Liability between Neighbours* (Cambridge University Press, 2010), pp. 1 ff.

[29] For a discussion of the statutes, which were often ineffective in preventing harms, see P. W. J. Bartrip and S. Burman, *The Wounded Soldiers of Industry: Industrial Compensation Policy, 1833–1897* (Oxford: Clarendon Press, 1983); and W. Cornish, J. S. Anderson, R. Cocks, M. Lobban, P. Polden and K. Smith, *The Oxford History of the Laws of England*, vol. XIII (Oxford University Press, 2010), pp. 558–79.

[30] See H. Parris, *Government and the Railways in the Nineteenth Century* (London: Routledge & Kegan Paul, 1965).

[31] See P. Giliker, 'Relationships between neighbours: England and Wales 1850–2000', in Gordley, *The Development of Liability between Neighbours*, pp. 29 ff.; and Cornish *et al.*, *Oxford History*, vol. XII, pp. 1068–111, vol. XIII, pp. 535–57.

[32] See J. Morgan, 'Technological change and the development of liability for fault in England and Wales', in Martin-Casals, *The Development of Liability in Relation to Technological Change*, pp. 40 ff., pp. 58–64, on legislation relating to exploding boilers.

in industrial accidents, by legislation passed at the end of the century in Germany (1884), Britain (1897) and France (1898).[33]

Such legislation has often been seen as having resulted from the identification of new problems (and possible solutions). The emergence of new professionals, such as statisticians and psychiatrists, paralleled the professionalisation of legal education and the increasing specialisation in private law over the course of the nineteenth and twentieth centuries. Expert opinion, either in the courtroom or in government, became more and more important for legitimating decisions about the potential dangers related to urbanisation and industrialisation.[34] However, as the chapters by Peter Bartrip and Paul-André Rosental (11 and 12, respectively) show, the process of obtaining official recognition of dangers, whether at the workplace or in the market, was complex. Experts advising the state played some role in this, but it also took social pressure from interest groups, and negotiation between interested parties, to force governments to take note of new dangers.[35]

These debates and changes took place at a time when traditional ideas about the role of government and the nature of society were being rethought. In the new industrial and urban age, in which the working classes were obtaining an ever stronger political voice, social and philosophical theorists began to rethink the nature of law, both as a means to nurture social solidarity and as a technique of government. There was an increasing focus on social science, looking at society as a whole. Developments in social theory are explored in this volume in the chapters by Roger Cotterrell, Sandra den Otter and Jose Harris (2, 3 and 4, respectively). As Cotterrell shows, the middle of the nineteenth century saw the rise of the new science of sociology. Auguste Comte developed

[33] On Germany, see Scherpe, 'Technological change...in Germany'; on France, see Y. Salmon, 'Technological change and the development of liability for fault in France', in Martin-Casals, *The Development of Liability in Relation to Technological Change*, pp. 89 ff., pp. 115–17.

[34] On the increasing importance of specialist knowledge during this period, see L. Raphael, 'Die Verwissenschaftlichung des Sozialen als methodische und konzeptionelle Herausforderung für eine Sozialgeschichte des 20. Jahrhunderts' (1996) 22 *Geschichte und Gesellschaft* 165 ff.

[35] In this world, litigation under tort law proved a useful supplement to political pressure, and the testimony of experts could play a critical, if contentious, role. Although specialists seemed to endow programmes for regulation or the decisions in court cases with scientific objectivity, the methods and personal biases of individual experts could come under attack. See, for example, S. Jasanoff, *Science at the Bar: Law, Science and Technology in America* (Cambridge, MA: Harvard University Press, 1997); and P. W. Huber, *Galileo's Revenge: Junk Science in the Courtroom* (New York: Basic Books, 1993).

a 'positivist' sociology, which sought to uncover the empirical laws of society and reveal the mechanisms of the social order, in works that were influential not only in France but in England as well. Other writers in the second half of the nineteenth century were also interested in theories of how societies evolved and developed. They turned their attention away from philosophy and towards the empirical study of the development of societies. Rather than seeing law in formalistic or abstract terms, centred on the free individual, thinkers now looked at the function of law in society, as an instrument of unity or as reflecting the needs of the people. This sociological turn was taken up in juristic circles, by writers such as Sir Henry Maine in England and Rudolf von Jhering in Germany.

In the field of social theory, the sociological turn led to more thinking about social solidarity. Later nineteenth-century social theorists sought to explain the role of law in maintaining complex modern industrial societies. On the one hand, some German theorists (such as Max Weber) took the view that modern societies needed a formally rational law in order to create a framework of rules to coordinate social interaction. As Ferdinand Tönnies saw it, modern society was a kind of *Gesellschaft* (society) that needed law – most prominently, the law of contract – to hold it together, because it was no longer sufficiently governed by the bonds of a traditional *Gemeinschaft* (community). On the other hand, the later work of the French theorist Émile Durkheim moved away from seeing law as a mechanism for efficient government in a society marked by the division of labour. Instead, Durkheim came to argue that there was a moral order that underpinned society. Durkheim's theory was rich and complex, putting at its heart a 'cult of the individual' that also required active democratic participation to discover the unity of thought among a people.[36] Durkheim's work had a direct influence on French jurists such as Léon Duguit and Emmanuel Levy,[37] and there is to be found in late nineteenth- and early twentieth-century French thought a continuous theme of social solidarity, which defined social rights and responsibilities. By contrast, German thought was more divided between the formal rationalism of Weber and a nostalgia for earlier forms of community found in the work of the sociologist Tönnies and the historicist legal scholar Gierke.

[36] See R. Cotterrell, *Émile Durkheim: Law in a Moral Domain* (Edinburgh University Press, 1999).

[37] See R. Cotterrell, *Living Law: Studies in Legal and Social Theory* (Aldershot: Ashgate, 2008), ch. 6.

In England, as den Otter shows, the late nineteenth century also saw a turn to collectivism. As she demonstrates, care needs to be taken not to attribute a crude form of individualism to mid-Victorian thinkers, such as John Stuart Mill. Writing in the era of the growth of sociology and evolutionary theory, Mill was very aware of the need for the individual to be mindful of others; indeed, his version of utilitarianism was premised on the existence of 'a powerful natural sentiment' that recognised general happiness as an ethical standard.[38] Mill's example (and, more strikingly, Herbert Spencer's) might be taken to show that one could readily accept the need for altruism without seeking an interventionist state. Indeed, in the sphere of corrective justice, such an approach might well justify the development of rules that broadened the scope of fault, requiring people to take greater care in their actions to foresee possible harms to others, without entailing a commitment to greater social intervention.[39] By contrast, the next generation of social thinkers – the idealist philosophers who followed T. H. Green, the broad range of philosophers and sociologists who provided intellectual ammunition for the 'new liberals', and the Fabians and early socialist thinkers – saw a far larger role for the state. In contrast to the Continental sociologists, Green and his followers built on early nineteenth-century German philosophy (notably G. W. F. Hegel) to develop the notion of society as a moral community. The state, rather than being a neutral arbiter – as the classic private lawyers saw it – was a moral entity that should facilitate each individual's (and the community's) progression to his ideal end. As den Otter shows, some theorists, such as Green, wove the common law into this philosophy, as embodying the general will of the community.

The turn of social theory to collectivism and social solidarity helped pave the intellectual way for the development of a welfare state that would operate parallel to the realm of private law. Each of our countries saw the rise of state-supported welfare in the century after 1870 that was different in nature and scale from earlier local provisions. Nevertheless, as Harris shows in her contribution, we need to be cautious before attributing too direct an influence to theory on the development of welfare policy. The idea that the poor needed to be given welfare provision was hardly new

[38] J. S. Mill, 'Utilitarianism (1863)', in J. M. Robson (ed.), *Collected Works of John Stuart Mill* (33 vols.), vol. X, *Essays on Ethics, Religion and Society* (University of Toronto Press, 1969), pp. 203 ff., p. 231.

[39] This might reflect the position of W. B. Brett, whose judgments in the 1880s helped develop a broad notion of the duty of care, but who was a conservative judge, hostile to all forms of socialism.

to the late nineteenth century – and, moreover, the way that theorists and policy-makers responded to problems of welfare was complex and varied. Indeed, the shape of social theory in France, Germany and Britain might be said to have reflected the distinct political and social cultures of these countries as much as it influenced the development of the cultures.

Nor should we overlook the fact that the history of the rise of the welfare state is not monolithic: if the European welfare states after the Second World War often looked strikingly similar, the paths they had followed to get there were varied. The immediate political motivations behind particular reforms were also varied. In Germany – the pioneer of welfarism – the rise of social democracy was an important context for the adoption of social insurance over the course of the 1880s. The conservative Chancellor, Bismarck, sought to stave off political unrest by promoting welfare policy as a hallmark of 'state socialism', which would contrast with the political socialism of the left. One of Bismarck's aims was to strengthen the German state, by making the industrial working class loyal to it. This entailed introducing public health insurance (1883), accident insurance (1884) and old-age pension insurance (1889).[40] Late nineteenth-century German theorists were hence writing in a context in which the state's intervention was already comparatively strong. The welfare system expanded during the Weimar era, with, for instance, the introduction of unemployment insurance in 1927.[41] In this era, though, the main motor for welfare reform was the Social Democratic Party, whose policies provoked a hostile reaction from conservative industrialists and further contributed to the political instability of the time. After the Second World War the new constitution, or Basic Law, proclaimed (in article 20) that the Federal Republic was a 'democratic and social federal state': democracy and social welfare were integral to the constitution.[42] Postwar West Germany was to be a market economy, but one with a

[40] In this process, Bismarck was not motivated entirely by his own ideas but, rather, reacted to the potential challenge of social democracy by usurping some of that movement's ideas. In turn, these reflected the philosophical writings of a range of theorists from the middle of the nineteenth century. See H.-U. Wehler, *Deutsche Gesellschaftsgeschichte*, vol. III, *Von der Deutschen Doppelrevolution bis zum Beginn des Ersten Weltkrieges, 1849–1914* (Munich: Beck, 1995), p. 803; O. Pflanze, *Bismarck: Der Reichskanzler* (Munich: Beck, 2008), pp. 399–434; and J. A. Moses, 'German social policy (*Sozialpolitik*) in the Weimar Republic, 1919–1933' (1982) 42 *Labour History* 83 ff.

[41] See D. F. Crew, *Germans on Welfare: From Weimar to Hitler* (New York: Oxford University Press, 1998).

[42] V. R. Berghahn, *Modern Germany: Society, Economy and Politics in the Twentieth Century* (Cambridge University Press, 1982), pp. 198–9.

strong welfarist tinge: one of the aims of the new constitution was to promote uniform living conditions throughout the country. Accordingly, postwar governments built on Bismarck's foundations, reintroducing the federal structures that had been undermined under the National Socialist government, reforming pensions in 1957 and introducing housing benefit in 1960.

In contrast to Germany, France's welfare state took longer to establish. Whereas Bismarck's aim was to forge a strong central state, the political classes of the French Third Republic, fearful of the revolutionary precedent of the Paris Commune, resisted a state-initiated system of national insurance, preferring to express social solidarity through charity or voluntary associations.[43] Although legislation was passed in 1898 to impose liability on employers for industrial accidents that were not the fault of workers, there was no wider form of social insurance. A pension law was passed in 1910, but it was effectively neutered by a judgment that contributions were not compulsory.[44] It was not until 1928 that legislation was passed providing for a national compulsory scheme for health, disability and pension insurance. As in many other countries, the end of the Second World War saw a renewed interest in building a welfare state. The wartime Resistance had advocated a comprehensive plan of social security, which would 'assure all citizens of the means of subsistence in every case where they are unable to secure them by working'.[45] In July 1945 the provisional government proposed the introduction of a system of social insurance, work disability insurance and family allowances, which would gradually be extended to provide for unemployment benefit.[46] The dominance of parties of the left at the start of the Fourth Republic ensured its passing, and the affluence of the postwar era ensured its growth.[47]

In Britain, governments from the 1870s had turned their attention increasingly to social questions, with, for instance, public health legislation in 1875 laying down minimal standards for housing. It is not until

43 See F. Ewald, *L'État providence* (Paris: Grasset, 1986).

44 H. Hatzfeld, *Du pauperisme à la Sécurité Sociale: Essai sur les origines de la Sécurité Sociale en France, 1850–1940* (Paris: Colin, 1971), pp. 134–5.

45 E. Cahm, 'The economic and social programme of the Resistance, 1944', in E. Cahm, *Politics and Society in Contemporary France (1789–1971): A Documentary History* (London: George Harrap, 1972), p. 491.

46 A. Shennan, *Rethinking France: Plans for Renewal 1940–1946* (Oxford: Clarendon Press, 1989), pp. 212–16.

47 D. R. Cameron, 'Continuity and change in French welfare policy: the welfare state under Gaullism, liberalism, socialism', in J. S. Ambler (ed.), *The French Welfare State: Surviving Social and Ideological Change* (New York University Press, 1991), pp. 58 ff.

the early twentieth century, however, that we can see the beginnings of a welfare state, with the Liberal government's introduction of old age pensions in 1908 and a National Insurance Act in 1911, which included provisions for health and unemployment insurance. The 'new liberal' reforms were undoubtedly informed by the new social theories discussed by den Otter, but they owed as much to new political pressures as to intellectual ones. These early schemes were reformed and expanded in the 1920s and 1930s, and they were replaced in 1948 by the creation of the modern welfare state, which set up a National Health Service (NHS) and reformed the system of social security benefits. This welfare state continued to grow in the following decades, with the range of benefits expanded in the 1960s. The postwar welfare state was linked to the idea that the policy of government would be to promote full employment and take a strong role in the economy, parts of which would be nationalised. By the mid-1970s, however, political parties of all stripes in Britain were admitting the impossibility of maintaining full employment; and by the 1980s the commitment to an interventionist welfare state had come under a stronger attack than was the case in France or Germany.

The effect of these reforms was to create a safety net, provided by the state. From the late nineteenth century workers injured in industrial accidents obtained statutory compensation without needing to litigate in private law. Social insurance provided a cushion for those unable or too old to find work. With the coming of the postwar welfare state, shaped in Britain by the Beveridge Report of 1942, medical costs for those who fell ill or were injured were covered by a free system of national health. Legislation on housing and planning sought to ensure decent homes for the entire population, developed in coordinated ways that served the common good. As social legislation increased, so private law moved away from being of central interest to being more marginal: state regulation, whether of the environment at large, or of workplace conditions, was designed to prevent the occurrence of harms in the first place, and to provide a remedy when harms did occur.

The relationship between private law and social legislation has always been complex. By the early twentieth century it was increasingly evident that people could suffer forms of harm, particularly at the workplace, that traditional tort law had great difficulty in recognising. If it was easy enough for courts to attribute blame when a worker was injured by a defective machine, it was rather more difficult for the layman to know which diseases were attributable to the workplace environment, and how far any particular employer was responsible for the illness of a particular worker. As Bartrip and Rosental show in their studies of expertise in Britain and France, the recognition of these diseases required the intervention of medical experts, who were often employed by the state. Their impact was initially felt not via the courtroom but through administrative and governmental bodies, which had to determine whether particular diseases should be brought within a statutory regulatory scheme. As Bartrip shows, the end of the nineteenth century saw an injection of expertise that transformed the British factory inspectorate, which hitherto could hardly be described as a body of experts. Their twentieth-century successors, who were specialists in occupational diseases, were influential both in extending the range of diseases compensated under the workmen's compensation legislation and in developing the first set of regulations (in 1931) to control the creation of asbestos dust. Further advances in medical knowledge led to more stringent regulations in the 1960s and 1980s.

These developments did not, however, displace tort law. The upsurge in tort litigation in Britain involving asbestos-related illnesses (which commenced in the 1970s and expanded in the 1990s)[48] grew out of advances in medical knowledge that had already been acted on by government, rather than driving the process of itself. Similarly, in France, the struggle to recognise occupational diseases took place largely outside the courtroom. As Rosental shows, the process here was complicated by the fact that the body charged with establishing a list of such diseases (the Commission of Industrial Hygiene) was structured in such a way as to turn the process into a trial of strength between capital and labour, rather than leaving it as a purely technical, medical one. As in Britain, the last decades of the twentieth century saw an upsurge in asbestos-related litigation, which in France had the effect of bringing occupational diseases much more into the public mind than had hitherto been the case.

1.3 New theoretical approaches to private law

The development of new collectivist ideas also had an impact on thinking about private law itself. As John Bell shows in his chapter (5), the start of the twentieth century saw the development of new jurisprudential theories of how judges should operate, which challenged the formalism that

[48] A series of decisions after the turn of the century made it easier to bring claims: see *Lubbe* v. *Cape plc* [2000] 1 WLR 1545; and *Fairchild* v. *Glenhaven Funeral Services Ltd* [2002] 1 AC 32. Procedural changes have also helped encourage litigation.

had been so dominant in the nineteenth century. Influenced by the broad social theorists we have already discussed, a range of other thinkers, including jurists, began to conceive of society increasingly as an organism. Many of these developed reform programmes, in areas such as labour law and housing. Jurists looked to the practice of particular communities, seeking law in the norms that regulated their own practices.[49] They sought to recognise intermediate interest groups between the individual and the state, and to harmonise their interests with the wider public interest. In this context, much research by legal academics focused less on doctrinal exploration of the private law codes than on studies of legislation in particular areas, or empirical research on problems to be solved.

In France, the lessons of the exegetical school were challenged, notably by François Gény and Raymond Saleilles. These writers saw that the older approach to private law – with its emphasis on individual rights – clashed with the modern social changes. The law needed to adapt to current social requirements, to forestall revolution. These writers were not socialists, and did not feel that the state should take the place of the individual. They were, however, very influenced by ideas of social solidarity.[50] Saleilles pointed out that social conditions at the turn of the twentieth century were very different from those at the turn of the nineteenth. As a consequence, the notion that the law should be concerned primarily with the free play of individual wills was insufficient. Sociology showed that, 'outside free contract, there was room for legal creations born of customary and spontaneous developments, inspired by a feeling of justice and equity, by an understanding of a closer and more complete solidarity'.[51] Saleilles also praised the German historical school for pointing to the fact that law adapted to changing social phenomena: purely formalistic views of law had to come to terms with the nature of evolution.

These writers demanded a rethinking of judicial method. In his work *Méthode d'intérpretation*, published in 1899, Gény attacked the exegetical school's view that the law in the code was complete and contained no gaps. He dismissed the notion that any apparent gaps could be closed by a process involving the induction and deduction of rationally necessary answers. Gény argued that the system was not coherent, and so lacked

[49] See G. Gurvitch, *L'Idée du droit social* (Paris: Recueil Sirey, 1932). See also A. Broderick (ed.), *The French Institutionalists: Maurice Hauriou, Georges Renard, Joseph T. Delos*, trans. M. Welling (Cambridge, MA: Harvard University Press, 1970).

[50] M.-C. Belleau, 'The "*Juristes Inquiets*": legal classicism and criticism in early twentieth-century France' (1997) *Utah Law Review* 379 ff., 384.

[51] Belleau, 'The "*Juristes Inquiets*"', 401, fn 52.

determinacy. Judges filled gaps in the law by making choices. This was not inherently negative; what was objectionable was the fact that they pretended not to do so. The exegetical school (he argued) had therefore abused its own method, by making subjective decisions appear to be objective. For Gény, it was necessary to admit that the law might be indeterminate, and to develop a method to help judges fill gaps. In his view, although judges should look primarily to the text of the code, and to doctrine and decisions, to guide their judgments, when these sources failed they needed to search for a rule on which to base the decision, using the method of 'free scientific research'. That is, the judge should base his decision on social realities, needs and values: the *nature des choses positives*. The insights of sociology and history would thus contribute to the development of the law.

At the same time that these writers were turning French legal thought to new directions, so, in Germany, jurisprudence also took a sociological turn. The 'heaven of concepts' developed by Pandectists such as Puchta had already been criticised by Jhering.[52] In his early work, Jhering had been a follower of the school of Savigny and Puchta, attempting to develop a unified theory of German law based on a systematic study of concepts. In the 1860s, though, he changed his views. Whereas beforehand he had looked for law in legal materials, produced by the community over time, which could be described and analysed in terms of their natural history, he now began to argue that law was always a purposive thing, a means to an end. This was also a more statist view: law was what the state defined as such, and it was manifested though coercion. In 1872 he argued that law was a site of struggle, in which people struggled to have their interests and feelings respected. The life of the law was one of a struggle for rights. Individuals might struggle with the existing law, if they felt it harmed their interests; the state had to react. It had to channel these separate interests – which were based on self-interest – into social purposes via coercion.

After the passing of the BGB, a number of schools took up the challenge against its formalism. The first, the free law movement of Hermann Kantorowicz and Eugen Ehrlich not only wanted to free law from the shackles of conceptualism; it also sought to give the judge a radical degree of freedom in interpreting the law. For these writers, the code contained more gaps than rules. The judge needed to fill these gaps to promote social justice: and this was done by appealing to the common sense of the

[52] R. von Jhering, 'In the heaven of legal concepts: a fantasy', trans. C. L. Levy (1985) 58 *Temple Law Quarterly* 799 ff.

people (as Kantorowicz argued) or to the 'living law' of the community (in Ehrlich's view). As Ehrlich put it, 'The great mass of law arises immediately in society itself in the form of a spontaneous ordering of social relations and most of this Social Order has never been embraced in Legal Provisions.'[53] He called for a sociological understanding of law, which rejected the idea that law was a gapless, autonomous system. For some jurists, this might entail the judge modifying, or even disobeying, a statute when occasion required.

The second, less radical, response was the 'jurisprudence of interests' school of Philipp Heck. Heck began from Jhering's argument that interests competed with each other, and that the struggles in law were struggles for the protection of different interests. However, he felt that Jhering had not gone far enough: the jurist needed to look more deeply into the interests. Heck argued that it was clear that judges had to abide by the law; but it was equally clear that the law was not gapless. When a new case arose, the judge had to consider the interests that were in conflict and examine whether the law had resolved the clash between these interests in other factual situations. When this was not possible, the judge had to examine the interests himself. Thus, Heck observed, '[i]t is from the concrete facts of reality that the framing of legal commands proceeds, and it ends by remodeling that reality through decision of cases'.[54]

The theorists we have been discussing so far all accepted that the existing codes of private law were the starting points for legal reasoning. They were not revolutionaries but sought, rather, to address social problems in order to prevent revolutionary change. In contrast, by the early twentieth century, powerful socialist parties had been organised in many countries, whose adherents sought a more profound transformation of the legal order. Socialist theories, derived from Karl Marx's broader theory, were central to the political philosophy of these political movements. Although such theories did not tend directly to address the question of law, a socialist theory of law was developed, particularly in the Soviet Union by Evgeny Pashukanis. As Christine Sypnowich shows in

[53] E. Ehrlich, 'The sociology of law' (1922) 36 *Harvard Law Review* 130 ff., 136, quoted by M. Garcia-Villegas, 'Comparative sociology of law: legal fields, legal scholarships and social sciences in Europe and the United States' (2006) 31 *Law and Social Inquiry* 343 ff., 352. On Ehrlich, see M. Hertogh (ed.), *Living Law: Reconsidering Eugen Ehrlich* (Oxford: Hart, 2008).

[54] P. Heck, 'The jurisprudence of interests', in M. M. Schoch (ed. and trans.), *The Jurisprudence of Interests* (Cambridge, MA: Harvard University Press, 1948), pp. 31 ff., 47.

her contribution, in Chapter 7, this theory argued that law was inherently an instrument of class oppression – a mystifying ideology that masked substantive unfairness – that would disappear when the means of production had passed into the hands of the people. Pashukanis's theory did not find favour in Stalinist Russia, and he himself was denounced and executed. Law did not wither away in the Soviet Union, but was used as an instrument of state power. At the same time, the state maintained codes of law to regulate the legal relations of private individuals.[55] In the West, Marxist theories that saw private law – and especially the law of tort – as giving institutional expression to selfish and exploitative interests had little impact on the development of law itself. They did, however, raise important and widely discussed questions about the very nature of law and the place of private law. Not all followed the path of a complete rejection of law. Some Western theorists, such as Karl Renner, used Marxist premises and insights to argue that the form of private law no longer reflected its function, and he suggested that socialists should seek to create legal norms that adequately reflected modern social developments.[56] Moreover, as Sypnowich shows, questions about the nature of the rule of law, and the function of a law of torts, remain the subject of significant debate for the left.

Within the common law world, instrumentalist views of law dominated much of twentieth-century American (though not English) jurisprudence. By the early twentieth century American jurists had begun to rebel against the 'formalism' that remained so powerful in England.[57] The early twentieth century saw the development of the legal Realist movement (in which Karl Llewellyn was the central figure), as well as a sociological jurisprudence, associated with the work of Roscoe Pound. As Morton Horwitz has put it, these scholars 'ridiculed the invisible-hand premise behind any assumption that private law could be neutral and apolitical. All law was coercive and had distributive consequences, they argued. It must therefore be understood as a delegation of coercive public power

[55] According to Wolfgang Friedmann, writing in 1967, 'The [Soviet] Civil Code of 1964 is, like the 1923 Code which it succeeds, predominantly akin to the structure of Western Codes. Such problems as the question of individual guilt in criminal law, fault as a basis of tort liability, or illegality or impossibility in contract...are dealt with by arguments familiar to other legal systems.' W. Friedmann, *Legal Theory*, 5th edn (London: Stevens & Sons, 1967), p. 380.

[56] K. Renner, *The Institutions of Private Law and their Social Function* [1929], ed. O. Kahn-Freund, trans. A. Schwarzschild (London: Routledge & Kegan Paul, 1976).

[57] For a history, see N. Duxbury, *Patterns of American Jurisprudence* (Oxford: Clarendon Press, 1995).

to individuals, and could only be justified by public policies.'[58] Rejecting the formalist view of law as a self-contained system of coherent rules, the Realists argued that legal rules did not accurately describe what courts did. To understand the working of law, and predict how judges would behave in future cases, one needed to look more carefully at how judicial decisions were really made, which entailed considering non-legal factors that influenced decision-making. Realist lawyers also dismissed the idea that there was an autonomous sphere of private law, which was separate from public law. In their view, tort law was not merely a private system of corrective justice, but had distributive consequences.

In the second half of the twentieth century the domination of legal Realism gave way in the United States to other instrumentalist views of law. One of the heirs of Realism was the Critical Legal Studies (CLS) movement, whose explicit aim was to deconstruct the ideas of legal liberalism, by revealing law to be arbitrary, contingent and oppressive. The CLS movement also took some of its inspiration from Marxist theories of law that had been elaborated in early twentieth-century Europe. An altogether different heir of Realism was the Law and Economics movement. Although this was more conservative than Realism, and often suspicious of state regulation, adherents of this approach also looked at law through distributive lenses, seeing the law as a vehicle to ensure wealth maximisation. For theorists such as Richard Posner, the economic aim of promoting efficient outcomes is the true – but concealed – basis of legal decisions: and one of the aims of the movement is to make judges and jurists more aware of the economic consequences of their decisions. Despite the influence of these instrumentalist movements in the United States, and despite their intellectual links with Continental thought, neither the CLS nor the Law and Economics movement proved influential in continental Europe until at least the 1990s. Moreover, their influence has yet to be seen in Britain.

In fact, in contrast to both continental Europe and the United States, which saw a flourishing of jurisprudential theories over the course of the twentieth century, lawyers in England continued, as they had done so often in the past, to muddle along without much theory. On the one hand, lacking the thriving system of university education that was to be found both in the United States and on the Continent, which encouraged theoretical investigation into the law, academic lawyers in England continued

[58] M. J. Horwitz, 'The history of the public/private distinction' (1982) 130 *University of Pennsylvania Law Review* 1423 ff., 1426.

to see their principal task as digesting and commenting on case law. On the other hand, the insights of jurists such as Gény bore far less revolutionary force in a common law jurisdiction, which lacked a code that pretended to be gapless, and in which judges had always drawn on material from outside the formal sources of law, than it did in France.

1.4 The impact of theory on private law

The rise of new social theories encouraged the development of law in ways that took account of more social interests. What impact did the growing social theories have on private law? At the time that Gény was developing his critique of the code, French tort law was being redrawn by the courts, which used article 1384 to develop strict liabilities, based on a theory of risk creation rather than fault. The risk theory had been expounded by Saleilles and Louis Josserand in works written in 1897.[59] In the previous year, in the *Teffaine* case, the Court of Cassation had applied article 1384 to the case of an exploding boiler, suggesting that there could be liability without fault. The decision in effect challenged the accepted doctrine that employers were liable for harms suffered by workmen only if they had been at fault.[60] The decision attracted much attention in academic debate; though it was not until the 1920s, in the *Resins of Bordeaux*[61] case and the *Jand'heur* case,[62] that the notion of the liability of the guardian for harms done by things under his care began to flourish. Although the courts do not seem to have cited Gény's work in these cases,[63] the impact of these new jurisprudential theories is evident. After all, the first president of the Court of Cassation, in a speech in 1904, argued that the courts should interpret the code generously, adapting it to modern times.[64] Moreover, Josserand, one of the architects of the new risk theory, who was appointed to the Cour de Cassation after the *Jand'heur* case, had his own academic opinions used to support his decision in *Mercier* on medical liability in 1936.[65]

59 R. Saleilles, *Les accidents du travail et la responsabilité civile* (Paris: A. Rousseau, 1897); L. Josserand, *De la responsabilité du fait des choses inanimées* (Paris: A. Rousseau, 1897).

60 Cass. civ. 16 June 1896, *Oriolle, Guissez et Cousin* c. *Teffaine*, S.1897.1.17, note Esmein; D.1897.1.433, concl. Sarrut, note R. Saleilles. See also G. Viney, *Les conditions de la responsabilité*, 3rd edn (Paris, LGDJ, 2006), sect. 629; and Salmon, 'Technological change…in France', pp. 110–17.

61 Cass. civ., 21 Jan 1919, 1922 D.1922. I.169 (note Savatier), S.1922.I. 97 (note Hugueney).

62 *Jand'heur* c. *Les Galeries Belfortaises*, 13 February 1930, Cass. Ch. réun., S.1930.1.121.

63 Tomlinson, 'Tort liability in France', 1349.

64 Tomlinson, 'Tort liability in France', 1309.

65 Cass. civ. 20 May 1936, D. 1936.1.88.

French scholars identify the 1899 publication of Gény's work as the birth of a modern French legal consciousness, in which judges and jurists began to accept that the judiciary plays a crucial role in developing legal norms. As Mitchel Lasser has put it, 'French *doctrine* has come to accept free scientific research as a legitimate judicial practice.'[66] It is now accepted that judges develop the law, interpreting the code according to the social needs and values of the time. Although French legal judgments continue to take the form of syllogistic reasoning on the bases of the text of the code, when cases are argued, the participants draw on case law, as well as invoking policy arguments and the views of jurists. This is not to say that tort law was 'socialised', for, throughout the twentieth century, jurists have debated fault and risk theories, and there has been a strong defence of the notion of fault.

In Germany, the long-term impact of the new theoretical developments of the early twentieth century was very different, thanks to the major political upheavals experienced by that country. The destruction of the Weimar constitution in 1933 initiated twelve years of National Socialist rule, in which lawmaking power was given to the executive, fundamental rights were deprived of all force and constitutional control of the state was removed. National Socialist ideology rooted law in the collective unity of the people. But if the *völkisches Recht* represented the will of the community, according to the *Führerprinzip* this will was articulated by the Führer, who brought it to action. It was the Führer who embodied the will of the *Volk*, so that his orders had primacy over all other sources of law.[67] This was a view of law that undermined any commitment to the principles of the rule of law, or to the autonomy of law. Nonetheless, a large number of German jurists adopted National Socialist ideology, joining the party (and keeping their jobs in law faculties). The best-known jurist, Carl Schmitt, developed a theory of 'thinking in a concrete institutional order', which allowed old law to be interpreted in new ways that fitted the goals of the National Socialist state. Schmitt did not look for abstract normative principles; rather, he wanted a concrete legal order based on the interest of

[66] M. de S.-O.-l'E. Lasser, 'Judicial (self-)portraits: judicial discourse in the French legal system' (1995) 104 *Yale Law Review* 1325 ff., 1347; *doctrine* is the French word, not the English. See also M. de S.-O.-l'E. Lasser, *Judicial Deliberations: A Comparative Analysis of Judicial Transparency and Legitimacy* (Oxford University Press, 2004), pp. 45–6.

[67] See O. Lepsius, 'The problem of perceptions of National Socialist law or: was there a constitutional theory of National Socialism?', in C. Joerges and N. Singh Ghaleigh (eds.), *Darker Legacies of Law in Europe: The Shadow of National Socialism and Fascism over Europe and Its Legal Traditions* (Oxford: Hart, 2003), pp. 19 ff.

the national *völkisch* community. This theory presupposed the existence of institutions and concepts that could not be reduced to the language of legal rules, and these concepts were to be applied in accordance with the political will of the *Volk*. This allowed judges to invoke general principles such as good faith or good morals while simultaneously denying the protection of the BGB to Jews and other groups.[68]

When the German state was reconstructed, between 1945 and 1949, there was a strong reaction not only against National Socialist notions of law but against those jurisprudential theories that seemed to some to allow for the kind of legal regime operating from 1933 to 1945. On the one hand, there was an attack against positivism, notably from Gustav Radbruch, who looked to a form of natural law to control unjust states. Judges under the National Socialist regime could hardly be described as positivists in their method, for the validity of a law was tested by its compatibility with the *völkisch* order. In fact, the positivist notion that law was not to be judged by its morality was the target of attack. On the other, there was some criticism of the free law movement, whose view that judges should disregard the law in favour of social need seemed to some to be a dangerous abandonment of the rule of law. This, it was argued, had allowed conservative judges in the Weimar period to fight social legislation that they disliked, and had opened the way for National Socialist judges to apply rules in a *völkisch* way.[69] German jurists after 1945 preferred to look to constitutionalism and natural law. Moreover, there was little desire in law schools to attack traditional forms of legal analysis. Instead, the nineteenth-century view of private law, as a formal, technical system, independent from politics and social struggles, seemed attractive once more.[70]

German private law continued to be influenced by academic writers. Perhaps the most telling example of this, discussed by Nils Jansen, was the constitutionalisation of German private law in the 1950s, following on articles by Carl Friedrich Nipperdey and Günter Dürig. In the 1958 *Lüth* case, the Federal Constitutional Court held that the constitution's

[68] V. Grosswald Curran, 'Fear of formalism: indications from the Fascist period in France and Germany of judicial methodology's impact on substantive law' (2001) 35 *Cornell International Law Journal* 101 ff., 169 ff.; C. Möllers, *Der vermisste Leviathan: Staatstheorie in der Bundesrepublik* (Frankfurt: Suhrkamp, 2008), p. 28.

[69] See O. Behrends, *Von der Freirechtsbewegung zum konkreten Ordnungs- und Gestaltungsdenken*, in R. Dreier and W. Sellert (eds.), *Recht und Justiz im 'Dritten Reich'* (Frankfurt: Suhrkamp, 1989), pp. 34 ff.

[70] C. Joerges, 'History as non-history: points of divergence and time lags between Friedrich Kessler and German jurisprudence' (1994) 42 *Am. J. Comp. L.* 163 ff., 185.

section on fundamental rights established an objective order of values that should inform the interpretation of private law norms. This allowed for the development of new rights that had been explicitly excluded from the BGB, such as personality rights. Moreover, academics continued to develop principles of private law, much as they had done in the nineteenth century. If Jhering's theories of law had opened a path for the early twentieth-century sociological jurists, his dogmatic writing continued to be of interest to lawyers. One of his most influential ideas was the doctrine of *culpa in contrahendo*, which he had developed from a conceptual construction of the Roman sources. The doctrine had not been incorporated into the BGB, although judges and jurists after 1900 did develop the doctrine to cover negligence in pre-contractual situations. In the twentieth century this area of law was further theorised by Claus-Wilhelm Canaris and Werner Lorenz, whose ideas proved influential on courts.[71] German academic influence was also secured through the *Juristentag*, which was able to mobilise and express academic opinion, its collective form giving an authority to academic writing that went beyond the prestige of particular individuals.[72]

In contrast to the United States (where the influence of the Law and Economics movement on tort law in particular has been enormous), in England the direct influence of theoretical writers on judges was limited. For most of the twentieth century English judges desisted from citing living legal academic authors,[73] let alone those outside law faculties. Common lawyers developed their system through forensic argument while resolving cases. As F. H. Lawson observed, English judges 'do not go home to do extensive research and they have no one to help them like the American law clerks'.[74] Indeed, they often had to rely on the learning digested for them by barristers arguing cases in court. Nevertheless, if English judges did not seek to apply abstract speculations, the way in which the law developed may be said to have reflected broader trends in the political

[71] On Canaris's influence, see S. Vogenauer, 'An empire of light? II: learning and lawmaking in Germany today' (2006) 26 *OJLS* 627 ff., 644–5. On Lorenz, see B. S. Markesinis and H. Unberath, *The German Law of Torts: A Comparative Treatise*, 4th edn (Oxford: Hart, 2002), pp. 92 ff.

[72] This institutionalised form of doctrinal writing is not unique to Germany. See P. Jestaz and C. Jamin, 'The entity of French doctrine: some thoughts on the community of French legal writers' (1998) 18 *Legal Studies* 415 ff.

[73] On this, see A. Braun, 'Burying the living? The citation of legal writings in English courts' (2010) 58 *Am. J. Comp. L.* 27 ff.

[74] Quoted by N. Duxbury, *Judges and Jurists: An Essay on Influence* (Oxford: Hart, 2001), p. 68.

and intellectual culture. The development of the concept of fault, which underlay the expanding tort of negligence, mirrored the growing welfarist notion in the middle of the twentieth century that individuals should be secured against harms. Thus in the 1950s, after the establishment of the NHS, the common law courts used the doctrine of vicarious liability to allow patients who had suffered negligent treatment to sue the hospital at which they had been treated, so that it was the state, which employed the doctor, that compensated.[75] Judges in numerous cases treated the negligent doctor as, in effect, a civil servant, recognising the state's liability.[76] Moreover, in the 1970s (a time when the welfare state was reaching its apogee) judges developed the notion of a general duty of care, derived from *Donoghue* v. *Stevenson*[77] – a decision followed only patchily in the middle of the century – to offer remedies against public authorities whose lack of care had resulted in harm. Just as the British welfare state expanded in the 1960s, so the courts seemed to respond, by extending the liability of public authorities.[78] They did so explicitly on the grounds of policy.[79] English lawyers usually agree that the general duty of care in negligence, first articulated in *Donoghue*, reached its broadest formulation in 1978 in *Anns* v. *Merton London Borough Council*.[80]

1.5 After the welfare state?

The dominant language of most of the nineteenth century may be said to have been individualism, while the dominant language of much of the twentieth was welfarism or social solidarism. In the later twentieth century, however, there was a reaction against the strong welfarist state. As Harris shows in her chapter, the intellectual challenges to the welfare

[75] See W. Swain, 'The development of medical liability in England and Wales', in E. Hondius (ed.), *The Development of Medical Liability* (Cambridge University Press, 2010), pp. 27 ff.

[76] The establishment of the NHS therefore led to more claims being brought in tort – something that was assisted by the establishment of legal aid. H. Teff, *Reasonable Care: Legal Perspectives on the Doctor–Patient Relationship* (Oxford: Clarendon Press, 1994), p. 26.

[77] *Donoghue* v. *Stevenson* [1932] AC 562.

[78] See, especially, *Home Office* v. *Dorset Yacht Club Ltd* [1970] AC 1004.

[79] Thus, *Dutton* v. *Bognor Regis UDC* [1972] 1 QB 373, 398 imposed liability in tort on a local authority whose inspectors had been negligent in approving a house, with Lord Denning arguing that the council was 'entrusted by Parliament with the task of seeing that houses were properly built. They received public funds for the purpose. The very object was to protect purchasers and occupiers of houses. Yet they failed to protect them. Their shoulders are broad enough to bear the loss.'

[80] *Anns* v. *Merton Borough Council* [1978] AC 728.

state – from the point of view of both economic theory and political theory – dated from the 1940s. In England, Friedrich Hayek's *The Road to Serfdom* (1944) exerted an influence on the Institute of Economic Affairs in the 1950s, which in turn began to influence right-of-centre politicians, such as Keith Joseph, who argued that the free market was the most efficient way to obtain services. With the coming of the Conservative government headed by Margaret Thatcher in 1979, there was a rolling back of the state. At the same time, there was a growing interest in rights. At a philosophical level, works such as John Rawls' *A Theory of Justice* (1971) reinvigorated liberal political theory on the basis of individualist premises. On a more practical level, in the postwar era there was an increasing focus on transnational human rights, which were to be guaranteed by an international legal order that was not attached to a particular state. Furthermore, the prime focus of attention in this rights discourse, found in such instruments as the 1948 Universal Declaration of Human Rights and the 1950 European Convention on Human Rights, was on individual civil and political rights, rather than on social rights.

Just as there was a growing focus on the language of individual rights, so there was a concomitant focus on the notion of responsibility. In England, where the era up to the publication of the Pearson Report of 1978 on civil liability and compensation for personal injury was one that increasingly favoured social solutions to harms befalling individuals, the period thereafter saw greater stress on holding wrongdoers to account. By 1990 the relationship between tort law and social security had been rethought, as theorists looked again at the importance of individual responsibility. As one writer put it, 'The collectivisation of our responsibilities should not be taken lightly. The ease of collecting funds through taxation and the economies of scale and scope obtained by organising, for example, health care provision on a large scale have to be weighed against the effects of collectivisation on incentives to behave responsibly.'[81]

If the welfare state was being rolled back, tort law was expanding. Thus, whereas there were 700 medical negligence claims in 1973, there were 10,901 in 2000/2001.[82] Moreover, the era after 1985 also saw a marked increase in non-medical professional negligence claims. The greater willingness to sue professionals, notably in a commercial environment,

[81] D. Howarth, 'Tort law and the welfare state' (2001) 60 *Cambridge Law Journal* 553 ff., 575.

[82] A. Morris, 'Spiralling or stabilising? The compensation culture and our propensity to claim damages for personal injury' (2007) 70 *Modern Law Review* 349 ff., 358.

may have been consequent on particular economic developments, such as the crash in the housing market in the early 1990s. Its effect, though, was to ask private law courts to allocate risks in commercial transactions, in order to regulate business outside the frame of government. The late twentieth-century English 'compensation culture' may be said to reflect a new focus on the rights of the individual (reflected in policies such as the Citizen's Charter, launched in 1991 by the then prime minister, John Major), exercised and expressed through a private law, developed by the judiciary, with its own views of when remedies should be permitted, on policy grounds. It can also be viewed as the reflection of a more consumerist approach to public services, manifested not only in the Citizen's Charter in England but also in similar agreements for the use of public services on the Continent.

By the late twentieth century many more litigants were seeking compensation from the state in tort litigation, seeking remedies from judges applying private law.[83] In the 1980s the expansion of the fault principle was checked. This decade saw a 'retreat from *Anns*' (a decision overruled in 1990).[84] By the 1990s courts were taking the view that, rather than there being a single principle in negligence (that a duty existed to take care to avoid reasonably foreseeable harms, unless there were policy considerations to preclude its imposition), a new category of duty would be recognised only if it was analogous to an existing duty and if there were policy reasons in its favour. The law was henceforth to develop in small steps, as litigants went to court to claim rights invaded by these breaches of duty.

On the Continent, the movement of the late twentieth century towards individual rights, manifested in tort cases, and away from social rights, characterised by the welfare state, was more ambiguous. On the one hand, welfare states were necessarily rethought, as national economies slipped from the postwar 'miracle years' into the difficulties of the 1970s and 1980s. Both Germany and France saw welfare programmes cut back, but their cuts took a different form from those in England and were much less noticeable, both in terms of the rhetoric surrounding them and in terms of where they fell. The Continental systems were based on social security contributions rather than redistributed taxes, and they reached a crisis amid growing unemployment. Certain welfare sectors were, therefore, hit more dramatically than others, so that, for example, child and family

[83] There was a trend against the courts allowing claims to be brought against public authorities that had failed to deliver services that would have prevented a loss.

[84] *Murphy* v. *Brentwood District Council* [1991] 1 AC 398.

benefits continued to thrive in Germany while compensation for the able-bodied unemployed was reduced. In France, a variety of minor changes at the margins quietly eroded one of Europe's largest social nets.[85] On the other hand, individual claims through tort cases have become more prevalent in the last three decades, as evidenced in the earlier volumes in this series. Despite widespread concern in England about growing litigiousness and a 'culture of compensation', recourse to court for cases involving tort law has been, at times, even more prevalent in continental Europe. In part, the availability of inexpensive legal counsel has played a role in this development,[86] as has the wider availability of no-fault compensation funds,[87] but it is also likely that the different experience with litigation in Continental systems reflects the enduring strength of intellectual and legal traditions that have differed, often markedly, from those in England.

The seeming divide between English and Continental legal traditions has, however, been questioned consistently over the last two centuries. In numerous areas, scholars at the turn of the twentieth century were interested in the development of law beyond the nation state. Moreover, in the field of contract and commercial law, as has been noted, the development of global rules beyond the nation state acquired ever more importance. Scholars have paid less attention to international connections involving tort law than those involving contract and commercial law, however, perhaps because tort law is more concerned with correcting harms that have occurred than with creating frameworks for social interaction.[88] Nonetheless, as Lucinda Miller's contribution, chapter 13, shows, there has in recent years been a Europeanisation of private law, in which legal

[85] P. Starke, *Radical Welfare State Retrenchment: A Comparative Analysis* (Basingstoke: Palgrave Macmillan, 2008), ch. 7; J. Clasen, *Reforming European Welfare States: Germany and the United Kingdom Compared* (Oxford University Press, 2005); B. Palier, '"Defrosting" the French welfare state', in M. Ferrera and M. Rhodes (eds.), *Recasting European Welfare States* (London: Frank Cass, 2000), pp. 113 ff.

[86] B. S. Markesinis, 'Litigation-mania in England, Germany and the USA: are we so different?' (1990) 49 *Cambridge Law Journal* 233 ff.; E. Blankenburg, 'Judicial systems in western Europe: comparative indicators of legal professionals, courts, litigation and budgets in the 1990s', in E. G. Jensen and T. C. Heller (eds.), *Beyond Common Knowledge: Empirical Approaches to the Rule of Law* (Stanford University Press, 2003), pp. 63–96, esp. 69–75.

[87] For example, France instituted no-fault compensation funds for road accidents in 1985 and for certain illnesses in 2002, while Austria has taken similar measures in relation to medical liability.

[88] A recent exception is E. Hondius (ed.), *Towards a European Civil Code* (The Hague: Kluwer, 2004), part E.

academics and legal thinkers have played an increasingly strong role in developing new rules. Building on the heritage of earlier international codes, such as for maritime law, discussions within the European Union have highlighted the possibility of common standards for cases under private law. It is these current efforts for the harmonisation of private law that will provide a test for the heritage of what contemporaries and historians alike have often viewed as culturally specific legal and philosophical traditions.

2

Responsibility, solidarity and state regulation in classical Continental social theory

ROGER COTTERRELL*

How did contributions to social theory in France and Germany, in the period from the middle of the nineteenth century to the early twentieth century, address or reflect changing ideas about individual and social responsibility? In considering this question, my focus is limited to certain ideas about the role of the state, especially with regard to public service and social provision, and about the increasing importance (reflected in legal debates and law reform) of social, collective or state responsibility in opposition to earlier laissez-faire individualism.

Social theory can be defined as the systematic, empirically oriented study of the 'social' (the general range of recurring forms, or patterned features, of interactions and relations between people) in terms of its historical variation, and its variation between different societies. Why might this theory be significant in considering legal debates around responsibility and the role of the state? There is, after all, little evidence that social theory has directly influenced legal reform. Nevertheless, in the period addressed by this chapter, there was unquestionably some cross-influence between jurists and social theorists.

Max Weber, for example, interacted with leading German jurists of his day, and some key concepts in his social theory may have been formed in debate with the ideas of legal scholars such as Georg Jellinek and Rudolf von Jhering.[1] Similarly, the sociology of Émile Durkheim and his followers was developed partly through their commentaries on the work of jurists

* Queen Mary, University of London.

[1] See S. Turner and R. Factor, *Max Weber: The Lawyer as Social Thinker* (London: Routledge, 1994); P. Honigsheim, *On Max Weber*, trans. J. Rytina (New York: Free Press, 1968), pp. 68–75; J. Radkau, *Max Weber: A Biography*, trans. P. Camiller (Cambridge: Polity Press, 2009), pp. 258–9, pp. 261–6; and, generally, M. Weber, *Max Weber: A Biography*, trans. H. Zohn (New Brunswick, NJ: Transaction, 1988).

and legal historians in the review pages of Durkheim's *Année sociologique* publication.[2] At the same time, social theory directly inspired jurists. Durkheim's sociology, which dominated French social thought in the early decades of the twentieth century, powerfully influenced the work of such diverse and important jurists as Léon Duguit, Emmanuel Lévy and Paul Huvelin – the latter two actually being part of Durkheim's team of collaborators.[3] In an Anglophone context, Oliver Wendell Holmes read Herbert Spencer's social theory as a young man, and thirty years later told Sir Frederick Pollock that 'I doubt if any writer in English has done so much to affect our whole way of thinking about the universe'.[4] Famously, a decade after that, in *Lochner* v. *New York* (1905), Holmes cited Spencer's 1851 book *Social Statics* as characterising the entire laissez-faire philosophy of legal responsibility that Holmes' dissenting judgment in that case condemned.[5]

Philosophy was a much more important direct theoretical influence on jurists in this period, however, as, for example, in the Kantian and Hegelian bases of juristic legal theory especially in Germany. Moreover, whatever the intellectual formation of jurists, it is hard to assess with any precision their general influence on the practice of courts and lawyers – a matter that may vary greatly from one legal system to another.[6]

Certainly, social theorists have often written with the aim of promoting change or influencing public debate. They have frequently been animated by moral or policy concerns, by a sense of the deficiencies of the existing social order or by fears for its future. Many writers (notably Weber and Durkheim) have insisted that their commitment to social science was separate from any direct political engagement, but their preferences for practical legal/political reform were usually not well hidden. Sometimes, as with Karl Marx and his followers, theory was intended to aid revolutionary social change, rather than to interpret the

2 See, generally, R. Cotterrell, *Émile Durkheim: Law in a Moral Domain* (Edinburgh University Press, 1999), ch. 3.

3 R. Cotterrell, *Living Law: Studies in Legal and Social Theory* (Aldershot: Ashgate, 2008), chs. 6, 7.

4 C. D. Bowen, *Yankee from Olympus: Justice Holmes and his Family* (Boston: Little Brown, 1944), p. 187; M. deWolfe Howe (ed.), *Holmes–Pollock Letters: The Correspondence of Mr Justice Holmes and Sir Frederick Pollock, 1874–1932* (2 vols.), 2nd edn, vol. I (Cambridge, MA: Harvard University Press, 1961), p. 58.

5 198 US 45, 75 (1905).

6 See, for example, N. Duxbury, *Jurists and Judges: An Essay on Influence* (Oxford: Hart, 2001).

world as 'the philosophers' had done.[7] But distances between social theory and legal practice are considerable. Evidence of direct influence is likely to be rare. Far more important is the point that, by appreciating the different standpoints of lawyers, law reformers and social theorists, it may be possible to integrate different perspectives on a shared legal and social history.

Social theory, at least in its most prominent forms, reflects something of the generally felt problems, assumptions, aspirations and contradictions of its time. Typically, it seeks insight into the nature and sources of contemporary social conditions, and their possible future. It aims to capture the prevailing sense of movement in social life, and society's self-understandings. Legal thought also, in various ways, reflects these matters, but through the prism of professional and political priorities.[8] Perhaps, then, social theory can reveal something of a broader context of social experience in which legal issues arise, but its focus will always be on the social as a whole, and on law and the state only insofar as they are aspects of, or shaping influences on, the social. Familiar conflicts also exist between seeing a theory as a product of its times and assessing its unique explanatory power. Patterns of historical influence in the development of a theory are hard to keep clearly in view when it is treated (as it should be, to do justice to it) as a complete and integrated system of thought.

Faced with these difficulties, the aim can only be to tell a coherent story in the history of ideas and in the social theoretical interpretation of history. The themes focused on in this chapter are (i) the development of conceptions of law as a modern technical *instrument of government*, available to protect citizens' interests or arbitrate between them; and (ii) the development of ideas of law as existing to nurture and define *social solidarity* and *collective responsibility*. Both themes characterise major currents in social theory from the middle of the nineteenth century to the early twentieth century. A focus on them highlights significantly different emphases in French and German theory in this period. Indeed, the tension between these emphases may be especially revealing with respect to changing perceptions of responsibility and of the role of the state.

[7] See K. Marx, 'Theses on Feuerbach' [1845], in *Marx/Engels Collected Works* (50 vols.), vol. V (Moscow: Progress, 1976), pp. 3 ff., 4.

[8] R. Cotterrell, *The Politics of Jurisprudence: A Critical Introduction to Legal Philosophy*, 2nd edn (Oxford University Press, 2003).

2.1 Pioneer sociology: law as obstacle and solution

2.1.1 Comte

Sociology (the term was coined by Auguste Comte in the fourth volume of his *Cours de philosophie positive*, published in 1839) is said to have been 'born in a state of hostility to law'.[9] The hostility was not only that of Comte but also of earlier French social theorists, such as Claude-Henri Saint-Simon. Comte saw the progress of human thought as passing through theological and metaphysical stages to enter (at different times in the different sciences) a final, modern stage in which positivist thought – focusing only on observable facts and discarding metaphysical speculation – would triumph in all fields. According to Comte's prediction, all positivist sciences will 'converge on sociology, because the whole hierarchy of being culminates in the human species',[10] the life of which is to be studied by sociology, as well as rationally guided by it.

With regard to the responsibilities of the citizen, sociology will define these. It will reveal the mechanisms by which the social order sustains itself and the part that everyone is called on to play in sustaining these mechanisms. Duty therefore flows directly from social functions that sociology explains. Law retains no role in this scientifically regulated world because it purports to address, without scientific understanding but through 'the vague and turbulent discussion of rights',[11] conflicts that the positivist science of society will remove. Law is 'a metaphysical vestige..., absurd as well as immoral', and positivism 'causes the idea of law to disappear irretrievably'.[12]

In Comte's thought both conservatism (resignation to the existing order of society) and an idea of progress (the possibility of continuous rational reform) loom large, both being removed from the field of human will and located now in an impersonal science. It is easy to see therefore why Comte's sociology treats ideas of will and responsibility in legal thought as its enemies: Comtean responsibility does not originate in the

[9] N. Timasheff, *An Introduction to the Sociology of Law* (Cambridge, MA: Harvard University Press, 1939), p. 45.

[10] R. Aron, *Main Currents of Sociological Thought*, vol. I, *Montesquieu, Comte, Marx, de Tocqueville, and the Sociologists and the Revolution of 1848*, trans. R. Howard and H. Weaver (London: Weidenfeld & Nicolson, 1965), pp. 101–2.

[11] A. Comte, *Cours de philosophie positive* (6 vols.), vol. VI (Paris: Bachelier, 1842), pp. 651–2, as quoted by Timasheff, *An Introduction*, p. 45.

[12] Comte, quoted by G. Gurvitch, *Sociology of Law* (London: Kegan Paul, Trench, Trübner, 1947), p. 12.

individual's acts and motivations, but is fixed by the nature of society. It is established not juridically but by scientific laws that govern social cohesion and set its requirements.

In this context, governmental authority must be a unifying force. Comte saw that modern, large-scale societies required extensive occupational specialisation. However in contrast to the view that Durkheim would later take, he thought that the increasing division of labour could undermine social cohesion, decomposing society 'into a multitude of unconnected corporations which scarcely seem to belong to the same species'; governmental power must 'contain and so far as possible arrest this fatal disposition to the fundamental dispersion of ideas, sentiments and interests'; it would have to 'intervene appropriately in the daily performance of all the various functions of the social economy, to sustain continuously the idea of the whole and the sentiment of common solidarity'.[13] Thus, at the beginning of modern sociology, Comte called for government intervention in aid of solidarity – a theme that would resonate through much later French thought. He did not see law as important to this intervention, however; it could be only an arena of irrational conflict in which rights are fought over without knowledge of their wider social context. A challenge is thrown down – if a somewhat unclear one, given Comte's ultimately vague views on the future of the state and on appropriate structures of government[14] – to rethink issues of social responsibility outside the framework of rights and duties of private law.

2.1.2 Von Stein

At much the same time as Comte wrote, the writings of Lorenz von Stein contributed foundations for sociological thought in Germany. Von Stein's work is now virtually ignored but the 1850 edition of his *History of the Social Movement in France*[15] contained a general theory of social development that 'laid the cornerstone of what we today call "historical

[13] A. Comte, *Cours de philosophie positive* (6 vols.), 2nd edn, vol. IV (Paris: Bachelier, 1864), p. 429, pp. 430–1, as quoted by S. Lukes, *Émile Durkheim: His Life and Work* (London: Allen Lane, 1973), p. 141, p. 142.

[14] H. E. Barnes, 'The social and political philosophy of Auguste Comte', in *An Introduction to the History of Sociology* (University of Chicago Press, 1948), pp. 81 ff. For the apparent change over time in Comte's ideas on the organisation and radical decentralisation of governmental functions, see, for example, R. Vernon, 'Auguste Comte and the withering-away of the state' (1984) 45 *Journal of the History of Ideas* 549 ff.

[15] L. von Stein, *The History of the Social Movement in France, 1789–1850* [1850], trans. K. Mengelberg (Totowa, NJ: Bedminster Press, 1964).

sociology"'[16] and is 'the first German sociology'.[17] Influenced initially by G. W. F. Hegel's philosophy of history, von Stein replaced such philosophical speculation with a 'science of society', an enquiry into general, empirically identifiable processes of the development of social life into the form of modern industrial organisation.

The principles of the *Declaration des droits de l'homme et du citoyen* are the 'first basic law of the new society'[18] brought into being by the French Revolution of 1789. They express fundamental laws that are 'structurally separate from state and government' and rooted in society itself.[19] These principles are not primarily political but social – 'the constitution of *society*'[20] rather than of the state. They must be seen as antecedent to state action and can be asserted if necessary against it. They do not depend on a particular form of state, but should influence the development of equal political rights. Thus natural (scientific) 'laws' of society's development are the real motor of modern European history.

What are these scientific (sociological) 'laws'? The Declaration of the Rights of Man expressed a principle of equality before the law, which gives free rein to the pursuit of self-interest and provides the means of challenging established privileges and statuses. Thereafter, acquired property becomes the foundation of social order and organisation. 'For the liberated individual..., property became the natural and indeed primary means of shaping his own worth and individuality'[21] and the concrete expression of abstract, universal liberty. These conditions support 'economic society' based on free acquisition. This, in turn, becomes 'industrial society', based on capital accumulation that is made possible by the mechanisation of production. The contradictions of this society are expressed in the contrast between universal abstract freedom (in theory) and differential access to property (in practice). Hence the conflict of social classes (which are defined by this differential access) arises as the proletariat becomes conscious of its situation. The result is the threat of violence, civil war and

[16] K. Mengelberg, 'Lorenz von Stein and his contribution to historical sociology' (1961) 22 *Journal of the History of Ideas* 267 ff., 268.

[17] H. Marcuse, *Reason and Revolution: Hegel and the Rise of Social Theory*, 2nd edn (London: Routledge and Kegan Paul, 1955), p. 375.

[18] L. von Stein, *Geschichte der sozialen Bewegung in Frankreich von 1789 bis auf unserer Tage* [1850] (3 vols.), vol. I (Munich: Drei Masken Verlag, 1921), p. 209, as quoted by E.-W. Böckenförde, *State, Society and Liberty: Studies in Political Theory and Constitutional Law*, trans. J. A. Underwood (New York: Berg, 1991), p. 121.

[19] Böckenförde, *State, Society and Liberty*, p. 121.

[20] Böckenförde, *State, Society and Liberty*, p. 126.

[21] Böckenförde, *State, Society and Liberty*, p. 127.

the self-destruction of society; and this result is produced by the nature of the social – not by the nature of politics, law or the state.

If many of these ideas sound familiar it is, of course, because they are so close in outline to Marx's analysis of the historical trajectory of capitalist society. But they were presented by von Stein before Marx had set out his mature theories. There is clear evidence that Marx had read von Stein's work, perhaps drawing much from it,[22] while condemning it for its bourgeois defence of the state and the established order. Unlike Marx, von Stein sought to save industrial society from itself, enlisting the state as central to this rescue operation. His warnings of social unrest (influenced by the experience of the 1848 German revolution) were largely ignored, however, in the growing optimism in Germany, from the middle of the nineteenth century onwards, for national unity and a national state.[23]

Despite the utter disparity in their fame today, von Stein is more significant in the context of this chapter than Marx, because, as Ernst-Wolfgang Böckenförde has argued,[24] he can be seen as a proponent in 1850 of the social or welfare state and of a science of society to serve it. He combined a partially Hegelian idealisation of the state with sociological realism. The state's function is to guarantee liberty and property, and, in principle, it is above class antagonisms, as 'the community acting as a personality'.[25] This is an ethical ideal, though, 'merely an abstraction'.[26] In reality the state is subordinated to the interests of ruling classes, or becomes absolutist and remote, losing support in society. Its only possibility of retaining its authority and regulatory power is to become an organ of society as a whole, enlisting the support of wide social groupings by guaranteeing the practical (not just the formal) liberty of all, and facilitating their participation in economic and social life, in particular through the creation of opportunities for property acquisition. As Böckenförde remarks, 'The

[22] J. Singelmann and P. Singelmann, 'Lorenz von Stein and the paradigmatic bifurcation of social theory in the nineteenth century' (1986) 37 *British Journal of Sociology* 431 ff. 447; Marcuse, *Reason and Revolution*, p. 374. As Werner Cahnman puts it, 'Marx's sociology is therefore as Steinian as his economics is Ricardian': W. J. Cahnman, 'Book review: Lorenz von Stein, *The History of the Social Movement in France, 1789–1850*' (1966) 71 *American Journal of Sociology* 746 ff.

[23] Böckenförde, *State, Society and Liberty*, pp. 117–18.

[24] Böckenförde, *State, Society and Liberty*, ch. 6.

[25] Von Stein, *Geschichte*, p. 16, as quoted by Singelmann and Singelmann, 'Lorenz von Stein', 436. See also Mengelberg, 'Lorenz von Stein', 269; and Marcuse, *Reason and Revolution*, p. 381.

[26] Von Stein, *Geschichte*, p. 49, as quoted by Mengelberg, 'Lorenz von Stein', 269; see also Singelmann and Singelmann, 'Lorenz von Stein', 437–8.

logic of this idea, once grasped, took Lorenz von Stein beyond liberalism as early as 1850.'[27] Indeed, it led him, in his later work on 'administrative science' (*Verwaltungswissenschaft*), to develop what now appear as foundations of the modern discipline of public administration:[28] seeking to devise ideas and techniques for use in the management, within limits, of the social by the state.[29]

The work of Comte and von Stein contains ideas about law, society and the management of responsibility that reappear in new guises in later social theory up to the early twentieth century. Among these is the idea in Comte's work that responsibility should be seen as the consequence not of the individual's will and acts but of social conditions. Von Stein, again like many later theorists, saw the state as responsible for creating adequate conditions for individual participation in social and economic life. For both writers, moreover, governmental regulatory tasks are not to be set politically or determined by the form that the state or governing power takes in a certain time and place. They are to be set by what 'society' demands of this power – a matter that social theory, not juristic analysis, is to reveal. The displacement of the jurists[30] would allow the emergence of practical administrative sciences: sciences of social management that Comte envisaged in theory and von Stein devoted his later career to developing. One way or another, the private assertion of rights or of claims of responsibility would be subordinated to a scientifically directed regulation of the social.

[27] Böckenförde, *State, Society and Liberty*, p. 133.

[28] C. Thornhill, 'The domain of public administration' (2006) 41 *Journal of Public Administration* 793 ff., 794.

[29] M. R. Rutgers, 'Can the study of public administration do without a concept of the state? Reflections on the work of Lorenz von Stein' (1994) 26 *Administration and Society* 395 ff.

[30] In this perspective, social science overwhelms juristic science. Unsurprisingly, from the juristic side, the complaint was made that von Stein's 'conception of society shows the modern tendency unduly to extend its meaning, and to include [in it] the functions of government and law and national economics': F. Berolzheimer, *The World's Legal Philosophies*, trans. R. S. Jastrow (Boston Book Co., 1912), p. 327. Comte's subsuming of law and government in the social attracted the same criticism: Berolzheimer, *The World's Legal Philosophies*, pp. 311–12. Nevertheless, some jurists made similar claims for the precedence of the social: Otto von Gierke wrote, in *Natural Law and the Theory of Society* [1913], trans. E. Barker (Cambridge University Press, 1950), p. 224, 'We shall no longer ask whether the state is prior to law, or law is prior to the state. We shall regard them both as inherent functions of the common life which is inseparable from the idea of man.' However, such general juristic speculations (part of lawyers' 'internal' debates) posed no threat to lawyers' preserves, unlike the creation of entirely new research fields of sociology or social theory to study law and government historically as social phenomena.

2.2 Sociological pessimism: the inevitability of individualism and bureaucracy

Von Stein's urgent advocacy of state action is strikingly at odds with the seemingly resigned, almost fatalistic outlook of some influential later German social theory, especially that of Ferdinand Tönnies and Weber. In their best-known theoretical works, neither of these late nineteenth- and early twentieth-century writers sees modern society as oriented to developing social or collective responsibility, though both recognise some counter-tendencies to the dominant privatised lines of development. Tönnies expresses nostalgia for decaying social forms – the village and the close-knit kin group – in which common responsibility is natural and needs no formal embodiment in law. But he sees the dominant kinds of modern social organisation as entirely different. There are perhaps, at best, pockets of economic life, such as co-operative movements, in which something more than the atomistic individual existence characteristic of modern society might be created.[31]

Weber, correspondingly, analyses what he sees as cold, morally empty forms of modern routine: the bureaucratised, rule-bound organisation of the social. Again, the main focus is on individuals pursuing their own projects, fixing their responsibilities primarily in terms of contract and private law. When Weber observes new political or legal developments that challenge this individualistic universe with its formal, technical law, his response is ambivalent. Thus what both theorists offer, in the main, is a characterisation of a world of legally supervised individual responsibility and of the social conditions that sustain it, as well as grave doubts as to how far it might be possible to build anything different.

2.2.1 Tönnies

Tönnies' book *Gemeinschaft und Gesellschaft*, first published in 1887, attracted immediate attention, if some initial criticism for its 'tone of pessimistic resignation',[32] and it has remained influential to the present

[31] F. Tönnies, *Community and Association*, trans. C. P. Loomis (London: Routledge and Kegan Paul, 1955), pp. 227–8.

[32] H. Liebersohn, *Fate and Utopia in German Sociology 1870–1923* (Cambridge, MA: MIT Press, 1988), pp. 11–12. It has been argued, however, that, after the publication of his 1887 book, Tönnies' perspective gradually shifted towards greater optimism. This led him to a sustained search for opportunities to recover, perhaps in new forms, aspects of *Gemeinschaft* in modern conditions, or to transform *Gesellschaft* structures productively. See A. Mitzman, 'Tönnies and German society, 1887–1914: from cultural pessimism to

day. His dichotomy of *Gemeinschaft* (community) and *Gesellschaft* (association), which he uses to identify a fundamental change in the social, marking the transition to modern society, is paralleled by other such dichotomies in social theory (especially Durkheim's contrasting of mechanical and organic solidarity, discussed below). *Gemeinschaft* is a social bond or community of kinship intimacy ('blood'), closeness in a shared environment ('locality') and ideas held in common ('mind'), or, often, all three of these.[33] It is a social unity in which the main identity of individuals is as part of a communal totality. Built on a similarity of experience, thought and feeling, *Gemeinschaft* can flourish only in relatively small-scale social networks and so is becoming increasingly irrelevant to the large-scale networks of modern life, its place being usurped by *Gesellschaft*, the opposing social form.

Gesellschaft is a social bond based on calculation or rational will, in which individuals remain 'essentially separated in spite of all uniting factors...and there exists a tension against all others'.[34] The typical and fundamental social bond of *Gesellschaft* is contract, and its perfect legal embodiment is the joint-stock company.[35] Responsibility arises from deliberate undertakings or the necessity of protecting the space of the individual in the life of the association. *Gesellschaft* requires powerful state support, however, in a way that *Gemeinschaft* does not. The latter is a natural unity, but the former is an artificial one: '[I]ndividuals remain in isolation and veiled hostility toward each other so that only fear of clever retaliation restrains them from attacking one another.'[36] State power exercised through law is needed to protect and maintain *Gesellschaft* relations.

Ultimately, Tönnies, like von Stein, portrays modern capitalist society as unstable, dependent on state law for such stability as it can attain and needing increasingly extensive state intervention to achieve this. What the state will enforce, however, are the calculated, measured, private law responsibilities of isolated individuals, not the conditions for mutually supportive interaction typical of integrated communities.

celebration of the *Volksgemeinschaft*' (1971) 32 *Journal of the History of Ideas* 507 ff.; and C. Adair-Toteff, 'Ferdinand Tönnies: utopian visionary' (1995) 13 *Sociological Theory* 58 ff.

[33] Tönnies, *Community and Association*, p. 48.

[34] Tönnies, *Community and Association*, p. 74.

[35] Tönnies, *Community and Association*, pp. 225–7, p. 264.

[36] Tönnies, *Community and Association*, p. 262.

2.2.2 Weber

If Tönnies' most influential work expresses a longing for a pre-capitalist world no longer possible, Weber's rejects all utopias and shows a resignation to modern political, economic and social conditions that are, in his view, unlikely to change fundamentally. His great book *Economy and Society*, assembled from manuscripts after his death in 1920, has as its longest section the 260 pages headed 'Economy and law (sociology of law)'.[37] Much of this discusses historical processes of the rationalisation of law, presenting these partly through a self-contained comparative social history of types of legal thought and practice. Weber also portrays them, though, in terms of his overall project of tracking the historical processes of the rationalisation of economy, political organisation, religion, science and other fields, which produced, in his view, the unique character of the modern civilisation of the West.

For Weber, rational law is rule-governed law, and the bases of law's rational strength – its integrity and authority as a rule system – may be formal or substantive. Substantively rational law is determined and legitimated by the principles of an ideological system other than law itself – such as ethics, religion or political values. For a time, natural law doctrines in the West provided a general input of substantive rationality into law, and gave law's authority a foundation in ultimate values or beliefs. One of Weber's most important claims, however, is that this source of external validation and consistent determination of law's substantive content has ceased to be viable in modern conditions: 'The axioms of natural law have lost all capacity to provide the fundamental basis of a legal system... The disappearance of the old natural law conceptions has destroyed all possibility of providing the law with a metaphysical dignity by virtue of its immanent qualities. In the great majority of its most important provisions, it has been unmasked all too visibly, indeed, as the product or the technical means of a compromise between conflicting interests.'[38]

Although many factors influence the substantive content of modern law, its integrity and authority as a rule system have become primarily a matter of its *technical usefulness* as a means of 'compromise between conflicting interests' and of its *formal rationality*, in which 'definitely fixed legal concepts in the form of highly abstract rules are formulated

[37] M. Weber, *Economy and Society: An Outline of Interpretive Sociology* [1922] (3 vols.), vol. II (New York: Bedminster Press, 1968), ch. 8 (this chapter trans. by M. Rheinstein).

[38] Weber, *Economy and Society*, vol. II, pp. 874–5.

and applied'.[39] Legal thought, insofar as it is formally rational, tends to become a logical calculus of rules. While formal logical legal rationality is, for Weber, an ideal type never found in pure form in reality, it conceptualises for him a crucial, dominant characteristic of modern law. This formality allows the 'integration of all analytically derived legal propositions' into an 'internally consistent, and, at least in theory, gapless system of rules'.[40]

In Weber's social theory, the importance of modern law's tendency to formal rationality is that it removes the need for any consistent reference to 'external' moral or political sources of validation or legitimacy for this law. Modern law, for Weber, is a largely self-sustaining normative structure validated by its technical sophistication and overall usefulness in regulating the interplay of private interests. Beyond that, most importantly, it is the servant and support of the modern state. Its formal logic of rules defines structures of authority impersonally and so underpins modern bureaucracy and capitalistic business organisation, as well as the idea of the rule-governed state (*Rechtsstaat*), with its everyday administrative operations very much like those of a machine largely removed from human volition.

What is the significance of this portrayal of (especially German) law and state? It suggests, first, the morally impregnable, fortress-like character of the modern state, seemingly free to do good or evil without challenges to its legitimacy from moral or political critics or from the social convulsions that von Stein had feared. Weber was aware, like Tönnies, of the dissatisfactions of his time with capitalist society, served by seemingly morally cold law and relentless state power. Nonetheless, just eight pages of Weber's text on the sociology of law are devoted to 'The anti-formalistic tendencies of modern legal development'.[41] Here, he offers brief comments on juristic and political developments at the beginning of the twentieth century that challenge legal formalism's dominance and effects. These include the growth of legal principles of 'good faith and fair dealing'; demands for 'social law' in opposition to or supplementation of individual law and linked to 'the emergence of the modern class problem';[42] claims (such as Eugen Ehrlich's) that popular social norms of 'living law' are more fundamental than the law of the state; the revival

39 Weber, *Economy and Society*, vol. II, p. 657.
40 Weber, *Economy and Society*, vol. II, p. 656.
41 Weber, *Economy and Society*, vol. II, pp. 882–9.
42 Weber, *Economy and Society*, vol. II, p. 886.

of Catholic natural law doctrines; the Jhering-inspired 'jurisprudence of interests'; and the 'free law' movement in Germany.

He saw all these as fated to be ineffectual, however, when viewed sociologically in the wider perspective of the processes of rationalisation that have entrenched modern economic, legal and political forms. Terms and phrases such as 'value-irrationalism', 'anti-logical, 'anti-historical', 'self-defeating scientific rationalisation' and 'flight into the irrational' litter Weber's account of these critical tendencies. Like Tönnies in *Gemeinschaft und Gesellschaft*, he had little confidence in the possibilities of significant change in economic and social relations. 'Weber could not conceive of any genuine alternative to the capitalist economic system'[43] or of any radical reorientation of the private law serving it. Bureaucracy and economic routine increasingly made life seem like an 'iron cage',[44] but attempts to create a socialist order would merely produce, less efficiently, more bureaucracy and formal rules. Again like Tönnies, Weber was far from discounting the need for reform, but this would be in the context of 'an inevitable and prolonged capitalist era'.[45] Moreover, what may have concerned him far more than legal individualism's deafness to calls for a social law of collective responsibility was the ultimately poor adaptability of juristic formal legal reasoning to the means/ends calculations of economic entrepreneurs.[46]

As social theorists, Tönnies and Weber have powerfully influenced general understandings of the legal and social changes that occurred in their era. There is little evidence, however, that they themselves contributed significantly to these changes. Rather, they wrote in ways that enable us now to gain a better perspective on some influences that did operate. Affinities might easily be found, for example, between Tönnies' evocation of pre-modern *Gemeinschaft* life and the jurist Otto von Gierke's erudite reconstruction of the communal forms of *Genossenschaft* (association) in old Germanic law.[47] Gierke's scholarly presentation of the legal past

[43] W. J. Mommsen, *Max Weber and German Politics 1890–1920*, trans. M. S. Steinberg (University of Chicago Press, 1984), p. 104.

[44] M. Weber, *The Protestant Ethic and the Spirit of Capitalism* [1905], trans. T. Parsons (London: Allen & Unwin, 1930), p. 181.

[45] Weber, quoted by Mommsen, *Max Weber and German Politics*, p. 105.

[46] See Weber, *Economy and Society*, vol. II, p. 885.

[47] See, for example, O. von Gierke, *Associations and Law: The Classical and Early Christian Stages* [1881], trans. G. Heiman (University of Toronto Press, 1977); O. von Gierke, *Community in Historical Perspective* [1868], ed. A. Black, trans. M. Fischer (Cambridge University Press, 1990); Gierke, *Natural Law*; O. von Gierke, *Political Theories of the Middle Age* [1881], trans. F. W. Maitland (Cambridge University Press, 1900); and O. von

reflected an emotional sense of a 'loss of community' directly comparable with that of Tönnies, and Gierke's rich, romantic evocation of half-forgotten characteristics of Germanic law had a powerful influence on debates about the appropriate content of the new German Civil Code of 1900.[48] Ultimately, neither Gierke nor Tönnies appear merely as reactionaries seeking to recover a golden past. Both of them eventually attacked the individualism of modern law for facilitating the exploitation of the socially disadvantaged.[49]

Gierke's influence on legal debates was mainly due to his juristic skill in presenting aspects of the reforms he advocated as being deeply rooted in national legal tradition. His efforts may have contributed to an outcome in which, although the Civil Code largely expressed Romanist legal individualism, it became accepted that legislation reflecting different (social) principles would be needed to supplement it.[50] Tönnies and Weber, both admirers of Gierke's juristic scholarship, saw his organic imagery of legal and social development as lacking adequate empirical foundation and being insufficiently informed about social (especially economic) forces of change.[51] Gierke's ideas were tailored to the political and juristic debates of his time and provided rhetorical ammunition for these in a way that Weber's and Tönnies' did not.[52] Weber's and Tönnies' characterisations of legal and social history retain a significant presence in scholarly debate, however, while Gierke's have ceased to do so. Weber, in particular, was able to see, more clearly than either Gierke or Tönnies, the capacity of modern law as an instrument of government, free of tradition and fixed moral points. Most importantly, he recognised the state's power to direct this instrument in hitherto inconceivable ways, yet to do so in the framework of a capitalist social order that legal reform would not significantly

Gierke, *The Development of Political Theory* [1878], trans. B. Freyd (New York: H. Fertig, 1966).

48 M. John, *Politics and the Law in Late Nineteenth-Century Germany: The Origins of the Civil Code* (Oxford: Clarendon Press, 1989), ch. 5.

49 John, *Politics and the Law*, pp. 109–11; Mitzman, 'Tönnies and German society'.

50 M. John, 'The politics of legal unity in Germany, 1870–1897' (1985) 28 *Historical Journal* 341 ff.

51 Mommsen, *Max Weber and German Politics*, p. 11; W. J. Cahnman and R. Heberle (eds.), *Ferdinand Toennies on Sociology: Pure, Applied and Empirical* (University of Chicago Press, 1971), p. 22, pp. 32–3; A. Brand, 'Against romanticism: Max Weber and the historical school of law' (1982) 1 *Australian Journal of Law and Society* 87 ff., 94.

52 See A. Black, 'Editor's introduction', in Gierke, *Community in Historical Perspective*, pp. xiv ff., p. xxx: 'Gierke furnishes a splendid example of the kind of thinking against which...Weber...reacted...; he was the type case of what Weber called "the professor carrying the marshal's baton of the statesman or reformer in his knapsack".'

disturb. This Weberian message was addressed to 'science' and the long term, though, not to 'politics' and the legal debates of the moment.[53]

2.3 Sociological optimism: solidarity and social responsibility

French social theory, developed during the first half-century of the Third Republic (from 1871 to the early decades of the twentieth century), offers a striking contrast to the dominant strands of German pessimism or ambivalence about possibilities for major social change, and also to German portrayals of the state's central significance, as guarantor of the social and as the sovereign source of all law. My concern here is merely to illustrate this difference by reference to some leading contributions to French theory in this period.

Informing them are (i) the continuing influence of Comte's positivism and of his conviction that social science could point to ultimate values on which modern society should be founded; (ii) echoes of Jean-Jacques Rousseau's idea of sovereignty not as the possession of a state apparatus but as the crystallising in legal form of a popular 'general will' – 'so that the natural relations [of social life] are always in agreement with the laws on every point, and law only serves…to assure, accompany and rectify them';[54] (iii) the legacy of the Declaration of the Rights of Man; and (iv) a widespread awareness (throughout much of the nineteenth century but especially after defeat in the Franco-Prussian War of 1870–1, the bitter experience of the Paris Commune in 1871, and ongoing economic unrest from the 1880s) of an urgent need for French national unity and a social solidarity capable of bridging class divides.

2.3.1 Solidarism

The last of these themes clearly informed the 'solidarism' of Charles Secrétan, Alfred Fouillée and Léon Bourgeois, spanning the period from the middle of the nineteenth century to the early decades of the twentieth. It reflected a need to circumvent and defuse the perceived threat of working-class agitation associated with socialism and radical syndicalism, and

[53] See M. Weber, 'Politics as a vocation' [1919], in H. H. Gerth and C. W. Mills (eds., trans.), *From Max Weber: Essays in Sociology* (London: Routledge & Kegan Paul, 1948), pp. 77 ff.; and M. Weber, 'Science as a vocation' [1918], in Gerth and Mills, *From Max Weber*, pp. 129 ff., esp. pp. 115–17, pp. 150–3.

[54] G. D. H. Cole (ed., trans.), *The Social Contract and Discourses of Jean-Jacques Rousseau* (London: Dent, 1973), p. 205.

to do so without recourse to authoritarian solutions. It sought to counter traditional conservative Catholic paternalism with a genuine reformism focused, inter alia, on changing conceptions of social responsibility and social entitlement. Solidarism is less a social theory than a political-moral philosophy, significant here not just for its general influence as 'a kind of official philosophy for the Third Republic'[55] but as an important part of the climate of thought in which Durkheim's social theory developed.[56]

The solidarists saw justice as governed by the need for social solidarity:[57] 'The justice of egoism is not justice'[58] and – significantly – the state is *not* the primary agent of solidarity, since it can create a kind of unity only through constraint. Justice is to be realised in free, egalitarian associations with the 'associationist principle' penetrating property relations. 'Participation in profits and in the management of enterprises will transform all industries into vast production cooperatives… The free cooperative association is…the future,' wrote Secrétan in 1889;[59] the state is not superior to other associations. Its right to exist comes from the fact that it is needed to enforce law, but law (*droit*) arises outside it, and rights express the sharing of liberty. Free association is an inalienable right. All voluntary associations are founded on contract, and contract is the basis of all solidarity. Society, for Fouillée, is a 'contractual organism…freely desired and consented to'.[60] Associations can and must flourish independently of the state, which, in itself, 'is not flexible enough to steer economic life'.[61] Justice, for Fouillée, 'is the obligation to give each person what is due to him by reason of his function in the living totality and his solidarity with the whole society'.[62] Bourgeois introduced the ideas of a 'social debt' owed

[55] C. Bouglé, *Le solidarisme*, 2nd edn (Paris: Marcel Giard, 1924), p. 7.

[56] See Lukes, *Émile Durkheim*, pp. 350–4.

[57] The following summary draws especially on G. Gurvitch, *L'idée du Droit Social: Notion et système du droit social: Histoire doctrinale depuis le 17e siècle jusqu'à la fin du 19e siècle* (Paris: J. Vrin, 1932), pp. 567–89; see also J. E. S. Hayward, 'Solidarity: the social history of an idea in nineteenth-century France' (1959) 4 *International Review of Social History* 261 ff.

[58] C. Secrétan, *La Philosophie de la liberté: Cours de philosophie morale fait à Lausanne* (2 vols.), 2nd edn, vol. II (Lausanne: Bridel, 1865), p. 471, as quoted by Gurvitch, *L'idée du Droit Social*, p. 572.

[59] C. Secrétan, *Études sociales* (Paris: F. Alcan, 1889), p. 176, p. 178, as quoted by Gurvitch, *L'idée du Droit Social*, p. 574.

[60] A. Fouillée, *La science sociale contemporaine*, 5th edn (Paris: Hachette, 1910), quoted by Gurvitch, *L'idée du Droit Social*, p. 577.

[61] Fouillée, as quoted by Gurvitch, *L'idée du Droit Social*, p. 580.

[62] A. Fouillée, *La democratie politique et sociale en France* [1910], 2nd edn (Paris: F. Alcan, 1923), p. 18, as quoted by Gurvitch, *L'idée du Droit Social*, p. 580. See, generally, J. E. S.

by and to all society's interdependent members, reflecting natural conditions of solidarity, and of a 'social quasi-contract' of membership in society – 'quasi' because it is based on what parties would have wanted had they been able to consent in advance to the regime of law under which they would live.[63]

In this way solidarism created a rhetoric of social unity across class divides – offered to dispel memories of a defeated (in 1870) and compromised state that had often appeared to betray revolutionary hopes of liberty, equality and fraternity. It sought to replace these memories with promises of a new social contract involving a sense of the responsibility of social elites to recognise workers' entitlement to decent life conditions in return for their productivity.

Georges Gurvitch, writing in the early 1930s, criticised solidarism's inconsistencies, especially its commitment to legal individualism (signalled by the basing of all analysis on contractual relations of individuals) despite its concern to transcend individualism as a foundation of social organisation.[64] Solidarism proposed that rights and responsibilities should be *socially* determined by the conditions of association. It saw these conditions, however, as originating in a real or 'quasi' expression of *individual* wills, founding a contract. Solidarism developed no social theory to explain the content or significance of solidarity as an idea. Ultimately, Fouillée admitted that solidarity was an ideal,[65] not a social fact.

2.3.2 Durkheim

It was left to Durkheim – who shared the solidarists' desire for a society aware of the conditions of its own moral cohesion – to provide a social theory to explain the nature of solidarity and its different forms. In his *De la division du travail social*, published in 1893 but originating in lectures in 1887–8, he identified two kinds of solidarity existing in societies: mechanical – based on shared values, experience and understandings

Hayward, '"Solidarity" and the reformist sociology of Alfred Fouillée', part 1 (1963) 22 *American Journal of Economics and Sociology* 205 ff.; part 2, 303 ff.

63 See M. Borgetto, 'La doctrine solidariste de Léon Bourgeois: une nouvelle definition des rapports entre le politique, le social et le droit', in C. M. Herrera (ed.), *Les juristes face au politique: Le droit, la gauche, la doctrine sous la IIIe République* (Paris: Kimé, 2003), pp. 35 ff.; Gurvitch, *L'idée du Droit Social*, pp. 582–5; and, generally, S. Audier, *Léon Bourgeois: fonder la solidarité* (Paris: Michalon, 2007).

64 Gurvitch, *L'idée du Droit Social*, p. 575, p. 589; see also Borgetto, 'La doctrine solidariste', 51–2.

65 Gurvitch, *L'idée du Droit Social*, p. 579.

uniting individuals or groups; and organic – based on the interdependence of individuals or groups having functionally differentiated roles.[66] If the solidarists saw solidarity as an ideal, Durkheim argued (against Comte and Marx) that it could exist as a natural condition of complex societies with a highly developed division of labour. In these societies, functional differentiation creates conditions of interdependence. He also argued, however, that social cohesion in modern industrial society is not (as Spencer had claimed) a natural consequence of the free play of individual interests. A *moral* framework enshrined in law is needed to guarantee solidarity. The cohesion of modern society is not based on contracts because contracts require non-contractual conditions of existence.[67] It is the moral phenomenon of organic solidarity, arising directly from the *social fact* of interdependence, that provides these conditions.

Tönnies, Durkheim suggested, had been right in his characterisation of *Gemeinschaft*, which is essentially mechanical solidarity, and right to see it as declining in modern industrial societies as networks of association become larger, and more intricate and varied. He was wrong, however, to see these societies as inherently unstable and held from self-destructive conflict only by the state. What Tönnies ignored, in Durkheim's view, was the bond of organic solidarity that arose from the specialisation of social and economic roles and functions in complex modern societies.[68] Organic solidarity created cohesion, but needed to be supported by law. Contrary to Tönnies' view, law is not required to compensate for a pervasive absence of solidarity as if this were an inevitable problem of modern society. Instead, law must guard against particular 'abnormal forms'[69] of social organisation that may disrupt solidarity, such as the isolation, repression or discriminatory treatment of particular social groups or classes, which will exclude them from society's networks of interdependence.

Durkheim's theory clearly signals a new sociological view of responsibility.[70] The meaning of responsibility is fixed by society, not by the

66 É. Durkheim, *The Division of Labour in Society* [1893], trans. W. D. Halls (Basingstoke: Macmillan, 1984).

67 Durkheim, *The Division of Labour*, p. 162.

68 É. Durkheim, 'Communauté et société selon Tönnies' [1889], reprinted in V. Karady (ed.), *Émile Durkheim, Textes I: Éléments d'une théorie sociale* (Paris: Éditions de Minuit, 1975).

69 Durkheim, *The Division of Labour*, book 3.

70 See J.-L. Génard, 'Responsabilité et normativité dans l'école et la pensée de Durkheim', in P. Robert, F. Soubiran-Paillet and M. van de Kerchove (eds.), *Normes, normes juridiques, normes pénales: Pour une sociologie des frontiers* (2 vols.), vol. II (Paris: l'Harmattan, 1997), pp. 9 ff.

expectations of individuals. Contracts, for example, are not merely private relations between the parties but depend on the regulation that society supplies. Accordingly, their terms should reflect the requirements of solidarity. They should be 'just contracts' that do not abuse unequal bargaining power.[71] What exactly are solidarity's requirements, however? In Durkheim's early writings the morality of modern society is presented as a kind of 'governmental morality' of good social management. In a society of complex specialisation, people have to fulfil their specialised roles conscientiously. Society, through the state and law, imposes the requirement to do so – adequately to fulfil one's function, or that of one's social group. This idea of functionally determined responsibility is close to Comte's.

Later, however, Durkheim's writings develop a different emphasis:[72] the unifying morality of a highly differentiated society can only be one that emphasises the equal humanity of all its members, as individuals entitled to dignity and respect.[73] Solidarity in modern society cannot be based on tradition, blind adherence to authority or the mere interplay of private interests, but only on universal respect for others as individual human beings – an ultimate value that must pervade modern law (requiring, for example, humane treatment of offenders). This value system of moral individualism (*le culte de l'individu*)[74] is not postulated by philosophy, but presented by Durkheim as a derivation from social theory. He sees it as the only universal, unifying morality fully consistent with the nature of solidarity in complex societies. It is not produced by social conditions, but given meaning and relevance by them.

Hence, in Durkheimian social theory, a sociological understanding of the nature of solidarity makes it possible to specify the ultimate parameters of individual rights and responsibilities, to be determined not juristically or philosophically but by the conditions of complex, modern social life. Durkheim's ideas were much discussed by jurists in France and beyond, and they have a clear bearing on the way ideas of legal responsibility might be reformed. Yet they cannot be said to have influenced

[71] É. Durkheim, *Professional Ethics and Civic Morals* [1900], trans. C. Brookfield (London: Routledge & Kegan Paul, 1957), ch. 18; Durkheim, *The Division of Labour*, pp. 316–22; See, generally, C. J. Sirianni, 'Justice and the division of labour: a reconsideration of Durkheim's *Division of Labour in Society*' (1984) 32 *Sociological Review* 449 ff.

[72] Cotterrell, *Émile Durkheim*, chs. 7–9.

[73] É. Durkheim, 'L'individualisme et les intellectuels' (1898), reprinted in J.-C. Filloux (ed.), *Émile Durkheim: La science sociale et l'action*, 2nd edn (Paris: Presses universitaires de France, 1987).

[74] See É. Durkheim, *Leçons de sociologie* [1895] (Paris: Presses universitaires de France, 1950), p. 199.

legal debate in the direct way that solidarism did. Solidarism postulated solidarity as an ideal, not as a sociological concept. As such, like Gierke's speculative appeal to history in Germany, solidarism in France offered an attractive rhetoric for political and legal debate (and had a major influence on legal reform campaigns in such areas as social welfare, health and safety, and industrial conditions).[75] Nonetheless, it was not rooted in a sociology that, like Durkheim's, sought to explain the historical developments it proclaimed.

At the same time, Durkheimian social theory lacked wide, direct influence partly because it did not provide an unambiguous rhetoric for law reform debates. Even among Durkheim's followers there was not necessarily agreement about conclusions to be drawn from theory. One of them, Paul Fauconnet, argued that modern legal ideas of responsibility, emphasising the subjective intentions of the individual wrongdoer, were 'an immense impoverishment',[76] because, from a sociological standpoint, attributions of responsibility had to be made to meet the needs of social solidarity as a whole, and could not be restricted by a subjective, 'spiritualised' emphasis on any particular individual's state of mind. The implication might be that Durkheim's outlook on the 'naturalness' of solidarity in modern society and the need only for legal action to correct 'abnormal' social developments was too complacent. A revolution in legal and social ideas might be needed. This was the conclusion of another Durkheimian, the jurist Paul Huvelin. Acknowledging Durkheim's sociological methods as fundamental, he nevertheless argued that organic solidarity is not a natural condition of modern societies (although interdependence is); therefore, law's directive, coercive power is essential to control the conflict that is endemic in modern social life.[77]

2.4 Conclusion: competing visions of law and state

Durkheim's writings on the state[78] emphasise in general terms, very much in the tradition of Comte and Rousseau, government's role as an agent of society. They offer no insights such as Weber's into the state's bureaucratic

[75] J. F. Stone, *The Search for Social Peace: Reform Legislation in France, 1890–1914* (Albany, NY: State University of New York Press, 1985).

[76] P. Fauconnet, *La responsabilité: Étude de sociologie*, 2nd edn (Paris: F. Alcan, 1928), p. 350; see also Cotterrell, *Émile Durkheim*, pp. 107–8; and J. Piaget, *The Moral Judgment of the Child* [1932], trans. M. Gabain (Harmondsworth: Penguin Books, 1977), pp. 315–28.

[77] On Huvelin's work, see Cotterrell, *Living Law*, ch. 7.

[78] Cotterrell, *Émile Durkheim*, chs. 10–11.

structure or legal foundations of its legitimacy. Since Durkheim and Weber never wrote about each other's work, the gulf in perceptions remains unbridged. That their social theories follow very different directions is clear, especially on matters of legal responsibility. For Durkheim, law and morality are always closely interrelated, and legal responsibility has to be shaped by the value system of moral individualism if it is to contribute to social solidarity. Even if some of his followers thought this approach might not go far enough to emphasise social bases of responsibility, they certainly agreed that responsibility is more than a matter between individuals, as portrayed in most modern legal conceptions of delict. Dictated by society for social ends, it is, by implication, capable of being adjusted into forms that best serve the needs of social solidarity.

Weber was silent on such matters, but one might presume to speak for him: Weberian responsibility is surely merely what law and state (rather than 'society') decree it to be. In Weber's view, since the demise of natural law, no consistent value orientations shape modern law; only a mass of disparate policy influences give it substance. Legal responsibility is thus the outcome of law's primarily formal-rational and pragmatic prescriptions. Like law itself, it is a technical instrument to serve the needs of the state and the task of compromising private interests. Separated from moral intuitions, legal responsibility is easily seen as merely a transaction cost in private dealings or a device for governmental coercion.

The theories of Tönnies and Weber present an image of the largely settled law, state and society of modern capitalism, especially as coloured by the experience of a new (German) political unity and centralised governmental power. By comparison, the ideas of the solidarists address the moral disquiet that was increasingly widespread about this modern social and political-legal order in the late nineteenth and early twentieth centuries. Correspondingly, the Durkheimians focused on the need to direct law and political power to meet the requirements of solidarity. Unsurprisingly, among social theorists, it was Durkheim who appealed most strongly to some reform-minded jurists in the period; but his ideas were useful to them mainly insofar as the sociological idea of solidarity could be turned into a philosophical justification for legal reform and a rhetorical tool in legal discourse.

By far the most important and influential appropriation of the concept of solidarity in this way was by the public lawyer Léon Duguit. A colleague of Durkheim for some years at the University of Bordeaux, Duguit enthusiastically adopted the Durkheimian view that law is both an instrument and a reflection of social solidarity. Duguit argued, like the solidarists, that the source of law, understood in this 'objective' way, is not the state but the conditions of life of the society in which law exists. As such it is 'contingent on social fact…, a spontaneous creation of social life'.[79] In his later writings, Duguit saw law as based in the consciousness of the mass of citizens who view it as necessary to maintain social solidarity. Clearly, positive law created by the state does not always correspond to this 'objective' law[80] rooted in social fact. The authority of the former ultimately depends on its congruence with the latter, however, and not on state sovereignty. Duguit, indeed, rejected the sovereignty of the state and claimed that the state retains authority only insofar as it acts to nurture solidarity. The state is subject to law – a social law dictated by the needs of solidarity. The modern state must become a public service state limited by law, its treasury being, 'so to speak, a friendly society' for the benefit of its citizens when they suffer harm in the ordinary course of social cooperation; in such circumstances 'society as a whole should intervene to repair the consequences'.[81]

Duguit assumed Durkheim's ideas about law as an expression of social solidarity without engaging with the sociology that underpins them, and his legal politics was close to that of the solidarists. Other jurists, notably Maurice Hauriou, strongly criticised Duguit's rejection, in his legal theory, of subjective rights (seen as expressions of individual will) in favour of his idea that law expresses objective social functions.[82] Duguit's arguments had a huge impact on French legal thought,[83] however, and were carried into Anglophone debates by Harold Laski[84] and others. They entrenched in juristic thought an understanding that responsibility is based in society, arising in the context of social associations of various kinds, and that the state has a new role as an instrument of collective wel-

[79] C. Eisenmann, 'Léon Duguit', in D. L. Sills (ed.), *International Encyclopedia of the Social Sciences*, vol. IV (New York: Free Press, 1968), pp. 305 ff., p. 306.

[80] L. Duguit, 'Objective law', part 1 (1920) 20 *Columbia Law Review* 817 ff.; part 2 (1921) 21 *Columbia Law Review* 17 ff.; part 3, 126 ff.; part 4, 242 ff.

[81] L. Duguit, *Souveraineté et liberté* (Paris: F. Alcan, 1922), p. 168, as quoted by J. E. S. Hayward, 'Solidarist syndicalism: Durkheim and Duguit', part 2 (1960) 8 *Sociological Review* 185 ff., 194.

[82] See, for example, M. Hauriou, 'The two realisms' [1912], trans. M. Welling, in A. Broderick (ed.), *The French Institutionalists: Maurice Hauriou, Georges Renard, Joseph T. Delos* (Cambridge, MA: Harvard University Press, 1970), pp. 45 ff.

[83] E. Pisier-Kouchner, *Le service public dans la théorie de l'état de Léon Duguit* (Paris: R. Vançon, 1972).

[84] H. Laski, 'Introduction', in L. Duguit, *Law in the Modern State*, trans. F. and H. Laski (London: Allen & Unwin, 1921), pp. ix ff.

fare: a role in which – in Durkheim's conception, influenced by Comte and Rousseau – the state 'thinks' solutions on behalf of society.[85]

All this is far removed from Tönnies', and especially Weber's, tendency to predict little long-term impact from demands for social law and social responsibility. Which of these visions was ultimately the more prescient? Perhaps only von Stein, among the major social theorists considered here, sensed clearly both the unavoidable modern need for some kind of social or welfare state and also the sheer difficulty of establishing such a state on a stable basis, given the organisational history of Western state forms, which Weber would explore. In juristic contexts, though, it was not difficult in the half-century after 1870 to adopt ideas (most fully developed in social theory) about law's foundations in society (rather than the state) and to use these to criticise individualistic orientations of legal thought and juristic fixations on state sovereignty.

The story of the most enduring forms of social theory in this period seems, however, to be one of voices talking past each other and of irreconcilable visions of the state. On one side was a recurring vision of a state that could – and must – be shaped to fulfil, as a central part of its task, an emerging expectation that responsibility would be shared *socially*, or determined by social need. Such a vision clearly implied the necessity, if not inevitability, of social legislation in many fields and a declining emphasis on private law solutions to issues of responsibility. On the other side were very different social-theoretical ideas that prefigured current neoliberal scepticisms about any such wider responsibility. These ideas portrayed the modern state as allied with forms of atomistic *individualism* reflecting increasing social complexity. In such a perspective, the task of managing innumerable, endlessly varied conflicts of individual interests appeared to be at the heart of that complexity. The implication was that an important part of the state's role would continue to be to provide reliable procedures and guarantees for private law claims of individual responsibility.

[85] Cotterrell, *Émile Durkheim*, ch. 10.

3

Individual and social responsibility in nineteenth-century British political thought

SANDRA DEN OTTER*

In *Law and Public Opinion in England*, the jurist Albert Venn Dicey drew a map of English thinking in the nineteenth century, through which a deep fault line ran: the era of individualism on one side of the gulf, and the era of collectivism on the other.[1] This notion of a seismic shift between the thinking of the middle of the century and the late nineteenth century on individual and social responsibility that undergirded law was almost axiomatic for a time. Two prominent commentators on the political landscape of their day, L. T. Hobhouse in his tract *Liberalism* (1911) and Ernest Barker in *Political Thought in England: From Spencer to the Present Day* (1915), traced a similar trajectory, though both were rather more certain than Dicey that this change was to be applauded. Several decades of scholarship on mid- to late Victorian political and legal theory have questioned just how radical a transition this was, however. Jose Harris, among others, has pointed instead to a much more nuanced intellectual landscape, much more variegated forms of Victorian liberalism and a political culture much less fiercely individualist in the middle of the nineteenth century and much less robustly collectivist in the twentieth than commonly thought. Herbert Spencer's advocacy of some forms of land nationalisation and Beatrice Webb's esteem for the virtues of individual self-help are just two of the intriguing paradoxes and continuities that a simple lineage from individualism to collectivism threatens to flatten away.[2]

* Department of History, Queen's University.

[1] Dicey recognised numerous inconsistencies in this broad outline of law and opinion: A. V. Dicey, *Law and Public Opinion in England during the Nineteenth Century* [1905] (London: Macmillan, 1962).

[2] J. Harris, *Private Lives, Public Spirit: A Social History of Britain, 1870–1914* (Oxford University Press, 1993); J. Harris, 'Political thought and the welfare state 1870–1940: an intellectual framework for British social policy' (1992) 135 *Past and Present* 116 ff.; M. Francis, *Herbert Spencer and the Invention of Modern Life* (London: Acumen, 2007); and H. S. Jones, *Victorian Political Thought* (London: Macmillan, 2000).

Shifts in jurisprudence and political theory were among the many elements that formed the English law of tort in the late nineteenth century, in tandem with the broad economic and social dynamics of industrialisation, trade union militancy and insurance provision, and distinctive features of the English legal profession.[3] Philosophical discussions about the nature of the individual, the state and their relative spheres of authority generated, albeit most often indirectly, the arsenal of dominant ideas and expectations of law that underpinned different understandings of justice and, in turn, took form in legal decisions and statutory law. The diffusion of these ideas across a broad legal culture in the nineteenth century was hastened in part by the absence both of separate professional schools within universities and of strong boundaries separating disciplines. The prominent stature of legal theorists such as Sir Henry Maine, Dicey, Fitzjames Stephen and other public intellectuals who cast philosophical debates about evolution, the individual and the state into a juridical idiom and who published vigorously in the periodical press (which was then widely read by fellow jurists) also assisted this diffusion. Jurists disseminated legal ideas and debates, and Continental and imperial legal innovations, across a wide audience. The subscriber to the 1877 editions of *The Fortnightly Review* could read Maine on feudal property in France and England, J. F. McLennan on endogamy and exogamy, Henry Sidgwick on Bentham and Benthamism, J. F. Stephen on a penal code and Mark Pattison on the 'age of reason', along side Sir John Lubbock on the habits of ants and Antony Trollope on Cicero. Autobiographies of Victorian jurists, letters, memoirs and histories of the bench attest to a highly literate and widely read elite, who were well acquainted – and, indeed, often actively engaged – with the dominant philosophical debates of the day. To insist on a precise circuitry leading from any single philosophical school to common law development, however, diminishes the heterogeneity, complexity and changeability of nineteenth-century legal cultures and runs the risk of underestimating the force of common sense in juridical practice. Sir Frederick Pollock, author of a treatise on Spinoza and for twenty years

[3] P. W. J. Bartrip and S. Burman, *The Wounded Soldiers of Industry: Industrial Compensation Policy, 1833–1897* (Oxford: Clarendon Press, 1983); D. Ibbetson, *A Historical Introduction to the Law of Obligations* (Oxford University Press, 1999); R. W. Kostal, *Law and English Railway Capitalism 1825–1875* (Oxford: Clarendon Press, 1994); P. Cane, *Atiyah's Accidents, Compensation and the Law*, 7th edn (Cambridge University Press, 2006); M. Taggart, *Private Property and the Abuse of Rights in Victorian England* (Oxford University Press, 2002); G. E. White, *Tort Law in America: An Intellectual History* (Oxford University Press, 2003), pp. 3–4; and N. Duxbury, *Frederick Pollock and the English Juristic Tradition* (Oxford University Press, 2004), p. 248.

the Corpus Professor of Jurisprudence at Oxford, described his interest in philosophy merely as a pastime and affirmed in 1932 to law students at the University of Birmingham: 'The older I grow, the less inclined I am to trust any general theories of jurisprudence.'[4] Although Pollock was notoriously opposed to Austinian positivism, and his dismissal of jurisprudence is in this sense unsurprising, he credited ideas with the authority and power to shape law, via the dominant expectations, principles and moral values of a community that judges articulated in their decisions.[5] Although the legal categories developed in tort law by Pollock and others were not often used by Victorian political philosophers, these philosophers articulated ideas of justice, duty, rights, the command of law and the relative spheres of individual and social responsibility that had an impact on the dominant expectations and values of their community.[6] Many Victorian theorists were engaged in active politics, in parliament (John Stuart Mill), in municipal government (T. H. Green) and in policy groups such as the National Association for the Promotion of Social Science and the Fabian Society. The wider political life of late Victorian and Edwardian Britain was also critical in framing these dominant expectations, because the rhetoric of freedom from what Victorians called 'the grandmother state' did not always dovetail with political or legal practice, even in the apparent heyday of the individual. The mid-nineteenth-century state was far from a hands-off, laissez-faire state, as it intervened far into the lives of citizens, fuelled at first partly by Tory paternalism and a juggernaut of social legislation that prompted some contemporary commentators to regard the advent of collectivism as almost inevitable.

3.1 Victorian individualism: J. S. Mill

Mill's *On Liberty* is most often read as a canonical text of Victorian liberalism, and more precisely as a canonical defence of the liberty of the individual from the interference of law and the state. Although several decades of scholarship on Mill have done much to complicate our understanding of *On Liberty*, its mythic status as an apology for negative liberty

[4] Sir Frederick Pollock (1932), cited by Duxbury, *Frederick Pollock*, p. 88.

[5] See Michael Lobban, 'English jurisprudence and tort theory', Chapter 6 in this volume.

[6] See G. P. Fletcher, 'Fairness and utility in tort theory' (1972) 85 *Harvard Law Review* 537 ff.; R. A. Posner 'The concept of corrective justice in recent theories of tort law' (1981) 10 *Journal of Legal Studies* 187 ff.; R. A. Posner, *Economic Analaysis of the Law* (London: Little, Brown, 1992); and P. Cane, 'Justice and justifications for tort liability' (1982) 2 *OJLS* 30 ff.

is remarkably resilient. But if we situate Mill fully within his age, with its complex and ambivalent wrestling with the ideas of progress, social evolution and moral character, some of the tensions that Mill encountered and that were to vex the next generation of liberal thinkers become more evident, for defining the relative spheres of the individual, the state and social authority was pivotal to changing ideas of tort law.[7]

Mill established as his starting point in *On Liberty* the principle 'that the sole end for which mankind are warranted, individually or collectively, in interfering with the liberty of action of any of their number, is self-protection. The only purpose for which power can be rightfully exercised over any member of a civilized community, against his will, is to prevent harm to others.' [8] This has often been interpreted to mean that there are two kinds of conduct, self-regarding and other-regarding, but scholars of Mill have challenged this interpretation and have argued instead that Mill was much more attentive to the ways in which the lines between so-called self-regarding and other-regarding activities are blurred.[9] Alan Ryan reminds readers that the primary target of Mill's attack in *On Liberty* was the tyranny of social conformity and homogeneity, rather than the coercion of the modern political state, and that Mill was defending individual liberty precisely because of its capacity to enlarge general well-being.[10] Believing, as he did, that 'the initiation of all wise or noble things comes and must come from the individual', conformity to religious thought or stultifying public opinion posed a monumental and almost unassailable threat to spontaneity, to the vigorous development of those unique qualities that make us human and, ultimately, to the progress and advancement of society as a whole. As Mill states:[11]

> Society can and does execute its own mandates: and if it issues wrong mandates instead of right, or any mandates at all in things with which it

[7] See J. Skorupski, 'The philosophy of John Stuart Mill' (2007) 15 *British Journal for the History of Philosophy* 181 ff., 183.

[8] J. S. Mill, *On Liberty* [1859], in J. M. Robson (ed.), *The Collected Works of John Stuart Mill*, vol. XVIII, *Essays on Politics and Society* (London: Routledge & Kegan Paul, 1977), pp. 213 ff., p. 223.

[9] See, for example, W. Donner, *The Liberal Self: John Stuart Mill's Moral and Political Philosophy* (Ithaca, NY: Cornell University Press, 1991); C. L. Ten, *Mill on Liberty* (Oxford University Press, 1980); J. Gray, *Mill on Liberty: A Defence* (London: Routledge, 1996); and C. McGann, *Individualism and the Social Order: The Social Element in Liberal Thought* (London: Routledge, 2004), ch. 2.

[10] A. Ryan, 'In a liberal landscape', in J. Skorupski (ed.), *The Cambridge Companion to Mill* (Cambridge University Press, 1998), pp. 497 ff., p. 498, p. 501, p. 516.

[11] Mill, *On Liberty*, p. 220.

> ought not to meddle, it practises a social tyranny more formidable than many kinds of political oppression, since, though not usually upheld by such extreme penalties, it leaves fewer means of escape, penetrating much more deeply into the details of life, and enslaving the soul itself. Protection, therefore, against the tyranny of the magistrate is not enough; there needs protection also against the tyranny of the prevailing opinion and feeling; against the tendency of society to impose, by other means than civil penalties, its own ideas and practices as rules of conduct on those who dissent from them; to fetter the development, and, if possible, prevent the formation, of any individuality not in harmony with its ways, and compel all characters to fashion themselves upon the model of its own.

Mill did not endorse a form of social atomism, in which he imagined the individual severed from connection to other citizens. To the contrary, in *On Liberty*, as well as across his writings spanning four decades, Mill describes the well-being of the individual as being closely tied, albeit awkwardly and dangerously, with other individuals and with society and civic institutions. As Mill emphatically states in *On Liberty*: 'It would be a great misunderstanding of this doctrine to suppose that it is one of selfish indifference, which pretends that human beings have no business with each other's conduct in life, and that they should not concern themselves about the well-doings or well-being of one another, unless their own interest is involved.'[12] Following the direction of contemporary evolutionary theories, Mill believed that mindfulness of others was a propensity in human nature that was strengthened in advanced societies by civilising institutions and education.[13] Mill connected individual development directly to the advancement of civilisation; social progress depended upon nurturing the liberty of the individual and thereby the development of their uniquely human capacities. His emphasis on exercising virtue in our personal and public lives recalled an older classical Greek notion in which the individual flourishes by being mindful of the social whole.

He remained opposed to incursions into private conduct on moral grounds. He reached for two particularly outrageous examples of legislative interference in the name of general welfare: temperance legislation, which attempted to limit the private consumption of alcohol, and sabbatarian legislation, to restrict trading, museum openings and railway travel on Sundays. He was therefore careful to identify when harmful

[12] Mill, *On Liberty*, pp. 276–7.

[13] J. S. Mill, 'Utilitarianism (1861)', in J. M. Robson (ed.), *The Collected Works of John Stuart Mill*, vol. X, *Essays on Ethics, Religion and Society* (London: Routledge & Kegan Paul, 1969), pp. 203 ff., p. 231.

actions should be censured by moral disapprobation and when they warranted the intervention of the state. He reminded readers that social disapprobation and 'remonstration' constituted a powerful influence on private conduct, and that these forms of preventing harm to others were often more effective that clumsy state initiatives such as those mentioned above.[14] But, when the predictable consequences of an action caused harm to others, 'the case is to be taken out of the province of liberty and placed in that of morality or law'.[15] Sometimes the state could intervene to ward off possible consequences by 'antecedent precautions', such as keeping a register of those buying poisons, or warning a recurrent public drunkard that repeated offences would be penalised. The state could also intervene in the apparently private realm of conduct to demand that a recipient of public money work (though, if he was not supported by the public purse, his idleness was his own affair), or it could order a father into compulsory labour to support his children (without children, his idleness would also be his own affair). It could command citizens to serve on juries or serve in municipal government, and in these latter cases the opportunities for active citizenship of an Athenian sort occasioned by these activities was a welcome additional benefit. These examples illustrate a fairly limited and minimalist level of intervention by the state, and the common law idea of duty to care that also undergirded employee liability in the middle of the century.

Take, for example, Mill's public campaign to repeal the Contagious Diseases Acts.[16] The Contagious Diseases Acts enabled the state in garrison towns to forcibly detain women suspected of prostitution in lock hospitals until their freedom from venereal diseases could either be determined or secured by medical treatment. On the one hand, Mill's harm principle might justify the Contagious Diseases Acts (and the intervention of the state in sexual conduct) on the grounds that these acts sought to prevent the spread of infection that was injurious not only to

[14] M. Freeden, 'Liberal passions: reason and emotion in late and post-Victorian liberal thought', in P. Ghosh and L. Goldman (eds.), *Politics and Culture in Victorian Britain: Essays in Memory of Colin Matthew* (Oxford University Press, 2006), pp. 136 ff., p. 142.

[15] Mill, *On Liberty*, p. 282.

[16] See J. S. Mill, 'The evidence of John Stuart Mill, taken before the Royal Commission of 1870, on the Administration and Operation of the Contagious Diseases Acts of 1866 and 1869', in J. M. Robson (ed.), *The Collected Works of John Stuart Mill*, vol. XXI, *Essays on Equality, Law, and Education* (London: Routledge & Kegan Paul, 1984), pp. 333 ff.; and J. Waldron, 'Mill on liberty and the Contagious Diseases Acts', in N. Urbinati and A. Zakaras (eds.), *J. S. Mill's Political Thought: A Bicentennial Reassessment* (Cambridge University Press, 2007), pp. 11 ff.

individuals but to the navy and army, and ultimately the security of the British nation – and, indeed, this was the rationale offered by the acts' defenders. But Mill, in the company of feminist opponents to the measures, argued instead that the coercive nature of the acts was so egregious and so unfairly borne by women rather than men that infringement of the liberty of the individual outweighed any social benefits. When asked before the Royal Commission on the Contagious Diseases Acts whether he agreed with the legislation on principle, Mill replied:[17]

> I do not consider it justifiable on principle, because it appears to me to be opposed to one of the greatest principles of legislation, the security of personal liberty. It appears to me that legislation of this sort takes away that security, almost entirely from a particular class of women intentionally, but incidentally and unintentionally, one may say, from all women whatever, inasmuch as it enables a woman to be apprehended by the police on suspicion and taken before a magistrate, and then by that magistrate she is liable to be confined for a term of imprisonment which may amount, I believe, to six months, for refusing to sign a declaration consenting to be examined.

Mill also objected that the acts constituted state patronage of prostitution, because they attempted to provide security against the consequences of injudicious sexual conduct, and thereby disturbed the intricate moral psychology that governed the will and so corrupted the development of the higher character.[18]

Mill nonetheless established a role for the state in preventing injury or harm that might ensue from otherwise unrestricted individual autonomy. He envisaged the state maintaining a vigilant control over the boundaries of individual liberty and social welfare: 'The state, while it respects the liberty of each in what specially regards himself, is bound to maintain a vigilant control over his exercise of any power which it allows him to possess over others.'[19] This might entail requiring proof that couples had financial resources to raise their children wisely and to educate them before giving out marriage licences; otherwise, the state would be derelict in its duty to prevent harm to the children of imprudent and hasty marriages. It might entail compulsory public examinations of all children to ensure

[17] Mill, 'The evidence of John Stuart Mill'.

[18] S. Collini, 'Introduction', in J. M. Robson (ed.), *The Collected Works of John Stuart Mill*, vol. XXI, *Essays on Equality, Law, and Education* (London: Routledge & Kegan Paul, 1984), pp. viii ff. What Mill proposed instead was to identify male users of prostitutes and to give wives the right of divorce with heavy damages.

[19] Mill, *On Liberty*, p. 297.

that they were being educated wisely and effectively (Mill was opposed to compulsory state-run schools because they would squash diversity and eccentricity).[20] It might entail some redistribution of land and resources. It might restrict procreation if a resultant child could be expected to be incapable of 'living a desirable existence', or when parents were unable to support the child or to prevent harm to society by adding to an overabundance of labour.[21] In these cases, Mill reached for utilitarian principles to explain the desirability of restricting the liberty of the individual in the name of the welfare of society as a whole. An example of the paternalistic possibilities of Mill's limited state was the question of whether the state ought to prevent individuals from causing harm to themselves by entering into a contract that would place them in lifelong servitude. There is good reason to think that Mill was not here invoking a 'hard paternalism' but was mindful of the public harm that could be occasioned by voluntary servitude.[22]

Although Mill demonstrated a strong sense of how much individuals in his society were harmed by inequities in the distribution of property, he saw a radical reorganisation of capitalism as more dangerous than the evils it might correct: 'The very idea of distributive justice or of any proportionality between success and merit, or between success and exertion, is in the present state of society so manifestly chimerical as to be relegated to the regions of romance.'[23] Mill's defence of the liberty of the individual set boundaries on how far he was prepared to travel in the direction of distributive justice. He was opposed to far-reaching state-operated schemes for a just distribution of economic resources, what he called 'state-managed socialism', because he feared the deadening weight of such a state on individuality and diversity of opinion.[24] He was convinced that individuals develop best when they freely exercise their own business, and that this liberty of action was a means to their own mental education. He found more sympathetic 'philosophic socialists' such as Robert Owen and Charles Fourier, and supported the idea of small worker

[20] Mill, *On Liberty*, pp. 302–5.

[21] McCann, *Individualism and the Social Order*, p. 62.

[22] J. Feinberg, *The Moral Limits of the Criminal Law* (Oxford University Press, 1986), pp. 72–81.

[23] J. S. Mill, 'Chapters on socialism (1879)', in J. M. Robson (ed.), *The Collected Works of John Stuart Mill*, vol. V, *Essays on Economics and Society Part II* (London: Routledge & Kegan Paul, 1967), pp. 703 ff., p. 714. J. A. Hobson cited this conclusion four decades later as still constituting an apt description of turn-of-the-century Britain.

[24] Mill, 'Chapters on socialism', p. 746. See also B. Baum, 'J. S. Mill and liberal socialism', in Urbinati and Zakaras, *J. S. Mill's Political Thought*, pp. 98 ff., pp. 119–20.

cooperatives governed by the kind of direct democracy that he favoured. Towards the end of his life he came to endorse some forms of state redistribution of wealth, primarily in the form of taxation on inheritance and land rents, and limited land nationalisation.[25] But he feared the instability of radical revolutionary change, not least because it threatened that security of expectation that was the chief end of political society. The bulwark of Mill's political economy remained as it had since first articulated in *Principles of Political Economy* in 1848: laws to govern the distribution of rights and duties that afforded security of expectation and ensured a certain level of well-being (above subsistence).[26]

Although Mill in his early life had been steeped in the legal reform campaigns of the philosophical radicals, and although he saw law as an essential curb on the self-regarding actions of individuals and a powerful vehicle for social change, the precise classifications of practical law did not figure prominently in his writings.[27] Mill's review essays on the jurists John Austin and Maine were notable exceptions. In an 1863 review essay, Mill endorses much of Austin's jurisprudential project, sanctioning his understanding of the law as a rational set of universal principles, modelled on Roman law, and his determination to simplify and codify law. He echoes Austin's call for a radical rethinking of the practical law of injury, harnessing this to a more wide-ranging critique of the prolixity of English law in contrast to the analytical simplicity of Austin's science of jurisprudence. He singled out Austin's analysis of wrong and injury, both civil and criminal. Austin had defined clearly the legal categories of will, motive, intention and negligence, upon which notions of wrong or injury depended, and from which, Mill argued, so much 'bad law and bad philosophy of law, have arisen from imperfect comprehension of them'. Mill regarded the practical law resulting from an imperfect comprehension of injury as a particularly vivid example of how sure the path from muddy juridical notions to bad law was:[28]

25 J. S. Mill, 'Land tenure reform (1871)', in J. M. Robson (ed.), *The Collected Works of John Stuart Mill*, vol. V, *Essays on Economics and Society Part II* (London: Routledge & Kegan Paul, 1967), pp. 687 ff.

26 J. Riley, 'Mill's political economy: Ricardian science and liberal utilitarian art', in J. Scorupski (ed.), *The Cambridge Companion to Mill* (Cambridge University Press, 1998), pp. 293 ff., pp. 315–17.

27 S. Collini, *Public Moralists: Political Thought and Intellectual Life in Britain, 1850–1930* (Oxford University Press, 1991), ch. 7.

28 J. S. Mill (1863), 'Austin on jurisprudence (1863)', in J. M. Robson (ed.), *The Collected Works of John Stuart Mill*, vol. XXI, *Essays on Equality, Law, and Education* (London: Routledge & Kegan Paul, 1984), pp. 165 ff., p. 201.

> The unhappy idea of classifying wrongs according to a difference which exists only in the modes appointed for redressing them, has raised up a notion in English lawyers that there is a distinction between civil injuries and crimes considered per se, which makes damages the proper remedy for the one, and punishment for the other. And hence that serious defect in English law, by which punishment eo nomine, and damages to the injured party, cannot both be awarded in the same cause; while in France, on the contrary, the sufferers by the crime can always be admitted as parties civiles, and compensation to them is habitually a part of the sentence. In England, whenever the wrong is of so grave a character as to require punishment over and above the obligation of making amends, the injured party loses the indemnity which he would have been able to exact for a less heinous injury; and the penalty on the criminal is deprived of one of its uses, that of being instrumental to the redress of the particular evil which the crime has inflicted upon an individual.

Mill was not advocating a radical reorganisation of the market economy animated by principles of distributive justice, and he defended vigorously the rights of individuals to pursue their own best interest within the parameters defined by the harm principle. He offered grounds for strengthening tort law to define liability and provide compensation, and for some limited state intervention through statutory protection to prevent individuals from harming each other. It fell to the next generation of British political thinkers, the idealists, to articulate a more expanded understanding of social responsibility, and to argue that law and the state had a moral purpose to prevent harm and injury.

3.2 The individual, community and the moral state: T. H. Green and philosophical idealism

Shifting understandings of the meaning of 'fault' articulated in late nineteenth-century legal decisions and in the new manuals on torts reflected a heightened sensibility about the interests of community as a whole, relative to an earlier attention to individual interests. The idealists had a potent impact on late nineteenth-century thought in generating these shifting understandings. Centred around the unlikely figures of Green, F. H. Bradley and, later, Edward Caird, a new kind of philosophical argument grew up through which the boundaries of liberal argument were expanded and reframed. As R. G. Collingwood remembered, 'The School of Green sent out into public life a stream of ex-pupils who carried with them the conviction that philosophy and in particular the philosophy they had learnt at Oxford was an important thing and their vocation was to put this into practice.'[29] Even though idealist metaphysics and epistemology were to falter under the attack of successive generations of philosophical critique, and the next generation of liberals and social democrats were to question whether some idealists had gone too far in sanctioning state totalitarianism, they had nonetheless authoritatively shifted the parameters of the debate about the relative spheres of the individual and the state, and opened up new ways of thinking, in their aspiration to build communities of moral individuals pursuing a common good. Several eminent jurists and judges were at Balliol College, Oxford, during the height of idealist influence, notably Sir Thomas Erskine Holland, Lord Coleridge, Justice Bowen, Sir Robert Samuel Wright and Dicey, though this did not turn them into idealists. Almost all the chief architects of the welfare state established in the 1940s (Sir William Beveridge, W. J. Braithwaite, R. Tawney, Clement Attlee) regarded the influence of philosophical idealism, either at Balliol College, South Place Ethical Society, Toynbee Hall or through reading Green and other idealists' writings, as formative.[30]

Although the metaphysical speculations of the Oxford idealists may have seemed remote, their view of society as a moral community that transcended the individual was urgent and compelling for many of their contemporaries. Their reinterpretation of state authority to encompass a general or communitarian will challenged Austinian notions of law as coercive command, which in its multiple forms had dominated Victorian jurisprudence. Green sought to modify Austin's view of sovereignty, as articulated in *Lectures on Jurisprudence* (1869 edition), incorporating Kantian moral philosophy and Maine's historical studies. Austinians erred, Green argued, by attributing to a determinate sovereign person the coercive power of law. The real source of the habitual obedience of people to the law was not the sovereign but 'that impalpable congeries of the hopes and fears of a people, bound together by common interests and sympathy, which we call the general will'.[31] Green described English

[29] R. G. Collingwood, *An Autobiography* (Oxford University Press, 1939), p. 16. This section draws on S. den Otter, '"Thinking in communities": late 19th-century liberals, idealists and the retrieval of community', in E. H. H. Green (ed.), *An Age of Transition: British Politics 1880–1914* (Edinburgh University Press, 1997), pp. 67 ff.; and S. den Otter, *British Idealism and Social Explanation* (Oxford: Clarendon Press, 1996). See also P. P. Nicholson, *The Political Philosophy of the British Idealists: Selected Studies* (Cambridge University Press, 1990).

[30] See Harris, 'Political thought and the welfare state', 124–5.

[31] T. H. Green, *Lectures on the Principles of Political Obligation*, vol. II, *The Works of T. H. Green*, ed. R. L. Nettleship (3 vols.) (London: Longmans, Green, 1886), p. 404. Green

common law, and the statutory laws that hedged it about, as an expression of this community will and collective sentiment, and not as the coercive command of a sovereign. He therefore viewed customary law in India as the expression of a general will, and mistakenly saw the imperial government there as a non-coercive entity that preserved customary law. This attention to communitarian themes suggested a new interpretation of individual responsibility, by arguing powerfully that the autonomy of the individual concealed duties and responsibilities to society.

Although the 'cult of character' so pivotal in Mill's defence of liberty resonated in idealist writings, the idealists did not echo Mill's caution against the repressive conformity of society, nor the necessity to be vigilant against the rapacious interference of the state. They saw no simple boundary between the individual and the rest of society, regarding it both as impossible and undesirable 'to treat the central life of the individual as something to be carefully fenced round against the impact of social forces'.[32] As Green, in uncharacteristic brevity, puts it: 'Without society, no persons.'[33] The Fabian idealist D. G. Ritchie maintained that 'the individual apart from all relations of community...is a mere abstraction – a logical ghost, a metaphysical spectre'.[34] This notion recalled Bradley's argument in *Ethical Studies* (1876) that any political theory that imagines the individual to be unencumbered and autonomous failed to recognize that the individual 'implies in every fibre relations of community'.[35] They drew on then pervasive forms of social organicism, drawn primarily from Platonism and German idealism, but also from naturalist versions then in currency, to frame a distinctive moral organicism. The key to ethical living was found in membership in some form of community, and individual virtue was best cultivated by citizenship.

Furthermore, the idealists challenged the assumption of individual natural rights that had been such a mainstay of liberal thought and

underestimated the idealist residue in Austin's own thinking and overestimated the naive positivist features that a more nuanced reading of Austin might furnish: M. Lobban, 'Was there a nineteenth-century "English school of jurisprudence"?' (1995) 16 *Journal of Legal History* 36 ff.

32 B. Bosanquet, *The Philosophical Theory of the State* [1899], 4th edn (London: Macmillan, 1930), p. 56.

33 T. H. Green, *Prolegomena to Ethics* (Oxford: Clarendon Press, 1883), sect. 288.

34 D. G. Ritchie, *The Principles of State Interference: Four Essays on the Political Philosophy of Mr Herbert Spencer, J. S. Mill and T. H. Green* [1891], 4th edn (London: Allen & Unwin, 1902), p. 11.

35 F. H. Bradley, *Ethical Studies* (London: Henry S. King & Co., 1876), p. 155.

practice, and argued instead that all rights are social rights, conferred by membership in society.[36] Green described rights as powers or faculties to contribute to a common good,[37] thereby translating the potentially divisive force of individual rights into a shared duty to contribute to the common good. Although later liberals were broadly sympathetic with Green's moral vision of individuals embedded in community, even before the outbreak of the First World War they found this view of rights alarming. Nor was Green's belief that the private good and the common good must be one and the same – 'in pursuit of which there can be no competition of interests' – without its difficulties, as later liberal theorists attempting to grapple with pluralism concluded.[38] In the intense climate of war, these early misgivings were to become more widely and deeply felt by liberals such as J. A. Hobson and Hobhouse.

Rather than regarding the state primarily as a neutral instrument for the preservation of order, as was the inclination of many earlier liberals, the idealists, to varying degrees, argued for a much more ardent, vigorous and moral conception of the state. Green's authority with a generation of young politicians and civil servants lay particularly in his conviction that the state and other civic institutions ought to lead individuals away from egotism to a mindfulness of a common and shared good. Recalling the Kantian principle that moral acts must be willed rather than compelled, Green explained that the state could nourish morality by enabling individuals to pursue common rather than private interests. Green was cautious, however, in extolling the virtues of an interventionist state, and other idealists, notably Bernard Bosanquet, were even more cautious. In Green's mind, state action that 'would interfere with the growth of self-reliance, with the formation of a manly conscience and the sense of moral dignity, – in short, with the moral autonomy which is the condition of highest goodness' was not desirable.[39] If the 'real function of government [is] to maintain conditions of life in which morality shall be possible', a paternalistic state would be counterproductive, for it would limit the

36 E. Caird, *The Moral Function of the State* (Glasgow: J. Maclehose & Sons, 1887), p. 9; D. G. Ritchie, 'Discussion: the rights of animals' (1900) 10 *International Journal of Ethics* 387 ff. See also J. Harris, 'Victorian interpretations of Hobbes', in Ghosh and Goldman, *Politics and Culture in Victorian Britain*, pp. 237 ff.

37 Green, *Lectures on the Principles of Political Obligation*, pp. 350–4.

38 Green, *Prolegomena to Ethics*, sect. 283

39 Green, *Lectures on the Principles of Political Obligation*, p. 345. Hobhouse used this principle later to oppose the compelling of conscientious objectors to undergo military service: M. Freeden, *Liberalism Divided: A Study in British Political Thought 1914–39* (Oxford University Press, 1986), p. 23.

space for unselfish, disinterested acts.[40] Although the state ought not to force its citizens to act in a moral manner – defined again by acting in concert with a common good – the state ought to remove obstacles to moral action. As Green himself realised, this could entail measures that at first glance seemed unduly authoritarian, notably compulsory education and restrictions of the freedom of contract in health, housing and property.[41]

Green drew immediate connections between this understanding of freedom and tort law. In a widely influential essay, 'Liberal legislation and freedom of contract', Green challenges the distinction drawn between private injury and public injury:[42]

> This is most plainly the case when a man bargains to work under conditions fatal to health, e.g. in an unventilated factory. Every injury to the health of the individual is, so far as it goes, a public injury. It is an impediment to the general freedom; so much deduction from our power, as members of a society, to make the best of ourselves. Society is, therefore, plainly within its right when it limits freedom of contract for the sale of labour, so far as is done by our laws for the sanitary regulations of factories, workshops, and mines.

Green nominated the law, as 'the deliberate voice of society', as the vehicle to ensure the 'general freedom of its members to make the best of themselves'.[43] Laws governing personal injury became a vehicle for enlarging the common good and ensuring the greater freedom of citizens. Green's reconfiguration of private harm and public harm thus provided a theoretical footing for demands for a universal insurance scheme to compensate for employment injury, ultimately embedded in the Workmen's Compensation Act 1897 – an act in which the competing claims of individual autonomy and communitarian interventions were simultaneously ensconced. Although they endorsed greater state responsibility for preventing harm to individuals, they at the same time continued to fear and reject unwarranted incursions into the autonomy of the individual. This finely tuned balancing of rights and duties, individual and social interest, within the idealist moral vision of a common good and the moral function of law and the state furnished grounds for tort theory and practice, in

[40] Green, *Lectures on the Principles of Political Obligation*, p. 346.

[41] Green, *Lectures on the Principles of Political Obligation*, p. 515.

[42] T. H. Green, 'Liberal legislation and freedom of contract', in *The Works of T. H. Green*, ed. R. L. Nettleship (3 vols.), vol. III, *Miscellanies and Memoir* (London: Longmans, Green, 1888), pp. 365 ff., p. 373.

[43] Green, 'Liberal legislation and the freedom of contract', p. 373.

particular for a conduct- or duty-based understanding of the just society and tort liability. The idealist moral vision of citizens who pursued a common good and shared interest seemed naively optimistic to some contemporaries, who argued for a more radical reorganisation of market society.

3.3 Social responsibility: new liberals and Fabian socialists

Although the idealists did not uniformly conclude from their communitarian position that the state ought to intervene in preventing harm to individuals, new liberal and Fabian thinkers and activists (many of whom carried an ambivalent debt to idealist thinking about moral communities and self-development) were less tentative. Most notably, they expanded the notion of what forms of individual actions might occasion 'harm' to others. From this perspective, chronic underemployment and the inequitable distribution of wealth caused harm to the capacity of individuals to live a full life. Hobson was particularly influential in advancing this line of investigation. In his writings of the early 1890s and 1900s, he argued that the growth of monopoly and inequitable distribution had led to underconsumption, large-scale unemployment and imperialist ambitions. He sought to define an ethical political economy that measured 'social utility', and enlarged the understanding of 'harm' to include 'unsanitary, dangerous and degrading work', 'chronic poverty', a lack of education and deprivation of culture.[44] He explains: 'When society leaves some individuals free, through the action of competitive industry, to encroach upon this property when it is produced, or to prevent its being produced, by depressing the physical efficiency of workers it fails to maintain "social utility", and condones infractions of a natural right of property.'[45] Accordingly, he advocated factory and public health acts, employer liability acts, industrial legislation, education acts and public dispensaries acts. He continued a campaign for law reform that had begun in the 1870s and 1880s under liberalism, to increase state control over property in order to secure fair rent.[46]

Like Hobson, Beatrice and Sidney Webb used William Stanley Jevons' theory of marginal value to argue that profit was not invariably related to

[44] J. A. Hobson, *The Social Problem* [1901], ed. J. Meadowcroft (Bristol: Thoemmes, 1996), pp. 10–12.

[45] Hobson, *The Social Problem*, p. 103.

[46] Hobson, *The Social Problem*, p. 193: '[A] sound progressive social policy will confine itself to such increased control over property in land as is required to secure security of tenure upon moderate terms of payment and such freedom and encouragement of cultivation.'

effort or labour, and that economic inequalities constituted 'harm' that the state and civil society had the responsibility to prevent.[47] This was pungently argued in the *Minority Report on Poor Law Reform*, drafted by Beatrice Webb and others, as the outcome of a Royal Commission struck in 1905. Webb adamantly rejected attributing to poor character the dismal prospects of London labourers. The question of character remained at the heart of their report, however, for they were not at all sanguine that the chronically underemployed could escape the moral deterioration that usually followed. As the commissioners noted, '[T]he enforced idleness and prolonged private characteristic of Unemployment have on both the strong man and the weak, on the man of character and conduct and on the dissolute, a gravely deteriorating effect on body and mind, on muscle and will.'[48] Accordingly the commissioners required the establishment across Britain of labour exchanges, on the German model. They demanded a reduction of hours of labour across occupations, notably for railway and tramway servants, and the wage-earning labour of mothers of young children to be replaced with public assistance. They required further amendments to existing Factory Acts and Education Acts that would make it illegal to employ boys, and to restrict hours of youths between fifteen and eighteen years of age, while requiring the employer to ensure that such youths remained in schooling, provided by the local education authorities, for at least thirty hours a week. Girls would be required to attend training in home economics and 'how to rear a baby'.[49] They proposed trade union insurance against unemployment, supported, as on the Continent, by public funds.[50] They also suggested that the residuum – those permanently unemployed and desperately poor – be taken to 'a Human Sorting House where each man's faculties would be tested to see what could be made of him' and then to 'Training Establishments' where they would be

[47] N. Thompson, *Political Economy and the Labour Party: The Economics of Democratic Socialism, 1884–2005* (London: Routledge, 2006), pp. 23–4; R. Harrison, *The Life and Times of Sidney and Beatrice Webb: 1858–1905* (Basingstoke: Macmillan, 1999), p. 237.

[48] B. Webb and S. Webb (eds.), *Public Organization of the Labour Market: Being Part Two of the Minority Report of the Royal Commission on Poor Laws and Unemployed* (London: Longman, 1909), pp. 241–2. See A. M. McBriar, *An Edwardian Mixed Doubles: The Bosanquets versus the Webbs: A Study in British Social Policy 1890–1929* (Oxford: Clarendon Press, 1987).

[49] Webb and Webb, *Public Organization of the Labour Market*, p. 274.

[50] The commissioners (Wakefield, Chandler, Lansbury and B. Webb) referred specifically to what they termed the 'Ghent system', introduced in Ghent in 1901 and then adopted across Belgium, France (from 1905), Norway, Denmark, Basle and Strasbourg, in which the state provided funds to trade unions for out of work benefits.

trained – rigorously – in new occupations. A newly created Ministry of Labour would manage all this.[51] These proposals envisaged radical, broad and sweeping state intervention in the labour market on a scale only dimly imagined by labour union activists fifty years earlier. It sustained the idea of character development but went much further in requiring local and national governments to create the conditions in which the individual might flourish. Writing in *Industrial Democracy*, the Webbs explain: 'We ourselves understand by the words "Liberty" or "Freedom", not any quantum of natural or inalienable rights, but such conditions of existence in the community as do, in practice, result in the utmost possible development of faculty in the individual human being.'[52] In short, they were proposing a national minimum. Although collective bargaining was a vital tool (and growing trade union membership gave them some confidence in this regard), they imagined that the national minimum would be secured by enacting legislation, notably a labour code, education law and sanitation legislation. As Alan Kidd argues, the '"policy of the national minimum" was at heart a plan for the moralisation of society, enshrining a conception of the reciprocal relationship between the community and the individual'.[53] By the 1930s the Webbs had turned to a Marxist ideology of law and specifically to Soviet communism, primarily because it was able to impose upon individuals the moral obligations of service to the community, and they had become ever more sceptical that individual self-interest would fold ineluctably into a desire for a shared or common good.

The new liberal and Fabian discussion of harm and injury did not adopt the technical-legal categories articulated in tort law and in law treatises, and a distinction should be drawn between the forms of distributive justice that these theorists had begun to articulate and the kind of corrective justice targeted by tort law. Nonetheless, their analysis of the dilemmas of justice in modern society furnished a conceptual foundation for adjudicating harm and injury in which blame to some extent shifted away from individuals to the inequities of modern market-driven societies and the risk of living in these societies. This transition should not be overstated, however, because a desire to protect the autonomy and independence of

[51] In contrast, the Majority Report called for labour exchanges, industry-specific voluntary insurance schemes and raising the school leaving age of boys to fifteen years.

[52] B. Webb and S. Webb, *Industrial Democracy* (2 vols.), 2nd edn, vol. II (London: Longman, 1911), p. 847.

[53] A. J. Kidd, 'The state and moral progress: the Webbs' case for social reform *c.*1905 to 1940' (1996) 7 *Twentieth Century History* 189 ff., 205.

the individual retained a vibrancy belied by the strong communitarian and welfarist themes of the early twentieth century. Mill's observation in *On Liberty* that the vexed question of 'how to make the fitting adjustment between individual independence and social control…is a subject on which nearly everything remains to be done' turns out to have a striking resilience, even if his own liberal individualist response to this vexed question did not.[54]

[54] Mill, *On Liberty*, p. 220.

4

The 'welfare state' in legal and social philosophy: origins and controversies

JOSE HARRIS*

4.1 The origins and evolution of 'welfare'

In this chapter I explore the history of the welfare state through the perspective of different legal, social and political theories and ideologies. In order to do this I look at the subject from two rather different angles. Although my remit is to consider the welfare state mainly after 1920, I also refer back to a number of earlier thinkers whose ideas have continued to resonate in debates on public welfare provision into more recent periods. I consider first the direct contribution to thinking about social welfare and its underlying norms made by legal, social and political theorists (including, when relevant, economic theorists as well). I also glance at the history of different conceptions of welfare state principles as tacitly embodied in public policy and in administrative and legal practice. In doing this I hope to draw out a number of themes that may help to give shape to an area of enquiry that is too often dominated either by built-in assumptions about social progress or by a sort of 'patchwork quilt' empiricism that obscures any overall picture. I try to avoid the narrative of 'from poor law to welfare state', from ignorance to enlightenment, that has characterised some strands of writing on the history of social welfare policy in Britain, Europe and the United States. Instead, I suggest that there have been many different notions of public welfare provision; that the very language of 'welfare' has varied in meaning and content within different intellectual traditions; and that policies and principles perceived at a particular time as benevolent and progressive (or vice versa) have often come to be seen as the opposite in other periods and contexts.

Many readers will doubtless already be familiar with the influential categorisation of the 'three worlds of welfare capitalism' invoked by

* St Catherine's College and Faculty of History, University of Oxford.

Gøsta Esping-Andersen and others in relation to Scandinavia, continental Europe and the Anglo-American world; and this categorisation clearly bears some relation to the various models and philosophies of welfare provision prevailing in the early twenty-first century.[1] But this is not quite the point I am making here. Instead, I want to suggest that, even within a single culture, there may be many different understandings of the role of social policy; that different welfare philosophies constantly compete and interact with each other; and that ideas, practices and moral imperatives may migrate across the boundaries of historic periods, cultures and rival intellectual traditions in quite unexpected ways. I also comment on some lost or forgotten strands in both 'populist' and 'specialist' welfare state thinking of earlier eras – strands that may perhaps help to inform and illuminate certain contradictions and dilemmas in thinking about public welfare policy in the modern world.

A rather stark example of these complexities is offered by the very terms 'welfare', 'social welfare' and 'welfare state': three concepts that in present-day speech are often used interchangeably, but that are nevertheless rooted in a very diverse range of earlier meanings and concerns. 'Welfare' itself was an Old English word that traditionally implied both personal and communal 'well-being', spiritual as well as material. With the rise of liberal political economy, however, it came increasingly to be used in a narrower and more technical sense, to refer to subjective units of personal utility that enabled individuals to calculate and exercise 'rational' market choice. This 'liberal-economic' understanding of 'welfare' was, in turn, challenged by the rise of the concept of '*social* welfare', a term inseminated into Victorian public debate by conservative paternalists such as James Froude and John Ruskin, as a deliberate critique of what they saw as the atomistic and asocial understanding of human well-being conjured up by the political economists.[2] The early twentieth century saw many attempts by British and European 'welfare economists' (many, but not all, of a socialist inclination) to effect a reconciliation between the two.[3] In North

[1] G. Esping-Andersen, *The Three Worlds of Welfare Capitalism* (Cambridge: Polity Press, 1990).

[2] J. Froude, *The Influence of the Science of Political Economy on the Moral and Social Welfare of a Nation* (Oxford: J. Vincent, 1842); J. Ruskin, 'The crown of wild olive: three lectures on work, traffic and war' [1866], in E. T. Cook and A. Wedderburn (eds.), *Library Edition of the Works of John Ruskin* (39 vols.), vol. XVIII (London: Allen & Unwin, 1905), pp. 385 ff.

[3] J. M. Keynes (ed.), *Official Papers by Alfred Marshall* (London: Macmillan, 1926); A. C. Pigou, *Wealth and Welfare* (London: Macmillan, 1912); T. W. Hutchison, *A Review of Economic Doctrines, 1870–1929* (Oxford: Clarendon Press, 1953), pp. 280–302.

America, meanwhile, and in parts of the British Empire, the concept of 'welfare' evolved along rather different lines. It was a term widely applied to philanthropic social service provision, not so much for 'the poor' in general but, more particularly, for groups in society deemed intrinsically unable to help themselves (such as the blind, the deaf, orphans, cripples and 'moral incapables'). This American usage was imported back into Britain in the early twentieth century, where it likewise became closely associated with care for dependent, 'deprived' and 'handicapped' groups (including, paradoxically, those specifically not eligible for the more mainstream contractual 'social services' being introduced at this time in the form of workmen's compensation and contributory social insurance).[4]

Even in the nineteenth century, therefore, the seemingly simple notions of 'welfare' and 'social welfare' carried a wide range of divergent meanings; and further ambiguities were to arise with the emergence of the concept of a 'welfare state'. The label of '*der Wohlfahrtsstaat*' was widely supposed to have been invented in the Weimar Republic during the 1920s, as a term of abuse coined by reactionary and pro-monarchist factions in order to discredit the continuous extension by the Social Democratic Party (Sozialdemokratische Partei Deutschlands: SPD) of state social insurance schemes (schemes that had originally been introduced in Germany under Otto von Bismarck forty years beforehand). The term was subsequently imported into England during the 1920s and 1930s by a small handful of reformist intellectuals, notably William Temple and Alfred Zimmern, who used it in a much more positive sense, to distinguish democratic governance 'for the welfare of the people at large' from the authoritarian 'warfare state' seen as emerging in Germany under the Third Reich.[5] Nevertheless, the phrase 'welfare state' did not enter into popular currency in Britain until the latter half of the 1940s, when it was initially revived not by champions of public services but by their free market antagonists, who invoked it to pour scorn on the new 'universalist' health and social security schemes introduced by the Labour government headed by Clement Attlee on the lines of the Beveridge Plan. Almost immediately, however, the more positive connotations of the phrase prevailed. The 'welfare state' rapidly became embedded in popular consciousness, not as a derogatory

[4] T. N. Kelynack (ed.), *The Child Welfare Annual* (London: John Bale, Sons & Danielsson, 1916); J. E. Lane-Claypon, *The Child Welfare Movement* (London: G. E. Bell, 1920); S. Gilford, *The Welfare Movement* (London: People's League of Health, 1921).

[5] P. Hennessey, *Never Again: Britain 1945–1951* (London: Cape, 1992), p. 121; M. Grimley, *Citizenship, Community, and the Church of England: Liberal Anglican Theories of the State between the Wars* (Oxford: Clarendon Press, 2004), pp. 1–2.

term but as a humane and democratic alternative both to unlimited capitalism and to the recently abolished Poor Law system, which had dominated English public welfare provision since the early sixteenth century.[6] This populist conception of the welfare state, as a system based on universal 'as-of-right' civic *entitlement* to welfare benefits (in stark contrast to the selective, means-tested and stigmatising Poor Laws), was to dominate much political and academic understanding of recent British history for the next half-century; and, despite the enormous changes that have occurred in the character of more recent welfare provision, it has continued to do so in much discussion of social policy down to the present day. Moreover, the more benevolent usage of the term was rapidly re-exported back to the Continent, where in the 1950s and 1960s some European 'welfare states' began to far outstrip the British model in their provision of universal insurance coverage, superannuation, health care and other extensive welfare entitlements.[7]

All this may seem very untidy and paradoxical, as history often is. Yet there is much in the origins of welfare state history that is even *more* paradoxical than the story so far, not least the fact that a much earlier German conception of a *Wohlfahrtsstaat* dated back not just to republican Weimar, nor even to the reforms of Bismarck in the 1880s, but to the Prussian 'welfare monarchy' of half a century earlier. In the 1830s and 1840s the phrase had been applied to attempts by Prussian royal officials to revive and reinforce the ancient social welfare obligations of local communities, just at the time when local and parish-based authorities were under similar pressures from central government in rapidly industrialising liberal Britain.[8] In other words, the German term '*der Wohlfahrtsstaat*' had been invoked to describe a process that had many close parallels to the English New Poor Law policies of 1834 (i.e. those deterrent and institutional

[6] R. M. Titmuss, *Essays on 'the Welfare State'* (London: Allen & Unwin, 1959); M. Bruce, *The Coming of the Welfare State* (London: Batsford, 1961).

[7] P. Flora, Franz Kraus and Winfried Pfenning, *State, Economy, and Society in Western Europe 1815–1975: A Data Handbook in Two Volumes* (London: Macmillan, 1987); P. Baldwin, *The Politics of Social Solidarity: Class Bases of the European Welfare State, 1875–1975* (Cambridge University Press, 1990); R. Disney and P. Johnson, *Pensions Systems and Retirement Incomes across OECD Countries* (Cheltenham: Edward Elgar, 2001); D. G. Green, *Benefit Dependency: How Welfare Undermines Independence* (London: IEA [Institute of Economic Affairs] Health and Welfare Unit, 1998).

[8] H. Beck, *The Origins of the Authoritarian Welfare State in Prussia: Conservatives, Bureaucracy and the Social Question, 1817–70* (Ann Arbor: University of Michigan Press, 1995).

reforms that have almost invariably been seen as the stark *antithesis* of what later British, American and European historians have come to understand as the 'welfare state' in its modern conception). Perhaps even more surprisingly, moreover, the compulsory state insurance schemes of the Wilhelmine empire, launched by Bismarckian civil servants in the 1880s, and still widely viewed today as the cradle of modern welfare-statism, were interpreted at the time by some commentators in a quite different light. On the contrary, compulsory state insurance, jointly managed by expert public officials and representative panels of employers and workers, was viewed in some quarters not as an evolutionary *development* from the welfare monarchy of the pre-unification era but as its modernising, progressive, legally regulated, democratic *alternative*. Thus a conference of German legal, sociological and historical scholars meeting on the eve of the First World War heard papers on the progressive transformation of the German state from its Prussian antecedents as a conservative *Wohlfahrtsstaat* into a modern liberal *Rechtsstaat*. The latter was seen as a state in which not just welfare provision but public administration of all kinds was being progressively transformed from a system of monarchical and aristocratic paternalism into one of universal civic rights and duties, mediated and enforced by professional administrators, public lawyers and formal tribunals and courts.[9] A rather different but parallel evolution appeared to be taking place in early twentieth-century France under the regime of the Third Republic, where *l'État providence* (a phrase still sometimes used to refer to the 'welfare state' in France at the present day) was increasingly shifting away from the provision of personal relief for the very poor, delivered largely by state-licensed private charities, towards administration by workers' and employers' syndicates and appellate administrative tribunals, and control by the civil courts.[10] The welfare state in its different historical guises has thus been a coat of many colours, with monarchical, traditionalist, liberal and charitable roots, as well as

[9] F. Tönnies, 'Rechtsstaat und Wohlfahrtsstaat' (1914) 8 *Archiv für Rechts- und Wirtschaftsphilosophie* 65 ff.

[10] On French uses of the term, see F. Ewald, *L'État providence* (Paris: Grasset, 1986); and P. Bourdelais, Jean-Marie Poursin, Denis Olivennes and Xavier Gaullier, *L'État-providence: arguments pour une réforme* (Paris: Gallimard, 1996). Many modern French commentators nevertheless prefer the term *le solidarité* to *l'état providence*, the latter being seen as having *une connotation négative*: J.-P. Révauger and P. Spicker, *Glossaire bilingue de la protection sociale*, vol. II, *Les termes anglais* (Paris: MIRE, 1998), p. 251. On earlier legal and historical developments in French welfare provision, see J. E. S. Hayward, 'Solidarity:

the more bureaucratic, universalist and 'rights-based' connotations that it carries at the present day.

4.2 'Welfare' in legal, social and political theory

Let us turn now to the impact on, and dissemination of, ideas about public welfare provision in the writings of social and legal philosophers. This is an under-researched subject, partly because – during the period associated with the 'rise of the welfare state' – writings by major socio-political and legal theorists on welfare issues were relatively scarce and partly because, when major theorists did turn their attention to such matters, their views on welfare were rarely directly influential – or were mediated in ways rather different from what their authors expected or imagined. Among the lesser ranks of theorists, writing on social welfare issues has been much more common, but interaction between their ideas and enacted social policies has often been relatively transient (with a few noteworthy exceptions, to whom I return in more detail below).

First, then, let us take a few brief examples among major legal, social and political theorists of the 'modern' era. Prior to the second half of the twentieth century the volume of specifically 'jurisprudential' writing on the public provision of welfare was surprisingly small. This was particularly so in Britain, where major legal theorists simply did not address social welfare questions in their jurisprudential writings (Jeremy Bentham, for example, discharged his views on the management of poor relief not in his systematic analyses of law and jurisprudence but in ephemeral political tracts).[11] Moreover, in a British context many experts on social policy from the middle of the nineteenth century onwards were inclined to view the principles and practices of the English common law not as aids but as major hindrances to the advance of social welfare, and as the very last place to which they would look for inspiration and guidance on questions of social reform. This prejudice was coloured by the striking failure of attempts to implement social welfare legislation through the English

the social history of an idea in nineteenth-century France' (1959) 4 *International Review of Social History* 261 ff.; T. Lynes, *French Pensions* (London: George Bell, 1967); E. Jabbari, 'Pierre Laroque and the origins of French social security, 1934–1948' (1999), D.Phil. thesis, University of Oxford; and L. Layet, 'Le société de Saint-Vincent de Paul en Angleterre 1869–1914: un modèle de charité catholique' (2006), Maîtrise d'Histoire, Université Paris X Nanterre.

[11] J. Bentham, *Panopticon, or the Inspection House* (London: T. Payne, 1791); and J. Bentham, *Observations on the Poor Bill* (London: privately printed, 1797).

law courts, and reinforced by the polemical stance *against* new forms of statutory public welfare provision taken up over many decades by certain prominent jurisprudential defenders of the common law.[12] Both the Royal Commission on the Poor Laws of 1834, and its Edwardian successor of 1905–9, bore witness to the existence of a body of largely forgotten common law decisions that over many centuries had endorsed the principle of poor relief as a fundamental citizen 'right'.[13] This evidence was largely ignored, however, by British social reformers of the period, to whom the very mention of 'rights' often signalled not the 'promotion of claims to social welfare' but the 'defence of the inalienable rights of property'.[14] The situation was rather different in civil law countries, where many prominent theorists of social policy were also public lawyers, actively engaged in the technical drafting and practical delivery of welfare legislation.[15] Moreover, on the Continent contemporary legal treatises that addressed social welfare questions were often confined to factual analyses of the duties of public officials, and to penalties for administrative failure, rather than engaging in discussion of the basic principles of public relief. Such treatises thus in turn confirmed the prejudices of many English common lawyers, that 'social legislation' was simply a cloak and an excuse, not for enhancement of the common good but for undemocratic 'diktats' by the ever-advancing 'administrative state'.[16]

Philosophical discussion of the nature and principles of public welfare provision must therefore be sought, until quite recently, largely outside the boundaries of formal writings on the law. Even here the nature

[12] R. Lambert, *Sir John Simon, 1816–1904, and English Social Administration* (London: MacGibbon & Kee, 1963), pp. 396–9; P. W. J. Bartrip and S. Burman, *The Wounded Soldiers of Industry: Industrial Compensation Policy, 1833–1897* (Oxford: Clarendon Press, 1983); A. V. Dicey, *Lectures on the Relation between Law and Public Opinion in England* (London: Macmillan, 1905); G. Hewart, *The New Despotism* (London: Ernest Benn, 1929).

[13] J. Harris, 'From poor law to welfare state? A European perspective', in D. Winch and P. K. O'Brien (eds.), *The Political Economy of British Economic Experience 1688–1914* (Oxford University Press, 2002), pp. 409 ff., pp. 415–17.

[14] C. Gore (ed.), *Property: Its Duties and Rights, Philosophically Regarded* (London: Macmillan, 1913); J. A. Hobson, *Property and Improperty* (London: Victor Gollancz, 1937).

[15] L. Duguit, *Law in the Modern State*, trans. F. and H. Laski (London: Allen & Unwin, 1921); F. Netter, *Notions essentielles de securité sociale* (Paris: Recueil Sirey, 1951); P. Laroque, *Les Institutions sociales de la France* (Paris: Documentation française, 1963); E. P. Hennock, *The Origin of the Welfare State in England and Germany, 1850–1914: Social Policies Compared* (Cambridge University Press, 2007).

[16] Dicey, *Lectures on the Relation between Law and Public Opinion*, pp. 217–40, pp. 259–302; Hewart, *New Despotism*, pp. 60–8, pp. 72–3, p. 99, pp. 239–305.

of the practical impact of such writings was often quite different from what the authors of such writing hoped for, or from what contemporaries supposed. Bentham in his writings on the 'Panopticon', for example, was often seen as the *eminence grise* behind the notorious Poor Law reforms of 1834, and the Victorian workhouse was long believed to have been a direct institutional embodiment of his principle of 'less eligibility'. Much detailed research into Poor Law legal and administrative records has suggested, however, that both these beliefs were ill-founded. It has indicated instead that Benthamism was marginal to the legislation of 1834, and that 'less eligibility' in the strictly material sense was explicitly ruled out as an instrument of workhouse policy. Victorian public welfare institutions were undoubtedly, by modern standards, unpleasant places to live in; but so were the private dwellings of the destitute poor. Some workhouses were ramshackle and disorderly, some resembled army barracks, while towards the end of the century a few began to resemble comfortable cottage homes; but none of them ever attained the state of fine-tuned deterrent emptiness conjured up (more as a theorem in geometry than as a human institution) in Bentham's imagination.[17] Instead, it may be argued that Bentham's serious influence on ideas about social welfare provision lay in quite another sphere. This was in his forging of the intellectual tools that led to the eventual formulation of the theory of marginal utility, with all the implications for differential rates of taxation and redistribution of income that marginalism historically entailed.[18] More speculatively, Bentham's influence lay in his insistence on rational choice as a universal human attribute and capacity, characteristic of the clients and beneficiaries of welfare schemes no less than of human actors in any other sphere.[19]

Another nineteenth-century key theorist who made important, though brief, comments on welfare was G. W. F. Hegel, whose analysis of poverty and property in the *Philosophy of Right* drew attention to what he saw as a painful and prolonged crisis of transition in contemporary civilisation. This was embodied in popular estrangement from the age-old

[17] S. Webb and B. Webb, *English Poor Law History*, part II, *The Last Hundred Years*, 2 vols. (London: Longman, 1929); A. Digby, *Pauper Palaces* (London: Routledge, 1978); M. A. Crowther, *The Workhouse System, 1834–1929: The History of an English Social Institution* (London: Methuen, 1983).

[18] On the historic impact of marginal utility theory (now largely discarded by economists as a basis for social policy), see W. Stark, 'Jeremy Bentham as an economist' (1941) 51 *Economic Journal* 56 ff.; and B. Jackson, 'The uses of utilitarianism: social justice, welfare economics and British socialism 1931–48' (2004) 25 *History of Political Thought* 508 ff.

[19] J. Bentham, *Introduction to the Principles of Morals and Legislation* [1789] (Oxford: Basil Blackwell, 1960), pp. 155–63.

shared ownership of the soil, the displacement of the duties of family life by impersonal civil society, the declining effectiveness of charity and an urgent need for supplementing private support of the needy by some form of disinterested public provision (a provision that Hegel himself hoped might be mediated through a self-regulating public welfare corporation, rather than the starker and more anonymous medium of a bureaucratic state).[20] Hegel's thoughts on these matters have long been seen as influential in the rise of later idealist and communitarian schools of political thought, in which many of the precursors of twentieth-century welfare state thinking were to be found. And, more recently, Hegel's conception of 'civil society', as an intermediate site of social provision lying somewhere between the market and the state, has found much favour with proponents of a 'mixed economy of welfare'.[21] Yet it might be argued that Hegel's most important contribution to social welfare thought, though muted in tone, was implicitly a much more radical one: his assertion of the principle that life in a modern 'civil society' (no less than in a traditional face-to-face 'community') automatically entailed an abstract ethical right to subsistence, as the basis of public obligation to those in need.[22] Poor Law and prison records both in Britain and elsewhere suggest that, at a very low-key and only half-articulated level, this sentiment long remained endemic in nineteenth- and early twentieth-century social services, and was far more pervasive than the much more sharply articulated philosophies of utilitarianism, Darwinism, Marxism or market liberalism.[23] To some, however, it seemed that such a principle simply ducked the whole issue of modern poverty, and was a throwback to 'mediaeval fatalism'. In the words of the German sociologist Georg Simmel, it acquiesced in the creation of a specific class whose sole identity, occupation and self-interest was to be poor; a condition determined not by the intrinsic nature of poverty but, rather, 'by the fact that others – individuals, associations,

20 G. W. F. Hegel, *Hegel's Philosophy of Right* [1819], trans. T. M. Knox (Oxford: Clarendon Press, 1967), pp. 145–55.

21 A. Vincent and R. Plant, *Philosophy, Politics and Citizenship: The Life and Thought of the British Idealists* (Oxford: Basil Blackwell, 1984); S. den Otter, *British Idealism and Social Explanation: A Study in Late Victorian Thought* (Oxford: Clarendon Press, 1996); M. Katz and C. Sachsse (eds.), *The Mixed Economy of Social Welfare: Public/Private Relations in England, Germany and the United States from the 1870s to the 1930s* (Baden-Baden: Nomos, 1996).

22 Hegel, *Hegel's Philosophy of Right*, p. 44, p. 123, p. 146.

23 J. Webster, 'Reason, character, evolution and environment: theory and policy in Victorian social science, *c*.1860–*c*.1895' (1993), D.Phil. thesis, University of Oxford; Layet, 'Le société de Saint-Vincent de Paul'.

communities – were available to correct this condition'.[24] Social need in this latter perspective was therefore not the *cause* but the *effect* of the organised provision of private and public relief: it was a 'niche' in the social system that some people filled, just as others occupied the niches of doctors, doormen or debutantes. This judgement was long seen by historians as discredited, but it has increasingly been revived, even by commentators sympathetic to the poor (as, indeed, was Simmel himself), with reference to the persistence of poverty in advanced industrialised economies to the present day.[25]

A further nineteenth-century theorist whose writings on social welfare also remain of substantial interest was the French social philosopher Pierre-Joseph Proudhon. Proudhon – despite his proclaimed hostility to all forms of government and law – has nevertheless been portrayed as the prime inspiration behind the peculiarly syndicalist and self-governing character of welfare provision in twentieth-century France, and as a direct influence upon the administrative philosophy of the post-1945 French welfare state. Moreover, at least as influential as any of the above were two social theorists who wrote virtually nothing of a detailed kind about social welfare arrangements, namely Auguste Comte and Karl Marx. Marx, as is well known, treated discussion of social welfare provision as largely irrelevant – even positively obstructive – to the pursuit of revolutionary goals, and as not needing to be specified in detail for a post-revolutionary society, in which all 'scarcity' in goods and services would have vanished.[26] Comte, by contrast, favoured a system based on large-scale concentrations of wealth in conjunction with extensive 'social reorganisation', whereby massive expansion of the 'gift relationship' would help to 'make riches more useful as well as more respected'. Such developments were envisaged as essential components of the future 'positivist polity' (a polity whose goal, it should not be forgotten, was to be the eventual political, economic and legal union of all the major and minor European states, extending even to Turkey). Comte wrote little in detail about such reorganisation, however, other than linking it to the supreme

[24] D. Levine (ed.), *Georg Simmel on Individuality and Social Forms* (University of Chicago Press, 1971), pp. 150–78.

[25] Green, *Benefit Dependency*.

[26] K. Marx, *Value, Price and Profit: Addressed to Working Men* [1865], trans., ed. E. Aveling (London: Allen & Unwin, 1899). On occasion, however, Marx did write generously about the benevolent impact, even under capitalism, on working-class lives of the English factory laws and factory inspectorate: K. Marx, *Capital* [1867], trans. B. Fowkes (Harmondsworth: Penguin Books, 1976), pp. 349–50, pp. 402–3, p. 542.

positivist virtue of 'altruism', which in the society of the future was to replace self-love and supernatural religion as the primary motor and moral code of the individual human psyche.[27]

Marx and Comte each had only a marginal impact on the social welfare theories and practices of their own day. Both of them, however, generated numerous disciples, less theoretically purist than themselves, who were only too willing to harness the writings of their respective masters to the promotion and defence of public social services. Indeed, throughout the later nineteenth and earlier twentieth centuries pragmatic revisionists in both positivist and Marxian camps were to be the authors of many major contributions to welfare state ideas and policies – not least among them Beatrice Webb, who started her career as a social reformer in the 1880s as a dedicated adherent of Comtean positivism and concluded it in the 1930s as a convert to Soviet-style Marxism (though always maintaining that the one was merely a practical fulfilment of the other).[28] Other prominent British reformers and welfare theorists who had links with the Comtean positivist tradition included the sociologist Charles Booth, the 'new liberal' economists J. A. Hobson and Leo Chiozza Money, the young William Beveridge, the young Richard Titmuss and the social demographer David Glass. In France, Comtean positivism was prominent in the turn-of-the-century 'solidarist' movement, among graduates of the grandes écoles and, above all, in the administrative philosophy of the welfare and public law specialist Pierre Laroque.[29] Laroque, often referred to as the 'French Beveridge', was to become the chief theorist and designer of the extended French welfare state system after 1945. All these figures pursued differing priorities in their social writings; but they all had certain characteristics in common that echoed many of the doctrines of Comte – among them the use of social security policies as a medium

[27] A. Comte, *A General View of Positivism* [1844], trans. J. H. Bridges (London: Trübner, 1865), pp. 140–226; *Auguste Comte and Positivism: The Essential Writings*, ed. G. Lenzer (New York: Harper & Row, 1975), pp. 404–12.

[28] S. Webb and B. Webb, *Soviet Communism: A New Civilisation?*, 2nd edn (London: Longman, 1940), p. 745; N. I. Mackenzie and J. Mackenzie (eds.), *The Diary of Beatrice Webb*, vol. IV, *1924–1943* (London: Virago, 1985), p. xii, p. xv, p. 280.

[29] T. R. Wright, *The Religion of Humanity: The Impact of Comtean Positivism on Victorian Britain* (Cambridge University Press, 1986); T. S. Simey and M. Simey, *Charles Booth: Social Scientist* (Oxford University Press, 1960); J. Harris, *William Beveridge: A Biography*, 2nd edn (Oxford: Clarendon Press, 1997); R. M. Titmuss, *The Gift Relationship* (London: Allen & Unwin, 1970); H. S. Jones, *The French State in Question: Public Law and Political Argument in the Third Republic* (Cambridge University Press, 1993); P. Laroque, *Au service de l'homme et du droit: souverirs et reflexions* (Paris: Association pour l'étude de l'histoire de la sécurité sociale, 1993).

of social and cross-class integration, an interest in popular participation in social service management, an idealised view of the traditional child-rearing functions of women and a commitment to 'altruism' as much more than a merely private virtue but a guiding philosophy for national and international public life. Thus, when Webb visited the Soviet Union as a convert to Marxism in the mid-1930s, she was far more impressed by the 'altruism', 'social virtue', 'scientific ethics' and 'public philanthropy' of the people's commissars, the local soviets and the Red Army than by other, more explicitly 'revolutionary', aspects of the Stalinist regime.[30]

Identifying direct Marxian influences in social welfare thought is more difficult than with Comtean positivism, since for Marxists support of 'social welfare' schemes usually entailed more of a tacit repudiation, rather than a refinement, of 'orthodox' Marxian theory. Nevertheless, in all major European countries during the early and middle years of the twentieth century, substantial contributions to discussion of proto-welfare-state principles came from people who had once been, or in many cases still thought of themselves as, close disciples of Marx. The German 'revisionist' socialist Eduard Bernstein regularly claimed social welfare issues (particularly those concerning child labour, workplace conditions and industrial accidents) as part of an authentic Marxian socialist tradition.[31] In the later stages of the Wilhelmine empire, many Marxian-inclined SPD trade unionists sat on public social insurance tribunals, and in the 1920s many of the innovations in social insurance and unemployment provision that so annoyed aristocratic critics in the Weimar Republic (see above) came not just from the SPD but from much more radical Marxian breakaway groups.[32] Similarly, in the Third Republic, the powerful syndicalist movement that dominated grass-roots management of French contributory insurance schemes managed to maintain regular if uneasy cooperation between corporately inclined cross-class 'solidarists', on the one hand, and its own founding myth of 'revolutionary violence', on the other.[33] In Britain, working-class Marxists during the interwar years were simultaneously involved in protest movements against benefit cuts,

[30] Webb and Webb, *Soviet Communism*, p. 84, pp. 94–8, pp. 618–23, pp. 677–81.

[31] H. Tudor and J. M. Tudor (eds.), *Marxism and Social Democracy: The Revisionist Debate, 1896–1898* (Cambridge University Press, 1988).

[32] G. Steinmetz, *Regulating the Social: The Welfare State and Local Politics in Imperial Germany* (Princeton University Press, 1993); W. J. Mommsen (ed.), *The Emergence of the Welfare State in Britain and Germany, 1850–1950* (London: Croom Helm, 1981); Hennock, *Origin of the Welfare State*.

[33] Hayward, 'Solidarity', 17–33; Lynes, *French Pensions*; Jabbari, *Pierre Laroque*.

in the management of public benefit schemes and in campaigning for a statutory 'right to work'.[34] Academic Marxists in interwar Britain, such as Harold Laski and G. D. H. Cole, likewise wrote about and campaigned for measures against unemployment that involved increased government spending on public works, an expansion of consumer demand, the extension of social insurance provision and a general reflation of the British economy.[35] These policies were all part of the intense ferment of social reconstructionist ideas that characterised the late 1930s and early war years; but it is difficult to see how, with respect to social welfare if not to other spheres, their remedies differed in any substantial way from those of advanced liberals and other non-Marxist radicals of the same period.[36]

Liberal theorists have been rather sidelined in this discussion so far, but their numbers included both powerful *critics* of extended state welfare and also some of its most passionate *supporters*. As indicated above, much mid-nineteenth-century liberal opinion in Britain and elsewhere had favoured leaving welfare issues as far as possible to the care of philanthropy, voluntarism and remedies at common law, while the very notion of '*social* welfare' (as opposed to mere *individual* welfare) had been introduced into public debate not by reformist liberals but by paternalist high Tories, as a deliberate critique of the liberal laissez-faire position. Progressive liberals had begun to shift their allegiances during the 1870s, however, though perhaps more slowly than is often supposed. It was William Stanley Jevons' *Theory of Political Economy* in 1871 that first introduced English readers to the notion that the 'marginal utility' of goods or money diminished the more one had of them; and, although there was no hint from Jevons himself that such a rule might sanction politically induced 'redistribution', this point was to be taken up by a new generation of liberal theorists shocked by the revelations of mass poverty that emerged in the 1880s and 1890s. This new generation of liberal theorists – among them Alfred Marshall, Hobson, J. M. Robertson, Money and Arthur C. Pigou – all identified an '*error*' or '*faultline*' in the 'natural' distribution of income, not just as a prime cause of poverty and unemployment but

[34] W. Hannington, *Unemployed Struggles 1919–1936* (London: Lawrence & Wishart, 1936); W. Hannington, *Ten Lean Years: An Examination of the Record of the National Government in the Field of Unemployment* (London: Victor Gollancz, 1940).

[35] H. Laski, *Democracy at the Crossroads* (London: National Council of Labour Colleges, 1934); G. D. H. Cole, *The Machinery of Socialist Planning* (London: Hogarth Press, 1938).

[36] S. Brooke, *Labour's War: The Labour Party during the Second World War* (Oxford: Clarendon Press, 1992); D. Ritschel, *The Politics of Planning: The Debate on Economic Planning in Britain in the 1930s* (Oxford: Clarendon Press, 1997).

also as the root of stagnation in the growth of national wealth. If surplus incomes were to be subject to progressive taxation, so their argument ran, then more could be spent on both public investment and help to the poor; as a result, employment would rise, generating more consumption and demand for goods, and thereby stimulating further investment and overall economic growth. Thus not just the poorer classes but the whole national economy would benefit from progressively graduated taxation on higher levels of income and wealth.[37] This cycle of argument was to be severely criticised in the middle and later years of the twentieth century by economists who claimed that the opposite sequence of causation was no less plausible, and that differential tax rates on higher incomes could *depress* rather than stimulate the generation of wealth, thereby *reinforcing* the downward spiral of unemployment and poverty. 'Marginalist' claims were also dismissed on the grounds that interpersonal comparisons of the relative 'utility' of units of income and wealth as between different individuals were inherently subjective and incapable of proof, and thus arbitrary as a basis for the promotion of 'welfare'. Some degree of redistributive taxation might be desirable on other grounds; but only markets could provide objective criteria for economic rewards, not as a matter of 'social justice' but simply as a benchmark of efficiency and utility.[38]

More recent interpreters have suggested, however, that, whether or not their claims were ill-founded, the liberal 'maldistribution' theorists *did* have a profound *practical* influence both on the social welfare thinking of the interwar period and on the social and fiscal innovations of the post-war welfare state.[39] John Maynard Keynes himself acknowledged his debt to the theoretical 'intuitions' of the underconsumptionist school, though he was always more wary than they were of the hazard of *accidentally* siphoning away the sources of a nation's public and private investment.[40] At the very height of the Edwardian redistribution debate, moreover, the

[37] A. Marshall, 'Preliminary statement and evidence before the Royal Commission on the Aged Poor' [1893], in J. M. Keynes (ed.), *Official Papers by Alfred Marshall* (London: Macmillan, 1926), pp. 199 ff.; J. A. Hobson, *The Economics of Redistribution* (London: Macmillan, 1900); L. C. Money, *Riches and Poverty* (London: Methuen, 1905); Pigou, *Wealth and Welfare*.

[38] L. Robbins, *An Essay on the Nature and Significance of Economic Science* (London: Macmillan, 1932); I. Little, *A Critique of Welfare Economics* (Oxford: Clarendon Press, 1950); W. J. Baumol, *Welfare Economics and the Theory of the State*, 2nd edn (Cambridge, MA: Harvard University Press, 1965).

[39] Ritschel, *The Politics of Planning*; Jackson, 'The uses of utilitarianism'.

[40] J. M. Keynes, *General Theory of Employment, Interest and Money* (London: Macmillan, 1936), pp. 24–5, pp. 359–71.

Italian economist and philosopher Vilfredo Pareto had dismissed attempts on both sides to find objective criteria for a 'just' distribution of material resources as mere bogus 'metaphysics'. 'All these pseudo-scientific reasonings,' Pareto claimed, 'are less clear and have less value than the Christian maxim: "love thy neighbour as thyself". Moreover we find this maxim in very different epochs and among totally distinct peoples; one can even find it in the Chinese… The Salvation Army, by using means appropriate to the persons it wants to reach, has a social effectiveness much greater than that of the most learned and subtle metaphysical discussions.'[41]

4.3 From 'warfare' to 'welfare'? Social policy in theory and practice

Such controversies underpinned the ebb and flow of debate on welfare state provision in many countries during the course of the twentieth century, though with something of a lull in the era after the Second World War, when the apparent eclipse of normative 'grand theory' in many Western cultures fostered the view that social policy had become largely a matter of pragmatic 'social engineering', rather than a focus for 'philosophical' concerns such as liberty and justice, obligations and rights.[42] Nevertheless, certain contentious intellectual assumptions made by welfare state writers of the postwar epoch may briefly be commented on here. In relation to Britain, one of these was the very widespread belief (represented in all parties in the 1950s) that the prolonged prosperity, high wages and full employment of the period (contrasted for many with memories of the 1930s) were causally linked to Keynesian demand management, postwar socio-economic planning and the redistributive impact of the 'universalist' welfare state.[43] More recent research has suggested that at least part of this analysis was false, the crucial factor being the continued high expenditure on the postwar British armaments industry, which undoubtedly generated secure jobs, high wages and certain forms of advanced technology but did so, arguably, so at the expense of investment in new skills, new companies and the new consumer-oriented industries

[41] V. Pareto, *Manual of Political Economy* [1906], eds. A. S. Schwier and A. N. Page, trans. A.S. Schwier (New York: A. M. Kelley, 1971), pp. 47–53.

[42] E. H. Carr, *The New Society* (London: Macmillan, 1951); I. Berlin, 'Does political theory still exist?', in P. Laslett and W. G. Runciman (eds.), *Philosophy, Politics and Society* (Oxford: Basil Blackwell, 1962), pp. 1 ff.

[43] D. Worswick and P. Ady (eds.), *The British Economy in the Nineteen-Fifties* (Oxford: Clarendon Press, 1962); Bruce, *The Coming of the Welfare State*; A. Cairncross, *Years of Recovery: British Economic Policy 1945–51* (London: Methuen, 1985), pp. 17–46.

of the future, in all of which fields Britain's international competitors by the mid-1950s were racing ahead.[44] The significance of this more recent account (which implicitly subverts the virtuous dichotomy between 'welfare state' versus 'warfare state' conjured up by progressive commentators of the 1930s) has still to be absorbed into current British historiography. Certainly, though, little hint of such an interpretation was ever reflected in social welfare writings of the postwar period, in which the unexpected revival of Britain's old heavy industries was widely interpreted as a near-miraculous consequence not of the economy of the Cold War but of the fortuitous impact of the 'full employment' and 'demand management' strategies of the postwar welfare state.

Another questionable assumption of the postwar period was the common view, classically stated by Titmuss in *Problems of Social Policy*, that 'human nature' and citizen expectations had fundamentally changed during the course of the 1940s – a change ascribed partly to the impact of Nazism and the horrors of war, but partly also to the massive organisational and redistributive achievements of the wartime public services. Ordinary people in the 'new society', so it was thought, would never again countenance a return to the gigantic social lottery of life in the pre-war era: a vision of the past famously conjured up in the writings of George Orwell and by the messianic imagery of Beveridge's 'Five Giants'.[45] Instead, democratic peoples (in Britain and elsewhere) would demand fair shares for all, job security and universal social services available 'as of right', rather than through the uncertain media of markets, means tests, private charity and philanthropy. In return, they would continue to support many of the social constraints of wartime, including high taxation, work discipline and continuing government controls over capital and labour; in other words, they would endorse the public philosophy of 'altruism' and 'social solidarity' that many of its protagonists, consciously or unconsciously, echoed from the classic writings of Auguste Comte. Such a picture was conjured up not just by British welfare experts such as Titmuss, Beveridge and Barbara Wootton but by commentators of a similar outlook in postwar Europe, such as Gunnar and Alva Myrdal in Scandinavia and Laroque in France.[46]

[44] D. Edgerton, *Warfare State: Britain, 1920–1970* (Cambridge University Press, 2006).

[45] W. Beveridge, *Social Insurance and Allied Services* (London: HMSO, 1942); G. Orwell, *The English People* (London: Collins, 1947); R. M. Titmuss, *Problems of Social Policy* (London: HMSO, 1950).

[46] G. Myrdal, *The Political Element in the Development of Economic Theory* [1930], trans. P. Streeten (London: Routledge, 1953); P. Laroque, *Réflexions sur le problème sociale* (Paris: Éditions sociales françaises, 1953).

For a time, moreover, it seemed a not unrealistic vision. The widespread acquiescence of both employers and trade unionists in postwar state controls, the gratitude of many people (middle- as well as working-class) for the new social services, and the decisive popular rejection of negative 'libertarian' portrayals of the welfare state all suggested that the writings of social security theorists were in tune with public opinion.

There was much less consensus, however, about the relation between social welfare and economic theory. Even during the war there had been deep divisions between economists about the implications of 'universalist' social welfare services both for the collective 'welfare' of society as a whole and for the 'welfare' of individuals. Although there were some who saw wartime controls as prototypes for a new, fully socialised, permanent peacetime economy, predominantly run by the state, there were others for whom such controls were mere temporary aberrations in what was fundamentally a competitive market economy. Furthermore, there was a third, more pragmatic, group who viewed the new social services as useful junior partners in a programme of Keynesian economic management – doubtless as 'goods' in their own right, but significant in economic terms mainly as a sphere in which public spending and consumer demand could be expanded or contracted by government intervention and planning as circumstances required. Within this third group there were also many who, like Keynes himself, had been influenced by the Edwardian 'marginal utility' approach and by Hobsonian 'underconsumptionism'; namely by those theories (mentioned above) that redistribution from larger to lesser incomes was not merely a question of 'social justice' (always a problematic term) but was acceptable in more orthodox terms, as conducive to greater *overall* welfare, insofar as it generated a greater sum of total human satisfactions.

The first and third of these approaches were by far the most commonly expressed during the 1940s and 1950s (with much debate about the social and economic policies of the period oscillating between these rival views). Nevertheless, as indicated above, there was throughout the period a significant body of liberal opinion that dissented radically from both these redistributive positions. The most vociferous of these dissenters was Friedrich Hayek, whose wartime treatise *The Road to Serfdom* had caused a publishing stir in 1944, though it appeared to have little immediate impact on public policy. Nonetheless, Hayek's views on specifically social welfare issues and their subsequent development merit closer attention than they usually receive. Hayek was not initially hostile to Keynes' family allowance scheme, to compulsory wartime savings or to Beveridge's proposals for subsistence-level social insurance; and even wartime plans for a comprehensive 'national health service' (which he later came to condemn as having 'no relation to reality') at the time escaped his criticism.[47] What seems to have turned Hayek into an enraged critic of wartime planning was not the Social Insurance Report of 1942 but more holistic schemes such as Beveridge's subsequent (private) report on *Full Employment in a Free Society*, published in 1944. The economic sections of this second report were largely composed not by Beveridge himself but by a group of Cambridge-based 'Keynesian socialists' (among them Nicholas Kaldor, Joan Robinson and Wootton). The crime of this later work, in Hayek's eyes, was that, while purporting to be the harmless continuation of Beveridge's report on social services, it tipped over into being a set of recommendations that, if adopted, would fundamentally transform and destroy the very nature of British society and the state. In place of a polity whose defining functions were to maintain civic order and the 'rule of law' (within which social services were a possibly desirable but nevertheless secondary goal), what was now envisaged was a state whose primary raison d'être was the guaranteeing of public employment and overall structural equality, regardless of any possible impact on efficiency, legal order and personal freedoms. Such an approach, Hayek and his followers believed, betrayed a fundamental naivety about economic reality, and an incapacity to interpret anything so complex as a 'free society'.[48]

Beveridge's *Full Employment in a Free Society* enquiry seems to have been something of a turning point in Hayek's subsequent mission to convert not just economic theory but social and political philosophy as well, away from misguided notions about state-induced 'social welfare'. It is not difficult to detect, even in the mid-1940s, certain straws in the wind that indicated a reluctant concession on the part of some leading welfare theorists that the Hayekian position might have some purchase. Even during the war such a dedicated theorist of comprehensive social planning as Wootton herself acknowledged an intellectual debt to the critical impact of Hayek. Beveridge too, when launching his *Voluntary Action* enquiry in 1946, signalled his rejection of the kind of all-encompassing state planning

[47] J. M. Keynes, *Collected Writings* (30 vols.), vol. XXII, *Activities, 1939–1945: Internal War Finance*, eds. E. Johnson and D. Moggridge (London: Macmillan, 1978), pp. 73–4, p. 92, p. 102, pp. 106–7.

[48] F. A. Hayek, *The Constitution of Liberty* (London: Routledge, 1960), pp. 253–66; A. Seldon (ed.), *Agenda for a Free Society: Essays on Hayek's 'The Constitution of Liberty'* (London: Hutchison, 1961), p. 120, p. 128, p. 139.

that many had read into his 'full employment' proposals of only two years earlier.[49] The postwar writings of T. H. Marshall on social welfare and citizenship likewise argued that – far from negating earlier models of freedom – the welfare state was a consummation and fulfilment of the legal, personal, economic and civic liberties that the British people had been progressively acquiring ever since the eighteenth century and even earlier.[50] Moreover, as indicated above, economists of the 1950s increasingly questioned the claims of earlier theorists that concepts of marginal utility and underconsumption could automatically be harnessed to social welfare goals, desirable as the latter might or might not be in their own political and moral right.[51] No welfare state theorist of the period adequately answered these criticisms. But supporters of redistribution during the course of the 1960s significantly shifted their ground, either by adopting a different *type* of economic claim (e.g. that public welfare services were cheaper and more efficient than private ones, because their overhead costs were lower) or by moving away from 'economic' arguments towards other more subjective or normative rationales for redistributive social policies. These included appeals to the old ethical and Comtean goals of 'altruism' and social service, and a revival of interest in theories of 'citizenship' and 'community'. They also invoked a series of more ambitious strategies, however, for combating 'structural inequalities' newly identified as linked to education, race and gender, as well as to the older variable of economic class.[52] Finally, and most importantly for the themes discussed in this chapter, there was a resurgence of academic and popular concern with the long-neglected relationship between 'social welfare', social 'rights', procedural 'fairness' and the principle of 'justice'.[53]

[49] B. Wootton, *Freedom under Planning* (London: Allen & Unwin, 1945), preface, passim; W. Beveridge, *Voluntary Action: A Report on Methods of Social Advance* (London: Allen & Unwin, 1948), pp. 268–318.

[50] T. H. Marshall, *Citizenship and Social Class: And Other Essays* (Cambridge University Press, 1950).

[51] I. Little, *A Critique of Welfare Economics* (Oxford: Clarendon Press, 1950); Baumol, *Welfare Economics*.

[52] Jean E. Floud, A. H. Halsey and F. M. Martin, *Social Class and Educational Opportunity* (London: Heinemann, 1957); T. H. Marshall, *Sociology at the Crossroads* (London: Heinemann, 1963); J. Rex and R. Moore, *Race, Community and Conflict: A Study of Sparkbrook* (Oxford University Press, 1967).

[53] This resurgence was signalled by John Rawls' article 'Justice as fairness' (1958) 67 *Philosophical Review* 164 ff., which was reprinted for a wider audience in Laslett and Runciman, *Philosophy, Politics and Society*, pp. 132 ff.

4.4 Conclusion

Thus a central feature of the shifting ground of welfare state discussion during and after the 1960s was to be the increasing prominence of the relationship between social welfare policies, law and rights. As indicated above, such a connection had always been present in civil law jurisdictions, in which civil servants concerned with the administration of social services were routinely trained in public law. Even on the Continent, however, works on social welfare law had often consisted largely of textbooks or handbooks on current legal and administrative rules (only in France were there faculties where professors in the tradition of Émile Durkheim and Léon Duguit studied social welfare provision as an aspect of 'legal sociology'). In Britain academic studies of welfare law before 1960 were virtually unknown, and welfare issues of the kind debated by economists were largely ignored in writings on jurisprudence. When, in 1959, Titmuss produced what was seen at the time as a path-breaking account of 'law and public opinion' in the making of social policy, he focused almost exclusively on a case study in a particular area of social welfare *legislation*. Such an approach accurately reflected what had been a central assumption of most British socio-legal commentators over the previous hundred years, namely that – insofar as they were affected by the law at all – substantive improvements in welfare provision were to be brought about mainly through the agency of *Acts of Parliament*.[54] By contrast, other aspects of the legal system – such as courts, tribunals, case law, access to legal advice and the face-to-face working of the law in action – had, with few exceptions, all been widely taken for granted as routine and uncontentious in their relation to the actual delivery of social services.[55] This perspective

[54] R. M. Titmuss, 'Health', in M. Ginsberg (ed.), *Law and Opinion in England in the Twentieth Century* (London: Stevens, 1959), p. 299 ff. Ten years later Titmuss was to take up an unpaid post as deputy chairman of the Supplementary Benefits Commission (the welfare state's heir to the Victorian Poor Law) in order to find out, as he put it, 'what really happens at the coal-face' of social legislation in practice. This humble action by a great man puts in a nutshell the cultural transition that I am trying to describe.

[55] E. A. Parry, *The Law and the Poor* (London: Smith, Elder, 1914); C. Chapman, *The Poor Man's Court of Justice: Twenty-Five Years as a Metropolitan Magistrate* (London: Hodder & Stoughton, 1925); C. K. Allen, *Law in the Making* (Oxford: Clarendon Press, 1927). Thus, even a work as sympathetic to the poor as Chapman's *The Poor Man's Court of Justice* discussed the law in relation to 'the social question' exclusively with respect to neglected and sexually abused children: pp. 77–83, pp. 90–7. Chapman had been one of the assistant commissioners who carried out research for the 1905–9 Royal Commission on the Poor Laws, but the possibility that such research might have included enquiry into the Poor Law as an aspect of the 'legal system' (which Chapman himself was well

was to be radically challenged and transformed, however, over the following decades – a period in which the historic identity of the British welfare state, as an embodiment of democratic consensus, fair shares for all and universal access to social services, was to become increasingly questioned and contested. Administrators, social workers, trade unionists and democratic representatives found themselves increasingly caught up in disputes about benefit claims and access to other welfare state services. A striking index of these changes was that books, articles and academic treatises on 'welfare law' (a neologism of the 1960s) began to be published not just in English but in many other languages, in ever-increasing numbers.

How did this 'legalisation' of the practices and culture of the welfare state come about, and what was its significance? To some extent it was simply a reflection of trends in wider society, as the regulatory controls, consensual values and modest expectations inherited from the Second World War gradually gave way to more controversy and diversity. But this cannot be the sole explanation, since the post-1960s explosion of public interest in the legal dimension of welfare bore little relation to anything in British, European or North American public culture that had existed in earlier, more peaceful and less regulated periods.[56] As a wider historical question, the increasing cultural centrality of law as an active rather than a passive force in social welfare politics deserves much more detailed investigation than can be undertaken here, but a few possible lines of explanation may be tentatively suggested.

One important catalyst appears to have been the rise of the American civil rights movement, which was to transform public thinking about 'rights' of all kinds, in relation not just to race issues but to social relations in general, and not just in the United States but throughout the Western world. A second important influence was to be the European Court of Human Rights, though this did not begin to make a major impact on social welfare enactments and entitlements until the late 1980s. Another significant factor was simply generational change, as the 1960s and 1970s brought to the fore a new cohort of university-trained lawyers and social scientists, who were themselves beneficiaries of public social services

equipped to carry out) never crossed his or the commissioners' minds. This comment is not made in any anachronistic spirit of criticism of the work of the 1909 Commission; it is meant simply to draw attention to our changed awareness of the all-pervasive impact of law on humdrum aspects of people's lives.

[56] In the United States there had been some pre-war interest in 'law and social policy' as a theme in political science, but there was virtually no practical case law on the subject: see, for example, J. S. Bradway (ed.), *Law and Social Welfare* (Philadelphia: American Academy of Political and Social Science, 1929).

(particularly universal secondary education) and whose backgrounds and aspirations were quite different from those of their counterparts only a short generation ago. A fourth, more intangible, influence was the cumulative impact of the welfare state itself, as a force for changing wider cultural expectations about 'entitlement' to public services. Such expectations had been largely satisfied during the 1950s, but were to become much more vocal and contentious in the 1960s and 1970s, particularly as the rising costs of social services meant that the assumption of 'universalism' came under increased political strain. In the specific context of Britain, it was no coincidence that the eruption of law into social welfare issues coincided with a period of prolonged public expenditure crisis, which brought in its train a large-scale administrative revival of the older, *means-tested* model of benefit systems that had supposedly fallen into abeyance with the abolition of the Poor Law in 1948.[57] The subsequent steep rise in benefit disputes for the first time attracted lawyers and legal aid workers into the settlement of social security questions in significant numbers, which in turn led to the growth of welfare 'case law' and to the emergence of an organised movement for the promotion and protection of 'welfare rights'.

Such changes also coincided with, and were fuelled by, new movements in social, political and legal theory, after several decades during which all academic disciplines with a 'normative' or 'philosophical' bent had been deeply constrained by the prevailing fashion for 'positivism' and 'value-free' social science.[58] Debates about 'citizenship', which in the past had been largely concerned either with voting rights or with the promotion of 'public-spirited' civic behaviour, now became increasingly caught up in questions about the legal entitlement of citizens to a share in social welfare schemes and in wider national prosperity.[59] At

[57] Certain aspects of the former poor law services had been transferred in 1948 to a body known as the National Assistance Board, designed to cater for 'transitional' groups such as old people and the seriously disabled, who could not be immediately absorbed into the new contributory insurance-based welfare system. From the early 1960s British public expenditure patterns showed a gradual reversion towards spending on 'selective', means-tested benefits, as opposed to 'universal' social services. This was partly because, in terms of aggregate expenditure, selective means testing was much cheaper than raising the level of 'universal' benefits; but it happened also because there were increasing numbers of people (among them the long-term disabled, recent immigrants and old people living longer than expected) whose contributions were inadequate for full 'National Insurance' entitlement.

[58] Berlin, 'Does political theory still exist?'.

[59] Marshall, *Sociology at the Crossroads*; E. Low, 'A tale of two citizenships: H. Jones, T. H. Marshall and the changing conceptions of citizenship in twentieth-century Britain' (2000), D.Phil. thesis, University of Oxford.

the same time, 'social justice' (in itself a deeply contentious philosophical term) crept into the language of academic jurisprudence in Europe, Britain and North America to an extent that would have been unthinkable a generation beforehand.[60] These shifts in ideas came about partly through the emergence of new forms of 'humanistic' Marxism, which (unlike the eastern European variant) were unabashed about pursuing such themes as the promotion of individual rights and the defence of social and procedural justice within a predominantly market economy. Of equal or greater importance, however, were developments within more broadly 'liberal' political thought that re-engaged with welfare issues from a variety of directions, each of which was to have lasting implications for both popular and academic debates on the role and nature of a welfare state. By contrast with the wartime and post-war periods, these legal and philosophical perspectives were to play an increasingly seminal role in welfare state controversies for the rest of the twentieth century.

Thus John Rawls' 'theory of justice' (first sketched out in the early 1960s but refined and extended over several subsequent decades) pursued the questions, posed earlier by Pareto, of how to reconcile the competing claims of liberty, efficiency and justice within both 'advanced' and 'developing' political societies. Rawls concluded that, in a liberal society (i.e. one characterised by 'equal liberty' and 'respect' for all), 'inequality' was justified insofar (but only insofar) as it sustained a pattern of distribution that benefited the 'least well off'. In other words, great wealth and higher incomes were legitimate if they generated jobs, security and prosperity for the poor, but not if they did not.[61] This analysis was to become widely incorporated into philosophical, jurisprudential and welfare state thinking in many parts of the Western world, though not without intense ongoing debate about its normative and practical implications. Many democratic socialists, for example, interpreted Rawls' formula as a recipe for a mixed economy with a strongly redistributive public sector, buttressed by compensatory services for the disadvantaged and an extensive system of judiciable 'welfare rights'.[62] Many more orthodox liberals claimed, on the other hand, that Rawls' conditions were perfectly

[60] D. Miller, *Social Justice* (Oxford: Clarendon Press, 1976); J. Broekman (ed.), *Social Justice and Individual Responsibility in the Welfare State* (Stuttgart: F. Steiner Verlag, 1985).

[61] Rawls, 'Justice as fairness'; J. Rawls, *A Theory of Justice* (Oxford University Press, 1972), passim, but esp. 258–332.

[62] T. Burchardt, 'Welfare: what for?', in J. Hills, J. Le Grand and D. Piachaud (eds.), *Making Social Policy Work: Essays in Honour of Howard Glennerster* (Bristol: Policy Press, 2007), pp. 35 ff.

compatible with an open 'market economy', operating a humane but residual 'welfare safety net', in which bottom-line welfare claims were treated as indistinguishable from other rights at common law. Hayekians in particular also argued that both 'welfare' and 'equal liberty' would best be enhanced not by spurious and paternalist welfare rights but by a radical extension of personal choice, operating particularly in such spheres as education, the environment and owner occupation of private housing.[63]

Another important strand in the political thought of the period was a resurgence of 'communitarian' ideas, variously emanating from the 'left', 'right' and 'centre' of the political spectrum. Protagonists of this trend increasingly attacked the ontological individualism and 'abstract justice' of much liberal and democratic-socialist social thought, claiming instead that human flourishing was possible only in a context of integrated 'face-to-face' communities – as against the increasingly fragmented and atomistic patterns of human life that appeared to be endemic in the emergence of 'global' market society.[64] Some strands of communitarian thought portrayed overextended state welfare services as in themselves a powerful causal element in this perceived process of societal disintegration, and called for their replacement by more voluntarist, less bureaucratised and less 'perfectionist' forms of community development. Many communitarians, however, did not abandon more conventional welfare state policies of income support and health care, instead, they pressed for their supplementation and reinforcement by 'welfare to work' schemes, credit unions, incentives to saving, the revival of dying neighbourhoods and social support services for both traditional and newer models of integrated family life.

Aspects of all these different strands of thought were increasingly incorporated into more programmatic writings about social welfare services during the last three decades of the twentieth century. One consequence has been that, despite the intense specialisation that occurred during this period in many academic disciplines, in the analysis of 'welfare states' perspectives from previously disparate intellectual traditions have become increasingly fused together. Authors assessing the economic implications

[63] F. G. Pennance and W. A. West, *Housing Market Analysis and Policy, with an Essay on the Legal Framework* (London: IEA, 1969); B. Bracewell-Milnes, *Land and Heritage: The Public Interest in Personal Ownership* (London: IEA, 1983).

[64] A. MacIntyre, *After Virtue: A Study in Moral Theory* (London: Duckworth, 1981); M. Sandel, *Liberalism and the Limits of Justice* (Cambridge University Press, 1982); M. Sandel, *What's the Right Thing to Do?* (London: Allen Lane, 2009); A. Etzioni, *The Common Good* (Oxford: Polity Press, 2004).

of welfare policies, for example, have increasingly done so as serious economists (rather than by smuggling in unexamined assumptions from other disciplinary or ethical frameworks). In the same way, lawyers and legal theorists now contribute much more substantially than was the case half a century ago both to debate on the overall goals of social policies and to procedural questions involving benefit entitlement and practical implementation – a trend strongly reinforced in a British and European context by the need to interpret social policy directives emanating from the European Union and the Court of Human Rights. Parallel changes have occurred in the spheres of political theory and moral philosophy, not simply in the sense indicated above – that writers in these areas have had direct influence on social welfare debates – but in the sense that questions of human 'welfare' have in turn become an intrinsically important strand in the substantive content of these disciplines. This has been so not just in the case of 'grand theory', as practised by followers of Rawls and his critics but in a more empirical and institutional sense, with the very concept of a 'welfare state' being increasingly categorised as a major 'type' or 'model' of a modern political 'system'.[65] Such developments may perhaps be seen simply as part of the ever-increasing centrality of law and the social sciences within the value systems and practical management of advanced industrial and information-based societies. But a historical perspective also suggests a quite different point: that the restoration of 'welfare' issues to a central place in legal, social and political thought can equally be seen as marking a return to the position that they occupied in some of the great seminal texts of the pre-modern and early modern eras – in, for example, the writings of Thomas Aquinas, Thomas More, Richard Hooker, John Locke, Hugo Grotius and William Blackstone. Whether such developments have also substantially enhanced either the 'welfare' or the 'social welfare' of societies, classes and individual citizens is, of course, quite another question, and beyond the remit of this chapter to determine. Undoubtedly, however, they have immensely enlarged the range, variety and intellectual interest of writings on law and social policy in recent decades, across the spectrum of many different contexts, problems, policies and national cultures.

[65] See, for example, J. S. Hacker, 'The welfare state', in R. A. W. Rhodes, S. A. Binder and B. A. Rockman (eds.), *The Oxford Handbook of Political Institutions* (Oxford University Press, 2006), pp. 385 ff.

5

Continental European jurisprudence 1850–2000

JOHN BELL*

In Chapter 2, Roger Cotterrell identifies the trends within general philosophy that impacted on lawyers and the law in the nineteenth and twentieth centuries. This chapter focuses particularly on jurisprudential ideas within the legal community. Writing about the law takes three major forms: doctrinal writing (the analysis of and theory about the rules and principles of specific branches of the law); legal theory (general reflections on the structure of the law in terms of principles and concepts); and legal philosophy (writing that reflects on the social and moral purpose and justification of the law). The contention in this chapter is that there is little in the major countries that merits the label 'legal philosophy' coming from within the legal community. For the most part, such writing is produced within the broader philosophical community discussed by Cotterrell. I argue that this is the result of the interest of lawyers not only with practice (what the law does, rather than why it does it) but also with the institutional structures of the academic community. For the most part, the concern of legal theory has been with the legitimacy of judicial lawmaking and with the conceptual structure of the law.

In broad terms, key jurisprudential writing of the period can be identified from textbooks and articles that are widely cited. The work is essentially about legal theory in part because of the definition of law that was adopted and in part because of the issues that were the focus of attention.

The definition of law is important in this series of works. In the first six volumes of the 'European legal development' series,[1] the authors spend

* University of Cambridge.

[1] S. Whittaker (ed.), *The Development of Product Liability* (Cambridge University Press, 2010); W. Ernst (ed.), *The Development of Liability* (Cambridge University Press, 2010); E. Hondius (ed.), *The Development of Medical Liability* (Cambridge University Press, 2010); J. Gordley (ed.), *The Development of Liability between Neighbours* (Cambridge University Press, 2010); M. Martin-Casals (ed.), *The Development of Liability in Relation to Technological Change* (Cambridge University Press, 2010); N. Jansen (ed.), *The Development and Making of Legal Doctrine* (Cambridge University Press, 2010).

much time discussing how the rules of tort developed in a context in which the state regulation of activities (e.g. in product safety or land use planning) became increasingly important and in which alternative compensation systems (e.g. workmen's compensation and no-fault road traffic compensation schemes) were being developed. In many ways, the conclusions of those books suggest that tort rules and concepts remained fairly stable in their formulations but that the context in which they operated changed markedly during the period from 1850 to 2000. Doctrinal writing on classical tort law retained a remarkable similarity over the period, but the 'law', in its widest sense of an integrated body of norms and practices authorised by the law, actually changed in remarkable fashion. This is best illustrated by *Technological Change and the Development of Tort Law.*[2] The reporters on the various legal systems relate that there was little litigation for exploding boilers, even though thousands of people died as a result of such explosions. In most cases, employees (the principal victims) were unable to sue either because of legal rules or because of practical constraints, such as not wishing to offend their employer or because of the cost of litigation. From the end of the nineteenth century, however, these principal victims were able to obtain compensation through workmen's compensation, and the incidence of explosions was reduced because of inspections introduced by the state and, more importantly, by insurers and professional associations of boiler owners.[3]

On the whole, the reader of the tort textbook gets little insight into the wider world of regulation and alternative compensation systems. Something similar happens when it comes to works of legal theory. The illustrations are drawn heavily from the classical areas of civil and criminal law, often harking back to the rules of Roman law or the medieval and early modern *ius commune*. On the whole, regulatory law is ignored. It was defined as public law, and was not applied by the classical legal professions (advocates and notaries) but by state officials, such as inspectors.[4] If there are individuals who mention this area, it is often to warn about the increasing power of the administration and the need to control it through public law. Equally, the importance of compensation and social security systems does not feature significantly in legal theory. Even the work of Léon Duguit, which Roger Cotterrell mentions at length and

[2] Whittaker, *The Development of Product Liability*, esp. pp. 15–17.

[3] Whittaker, *The Development of Product Liability*, pp. 14–15.

[4] In this volume, the chapters by P. W. J. Bartrip and Paul-André Rosental (11 and 12, respectively) provide us with insights into these communities and their influence on the practical application of law.

which is discussed later in this chapter,[5] does not talk about the important contemporary topic of workmen's compensation as a sign of the way the law embraces social solidarity. In crude terms, law is defined as what the classical legal professions (judges, professors, advocates and notaries) do. Welfare law and regulatory law were not topics in law schools and did not feature in the books written by academics for the formation of lawyers. Legal theory (*la théorie générale du droit* or *Rechtstheorie*) that is taught to young law students was to be the foundation of the subjects that they studied and practised later.

If we then look at the topics that they discussed, we can see that their writings reflect this basic preoccupation and the narrow concerns of doctrinal legal writing. The sections below focus, in particular, on the interpretation of law and how judicial interpretation and the expansion of the law can be treated as legitimate within the constitutional framework governing the work of judges. In addition, there is analysis of legal concepts that demonstrate the consistency of the way in which the law is applied.

The core approach of Continental lawyers is to adopt an instrumental theory of law. Developed against a background of reaction to natural law, the growth of legislative codification and law reform, as well as secular ideas of progress, especially through science, the law is not seen as having its own values but, rather, as serving the values espoused by the legislator. The French Revolution and nineteenth-century reforms reflect a liberal revolution. In the first place, this entailed the abolition of privileges arising from class or religion (and hence the abolition of the privileged position of lawyers). In the second place, it laid stress on the importance of the legislator (and often democracy) such that lawyers were under the law and were called upon to ensure that everyone else was also under the law. Both of these conspired with the utilitarian ideas that Cotterrell mentions to encourage an amoral, instrumental theory of the law. Such ideas (except the rule of law) are rarely the subject of direct discussion in the jurisprudential literature, but they form a tacit background. An illustration would be the work of Hans Kelsen, who wrote between the 1920s and the 1970s.

This chapter focuses principally on the period 1850 to 1960. This was a period that saw the gradual professionalisation of legal scholarship in the universities. It would be fair to say that many countries did not have an active legal theory or jurisprudence tradition. The purges that led the Austrians (in the 1780s), the Spanish (in the 1840s) and the Piedmontese

[5] See the contribution in this volume by Alexandra Braun (Chapter 10).

(in the 1860s) to expel religious orders and to close some universities removed a source of legal philosophers, as opposed to legal practitioners and theorists connected with their view. Political conditions often did not favour broader speculative reasoning. Italy and Spain suffered under dictatorships in much of the first part of the twentieth century, and so were not congenial centres for theoretical (and potentially critical) thinking. As state employees, professors had to conform to some extent. In many ways, therefore, the story of European jurisprudence as a body of ideas capable of influencing the development of delict law is deeply disappointing.

Tony Becher has argued that softer and less compact disciplines such as law enjoy a lower reputation within the academic community and tend to compensate by seeking to model themselves on high-status subjects with a reputation for rigour and objectivity.[6] Whereas the identification of legal rules and the application of them in routine situations may have an aspect of technique that is appropriate to legal training, education and scholarship have higher aspirations: to produce critically reflective individuals who can examine the content of the law and its place within society. In order to escape the realm of technique and gain an academic reputation, legal theory (*Rechtstheorie*) and jurisprudence (*Rechtswissenschaft*)[7] have sought to align the study of law to the paradigms of other disciplines. This chapter argues that empirical science and analytical philosophy provided the early reference points for academic legal writing and that empirical social science was a later reference point, when it gained respectability as an academic discipline. Law is inescapably a branch of practical ethics, though, whose paradigm is inevitably soft and lacking firm boundaries. Political theory is perhaps a missing element. Cotterrell argues in his contribution[8] that sociology offered an alternative paradigm in the work of Émile Durkheim, and this chapter reflects on legal sociology. All the same, I argue that this serves far more as an analytical rather than a normative model for the paradigms of jurisprudence. The tension between an objective or 'scientific'[9] model of resolving legal problems and a softer, dis-

[6] T. Becher and P. R. Trowler, *Academic Tribes and Territories*, 2nd edn (Milton Keynes: Open University Press, 2001), pp. 183–5.

[7] On the difference, see J. Bell, 'Introduction', in M. Van Hoecke, *What Is Legal Theory?* (Antwerp: Acco, 1985), pp. 11 ff.

[8] See the contribution in this volume by Roger Cotterrell (Chapter 2).

[9] The resonance of the word 'scientific' in English is different from the homologues *scientifique* or *wissenschaftlich* in French, German and cognate languages. The English term has come to mean 'empirically grounded' or 'experimentally testable', whereas the terms in other languages convey the broader sense of 'objective' or 'rigorous'.

cursive model is something that lawyers and legal theorists have struggled to resolve, however, or at least to balance.

This chapter reflects my selection of key themes of the period. The principal issues to be considered were, first, the scope for interpretative freedom: how far there is scope for interpretation by the judge or doctrinal writer. Second, when there is freedom to interpret, on what basis is the interpretation made? Third, should one study law simply in terms of rules and concepts or in terms of the social impact of law?

5.1 Institutional background: why jurisprudence is patchy

The argument of this section is that the institutional structure of universities and academic careers has not fostered broader-ranging thought by academic lawyers about the social function of law. Rather, the topics predominantly reflect the work and practice of professional lawyers.

France is the clearest exemplar, even though it is the home for many of the most inventive legal solutions in tort law of the period. French universities were re-established in 1808, but with a very centrally defined programme. As a result, there was not much theory, either of the law in general or of specific areas of law. The succession of authoritarian regimes and purges was not congenial to the development of potentially controversial theories. Legal writing focused mainly on expounding and systematising the law, often based on Roman law principles. It was not really until the Third Republic became established and freedom of university teaching was legislatively enshrined that theory emerged from the law schools and the legal community. Judges had been the subject of too many purges (the last being in 1879–81) for independent writing to come from that quarter of the legal community.

The security of the liberal state from about 1880 gave academics the freedom to publish without censorship (the Press Law of 1881), to teach (the Universities Law of 1884) and to restructure the law course, rather than simply conform to the central requirement of teaching according to the structure of the *Code civil*. The development of doctrinal commentary on the law (especially with the notes of Léon Labbé and other *arrêtistes* from the 1860s in the Recueils Dalloz and Sirey) enabled a new range of more theoretically inclined lawyers to have an outlet for their ideas.[10] This

[10] P. Jestaz and C. Jamin, *La Doctrine* (Paris: Dalloz, 2004), pp. 104–8. On the *note d'arrêt*, see N. Duxbury, *Jurists and Judges: An Essay on Influence* (Oxford: Hart, 2001), pp. 48–54.

represented a paradigm shift in legal writing. Rather than focusing on the internal logic of the code, the attention of commentators moved towards changes in everyday life and the reaction of the law to them.[11] There were also the new breed of textbooks, which broke with the tradition of exposition of the code (*école de l'exégèse*) and provided a systematic presentation of the principles of the law, often providing new ideas about how to develop it. The Strasbourg-based professors Charles Aubry and Charles Rau were strongly influenced by German writings on civil law and on the French *Code civil*, which was in force in a number of German territories, and rejected the exegetical method in favour of a more principled analysis of the law. The first edition of their *Cours de droit civil français*, published in 1838, was a translation of Karl Salomo Zachariae with notes.[12] It was only really with the fourth edition, in 1869, that it became a distinctively French textbook.[13] Because of the annexation of Alsace by the Germans in 1870–1, Aubry and Rau became members of the Cour de Cassation in Paris and were able to exercise significant influence over the development of private law that complemented their academic writings. There were similar developments in administrative law with the work of Édouard Lafferière (vice-president of the Conseil d'État and later president of the Cour de Cassation) in 1887.[14] The creation of the *agrégation* as a competitive entry into the professoriate and the launching of academic careers encouraged the bolder academic spirits. The 1895 structure (still in place) provided competitions for history, public law, international law and private law. But there was no place for legal theory. Any person who had a theoretical cast of mind had to earn his keep by being a specialist in another field. Although France has had a number of legal theorists, there has never been a school, as in England, Germany or even in post-1950 Belgium, in which many of the writers have been francophone (e.g. Chaïm Perelman, François Ost, Michel van de Kerchove, Philippe van Parijs). In particular, the lack of institutional structure to support legal theory and a greater focus on specialism in initial doctoral theses has meant that there have been hardly any French legal theorists with major influence since 1945,

[11] Jestaz and Jamin, *La Doctrine*, p. 107.

[12] K. S. Zachariae, *Handbuch des französischen Zivilrechts* (Heidelberg: Ernst Mohr's Verlag, 1808): see É. Bartin, 'Preface', in C. Aubry and C.-F. Rau, *Cours de droit civil français*, 6th edn (3 vols.), vol. I (Paris: Marchal & Billard, 1936), pp. 9 ff., pp. 11–12.

[13] See C. Aubry and C.-F. Rau, 'Preface', in Aubry and Rau, *Cours de droit civil français*, 4th edn (3 vols.), vol. I (1869), reproduced in 6th edn, pp. 15 ff., p. 19.

[14] L.-É. J. Laferrière, *Traité de la jurisdiction administrative et du recours contentieux* (2 vols.) (Paris: Berger-Levrault, 1887–8).

certainly none on private law since René Savatier and Jean Carbonnier. Existentialist philosophy does not breed jurisprudence.[15]

None of this implies that French academics have stood apart from political action to develop the law. André Tunc developed the plan for no-fault road traffic liability in 1965 and campaigned hard until its adoption in 1985. Geneviève Viney has been heavily involved in commissions on consumer protection. The same was true in earlier periods, when professors were deputies or ministers. It does not translate into the character of the writing by these academics about law, however.[16] The themes that do emerge in French writing are (i) the theory of interpretation, (ii) the sociology of law, (iii) the theory of the state and liberalism and (iv) the theory of law and society.[17]

It is notable that a history of Italian legal philosophy will talk predominantly about Austrian and German writers and some French writers, with little scope left for Italians.[18] That mirrors the influence of German and French writers on Italian law, but it also points to the limitations of Italian jurisprudence. There are Italian theorists of liberalism whose work is influential in public law, such as Santi Romano, but the legal theory and legal philosophy that is presented here is limited. The freedom of Italian professors from the 1870s was substantial, but most were in legal practice, and the writing about the law that there was reflected the preoccupations of lawyers. With the Fascist dictatorship from the beginning of the 1920s, the writing about law was much more focused on the revisions of the civil code than on controversial issues concerning the philosophical purposes of the law.

Spain had one of the highest attendances at university in the middle of the nineteenth century and a high number of law students. Legal philosophy was not one of the main fields that was developed, however, particularly with the pressure on Catholic viewpoints in much of the period.

15 R. Savatier, *Les métamorphoses économiques et sociales du droit civil d'aujourd'hui*, 3rd edn (Paris: Dalloz, 1964); J. Carbonnier, *Flexible Droit: Textes pour une sociologie du droit sans rigueur* (Paris: LGDJ, 1969).

16 A. Tunc, 'Tort law and the moral law' (1972) 31 *Cambridge Law Journal* 247 ff., would be an exception; typically, for a non-French audience!

17 F. Gény, *Méthode d'interprétation et sources en droit privé* (2 vols.) (Paris: A. Chevalier-Marescq, 1899); Carbonnier, *Flexible Droit*; M. Hauriou, *Cours de science sociale* (Paris: Larose, 1896); L. Duguit, *L'État, le droit objectif et la loi positive* (Paris: A. Fontemoing, 1901); G. Ripert, *Les forces créatrices du droit* (Paris: LGDJ, 1955).

18 See G. Fassò, *Storia della filosofia del diritto* (3 vols.), vol. III (Bologna: Società editrice il Mulino, 1966–70).

Germany, by contrast, made great strides, in part because of the reforms in Prussian universities introduced from 1809 onwards by Wilhelm von Humboldt. This produced a structure of posts and encouraged young men to attend university in ways that were less familiar in other countries. The result was a large number of professorships and guarantees of freedom of teaching. This was then combined with a very lively philosophical and, later, psychological tradition. These reforms in Prussia were gradually rolled out to other parts of Germany up until the late 1870s. They involved young lawyers sitting a state examination in order to qualify for the legal profession, rather than a university examination. This freed the universities to teach what they thought important, providing students with the prerequisites for sitting the professional examinations, without being required to prepare them for these examinations. Indeed, in the nineteenth century there was little local (state) law taught in the German law schools.[19]

5.2 Interpretative freedom and 'free legal research'

The starting point for French legal scholarship in the later nineteenth century is in the exegetical approach to the civil code. Their approach was not the one taken by the makers of the code, who were committed to the idea that legislation should strive to reflect principles that could be derived from reason. As James Gordley suggests, later writers adopted a more expository approach for reasons of principle: 'They treated the Code as self-sufficient because they did not believe, as Portalis had, in the possibility of a transnational, transtemporal legal scholarship that could give the texts meaning. Since there was nowhere else to look except the texts of the Code, the Code had to be self-sufficient. So they created the myth that it was.'[20] He points to the way in which leading jurists such as Raymond-Théodore Troplong, Charles Demolombe, Aubry and Rau (from 1869) and François Laurent (1869)[21] all emphasised that the role of the lawyer was to see the law in the text, rather than in external sources such as principles of natural law. This firmly positivist approach was a way of coping with a

[19] F. Ranieri, 'Juristen für Europa: Wahre und falsche Probleme in der derzeitigen Reformdiskussion zur deutschen Juristenausbildung' (1997) 52 *JZ* 801 ff., 804–5, 807–8.

[20] J. Gordley, 'Myths of the French civil code' (1994) 42 *Am. J. Comp. L.* 459 ff., 491.

[21] R.-T. Troplong, *De la Vente, ou commentaire du titre VI du livre II du code civil*, 3rd edn (Paris: C. Hingray, 1837); C. Demolombe, *Cours de code civil* (31 vols.) (Paris: A. Durand, 1845–82); Aubry and Rau, *Cours de droit civil français*, 4th edn; F. Laurent, *Principes de droit civil* (33 vols.) (Paris: A. Durand, 1869–78).

more diverse and secular society. This culture became pervasive and was very atheoretical. It fitted the revolution-derived suspicion of judges and their power to block reform. Judges were to be limited to giving judgment according to law or referring cases to the legislature by way of a reference procedure (which lasted until 1837).

It should not be thought that the jurists of the period before 1880 were unimaginative. Troplong was creative as a writer and a judge, laying the seeds for the development of product liability into the twentieth century, and *arrêtistes* such as Labbé shaped branches of law for many years to come. They felt constrained to present their work as firmly embedded in an exegesis of the civil code, however, rather than based on some other principles.

In the 1880s it became more accepted that judges made law. As French society changed in a more industrial period and through colonial expansion, new rules were needed. The democratic, parliamentary system made it more difficult to obtain legislation, and so other forms of lawmaking were needed. It was recognised that, in any case, legislation is not sufficiently precise to cover all eventualities without further interpretation. The development of public law in the 1880s demonstrated this most effectively. A landmark was article 1 paragraph 2 of the Swiss Civil Code of 1907, which authorised the judge explicitly to fill gaps in the law on the basis of what he considered that the legislator would have done.[22]

The school of 'free legal research' was developed in both France and Germany at the end of the nineteenth century. One of its leading exponents was François Gény, whose major work appeared in 1899.[23] Having pointed out the impossibility of the legislator foreseeing everything, he argued that judicial creativity was inevitable. He demolished the constitutional objections, often based on the prohibition, in article 5 of the *Code civil*, of judges making regulatory decisions. The sovereignty of parliament could be secured by giving the legislature the power to override the judges. Having established that position, Gény then set about explaining

[22] 'Statute governs all matters within the letter or spirit of any of its provisions. In the absence of any applicable statutory provision, the judge shall decide according to customary law, and in its absence according to the rules that he would enact as a legislator. In this he shall follow established doctrine and case-law.'

[23] Gény, *Méthode d'interprétation*. On this movement and its links with Pound and other members of the American realist movement, see J. E. Herget and S. Wallace, 'The German free law movement as the source of American legal realism' (1987) 73 *Virginia Law Review* 399 ff. On pages 412 and 413 they show how Gény, a native of Alsace, was aware of German literature and debates.

that this did not entail judges having the power to decide according to personal whim:[24]

> However, where all formal support is missing, the interpreter is completely handed over to the inspiration of his individual conscience. But this conscience cannot decide according to its own fantasies or, so as to say, according to its whim. It is necessary to draw out from the common source of the nature of things the objective rules which can guide it and will guarantee it against the subjectivity of its judgments.

Gény called his approach to gap-filling 'free scientific research'. Wolfgang Friedmann, among others, criticised this as a kind of secular natural law.[25] This does not fully characterise the paradigm to which he was relating his work, however. It is clear that the natural sciences of his day set a paradigm for 'scientific' or objective study. He was invoking the idea that there are patterns in the nature of social interactions or transactions to which the law ought to conform, if it is going to work effectively, just as there are patterns in the development of species or in nature. He rejected applying public opinion (even if it could be discovered), because it has no authority until it has become custom. Instead, he talked of a *technique* for discerning 'the laws of the phenomena' that the interpreter is studying, a kind of rule that is in harmony with the realities of social life.[26] He rejected Rudolf von Jhering's idea that one should look to the purposes of the law, because it is a question first of deciding what the purposes are to be, and that can happen only when one has studied the nature of the social reality with its inherent purposes.[27] Concepts of justice and fairness (*équité*) also have to be interpreted in light of the nature of that (social) reality.

Gény's critique of a textual focus for law was accepted. Among leading private lawyers, Georges Ripert argued for the role of case law as a conservative force in legal development. Society needs stability. Although the law must adapt to social developments, progress should come principally through legislation, which is where the jurist should expend his efforts:[28] 'Parliament is sensitive to the strength of claims and to the ideology of

[24] F. Gény, *Méthode d'interprétation et sources en droit privé*, 2nd edn (2 vols.), vol. I (Paris: A. Chevalier-Marescq, 1919), p. 221. On the impact of commentaries on cases within the legal community, see Duxbury, *Jurists and Judges*, pp. 54–9.

[25] W. Friedmann, *Legal Theory*, 5th edn (London: Stevens, 1967), p. 263. This label is also given by B. Gény, 'De la méthode et de la technique du droit privé positif à celles du droit administratif', in Conseil d'État, *Livre jubilaire publié pour commémorer son cent cinquantième anniversaire* (Paris: Recueil Sirey, 1952), pp. 277ff., p. 279.

[26] Gény, *Méthode d'interprétation*, 2nd edn, vol. I, p. 80, pp. 90–1.

[27] Gény, *Méthode d'interprétation*, 2nd edn, vol. I, p. 91.

[28] Ripert, *Les forces créatrices du droit*, p. 26.

social progress. Judges recognise the value of the existing law and seek to preserve it.'[29] Gény's idea of a scientifically discoverable standard outside the law was rejected by Ripert in favour of a strict positivism, however. He recognised the ideals, but preferred a certain scepticism in relation to ideas of perfection. It is this approach that has been more dominant in France.

The debates in other countries were similar. The Prussian Allgemeines Landrecht of 1794 declared that the opinions of law teachers and the previous decisions of judges should not be taken into account when interpreting that code (introduction, § 6), and paragraph 12 of the Austrian Civil Code of 1811 had a similar stipulation. The aspiration of much legal writing was to find coherence either within the relevant code or within the scholarly restatement of Roman law. The character of the legal writing paralleled the French *école de l'exégèse*. In order to establish academic credibility, problems were to be solved by reinterpreting the code or by developing the concepts within the existing law. For that reason, it was caricatured by critics as 'concept legal theory' (*Begriffsjurisprudenz*). The alternative 'historical school', developed by Friedrich Carl von Savigny, had paid attention to the need to situate codification and legislation within the character and needs of a particular nation. Again, this was a predominantly conservative approach. By and large, the impact of that approach had receded significantly by 1850. In the study of Roman law, which remained dominant until the process of adopting a national civil code for Germany in 1900, much of the work was also conceptually based. Rigour in the analysis of concepts was seen as attempting to make law self-sufficient and remote from the debates of ordinary life. With natural law in decline, this kind of positivism eclipsed the historical approach.

By way of reaction in a period of significant legal change brought about by industrialisation as well as unification, Josef Kohler suggested in 1886 that judges could resolve new problems by broadening the meaning of the statute by having regard to the social and economic purposes it was meant to pursue, and Eugen Ehrlich in 1888 pointed to the scope for judicial creativity in the interpretation of general clauses in legislation or general principles of law.[30] At the turn of the century the draft of the Swiss Civil Code was circulating, with its provision on the filling of gaps by the judge. This provoked a further reaction among legal theorists. Those in favour of the recognition of judicial creativity included Ernst Zitelmann (1902), Ehrlich (1903) and Hermann Kantorowicz (1906). Parallel to Gény,

[29] Ripert, *Les forces créatrices du droit*, p. 390.

[30] See Herget and Wallace, 'German free law movement', 408.

Ehrlich argued for the principles of 'free interpretation' of law' (*freie Rechtsfindung*).[31] He recognised the importance of statute law enacted by the legislator, but also accepted that judges were not bound hand and foot, so that there was freedom for judges as interpreters. Terms such as 'good faith' (*Treu und Glauben*), 'custom of the trade' and 'implied intention' all gave the judge scope for decision. As a result, '[t]here is no guaranty of justice except the personality of the judge'.[32] The role of the judge was not purely bureaucratic or technical, but creative. The discretion of the judge was not unconstrained, though, but focused on conformity with 'the living law' within society. For him, '[i]t is the business of legal science to teach the law as it actually works'.[33]

The judicial decision had to reflect a number of factors, only one of which was the legal rules, and law should mirror social movements. Ehrlich saw a close connection between legal norms and other social norms ('the living law') that regulate conduct in society. For him, the state was only one social organisation among many competing for influence over what happens in society. The essential body of legal rules was always based on the 'social facts of law' (*Tatsachen des Rechts*).[34] It would be wrong to argue (as R. W. M. Dias does) that Ehrlich was privileging customary law at a time when legislative law was very much in the ascendant. Rather, he is arguing, following Savigny, that the success of lawyer's law (which is not only legislation) depends on an understanding of the social context in which the law is operating and the competing standards in play. A key feature, as Friedmann points out, is that Ehrlich did not confine ideas of justice to a static description of how society now operates.[35] There is a dynamic perspective in which society is in continuous development and the law must adapt with it (a sense of social progress is a contrast to the extreme approaches of historical jurisprudence):[36]

> Ehrlich's work is full of stimulating suggestions for a scientific approach to law which relates the law more closely to the life of society. It has played a leading part in the reaction of legal thinking towards the turn of the century, against the surfeit of analytical jurisprudence which had

[31] E. Ehrlich, *Freie Rechtsfindung und freie Rechtswissenschaft* [1903], reprinted as 'Judicial freedom of decision: its principles and objects', in E. Bruncken and L. B. Register, *Science of Legal Method* (Boston Book Co., 1917), pp. 47 ff.

[32] Ehrlich, 'Judicial freedom of decision', p. 63.

[33] Ehrlich, 'Judicial freedom of decision', p. 77.

[34] See Friedmann, *Legal Theory*, p. 249.

[35] Friedmann, *Legal Theory*, p. 250.

[36] Friedmann, *Legal Theory*, p. 251.

> characterised the legal thinking of the preceding generation. If Ehrlich resumes Savigny's line of thinking, he does so with a much more practical and active purpose, with his eye on the present much more than on the past. Whenever legal science becomes too self-sufficient, too exclusively preoccupied with its technique as an end in itself, it is necessary to remind it of its social function.

The common element with Gény and Ehrlich is the belief in the existence of objective principles that underpinned social activity. The concept of the 'nature of things', or, better, the 'nature of reality', was central. It was developed further by Gustav Radbruch, who saw it as the motor force in the transformation of legal institutions in response to social change.[37] An example might be labour law, whereby the law adapts to changes in the relationships of capital and labour. Friedmann suggests that this forms a kind of phenomenological approach akin to natural law, but he notes that Radbruch wanted to separate the two, since natural law was, for him, grounded in metaphysics, rather than the physics of reality.[38]

Despite the scientific approach, Friedmann was right to identify that it was ultimately unsatisfactory. The existence of factual data, however well researched (and there was relatively little empirical research undertaken to back up these kinds of argument), left the ultimate problem as a conflict of values.[39] It was in relation to this issue that authors such as Philipp Heck intervened to suggest that the function of the judge was to weigh the interests in conflict.[40] The judge had to identify the underlying social conflicts and see how far these could be resolved by analogy from the provisions enacted by the legislator. The function of legal education was to inculcate a kind of 'sense of justice' in the judge for resolving the unregulated case.

The idea of system-based reasoning is not dead. The importance of positivism and doctrinal legal writing have contributed to the suggestion that fidelity to the law requires the interpreter to draw answers from the law, rather than from other values. Given the German and Italian experience of dictatorship, it is not surprising that this kind of approach has been important in the jurisprudence of these two countries since 1945. There

[37] See G. Radbruch, 'Die Natur der Sache als juristische Denkform', in G. C. Hernmarck (ed.), *Festschrift zu Ehren von Rudolf Laun* (Hamburg: J. P. Toth, 1948), pp. 157 ff.

[38] Friedmann, *Legal Theory*, p. 204.

[39] Friedmann, *Legal Theory*, p. 205.

[40] P. Heck, *Gesetzesauslegung und Interessenjurisprudenz* [1914], reprinted in P. Heck, *Das Problem der Rechtsgewinnung: Gesetzesauslegung und Interessenjurisprudenz: Begriffsbildung und Interessenjurisprudenz* (Bad Homburg: Gehlen, 1968), pp. 46 ff., pp. 129–41.

is significantly influential work that points to the importance of 'system rightness', which may conflict with substantive conceptions of justice.[41] Others would take the view, however, that the balancing of the system and external perspectives leads to a situation-based decision-making.[42] This tension is reflected in much writing on legal reasoning. Among the most influential writers have been Josef Esser[43] and Emilio Betti.[44] Both tried to argue that the incompleteness of the law does not leave the judge with unfettered discretion. Following Hans-Georg Gadamer's hermeneutics, the interpretative process takes place within a tradition. In order to understand the text, the interpreter must read it as part of a tradition that gives the rationale and meaning to the text.[45] This way of viewing the interpretative process situates the text within the body of the law and the traditions of legal scholarship and judicial decision-making of a particular community. Following Roscoe Pound, Esser used the distinction between 'rules' and 'principles' to express the idea that the law does not run out when the legal rules do not give an answer. The judge is required to fit within these principles, and this will reflect the best way of interpreting the dominant legal ethos.[46] As Betti puts it, 'We are not dealing with an autonomous, original and free creation, but with a subordinate, derived and bound recreation of something other and original: the precept to be interpreted, embedded in the legal order of which it is a part.'[47]

5.2.1 *Rechtsgefühl*

The other widely used idea to explain how judges should fill gaps in the law was that of a 'sense of justice' (*Rechtsgefühl*) among the people.

[41] See C.-W. Canaris, *Systemdenken und Systembegriff in der Jurisprudenz* (Berlin: Duncker & Humblot, 1969), pp. 104 ff. (Canaris has since become one of the leading private law academics in Germany, responsible for changes to the Civil Code in 2002.)

[42] P. Visser t'Hooft, 'On legal reasoning and the concept of practical reason' (1982) 13 *Rechtstheorie* 269 ff.

[43] J. Esser, *Grundsatz und Norm in der richterlichen Fortbildung des Privatrechts* (Tübingen: Mohr, 1956); J. Esser, *Vorverständnis und Methodenwahl in der richterlichen Fortbildung des Rechts* (Frankfurt: Athenäum Verlag, 1970).

[44] E. Betti, *Interpretazione della legge e degli atti giuridici*, 2nd edn (Milan: A. Giuffrè, 1971).

[45] Betti, *Interpretazione della legge*, p. 160.

[46] R. Zippelius, 'Rechtsnorm und richterliche Entscheidungsfreiheit' (1970) 25 *JZ* 241 ff.

[47] Betti, *Interpretazione della legge*, p. 144. He draws a distinction between 'discretionary evaluation' ('*apprezzamento discrezionale*') and 'bound evaluation' ('*apprezamento vincolato (interpretativo)*'): p. 157; see H.-G. Gadamer, *Truth and Method* (London: Sheed and Ward, 1975), p. 277.

The concept is first found in Heinrich von Kleist (1810), then in Gustav Rümelin (1871) and Jhering (1872), as an expression of the underpinning of positive law that bound the individual subjects to what the state enacted.[48] For Rümelin, it was not simply a description but a standard against which to judge positive law – the sense of justice of right-thinking people ('Rechtsgefühl aller billig und gerecht Denkenden').[49] In more modern times the idea has been used by Reinhold Zippelius (1970) and finds expression in the introductory article 7 of the New Dutch Civil Code. For Zippelius, the subjectivity of decision by judges in unregulated situations was overcome by its foundation in agreement with a broad consensus among others in society. Drawing on ideas going back to Friedrich Schleiermacher in the 1830s, Zippelius argued that the capacity of a solution for achieving consensus in society (*Konsensfähigkeit*) was the objective test of the judge's own sense of fairness.[50]

In its earlier formulation, the sense of justice was conceived as an innate way of thinking (Feuerbach and Savigny talk of *Rechtsbewusstsein*), but this was rejected by Jhering, who argued that 'Nicht das Rechsgefühl hat das Recht erzeugt, sondern das Recht das Rechtsgefühl'.[51] Law has had a civilising function. When analysed, it is objective, in the sense of being a typical reaction among a group of fellow citizens according to social position and type of activity. In terms of method, it means that the lawyer has to focus not on the abstract norm but on understanding the individual situations in which decisions arise.[52] This idea that the law creates values

[48] H. von Kleist, 'Michael Kohlhaas', in *Erzählungen* (Berlin: Realschulbuchhandlung, 1810), pp. 1 ff., p. 3; G. Rümelin, 'Über das Rechtsgefühl' [1871], in G. Rümelin, *Rechtsgefühl und Gerechtigkeit*, 2nd edn (Frankfurt: Klostermann, 1943), p. 5 ff.; R. von Jhering, *Der Kampf ums Recht* (Vienna: Manz, 1872). See C. Meier, *Zur Diskussion über das Rechtsgefühl* (Zurich: Thesis, 1985).

[49] BGHZ 52, 17, 20.

[50] See R. Zippelius, 'Rechtsgefühl und Rechtsgewissen', in E.-J. Lampe (ed.), *Das sogenannte Rechtsgefühl* (Opladen: Westdeutscher Verlag, 1985), pp. 12 ff., p. 14.

[51] 'It is not the sense of justice which has generated law, but law the sense of justice.' Cited by R. Weimar, 'Rechtsgefühl und Ordnungsbedürfnis', in Lampe, *Das sogenannte Rechtsgefühl*, pp. 158 ff., p. 161. Lampe and Eckensberger in the same collection argue that the concept embodies an idea of social learning – learning in a role: E.-J. Lampe, 'Rechtsgefühl und juristische Kognition', pp. 110 ff., pp. 118–19; L. H. Eckensberger, 'Das "Rechtsgefühl" aus entwicklungspsychologischer Perspektive', pp. 71 ff., pp. 80–1.

[52] See O. Bülow, *Gesetz und Richteramt* [1885], cited by L. Eley, 'Rechtsgefühl und materiale Werkethik', in Lampe, *Das sogenannte Rechtsgefühl*, pp. 136 ff., p. 140: 'Law is the product of experience. It must be tested out [*herausexperimentiert*]. It is a product of bitter need for justice, for which people have struggled from case to case, to resolve through the impartial judgment of state power the conflicts of human longing and suffering presented about property and life.'

is taken up by Rudolf Wiethölter, who argues that key ethical values in the modern law, such as autonomy and human dignity, are not metaphysical presuppositions of the law but are the product of the law and constructed by it.[53]

The discussion of gap-filling within a code and judicial lawmaking was the framework within which the connection between the law and wider values was looked at. Once the question of the legitimacy of gap-filling had been settled, then the question of how those gaps could be filled by judges (and also by academic writers) came into focus. The search for objective perspectives and socially acceptable views became significant. The methodology for deriving such values was, essentially, left to intuition, however, rather than to evidence, except insofar as those values could be identified through a systematic analysis of existing legal provisions.

5.3 Analytical jurisprudence and legal reasoning

A consequence of both legal positivism and conceptual jurisprudence was an emphasis on analytical approaches to the study of law and on an analysis of legal reasoning. In a sense, this is focused on the 'inner life of the law', rather than its external justification. Conceptual coherence pays attention to the meaning and boundaries of certain legal concepts, such as 'person' or 'property'. Doctrinal legal writing continued this pattern, but this chapter does not have the space to deal with this latter aspect, which is covered more fully in other volumes in this series.[54]

More important for the development of tort law is the area of legal reasoning. Given agreement that there are gaps in the law and that interpretation is necessary, then the theories of legal reasoning tried to explain this. The work on this field was developed in particular in Germany and Italy.

A preoccupation of German writing after the Nazi period has been with the way of preventing pure legal logic or pure respect for the will of the legislator from leading to unacceptable results. In this, the 'bureaucratic' model of Max Weber had to be complemented by recognition of the political dimension of decision-making. For Adolf Arndt, the political dimension of judicial decision-making was not an 'irritating itch' that one could get rid of but, rather, an integral part of democratic judging:[55]

[53] R. Wiethölter, *Rechtswissenschaft* (Frankfurt: Fischer, 1968), pp. 180–1.

[54] See Jansen, *The Development and Making of Legal Doctrine*; and P. Mitchell (ed.), *Institutions and Professions in the Development of Tort Law* (Cambridge University Press, forthcoming).

[55] A. Arndt, *Das Bild des Richters* (Karlsruhe: C. F. Muller, 1957), p. 17, p. 12.

> [T]here is no law that is comprehensible without political understanding for its specific task and without a view of the whole… The universal structural principle of partnership in constitutional democracy must rather lead to judging being not a process free from political responsibility, but that judge identify himself responsibly with the legally correct decision which he has shared in making.

In a word, the roles of the judge and legislator were complementary: the legislator sets out general principles and the judge renders these concrete. In this relationship, though, the personality of the responsible judge comes more to the fore.[56] The point is that the legal system is not a series of rules but is held together as an ethical-legal order by fundamental values. It is the application of these that gives the judge his charisma.[57] German scholarship in particular is unanimous in supporting this ethical interpretation.[58] Such an approach links conceptual analysis and interest analysis by a concentration on values as an interpretative scheme. There is a long-standing vein of wariness, however, in terms of giving too much place to values. Justus Wilhelm Hedemann's 1933 critique of judges for using the general clauses of the Civil Code is an example.[59] By contrast, others have tried to demonstrate that concepts such as 'fairness' are used in a careful and considered manner.[60]

The alternative, which many on the left proposed (including judges such as Rudolf Wassermann), was the model of the social judge, taking responsibility to achieve justice in individual cases and prepared to stand up to the public authorities in defence of individual freedoms.[61] This did not gain much favour, however. More traditional commentators criticised such judges on the left by arguing that to go beyond the normal judicial development of the law in line with legal values went too far into the role

[56] Arndt, *Das Bild des Richters*, p. 11; T. Rasehorn, *Im Namen des Volkes?* (Neuwied: Luchterhand, 1968), pp. 15–25.

[57] See K. Zweigert, 'Zum richterlichen Charisma in einer ethisierte Rechtsordnung', in T. Eschenburg and T. Heuss (eds.), *Festgabe für Carlo Schmid zum 65* (Tübingen: Mohr, 1962), pp. 299 ff., pp. 309–10. See also (1954) BVerfGE 7, 198 (*Kuppelei* decision): '[T]he Constitution consists not only in individual sentences, but also in general political guiding ideas, which stand behind the individual rules and have shaped them.'

[58] For example, K. Larenz's *Methodenlehre der Rechtswissenschaft* (Berlin: Springer, 1960) makes much use of this.

[59] J. W. Hedemann, *Die Flucht in die Generalklauseln: Eine Gefahr für Recht und Staat* (Tübingen: Mohr, 1933), suggests that the use of general clauses reflects the prevalence of uncertain 'sentiment' over the hardness of law.

[60] F. Henf, *Billigkeit und zivilrichterliche Argumentation* (Kiel: Thesis, 1978), p. 24, pp. 240 ff.

[61] See R. Wassermann, *Justizreform* (Neuwied: Luchterhand, 1970), ch. 1; and R. Wassermann, *Der politische Richter* (Munich: Piper, 1972), pp. 17–18.

of the social engineer in creating a new kind of society, which was not a proper role.[62] Judges had to anchor themselves firmly in legal texts in order to justify their creativity, rather than any ideals of a better society. At core, the judges, especially in the Bundesverfassungsgericht (Federal Constitutional Court), argue that the Basic Law establishes a kind of consensus. The role of the judge, in the view of Carl Friedrich Rudolf Smend and later constitutional judges, is to contribute towards a process of social integration.[63] Compromise and consensus are the social processes by which this is achieved. As Jutta Limbach puts it, '[E]ven though it is not the primary task of the Bundesverfassungsgerichtshof to create consensus in society, equally it cannot be its task to release productive unrest in society.'[64] An understanding of society and an ability to contribute to building consensus are seen here as ideals. It is not that there is an actual consensus that the judges are reproducing, but they are working with the grain so as to fashion a consensus. The task is to create the conditions for social stability, and to generate acceptance of the decisions, while at the same time this role of emphasising foundational values also means that the constitutional judges, at least, have the task of resisting the majority. On the other hand, if the judges ignore the sense of justice in the community, they create a gulf between themselves and the community. This leads to a delicate balance. In the view of its former president, Limbach, the job of the court is to lead a long-term policy role, not simply to be the guardian of the constitution.[65]

This conflict of views among judges is reflected in the academic literature. Robert Alexy has provided the most sophisticated modern theory of legal reasoning, the 'special case thesis'. In brief, this suggests that 'the claim to correctness [in a legal argument] is indeed...raised in legal discourse, but this claim, unlike that in general practical discourse, is not concerned with the absolute rationality of the normative statement in question, but only with showing that it can be rationally justified within the framework of the validly prevailing legal order'.[66] The idea of legal reasoning as an exercise in consensus-building is reflected in the highly influential work of the Belgian Chaïm Perelman.[67] His work on 'the new

62 W. Richter, 'Die Rolle des Richters in unserer Zeit' (1974) 29 *JZ* 345 ff., 348.

63 J. Limbach, *Im Namen des Volkes* (Stuttgart: Deutsche Verlagsanstalt, 1999), pp. 151–6.

64 Limbach, *Im Namen des Volkes*, p. 157.

65 Limbach, *Im Namen des Volkes*, pp. 158–62.

66 R. Alexy, *A Theory of Legal Argumentation* (Oxford: Clarendon Press, 1989), p. 220.

67 C. Perelman and L. Olbrechts-Tyteca, *The New Rhetoric: A Treatise on Argumentation* [1953], trans. J. Wilkinson and P. Weaver (University of Notre Dame Press, 1969).

rhetoric' provides a structure for understanding legal reasoning that goes beyond simply focusing on deduction from authoritative rules. In his model, the reasons presented by a judge are *topoi*, perspectives chosen because of their resonance within the audience to which the arguments are addressed. Now legal arguments are, in theory, addressed to the 'universal audience': anyone willing to listen. In practice, though, the actual audience is within the legal community. It is the legal community's reaction that determines the acceptability of the legal arguments. In this model, there is no externally identifiable truth; rather, a rightness that is determined essentially by the legal community. Of course, the claims of law are greater than simply convincing the legal audience, and so the notion of the 'universal audience' has the advantage of showing the wider community that has to be persuaded, but there is a strong emphasis on the relatively closed nature of the legal argument.

This relatively closed system approach has been challenged, however, by Jürgen Habermas and his procedural understanding of the constitution, in which it is instead the process of discussion and decision-making that is laid down, rather than the content of values.[68] Like Judge Wassermann and others, he is arguing for a deliberative process that engages the interested parties in society.[69] For the judges, the judge would stand at the centre; for Habermas, it is the citizenry. Thus, the debate between judges reflects broader philosophical debates about conceptions of the rule of law and democracy, and how far legal reasoning is constrained. It focuses on the process of deliberation in the broadest sense. Mitchel Lasser has rightly commented that the format of Continental decisions typically masks the intense substantive policy debates within the court with a veneer of formality.[70]

Within this debate, there remains a consensus in Germany that the judge then plays a creative part in giving effect to the framework thus established. To take Konrad Zweigert's term, there is an 'ethicised legal order' that affects the work of all lawyers.[71] The issue is how these values are identified and applied in a pluralistic society.[72] In this, the

[68] See, for example, J. Habermas, *Between Facts and Norms* [1992], trans. W. Rehg (Cambridge, MA: MIT Press, 1996), chs. 5.3–6.3.

[69] See R. Kühne, 'Die Richter und die Politisierung der Rechtsprechung' (1971) *DRiZ* 113 ff., who emphasises the principle of openness and specifically discusses the work of Habermas for a judicial audience.

[70] M. de S.-O.-l'E. Lasser, *Judicial Deliberations: A Comparative Analysis of Judicial Transparency and Legitimacy* (Oxford University Press, 2004), ch. 2.

[71] Zweigert, 'Zum richterlichen Charisma', p. 304.

[72] Wassermann, *Der politische Richter*, pp. 52–6.

Bundesverfassungsgericht took a stronger lead in the 1970s in having presented before it controversial political and social issues, and explaining its reasons for choices. Other judges remain more reticent to engage judicially in debates about the direction of society; but the existence of vigorous debate over many years about the judicial role is one clear way in which German judges have departed from the more formal and impersonal bureaucratic image of the past.

5.4 Sociology of law, law and psychology

It is clear from the discussion of gap-filling and 'the nature of reality' in section 5.2 that legal theory encouraged judges to look to an analysis of society in order to find reference points for solutions. As Raymond Saleilles points out in his preface to Gény's work of 1899, it is no longer possible to have a science of law that is isolated and that closes in on its own theses and formulae.[73] There was a tension between the Jhering tradition, which focused on the purpose that the legislator sought to realise, and that of Savigny, which looked to make legislative law conform to broader social norms. Sociology and psychology were developing in Germany as disciplines with scientific rigour, and these were seized on by some legal scholars. Cotterrell points to the important role of sociologists such as Durkheim and Ferdinand Tönnies in the intellectual climate of the 1880s. In 1910 Ehrlich established a seminar on legal sociology with limited resources and in 1913 he wrote a treatise on the foundations of legal sociology (*Grundlegung der Soziologie des Rechts*), both of which tried to give concrete shape to his advocacy of the study of 'living law'.

As Evelyne Serverin points out, 'We can affirm that the situation of lawyers as outsiders in relation to social phenomena belies their search for justification for their legal constructions, and not just for knowledge. This is clear in the teaching of case-law, where the subject-matter has never been to make social facts understood, but only to legitimate a social system.'[74] She notes how Duguit imported sociology into the teaching of law in Bordeaux from 1887, drawing on the work of Durkheim. Much of the discussion of sociology was social theory, though, since there was not (and never has been since in France) a major tradition of empirical research in law.

The major theorist of legal sociology was Weber, who was influential across a wide spectrum of jurisprudential approaches. Weber offered,

[73] Gény, *Méthode d'intérpretation*, 2nd ed, vol. I, pp. xxiv–xxv.

[74] E. Serverin, *La jurisprudence en droit privé* (Presses universitaires de Lyon, 1985), pp. 180–1.

essentially, a theory of social development, pointing to the important links between the economy, social organisation and law. Weber recognised that economic change need not entail legal change. Under certain conditions, the legal order might remain unchanged while the economy underwent radical transformation.[75] In his view, however, certain legal forms were more favourable to economic progress than others. For him, legal-rational authority was the most appropriate form of law for economic prosperity in capitalism. Legal-rational authority rested on the idea that norms are made by human beings and this alone confers on them their normative status. This removes them from traditional authority, which claims a timeless value transcending individuals. Formal rational law was to be applied in an impartial and predictable fashion, and this contrasted with charismatic authority, in which the will and status of the decision-maker conferred authority to make laws that were often unpredictable. Rational, bureaucratic law was more predictable, thereby creating the security needed for economic progress in capitalism.[76] The bureaucratic, rational form of law supported the rise of a rational economy and economic change. This best fitted Roman law systems, but he freely admitted that the less rational common law was also able to achieve economic development. The commitment to rationality limited judicial freedom. Although he recognised the impossibility of a gapless system and the need to tailor the law in some cases to individual circumstances, he also saw a tension between the inherent legal logic of rational law and the economic results that needed to be realised in practical situations. Formal justice provides predictability, but entrenches existing economic inequalities.[77] As a result, lawyers are not content with the 'slot machine' view presented by traditional formalism, but want to engage in more creative lawmaking (the free law movement). The solution was to allow limited creativity as a 'safety valve'.[78] The importance of explicit reasons open to inspection was the best way of controlling such discretion.[79]

[75] M. Rheinstein (ed.), *Max Weber on Law in Economy and Society*, trans. E. Shils and M. Rheinstein (Cambridge, MA: Harvard University Press, 1954), pp. 35–6. Weber gives as an example the case when the law retains its capitalist form, even though the ownership of the means of production has changed.

[76] A. T. Kronman, *Max Weber* (London: Edward Arnold, 1983), pp. 76–9.

[77] Rheinstein, *Max Weber on Law in Economy and Society*, p. 812, p. 980, pp. 887–91.

[78] Kronman, *Max Weber*, p. 90; Rheinstein, *Max Weber on Law in Economy and Society*, p. 317. Weber does not exclude applying a 'sense of justice' but recognises this is unstable and not highly desirable: Rheinstein, *Max Weber on Law in Economy and Society*, pp. 759–60.

[79] Rheinstein, *Max Weber on Law in Economy and Society*, p. 979.

The result is that Weber, on the one hand, gave a prominent place to law as a high point in social development, liberating society from random violence and the uncontrolled power of charismatic authority – a view that is picked up by Kelsen, among others. His approach thus contrasted with those of Ehrlich, Karl Marx, Benedetto Croce and Giovanni Gentile, who would minimise the differences between the law and other social systems.[80] On the other hand, he was clear that the law is there to serve economic development, although he did recognise that law serves other interests as well.[81] For him, the predictability provided by rule-based systems and organisations is more conducive to stability and economic development than a more unstructured and charismatic approach that seeks to do justice in the individual case.

Later legal sociology has been influenced strongly by Weber. The connection between law and society has been the subject of numerous theories. Among the more influential in the later part of the twentieth century were those of Niklas Luhmann[82] and Gunther Teubner. Each in their different ways has sought to argue that law is an independent system with its own internal logic and development. For Luhmann, the analogy is with a computer programme that can operate with its own internal logic. For Teubner, the analogy is with a biological system, which develops as a result of internal processes but which adapts to changes in the external environment. These theories are sociological, but argue in favour of an autonomy of law that fits some of the other modern theories of legal reasoning.

It would be fair to say that little of the sociological theories of law is based on direct empirical study. This has not been a strong feature of European legal study, though there have been empirical studies, predominantly in Germany in the period after 1960, strongly under US methodological influence. The sociology of law about which French *civiliste* authors such as François Terré and Jean Carbonnier have written is theoretical and about the nature of social formation. On the whole, this kind of work has informed some aspects of legal education and had some effect on legislation, but it has had only a limited impact on judicial decision-making and debate.

[80] Croce refused to write a theory specifically of law, preferring to include it within a study of the economy in society, and Gentile did the same with his focus on social formation. Therefore, there are a number of theories, like those of Marx, that do not see the value of a distinctive *legal* theory.

[81] Rheinstein, *Max Weber on Law in Economy and Society*, p. 333.

[82] N. Luhmann, *A Sociological Theory of Law* [1972], trans. E. King and M. Albrow (London: Routledge & Kegan Paul, 1985).

5.5 Instrumental theories of law

Legal positivism emphasises that law is the creation of the state. Jhering took this further by pointing to the essentially instrumental function of law, as a vehicle to achieve purposes that human leaders have determined. In Scandinavia, positivism was linked to understandings of contemporary psychology to agree with Jhering that a sense of justice is a product of the law, rather than something to which the law needs to conform. Scandinavian Realism was an indigenous theory of law developed at Uppsala University.[83] The leading writer was Axel Hägerström (professor 1911–33),[84] together with his disciples Vilhelm Lundstedt (professor 1914–48) in Uppsala and Karl Olivecrona (professor 1933–64) in Lund. These realists challenged metaphysical ideas and emphasised the human creation of moral ideas. This gave law an important place in the creation of a social climate of ideas.

Their writings are based on two concepts. First, metaphysical notions of 'ought' and 'right' have no existence in the world of fact and are, essentially, superstitious notions. The only reality to which they correspond is in the minds of citizens. In other words, there is no objective moral order that requires certain actions to be performed. A person is obliged because he feels obligated. The task of legal theory is not to determine what an objective moral order demands, as natural lawyers suggest, but to explain how people come to acquire a sense of obligation. Second, legal utterances are in the form of commands to citizens, and this form of words encourages them to adopt an attitude of willingness to comply with what is required. Rules of law are designed to change people's attitudes: 'The word "ought" and the like are imperative expressions… Their sole function is to work on the minds of people, directing them to do this or that or to refrain from something else – not to communicate knowledge about the state of things.'[85]

This approach of demythologising the normative aspects of law leads to a strong positivism. Law reflects the will of the legislator, not some higher standard. Law is also an important mechanism for changing the

[83] See F. Schmidt, 'The Uppsala school of legal thinking' (1976) 22 *Scandinavian Studies in Law* 149 ff.

[84] See, generally, J. Bjarup, 'Epistemology and law according to Axel Hägerström' (1985) 29 *Scandinavian Studies in Law* 11 ff.

[85] K. Olivecrona, *Law as Fact* (London: Oxford University Press, 1939), p. 21; see also A. Hägerström, *Inquiries into the Nature of Law and Morals* [1917], ed. K. Olivecrona, trans. C. D. Broad (Uppsala: Almqvist & Wiksell, 1953), pp. 192–6.

climate of ideas in society. According to Olivecrona, '[T]he use of force [by the law] is one of the chief factors in moulding our moral standards, and not the other way round.'[86] For Lundstedt, legal theory was required to study these psychological processes and to see how the law can change behaviour. For example, there might be controls on alcohol and attempts to deal with those who are alcoholics. Such an instrumentalist view of law provides scope for the legislator to define and achieve social change, and gives the judge no independent role to challenge this. The judge is there to carry out what the legislator has willed.

5.6 Justice and natural law

Natural law theories went out of favour with the French Revolution and its aftermath. The claims made in the name of 'reason' came to seem exaggerated, if not malevolent. The Catholic Church found many of its universities closed. The Catholic revival of natural law began in the final part of the nineteenth century, and it had some impact on legal thinkers. Many more were inspired to look beyond positivism as a result of the totalitarian regimes in power between the 1920s and the 1940s. One of the important themes to emerge from the natural law discussions was the importance of the human person. Paralleling the papal encyclical *Rerum Novarum* (1891), there was a concern that the expanding state should not take decisions that focused on the collective good and failed to give due respect to the individual.[87] Giorgio del Vecchio offered an attempt in the 1920s to ground an objective morality based on the human person that could act as a standard to judge state law. These could give content to the notion of 'general principles of law' that contrasted with the draft of the Civil Code then circulating, under which legal interpretation and gaps in the law were to be resolved 'according to the general principles of the legal order of the State'.[88] The trans-subjective conception of justice was that 'each individual must be recognised (by others) for what he is worth, and to each must be attributed (by others) what belongs to him'.[89] Clearly, this

[86] Olivecrona, *Law as Fact*, p. 156.

[87] See Adolfo Boistel (1899) and Viktor Cathrein (1901) in Fassò, *Storia della filosofia del diritto*, pp. 307–8.

[88] Fassò, *Storia della filosofia del diritto*, pp. 288–9; see also J. Bell, 'Justice and the law', in K. R. Scherer (ed.), *Justice: Interdisciplinary Perspectives* (Cambridge University Press, 1992), 114 ff., pp. 118–19.

[89] G. Del Vecchio, *La justice – la verité: Essais de philosophie juridique et morale* [in French] [1923] (Paris: Dalloz, 1955), p. 67.

has found much resonance in the postwar elevation of human rights to prominence within the pantheon of social and legal values.[90]

The idea of objective principles that go beyond human rights attracted other postwar writers, many of whom were aware of the limitations of abstract principles. As a result, many of the modern writers on natural law have seen justice not as an independent virtue but as a way of realising other values, such as human rights. Thus, Jean Dabin focused on the way that legal justice (*la justice légale*) needed to follow the rules of reason in the construction of legal rules and in the operation of institutions. This kind of minimum natural law morality was aligned to procedural justice (fair hearing, non-retrospectivity), rather than teleological ambitions such as realising basic goods – a view put by John Finnis.[91] Other authors, such as Michel Villey, who tried to revive natural law study in France (with very limited success), focused their treatment of justice on the organisation of institutions and relations between individuals – rather than on larger-scale questions of the distribution of resources in society. In this, they rejoined the ideas of Ripert.

5.7 Social solidarity

The theory of social solidarity espoused by Duguit[92] represented an important strand in values related to law. On the one hand, Duguit rejected the idea that the authority of law was simply based on the will of the legislator. Germanic theories originating with thinkers such as Georg Jellinek (later followed by Kelsen) focused on the idea that the law was the product of the state and thus of the will of the legislator. This was seen as too authoritarian and illiberal by Duguit. There needed to be limits on the state and its actions. On the other hand, he rejected the ideas of natural law focused on the innate value of the human person, since it was difficult to ground such metaphysical ideas. Instead, he founded his ideas on sociological observation. On the one hand, the individual wanted increasingly to determine his own life, and so individualism was important. On

90 See the works of I. Tebaldeschi, *La vocazione filosofica del diritto* (Milan: Giuffrè, 1979); A. D'Amato, *Jurisprudence: A Descriptive and Normative Analysis of Law* (The Hague: Martinus Nijhoff, 1984); and A. Zanfarino, *Pluralismo sociale e idée di giustizia* (Milan: Giuffrè, 1967); see also Bell, 'Justice and the law', pp. 118–19.

91 J. Dabin, *Théorie générale du droit* (Paris: Dalloz, 1969); J. Finnis, *Natural Law and Natural Rights* (Oxford: Clarendon Press, 1980). See also Bell, 'Justice and the law', p. 123, and the authors cited there.

92 Duguit, *L'état, le droit objectif et la loi positive*, pp. 69–78.

the other hand, drawing on Durkheim, he argued that society was held together by bonds of solidarity. It was true that the family and local communities were disintegrating as cohesive units. The family was becoming a group that was less and less coherent and supportive, and local communes were increasingly becoming mere administrative units. He saw solidarity through similar interest groups, however, and, as Durkheim had pointed out,[93] through the division of labour creating more complex forms of interconnectedness. These facts of interconnectedness gave rise to a principle of action, namely that one should try to act in a way that contributes to social solidarity: 'To act in conformity to law...is to act in conformity to what is social. The jural principle (*la règle du droit*) says: do a thing because it is social; refrain from doing a thing because it is anti-social. A juridical obligation is not an obligation to do what is good in itself but an obligation to do what has a social value, that is, not to do what is anti-social.'[94] In this sense, there are objective standards against which to judge the law and social conduct.

There was only a limited translation of this idea into national legislation. The idea of creating a social bond between employers and employees was mentioned by those promoting the German Accident Insurance Law of 1884.[95] The more frequently mentioned argument in relation to that law and the creation of strict liability for accidents, however, was that of 'justice' or 'fairness'.[96] The concern was that those who create a risk should also bear the burdens of that risk – a view shared by Saleilles and Louis Josserand. André Tunc,[97] in justifying road traffic liability, goes further and suggests a strong idea of social solidarity. Social insurance does contain a certain element of social solidarity, but this predominantly relates to the way in which legislation developed – the socialisation of risk – rather than to the transfer of risks back to the risk creator. There is a contrast with the way in which tort law has developed predominantly around ideas of fairness.

93 É. Durkheim, *De la division du travail social: Étude sur l'organisation des sociétés supérieures* (Paris: F. Alcan, 1893).

94 L. Duguit, 'The law and the state' (1917) 31 *Harvard Law Review* 1 ff., 181. He is struggling here to demonstrate that he is not deriving an 'ought' from an 'is'.

95 See J. Scherpe, 'Technological change and the development of liability for fault in Germany', in Martin-Casals, *The Development of Liability in Relation to Technological Change*, pp. 160–70.

96 See Scherpe, 'Technological change...in Germany', pp. 169–70; G. Viney and A. Guégan-Lécuyer, 'The development of traffic liability in France', in Ernst, *The Development of Traffic Liability*, pp. 50 ff.; and J.-L. Halpérin, 'French doctrinal writing', in Jansen, *The Development and Making of Legal Doctrine*, pp. 73 ff.

97 Tunc, 'Tort law and the moral law', 247.

5.8 Conclusion

What, then, are the conclusions to be drawn from this project? The biggest question discussed in the jurisprudential literature is the nature and limits of judicial discretion in interpreting the law. Once it had been permitted to admit judicial creativity, then the debate turned to the sources for the exercise of such creativity. There remains an unresolved tension between a substantial body of scholars who consider that solutions are found essentially within the dogma and value structure of the legal materials, properly interpreted, and those who argue that judges should look to outside values. Among these outside values, moral and social principles seem to rank more highly than economic objectives. Those who focus on legal certainty (Weber, Esser, Betti, Claus-Wilhelm Canaris and others) try to explain the internal logic of the law by seeing legal materials as more extensive than the rules. This argument focuses legal interpreters on the internal principles of the law, however, rather than evidencing it from other sources.

In terms of values, there is a strong resistance to see positive law as subordinated to the metaphysical principles of natural law, even if these principles, such as autonomy, human dignity and the value of the human person, have an attraction. In order to avoid the need to rely either on natural law or on conceptual jurisprudence, a number of authors sought some form of empirical grounding for their ideas, particularly during the period from 1880 to 1920. There was an attempt to see in the pattern of social interaction or organisation some 'laws' equivalent to scientific laws that provided a sensible way of resolving disputes – so that one could say that one way of dealing with a problem was more 'scientifically sound' than another. This seems to be the line that was adopted by Duguit and Gény. The more teleological approach suggested later by Jhering was developed in a different way by Weber in order to focus on the contribution to the economy.

Jurisprudential theory for the most part did not encourage much wider thinking on the development of tort law. There was much emphasis on conceptual coherence and fitting solutions into the broader context of the legal system. The philosophical and ethical approaches fitted within the view of law as an ethical order, which has developed in particular since 1945. Earlier ideas laid most stress on fitting social reality, but based this really on what one might term 'facts known to well-informed people generally'. There is less factual research to support it. Sensitivity to social or economic reality is encouraged by some authors as a major feature of thinking about law.

6

English jurisprudence and tort theory

MICHAEL LOBBAN*

6.1 Taking the politics out: nineteenth-century analytical jurisprudence and tort law

English jurisprudence was dominated by the approach of John Austin for a century after the publication in 1863 of his *Lectures on Jurisprudence*. For Austin, jurisprudence provided the tools both for the legislator and for the lawyer dealing with actual law; but it was clearly distinguished from the 'science of legislation', being concerned with law 'as it is' and not 'as it ought to be'.[1] Jurisprudence had two tasks. The first was to 'understand the laws, that men are...bound to observe' as members 'of a commonwealth'. This involved identifying what constituted a law. The second was to 'analyse certain notions which meet us at every step, as we travel through the science of law'.

Austin owed a great deal to the analytical work of his mentor, Jeremy Bentham. In Bentham's view, a proper analysis of legal concepts coupled to a clear understanding of the principle of utility would provide the basis of a science of legislation, permitting the enactment of a code.[2] Bentham's understanding of the 'province of jurisprudence' was much wider than Austin's. Having become convinced of the need for a code, Bentham's concerns after 1800 turned in large part towards constitutional and political theory. If – as his analysis established – law was the product of positive legislation, rather than the result of judges discovering or uncovering natural principles, and if judges and lawyers were only to apply rather than make the law, then securities had to be provided to ensure both that the law would reflect what utility required and that those administering the state would do so in a

* Queen Mary, University of London.

[1] J. Austin, *Lectures on Jurisprudence*, 5th edn (2 vols.), vol. I (London: J. Murray, 1885), p. 32.

[2] D. Lieberman, *The Province of Legislation Determined: Legal Theory in Eighteenth-Century Britain* (Cambridge University Press, 1989).

way that was not corrupt. Bentham's later *Constitutional Code* writings thus sought to develop a model and theory of administration that would promote accountability, democracy and transparency.[3] In this way, Bentham's jurisprudence engaged directly with wider theories of political organisation.

With Austin, the ambitions of jurisprudence narrowed. Although he was also a utilitarian, with unfulfilled ambitions to write a science of ethics, he defended the common law, and saw codification more as an ultimate goal than as an urgent necessity. Later jurists were puzzled by his extensive discussion of utility, arguing that his positivism was consistent with any ethical theory.[4] The lessons they drew from reading Austin were that law was distinct from morality, having to be traced to its source and not known by its content; and that morality, or the science of legislation, was not something for the lawyer to worry about. Austin seemed to have filleted the politics out of Bentham's work.

Austin's theory rooted law in the decisions of positive institutions, rather than in moral sense or theology. Although he argued that new rules of law could be made by the judges, he did not say very much about how they were to do this, for he eschewed the kind of discussion given to lawmaking engaged in by Bentham. For Austin, a judge making a new rule could draw from sources that did not have the force of law (such as custom), develop existing rules by 'consequence and analogy', or simply use 'his own views of what law ought to be (be the standard which he assumes, general utility or any other)'.[5] The implication from Austin's work was that a proper analysis of the necessary concepts would make the task of judicial legislation unproblematic.

Austin's late nineteenth-century jurisprudential successors showed no greater interest in reviving the political dimension of legislation. Bentham had begun to develop a modern theory of the state, but later jurists ran away from it. In part, this reflected a fear of democracy among commentators. One of these, Sir Henry Maine, who wrote a conservative political tract, was also Austin's best-known critic. Maine did not challenge Austin's modern analytical project, considering it to provide a suitable and necessary

[3] See, in general, P. Schofield, *Utility and Democracy: The Political Thought of Jeremy Bentham* (Oxford University Press, 2006). On Bentham and Austin, see also M. Lobban, *A History of the Philosophy of Law in the Common Law World, 1600–1900* (Dordrecht: Springer, 2007).

[4] H. S. Maine, *Lectures on the Early History of Institutions* (London: J. Murray, 1875), p. 369.

[5] Austin, *Lectures on Jurisprudence*, p. 639.

toolbox with which to understand current English law.[6] However, he did show that Austin's 'necessary' legal notions were in fact the product of particular developments over time, and argued that it was artificial to suggest, as Austin did, that custom became positive law only as a result of being incorporated by the decision of a judge into law. For Maine, law could be located in a community that was distinct from and anterior to the state. This point was accepted by later nineteenth-century jurists, who agreed that judges applied customary rules because they felt they were already bound to do so.[7] As Sir John Salmond explained, although the *formal* source of customary law was the state's power of enforcement, its material source was 'popular conscience embodie[d] in popular usage'.[8]

The focus on custom was in many ways odd, since judicial precedents and statutes were overwhelmingly more important in the working of the late nineteenth-century legal system than custom as found in the community. In fact, its importance was more ideological than practical. For these writers, the common law did not require Benthamic democracy and accountability to legitimate it, since it was legitimated by custom. Judges could therefore be seen as guardians of a tradition already rooted in popular consent. This focus on the customary roots of the common law also served to bring morals back into the law. Although jurists accepted that the law was distinct from private morality, they nonetheless saw it as a moral system. For Salmond, the primary function of the state was 'to maintain right, to uphold justice, to protect rights, to redress wrongs'. This was done through law, which emerged as fixed rules replaced individual judgments about justice. Custom fitted comfortably into this picture, being 'the embodiment of those principles which have commended themselves to the national conscience as principles of truth, justice, and public utility'.[9] It was the state, acting through judges, that gave custom its legal force; but, in applying custom, judges were articulating a broad and undifferentiated view of public morality.

Taking this view allowed later nineteenth-century jurists to develop a 'policy-free' theory of legal development. Sir Frederick Pollock, for

[6] H. S. Maine, *Village Communities in the East and West* (London: J. Murray, 1871), p. 67.

[7] See J. Bryce, *Studies in History and Jurisprudence* (2 vols.) (Oxford: Clarendon Press, 1901), p. 44; F. Pollock, *A First Book of Jurisprudence*, 6th edn (London: Macmillan, 1929), p. 24; T. E. Holland, *The Elements of Jurisprudence*, 13th edn (Oxford: Clarendon Press, 1924), pp. 60–1; and E. C. Clark, *Practical Jurisprudence: A Comment on Austin* (Cambridge University Press, 1883), p. 152.

[8] J. W. Salmond, *Jurisprudence or the Theory of the Law*, 3rd edn (London: Stevens and Haynes, 1910), pp. 49–50, p. 121.

[9] Salmond, *Jurisprudence*, pp. 13, pp. 145–6.

instance, argued that law developed from the community's legal disputes, without hard policy choices having to be made by judges. When judges decided cases of first impression, they followed arguments taken from 'the most general principles of justice and convenience'. This was the same as the law of nature, or the judgement of the reasonable man so beloved of English lawyers.[10] For Pollock, judges articulated moral values in their decisions, which fitted with the community's expectations and needs. Taking this approach, jurists could preserve Austin's formal jurisprudence, but replace his notion that judges were delegated legislators with the view that they articulated the customs of the people.

A generation of lawyers was also inspired by Maine to look to history, rather than policy, to understand law. Some, such as Sir Paul Vinogradoff, reiterated Maine's general point that 'legal observance' was not the product of litigated disputes but of 'the practices of every day directed by the give-and-take considerations of reasonable intercourse and social co-operation'.[11] Others looked more directly at the history of the common law and its doctrines, taking the view that only through a careful study of legal decisions over time could the jurist properly understand the common law. In 1929 A. L. Goodhart even described W. S. Holdsworth's *History of English Law* as 'the greatest legal work of the twentieth century'.[12] At the same time, those seeking to expound private law doctrines spent much of their time tracing the development of doctrines from historical cases.

Whereas, for Austin, the process of analysis would clarify issues for the judge to settle by considering the best answer suggested by utility, late nineteenth-century jurists preferred to use the tools of analytical jurisprudence to make sense of the materials generated by the history of the common law. They were influenced in part by the method outlined for the social scientist by John Stuart Mill's *System of Logic*.[13] The method was best exemplified by the dean of Harvard Law School, C. C. Langdell, who treated case law as the raw material that the legal scientist had to classify and arrange, just as the natural scientist classified and arranged data observed in the natural world. Just as Darwinian evolution had produced

[10] See F. Pollock, 'History of the law of nature', in *Essays in the Law* (London: Macmillan, 1922) pp. 62 ff., p. 70. See also F. Pollock, *The Expansion of the Common Law* (London: Stevens & Sons, 1904), p. 128.

[11] P. Vinogradoff, *Outlines of Historical Jurisprudence* (2 vols.), vol. I (Oxford University Press, 1920), p. 368.

[12] A. L. Goodhart, 'Recent tendencies in English jurisprudence', in *Essays in Jurisprudence and the Common Law* (Cambridge University Press, 1931), pp. 26 ff., p. 28.

[13] T. C. Grey, 'Langdell's orthodoxy' (1983) 45 *University of Pittsburgh Law Review* 1 ff., 18.

a coherent and well-ordered cosmos, so history would be revealed to have produced a coherent and well-ordered system of norms. This approach was taken by treatise writers such as Pollock and W. R. Anson, who applied the scientific method in England. For Pollock, '[t]he really scientific treatment of principles' began 'only with the decisions of the last fifty years', when the decline of the forms of action made judges and jurists take a broader view of principle, but by drawing on historical material.[14] The jurist could find legal principles in the historical materials provided by the common law, which could then be refined in future cases. Pollock argued that 'the practical branch of legal knowledge which is concerned with the decision of new cases has all the characteristics of inductive science, and proceeds on the scientific method'.[15] In using this method, the highest court was 'guided by an ideal standard of scientific fitness and harmony', which was 'nothing else than the objective side of the legal habit of mind itself', found in 'the collective opinion of legal experts'.[16] For Pollock, the law was in a constant process of approximation to an ideal certainty that could never be perfectly attained at any given moment. It was an artificial system always gathering new material, as '[t]he controverted points of one generation become the settled rules of the next, and fresh work is built up on them in turn'.[17] In his view, legal change was to be traced over the long term of generations, rather than the short time span of elections.

Considering that general principles could be figured out by looking at the nature of the subject, Pollock looked for a single principle behind the law of tort. In his view, the law of tort involved 'the technical working out of a moral idea by positive law, rather than the systematic application of any distinctly legal conception'.[18] The moral idea was that one should not harm one's neighbour: 'All members of a civilized commonwealth are under a general duty towards their neighbours to do them no hurt without lawful cause or excuse.'[19] It was for judges to identify and articulate this

[14] F. Pollock, *The Law of Torts: A Treatise on the Principles of Obligation Arising from Civil Wrongs in the Common Law* (London: Stevens & Sons, 1887), pp. vi–vii. Pollock praised Willes J – one of the heroes of the development of tort law, in his view – for teaching him to look at Year Book cases.

[15] F. Pollock, 'The casuistry of common sense', in *Essays in Jurisprudence and Ethics* (London: Macmillan, 1882), pp. 261 ff., p. 261. See also Pollock, 'The science of case law', in *Essays*, pp. 237 ff.

[16] Pollock, 'The science of case law', p. 251.

[17] Pollock, *A First Book of Jurisprudence*, p. 43.

[18] Pollock, *The Law of Torts*, p. 12.

[19] F. Pollock, *The Law of Torts*, 12th edn (London: Stevens, 1923), p. 1. Contrast Salmond's view that the law of tort was a catalogue of duties imposed by the law: J. W. Salmond, *The*

moral idea. Unlike his friend Oliver Wendell Holmes, Pollock remained untroubled by the idea that judges might be asked to make policy choices. Reflecting on divergent decisions in English trade combination cases in the 1890s,[20] Holmes suggested that disputes over whether an activity constituted an actionable harm could not be settled simply by referring to community morality. Rather, judges developing the law in future would have to look far more to policy questions.[21] By contrast, Pollock was wary of lawyers 'committing themselves to fashionable economic theories', which they were apt to misunderstand and which were in any event likely to go out of fashion.[22] Instead of admitting that judges might have to make policy choices in contentious cases involving trade unions or cartels, Pollock noted that, in reconciling the freedom of collective action and the freedom of the individual citizen, '[n]atural law will have…a large and probably dominant part in it'.[23]

Holmes' insight opened the path for the development of a Realist jurisprudence in the United States. Realism attracted few followers in England, however. Although Realist scholarship grew in the flourishing American law schools, English legal education was weak in the era before the Second World War,[24] with jurisprudence courses requiring only a rudimentary learning of Austinian analysis. Those legal scholars – including Salmond and Pollock – who did write academic works were primarily interested in writing treatises for the profession, designed to describe and explain the decisions of law courts. As a result, English jurisprudence seemed weak. 'While other countries have abounded in new philosophies of law,' C. K. Allen wrote in 1958, 'no Englishman in this century has founded a new legal "school of thought", and we are sometimes accused of inertia, or even sheer myopia, in this infertility.'[25]

Law of Torts: A Treatise on the English Law of Liability for Civil Injuries, 4th edn (London: Stevens & Haynes, 1916), pp. 9–10. Salmond did, however, agree with the notion that fault was central to tort liability: Salmond, *Jurisprudence*, p. 373.

20 *Mogul Steam Ship Co. Ltd* v. *McGregor* [1892] AC 44; *Temperton* v. *Russell* [1893] 1 QB 715 (CA).

21 O. W. Holmes, 'The path of the law' [1897], in S. M. Novick (ed.), *The Collected Works of Justice Holmes* (3 vols.), vol. III (University of Chicago Press, 1995), pp. 391 ff., 399.

22 F. Pollock, *The Genius of the Common Law* (New York: Columbia University Press, 1912), p. 108.

23 Pollock, *The Expansion of the Common Law*, pp. 131–2.

24 W. Twining, *Blackstone's Tower: The English Law School* (London: Stevens & Son, 1994), p. 26.

25 C. K. Allen, *Aspects of Justice* (London: Stevens, 1958), p. 81. See also D. Hughes Parry, 'Economic theories in English case law' (1931) 47 *Law Quarterly Review* (1931) 183 ff., 185.

In the early twentieth century Pollock's vision gained ascendancy, as a way of explaining both the common law and tort.[26] The most important champion of his view of tort in the next generation was Percy Winfield.[27] Winfield was more precise than his mentor, however, when it came to explaining how to distinguish those activities that did not attract liability from those that did. Pollock sought to solve this problem simply by saying that the 'precise extent of the duty [not to harm one's neighbour without lawful excuse], as well as the nature and extent of the recognized exceptions, varies according to the nature of the case'.[28] He did not explain how these exceptions would be determined, though it may be assumed that he felt they developed incrementally as judges expressed the good sense of the common law. By contrast, Winfield felt that the distinction was made by the policy choices of judges developing the law. Against those (such as Salmond) who felt that the law of tort comprised a series of static, defined duties, Winfield argued that history revealed that the province of torts was always expanding. He saw Pollock's view of the tort of negligence not as providing a blanket principle of corrective justice that every harm would be compensated but as offering a principle that allowed judges to develop the law. 'The courts have power to create new remedies for tortious injuries,' he wrote, 'but whether they will create them or not is a matter of judicial discretion.'[29] Judges were as free to create new torts now as they were in the past: 'And there is no remedy in tort at all for injuries which the Courts do not consider, in the interests of the community, to be unlawful acts.'[30]

Winfield admitted the role of public policy in influencing legal judgments. The common law, he said, 'would have been a stunted and flaccid affair if it had not been nourished by the power of public policy'. His acknowledgement of the role of policy did not encourage Winfield to take a Realist approach to legal development, however. Public policy, in his view, was simply 'a principle of judicial legislation or interpretation

[26] Although Pollock's view that there should be liability for intentional 'abuse of rights' was rejected, his views on negligence were accepted, most famously in *Donoghue* v. *Stevenson* [1932] AC 562. Even Salmond's editor, W. T. S. Stallybrass, conceded that the law was moving towards recognising Pollock's general principle. J. W. Salmond, *The Law of Torts*, 7th edn (London: Sweet & Maxwell, 1928), p. 67.

[27] See P. H. Winfield, 'The law of torts' (1935) 51 *Law Quarterly Review* 249 ff.

[28] F. Pollock, *The Law of Torts*, 6th edn (London: Stevens & Sons, 1901), p. 1.

[29] P. H. Winfield, *The Province of the Law of Tort* (Cambridge University Press, 1931), p. 37.

[30] P. H. Winfield, *A Text-Book of the Law of Tort* (London: Sweet & Maxwell, 1937), p. 19, p. 21.

founded on the current needs of the community'[31] – the traditional common lawyer's view. Other lawyers equally shied away from politics. Allen, for instance, noted that '[t]he public policy which [the judge] will apply to a new point is what he understands public policy to be from studying it in other legal connexions'.[32] Similarly, Lord Wright said that 'public policy is not a matter depending on the personal views of the individual judge, but a body of rules in some cases fixed, in other cases flexible, but governed by precedent and authority like other branches of the common law.'[33]

6.2 Putting politics back: jurists and the rise of the welfare state

The common lawyers discussed so far felt that the conscience of the community was embedded in an individualistic common law, rather than in an activist state. They were suspicious of state intervention. The common law, Pollock noted, 'does its best to secure equality of legal rights, but disclaims any power to secure equality of conditions for all men'.[34] It parted company 'with our modern Socialists who think that they can reduce all such problems to universal formulas, paying very little regard to the lessons of actual experience, and none at all to the dangers of red-tape despotism'.[35] Although Pollock saw a role for the state in 'suppressing unfavourable external conditions and equalizing opportunities',[36] his liberalism owed more to Mill than to T. H. Green. For him, and the common lawyers who followed him, the role of the law was to hold individuals responsible for the harms they caused to others, with the community, speaking through the court, determining what amounted to a harm. Common lawyers consequently saw the core of their subject matter to be private law, and either ignored the developing administrative state or wrote highly critical works of the regulatory state, which seemed to operate beyond the reach of the courts.[37]

31 P. H. Winfield, 'Public policy in the English common law' (1928) 42 *Harvard Law Review* 76 ff., 91, 92.

32 C. K. Allen, *Law in the Making*, 7th edn (Oxford: Clarendon Press, 1964), p. 307.

33 Lord [R. A.] Wright, 'Public policy', in *Legal Essays and Addresses* (Cambridge University Press, 1939), p. 95, quoted by N. Duxbury, 'English jurisprudence between Austin and Hart' (2005) 91 *Virginia Law Review* 57 ff.

34 Pollock, *The Genius of the Common Law*, p. 54.

35 *The Spectator*, 24 October 1925, quoted by N. Duxbury, *Frederick Pollock and the English Juristic Tradition* (Oxford University Press, 2004), p. 179.

36 Pollock, *The Genius of the Common Law*, p. 108.

37 See, for example, C. K. Allen, *Bureaucracy Triumphant* (Oxford University Press, 1931).

This dominant view was criticised in the 1930s by a small number of writers from outside the common law tradition. One such was the socialist Harold Laski, professor of government at the London School of Economics and book review editor of the *Harvard Law Review*. Laski found the ambitions of analytical jurisprudence to be unsatisfactory, and called for a more political theory of law. '[A] philosophy of the State can never rest satisfied with the axioms of formal jurisprudence,' he argued. 'It must seek a bridge between the purely logical world of ideal concepts, in which alone the juristic theory of the state dwells, and the actual world about us, in which the States that we know have to perform their function.'[38] It was not from their position in a logical hierarchy that institutions found their justification, but from 'their power to satisfy effective demand'.[39] For Laski, the state existed 'to satisfy the largest possible volume of demand in the community', and it was 'the organ through which the Government registers the fact that some given demand has secured a factual title to satisfaction'. Law was 'the operative satisfaction of effective demand, and its sources are as varied as life itself'.[40] A theory of law therefore needed to start by postulating the ends for which law existed – human satisfaction – and to evaluate institutions by their ability to satisfy these ends. This was, he said, 'a pluralistic theory of law'. Although Laski – unusually for a political scientist – engaged with juridical debates, his influence on legal thinking was minimal. Those political thinkers – such as the Fabians – who wrote more broadly about the state, but did not engage with juridical debates, made even less impact on the consciousness of the common lawyers.

The lawyer Wolfgang Friedmann, a German refugee who taught at University College after 1938, was more influential in legal circles.[41] In his 1944 textbook *Legal Theory,* he sought to introduce students to the work of François Gény, Eugen Ehrlich and Hermann Kantorowicz, as well as American writers such as Roscoe Pound. For Friedmann, law could not be studied as a closed logical system. Nor could the judge simply claim to articulate the moral consciousness of the community. The judge, he wrote,

[38] H. Laski, 'Law and the state', in *Studies in Law and Politics* (London: G. Allen & Unwin, 1932), pp. 237 ff., pp. 239–40.

[39] Laski, 'Law and the state', p. 244.

[40] Laski, 'Law and the state', p. 254, p. 273.

[41] See J. Bell, 'Wolfgang Friedmann (1907–1972)', in J. Beatson and R. Zimmermann (eds.), *Jurists Uprooted: German-Speaking Émigré Lawyers in Twentieth-Century Britain* (Oxford University Press, 2004), pp. 517 ff.

> cannot consider a single bold social innovation undertaken by a radical government as being an assured part of the social thinking of his generation and country. But he is no more justified in regarding principles accepted a century ago as being fixed for all time in the interpretation of the law. In trying to assess the assured results of social evolution for translation into legal judgments, the judge must look for aid not only to jurisprudential thought but also to the multitude of other sciences which influence the law.[42]

In his postwar editions, Friedmann noted that the age of the welfare state required new legal techniques that could not be divorced from the world of politics. Legal technique had always to be subordinate to social ideals. As he saw it, the study of law 'provides one avenue to the diagnosis of social crisis, no less so than any other social science'. It was hence appropriate for the lawyer to play a leading role in social reform. The lawyer 'has ample opportunity to assist social progress by developing and interpreting a widely framed legal principle in accordance with changing conditions'. He could also 'discover, through his particular way of contact with social reality, that a law fails to achieve its ostensible purpose and brings misery instead of welfare'.[43]

Friedmann sought to apply this method to the study of various areas of law, including tort. He argued that, after *Donoghue* v. *Stevenson*, courts had increased the range of liabilities towards consumers. In these developments, Friedmann identified a move away from the fault principle, which had been so championed by late nineteenth-century jurists, towards a stricter liability. At this time the judiciary seemed to be moving away from the world described by Holmes, in which the state did not see itself as 'a mutual insurance company against accidents', and in which losses should be left to lie where they fell, to one promising wider compensation.[44] Friedmann's work was rich and suggestive, and brought to England the sociological approach found in the work of some other German scholars who came to England in the 1930s, including Otto Kahn-Freund. However, he did not inspire a new school of jurists in England. Although Friedmann's works continued to be published in England he left England in 1947, for Australia, Canada and, finally, New York.

[42] W. Friedmann, *Legal Theory* (London: Stevens & Sons, 1949), p. 301.

[43] W. Friedmann, *Legal Theory*, 5th edn (London: Stevens & Sons, 1967), pp. 79–80.

[44] W. Friedmann, 'Social insurance and the principles of tort liability' (1949) 63 *Harvard Law Review* 241 ff., reproduced in his *Law and Social Change in Contemporary Britain* (London: Stevens & Sons, 1951), ch. 4.

The rise of private and social insurance in the twentieth century raised serious questions about how far the approach to tort pioneered by Pollock in the late nineteenth century remained appropriate half a century later. Thanks to the Road Traffic Act of 1930, and workmen's compensation legislation dating from 1897, the commonest kinds of accidents were already covered by insurance. The function of tort law was further put in question with the creation of the postwar welfare state, when a new, more comprehensive system of benefits was put in place, without displacing tort. In his 1942 report, William Beveridge wondered whether there was any reason to permit negligence suits to be brought, if victims of accidents were given adequate compensation from a social fund. Pointing out that negligence suits had 'something of the character of a lottery', he suggested that the role of deterrence against careless employers might be better served by criminal sanctions that could not be insured against.[45] When this question was referred to the Monckton Committee, however, the committee rejected abolishing the right to sue for negligence, since benefits given under the new system of social insurance would not match the sums recoverable at common law, and since they would not be universally obtainable.[46] When a new system of national insurance was introduced in 1948, not only were those who were entitled to claim benefits still to be permitted to sue in tort for industrial injuries, but the old rules under which claimants were required to choose between the common law and statutory schemes, and under which a defence of common employment was available to employers, were abolished. Moreover, rather than fully accepting the recommendation of the Monckton Committee that any damages assessment be reduced by the amount of benefits the claimant had received from social insurance, to avoid a double compensation,[47] legislation permitted claimants to receive damages as well as social security payments, with the former being only partially reduced on account of the latter. After the creation of the welfare state, the tort system of accident compensation was thus left in place, primarily as a system to permit accident victims to obtain compensation beyond the state-supplied baseline. Reformers seemed to have left tort as a satellite system of corrective justice, to supplement the distributive system set up on 5 July 1948.

[45] W. Beveridge, *Social Insurance and Allied Services* (London: HMSO, 1942), para. 262.

[46] W. Beveridge, *Final Report of the Departmental Committee on Alternative Remedies* (London: HMSO, 1946), paras. 23–30, paras. 68–74.

[47] Beveridge, *Final Report*, paras. 48–50, paras. 92–6.

In this new era, Glanville Williams surveyed four theories available to explain tort, and found none satisfactory. The first theory, according to which tort existed to appease the victim, was considered of limited importance in modern society. Williams also rejected a theory of deterrence, which saw tort law as 'designed to control the future conduct of the community in general'.[48] Such a theory was hard to square with the fact that victims, rather than the state, took the initiative and with the fact that the amount of damages awarded was designed to compensate victims rather than to deter wrongdoers. A third theory of 'justice', according to which the function of tort was to require a tortfeasor to make good wrongs done by his fault, was also rejected, since defendants who had acted with a good motive and took care were held liable. If men such as Pollock saw it as a system of justice rooted in morality, the law of tort clearly did not reflect morality perfectly. Moreover, each of the three theories was hard to square with the existence of insurance. The existence of insurance was consistent only with a fourth view, 'the compensation theory', according to which the tortfeasor had to compensate, whether or not he was at fault. Even this theory could not adequately explain tort, however, as it failed to answer why a defendant who was not at fault should pay for harms suffered by the plaintiff.

Having surveyed the various theories, Williams concluded that '[o]ur attempt to find a coherent purpose in the present law of tort cannot be said to have met with striking success'. The tendency of the law, he said, was to choose the deterrent purpose for torts of intention and the compensatory one for other torts. When it came to compensation, the choice between strict and fault liability reflected one's economic position. As he put it, '[T]he cry of "no liability without fault" comes from those who wish to maximize the national income, while the present apotheosis of strict liability is the result of a majority preference for security and broad equality.' In practice, however, the actual rules of strict liability were haphazard and could not be fitted into any rational pattern. But if, he went on, the purpose was seen as one of compensation, then the question arose as to whether this was not better secured through a system of social insurance. Administrative law and regulation, he suggested, might replace the haphazard law of tort, 'on the principle that prevention is better than punishment, control better than compensation'.[49] Tort's crisis of identity remained.

[48] G. Williams, 'The aims of the law of tort' (1951) 4 *Current Legal Problems* 137 ff., 144.

[49] Williams, 'The aims of the law of tort', 152, 172, 176.

6.3 The postwar philosophical turn

English jurisprudence in the second half of the twentieth century did not take up Friedmann's project but, instead, returned to analytical philosophy. The pivotal figure here was H. L. A. Hart, appointed to the chair of jurisprudence in Oxford in 1952. Hart brought the tools of postwar Oxford linguistic philosophy to jurisprudence. Despite his claim that his book *The Concept of Law* might 'be regarded as an essay in descriptive sociology',[50] Hart had no interest in the social study of law.[51] In fact, he noted that lawyers would regard this book as an essay in analytical jurisprudence, since it was 'concerned with the clarification of the general framework of legal thought'. It was not, however, the analytical jurisprudence of the previous generation of jurists.

The starting point of Hart's jurisprudence was the idea that law could be understood only by looking at the linguistic practices of people living in a legal system guided by rules, and adjusting their social activity in accordance with it. According to his theory, legal concepts such as 'right' and 'duty' cannot be understood through analysis *per genus et differentiam*, but only by specifying the conditions under which statements using the terms such as 'right' or 'duty' are true. A statement that 'X has a right' is true if a legal system exists, under which persons other than X are obliged to do or refrain from certain actions, if required by X to do so. To understand 'right', one therefore needs also to understand what is meant by being under an obligation, which in turn requires an understanding of the legal system that generates such obligations.

Hart aimed to provide a theory that could identify what constituted a legal system, and the rules that made it up. Finding Austin's command theory unsatisfactory, he instead described law as a system of rules. The rules of conduct enforced by courts, Hart explained, were identified and validated by a secondary 'rule of recognition'. The existence of this latter rule was a matter of social fact: it 'exists only as a complex, but normally concordant, practice of the courts, officials, and private persons in identifying the law by reference to certain criteria'.[52] Hart's theory reasserted the positivist view that law and morality were distinct bodies of norms, and that rules of law were identified not according to their content or by

[50] H. L. A. Hart, *The Concept of Law*, 2nd edn (Oxford: Clarendon Press, 1994), p. vi.

[51] See Hart's damning review of Friedmann's *Law and Social Change in Contemporary Britain*, in (1954) 70 *Law Quarterly Review* 115; see also R. Cotterrell, *The Politics of Jurisprudence*, 2nd edn (London: LexisNexis, 2003), p. 91.

[52] Hart, *The Concept of Law*, p. 110.

their moral quality but by the fact that they were to be sourced to the rule of recognition.

Hart's restatement of positivism had two targets in mind. The first was jurists, such as Salmond, who had encouraged the notion that the 'separation between law and morals is…superficial and wrong'. Hart dismissed Salmond's claim that the rules of a legal system had necessarily to be connected with principles of justice as simply wrong. He recognised that Salmond's move derived from his realisation that Austin's theory, which traced all law from sovereign commands, left no place for an explanation of rights. But Salmond's solution to this problem, that rights had to derive from moral sources, was confused. 'Rules that confer rights, though distinct from commands, need not be moral rules or coincide with them,' Hart wrote, '[n]or need rules which confer rights be just or morally good rules.'[53] The solution to Austin's problem was to rethink the nature of rules, and consequently rights.

The second target was the Realist critique, which associated positivism with the approach of formalists such as Langdell, who thought that legal answers could be deduced as a matter of logic, and who ignored the range of choices exercised by judges. Hart's response was to admit that judges exercised choice when adjudicating, albeit only in a 'penumbra of debatable cases', when the facts of the case did not fall within the core of settled legal meanings. In his view, positivism made no claim that judges exercised no choice in novel cases. But, for Hart, the fact 'that a judicial decision to be rational must be made in the light of some conception of what ought to be' did not mean that 'the social policies and purposes to which judges should appeal, if their decisions are to be rational, are themselves to be considered as part of the law'.[54]

Hart's point was that a legal system was made up of a body of rules that was distinct from the vague sense of justice invoked by Salmond, and from the policy choices invoked by the Realists. Salmond's jurisprudential error was to see the normativity of law as deriving simply from a wider sense of justice. The Realists, by contrast, failed to appreciate the normativity of law at all, as they ignored the internal point of view of participants in the legal system. They could therefore not explain why judges felt obliged to follow the rules of the system. Rule scepticism, which saw law as consisting only in 'the decisions of courts and the prediction of them',

[53] H. L. A. Hart, 'Positivism and the separation of law and morals' (1958) 71 *Harvard Law Review* 594 ff., 605–6.

[54] Hart, 'Positivism and the separation of law and morals', 612.

explained nothing, since laws functioned 'not merely as habits or the basis for predicting the decisions of courts or the actions of other officials, but as accepted legal standards of behaviour'.[55]

Hart's work, and the debates it generated, dominated English jurisprudence for the rest of the century. Even more than Austin, Hart took the politics out of law, for, although the *Concept of Law* taught the philosopher how to identify a legal system, it said nothing about its purposes or goals. It was as if, like Austin, he regarded this as part of a separate science of legislation or politics. Even so, his reluctance to address the question of goals made his theory look incomplete. He had introduced the notion of the internal point of view of participants in the practice, which assumed that they shared a notion of the purpose of the practice. Such an assumption suggested that the development of the law would not – as Realists thought – be radically indeterminate and random, but would be coherent. But since he offered neither a moral theory, nor a political theory nor one of adjudication, he did not explain how the law would be coherent. Hart's failure to provide a theory of how judges developed the law, and handled principles and rules, stimulated the critical response of his successor at Oxford, Ronald Dworkin.

Although Hart did not offer a theory of torts, his analytical approach to the subject can be seen in *Causation in the Law*, written with Tony Honoré in 1959. This work was written in part to challenge the views of the Realists, who argued that, when courts discussed matters of causation, they were not making factual judgments but, rather, were engaged in making policy judgments about liability. Against this, Hart and Honoré argued that questions of causation were not questions of legal policy but were factual questions, determined on 'common sense' principles, derived from 'the plain man's notion of causation'. This was not to say that a finding of causation was either 'always necessary or always sufficient for legal responsibility'. It was, instead, to insist that the limitations on liability 'imposed by legal policy are prima facie distinguishable from limitations due to the frequent requirement of legal rules that responsibility be limited to harm caused by wrongdoing'.[56] This work, like Hart's wider theory, was concerned with analysing and explaining the concepts used by lawyers, and clarifying their meanings, rather than answering policy questions. This approach, which began with the philosophical analysis of language, and

[55] Hart, *The Concept of Law*, p. 137.

[56] H. L. A. Hart and A. M. Honoré, *Causation and the Law*, 2nd edn (Oxford: Clarendon Press, 1985), p. 26, p. 1, p. 67.

which eschewed the creation of overarching explanatory systems, was taken up by a succeeding generation of theorists, who sought to examine the substantive concepts used in tort law, such as causation and responsibility, often with considerable influence.[57]

Philosophic approaches to tort law, which avoided political or sociological issues, continued to flourish at the end of the century. From the 1970s onwards a number of scholars, notably in North America, began to explore the normative foundations of tort law, in part in reaction to the dominance in US law schools of the economic analysis of law.[58] Critics of the economic approach argued that it failed to understand how participants in the practice understood tort law. Rather than being concerned with wider distributive questions about the allocation of resources, a number of theorists building on Aristotelian notions of corrective justice argued that 'the point of a tort action is to undo the injustice that the defendant has done to the plaintiff'.[59] For such thinkers, theories of deterrence or compensation could not explain the scope of tort law. A system aimed at deterrence would develop rules specifically designed for the purpose, instead of linking its rules to compensatable injuries. Equally, a system whose main aim was to compensate would not (as tort did) limit itself to helping only those victims who could find a responsible wrongdoer.[60] It was also pointed out that, when judges handled tort cases, they did not use the language of deterrence or compensation but spoke of causation, responsibility and fault. For corrective justice theorists, a theory of tort law had therefore to explain the correlative nature of tort law, whereby the plaintiff looks only to the defendant to correct the specific wrong he has done.

Some justice theorists, such as Ernest J. Weinrib, see corrective justice as wholly distinct from distributive justice, being concerned only with correcting imbalances caused to a notional (Aristotelian) equality set by the system of distributive justice, 'simultaneously taking away the defendant's excess and making good the plaintiff's deficiency'.[61] His part-

[57] See, for example, T. Honoré, *Responsibility and Fault* (Oxford: Hart, 1999).

[58] See, for example, R. Epstein, 'A theory of strict liability' (1973) 2 *Journal of Legal Studies* 151 ff.; and G. P. Fletcher, 'Fairness and utility in tort theory' (1972) 85 *Harvard Law Review* 537 ff.

[59] E. J. Weinrib, 'Correlativity, personality, and the emerging consensus on corrective justice' (2001) 2 *Theoretical Inquiries in Law*, 2 ff.

[60] E. J. Weinrib, *The Idea of Private Law* (Cambridge, MA: Harvard University Press, 1995).

[61] E. J. Weinrib, 'Corrective justice in a nutshell' (2002) 52 *University of Toronto Law Journal* 349 ff., 350.

Aristotelian, part-Kantian account is highly abstract, seeking to develop a moral theory entirely internal to tort.[62] Although it may explain the ethical significance of tort law, it offers no account of the substantive content of wrongs and wrongdoing.[63] Other justice theorists have doubted whether corrective justice can be autonomous of distributive justice. For instance, Jules Coleman has argued that there is a fundamental unity between them, since both are concerned with fairness. They are distinguished in that corrective justice is concerned with how society deals with misfortunes that result from the agency of others, while distributive justice deals with those that do not.[64] For Coleman, the concept of fairness that informs corrective justice 'is partly determined by tort law, but it is also determined in part by all of our other moral practices – legal, political, and private – in which fairness figures'.[65] For him, wrongs are not self-defining but have to be defined by society. Like Weinrib, though, Coleman does not give much guidance on the substantive nature of the rights to be protected.

Philosophers of private law have continued to debate the relationship between corrective justice and distributive justice. Since the moral basis of corrective justice depends on the existence of a morally defensible system of distributive justice that it seeks to defend, and since 'corrective' decisions in tort law have distributive effects,[66] the question has been raised as to whether tort theorists need to look more broadly at the nature of distributive justice, and whether they need to develop broader theories of their own.[67] Nonetheless, the impact of these philosophers on the broader legal community has been very limited, not least because they largely ignore the input of statute and omit the demands of policy, and fail to discuss the relationship of tort law even with other areas of private law, such as property.[68] Reviewing a collection edited by Weinrib, Tony

[62] For Weinrib, the justifications of tort law are internal to its practice and are 'normative in their own terms rather than as the disguised surrogates for extrinsically justifiable social goals': 'Correlativity, personality and the emerging consensus on corrective justice', 4.

[63] W. Lucy, *Philosophy of Private Law* (Oxford University Press, 2007), pp. 299–307.

[64] J. L. Coleman, *The Practice of Principle* (Oxford University Press, 2001), pp. 44–53.

[65] J. L. Coleman, 'Tort law and tort theory,' in G. Postema (ed.), *Philosophy and the Law of Torts* (Cambridge University Press, 2001), pp. 181 ff., 205.

[66] See P. Cane, 'Distributive justice and tort law' (2001) 4 *New Zealand Law Review* 401 ff., 404. For a good survey of the debates and issues, see P. Cane, 'The anatomy of private law theory: a 25th anniversary essay' (2005) 25 *Oxford Journal of Legal Studies* 203 ff.

[67] Some jurists have developed such theories: See, for example, R. Dworkin, *Sovereign Virtue* (Cambridge, MA: Harvard University Press, 2000).

[68] For a philosophically informed account that does take into account these wider issues, see P. Cane, *The Anatomy of Tort Law* (Oxford: Hart, 1997).

Weir therefore wrote in 1992 that 'there is nothing here of the slightest assistance on questions recently raised in this jurisdiction, the answers to which actually made some difference to real people'.[69]

6.4 Instrumental theories and the decline of the welfare state

If the philosophical turn in jurisprudence diverted mid-century juristic minds from instrumentalist approaches, by the 1970s policy was once more in the forefront of the minds of practitioners. Writing shortly after the postwar reforms that created the welfare state, Friedmann thought he could detect a change in the judicial approach to tort, towards 'a more cautious and conservative attitude as an ever-swelling number of statutes give articulate expression to new social policies'.[70] In fact, rather than taking a conservative approach to tort law (on the assumption that matters of compensation were better left to the welfare state), the postwar judiciary expanded liability, allowing remedies in negligence for purely economic losses[71] and allowing public authorities to be sued for failing to prevent harms.[72] Judges seemed to be making negligence liability ever stricter, safe in the knowledge that the defendant was either insured or a self-insurer. Some, like Lord Denning, were explicit in invoking policy considerations when developing the law.[73] Lord Atkin's broad principle appeared to be expanding expeditiously, but was applied to those who were either not morally at fault or who were able to shift the burden of paying onto others. It seemed to reach its apogee in 1978 in *Anns* v. *Merton London Borough Council*.[74]

Instrumentalist approaches to tort law became dominant in the United States in this era. From the middle of the century, American scholars began to see tort law as 'public law in disguise', essentially concerned with policy judgments about allocating the cost of injuries, making more powerful enterprises assume the cost of accidents to weaker victims. The developing law of product liability in the United States saw the judges' role as that of regulators of a market of potentially dangerous goods, in a situation in

[69] T. Weir, 'Book reviews: *Tort Law*, edited by Ernest J. Weinrib, and *Contract Law*, edited by Larry Alexander' (1992) 51 *Cambridge Law Journal* 388 ff., 388, 389. See also J. Stapleton, 'In restraint of tort', in P. Birks (ed.), *The Frontiers of Liability* (2 vols.), vol. II (Oxford University Press, 1994), pp. 83 ff., p. 100.

[70] Friedmann, *Law and Social Change*, p. 74.

[71] *Hedley Byrne & Co. Ltd* v. *Heller & Partners Ltd* [1964] AC 465.

[72] *Dorset Yacht Co. Ltd* v. *Home Office* [1970] AC 1004.

[73] For example, *Dutton* v. *Bognor Regis UDC* [1972] 1 QB 373, 397–8.

[74] *Anns* v. *Merton London Borough Council* [1978] AC 728.

which consumers did not have the ability to weigh the risks and protect themselves.[75] From the 1960s a number of US scholars, building on the theoretical work of Ronald Coase, began to develop an economic analysis of law, an instrumentalist theory that argued that the common law both had acted and should act in a manner to promote efficiency best.[76] According to economic analysis, when risks of loss were generated by the activities of two people, liability for accidents should be cast on the person who could avoid the loss more cheaply.[77] The leading exponent of this approach, Richard Posner, argued that the function of the law of negligence was to generate liability rules that would promote efficient levels of safety, with judges setting out incentives for economic actors. Rather than being an after-the-event reallocation of losses between litigants, lawsuits were signals to other economic actors designed to make them adjust their precautionary investments to the most efficient level. He found evidence that the common law did this in the formula articulated by Judge Learned Hand in 1947 in *United States* v. *Carroll Towing Co.*, according to which a party could be regarded negligent, and hence liable for harms, only if the cost of his taking precautions against the harm was less than the product of the probability of the harm and the magnitude of the loss.[78]

If economic analysis became dominant in US law schools, it made little impact on English judges or jurists. Whereas American jurists sought to develop an efficiency-oriented deterrence theory, many English policy-makers and jurists continued to conceive of tort law as a system of compensation. But the concerns about what tort law was for, which had worried mid-century jurists, continued to be felt. From the 1960s a number of academic criticisms were made of the capricious system of compensating accident victims by the law of negligence.[79] This critical approach was manifested in Patrick Atiyah's *Accidents, Compensation and the Law*, published in 1970. In contrast to all earlier textbooks on tort, this one sought both to set out the substantive law of tort in relation to personal injury and to compare its operation as a system of compensation with other forms. Atiyah's view of tort was heavily influenced by American Realist perspectives. In his view, judges determining liability for negligence were

[75] See G. E. White, *Tort Law in America: An Intellectual History* (Oxford University Press, 2003), chs. 5–6.

[76] For an early discussion, see I. Englard, 'The system builders: a critical appraisal of modern American tort theory' (1980) 9 *Journal of Legal Studies* 27 ff.

[77] See R. A. Posner, *Economic Analysis of Law*, 6th edn (New York: Aspen, 2003), p. 167.

[78] *United States* v. *Carroll Towing Co.* 159 F. 2d 169, 173 (2d Cir, 1947).

[79] T. G. Ison, *The Forensic Lottery* (London: Staples, 1967).

engaged in making policy decisions. When they invoked the notion of duty, it was to disguise policy decisions. Equally, their language of causation was not (as Hart and Honoré had argued) that of ordinary speech, but was replete with policy choices.[80] In Atiyah's view, tort law could not be understood without an awareness of the influence of insurance. It allowed judges to expand liability for personal injury, since plaintiffs would be paid large damages that would, in effect, be paid by the community, as the loss was passed on to consumers and taxpayers. For Atiyah, though, this was a troubling development. It meant that the accident victim who happened to be able to fix his misfortune on the fault of some insured person could get far greater compensation than the one who had to rely on welfare.[81] Besides analysing tort doctrine, the book compared the respective levels of compensation obtained by victims under the different schemes, and showed how many inconsistencies were thrown up by the failure to coordinate schemes. Having surveyed various aims of compensation, he concluded that compensation for personal injuries should not be handled through tort law at all, but that it should be replaced by social security compensation.

It was not only academics who expressed concern about the nature and function of tort law. In 1965 the Lord Chief Justice, Lord Parker of Waddington, called for a Royal Commission to investigate how to compensate road accident victims, suggesting that there should be a no-fault comprehensive insurance scheme.[82] The Robens Committee on Health and Safety at Work also expressed concern about the relationship between tort and work accidents, suggesting that the current system of civil damages had a distorting effect on accident prevention in the workplace.[83] Public concern for the thalidomide victims added pressure, and in 1972 – after New Zealand had introduced its pioneering no-fault accident compensation system – the whole question of accident compensation was referred to the Pearson Commission. If its appointment seemed to promise a radical rethinking of the role of tort law, however, its conclusions were far from radical. The commission rejected abolishing tort liability. In the absence of

[80] P. S. Atiyah, *Accidents, Compensation and the Law*, 2nd edn (London: Weidenfeld & Nicolson, 1975), pp. 66–7, p. 121.

[81] The need to find a tortfeasor at fault remained central, even though the real party being sued was an insurance company. See, for example, *Mansfield* v. *Weetabix Ltd* [1998] 1 WLR 1263.

[82] *The Times*, 17 February 1965, col. 5 a.

[83] Lord [A.] Robens, *Safety and Health at Work: Report of the Committee 1970–72* (London: HMSO, 1972), ch. 17.

a no-fault scheme covering all injuries – which it was not within its remit to consider – the commission felt the abolition of tort liability would deprive many of a potential source of compensation without putting anything in its place.[84] The commission also rejected abolishing the tort remedy when no-fault systems existed (such as with workplace injuries).[85] Even those members who were keen to see tort wither away as social security provision developed argued that the tort system should for the time being remain in place, first, because the present system of social security remained inadequate and, second, because the tort system permitted 'a degree of individualised justice which social security schemes find very difficult to operate'.[86] As in 1946, it was not ideology but the perceived incompleteness of the social security system that shielded the law of tort.

If Lord Pearson disappointed those who wanted radical reform, the ambition gradually to replace tort law's system of compensation with state-run welfarism was dealt a fatal blow with the sea change in economic thinking in the mid-1970s, when both major political parties abandoned the commitment to full employment on which welfarist thinking was premised. As the welfare state contracted, tort continued to expand. There were fifteen times as many clinical negligence claims in 2000/2001 as in 1973, while the number of professional negligence claims had also expanded dramatically since 1985.[87] The trend may be accounted for in part by new social attitudes, which concentrated on the legal rights of the consumer of services, and in part by the fact that the economic reforms that accompanied the move away from welfarism – including the expansion of the housing market consequent on the sale of council housing, or the expansion of the pension market after the 1986 Social Security Act – generated more disputes with professionals in the market. Whatever the causes, by 2000 a commonly held view had developed that Britain was in the grip of a compensation culture.

Whereas, before 1979, a slowly expanding tort could be seen as offering a supplement to the compensation supplied by the welfare state, the

[84] Lord [H. C.] Pearson, *Royal Commission on Civil Liability and Compensation for Personal Injury*, vol. I (London: HMSO, 1978), para. 275. It did recommend the introduction of a no-fault scheme for road injuries, however.

[85] Pearson, *Royal Commission*, para. 304.

[86] Pearson, *Royal Commission*, para. 450 (Prof. Olive Stevenson).

[87] A. Morris, 'Spiralling or stabilising? The compensation culture and our propensity to claim damages for personal injury' (2007) 70 *Modern Law Review* 349 ff., 358; H. Evans, 'The rise and fall of professional negligence: one practitioner's view' (2005) 21 *Professional Negligence* 27 ff.

withering of welfare and the expansion of the kind and number of tort claims posed new questions about the role of tort law. The period after 1978 saw a 'retreat' from the broad view of *Anns*. As Lord Hoffmann put it, by 1999 the view that tort should 'aspire to provide a comprehensive system of corrective justice, giving legal sanction to a moral obligation on the part of anyone who has caused injury to another without justification to offer restitution or compensation, had been abandoned in favour of a cautious pragmatism'.[88] Instead of beginning with the assumption that an injured person was prima facie entitled to compensation from a party causing him harm, courts began to look more closely at those situations in which the law recognised that a duty of care existed and 'then ask[ed] whether there are considerations of analogy, policy, fairness and justice for extending it to cover a new situation'.[89] Insofar as this invited extensions of liability, it invited judges to engage in policy-making or moral reasoning. At the end of this period, the basis on which judges were to decide whether a duty of care existed was far from clear. A menu of approaches was available for judges to choose from, some of which were more policy-oriented, some less.[90]

At the end of the twentieth century the theoretical dilemmas of tort law remained unresolved. Some scholars continued to doubt whether a system of compensation premised on the existence of fault should be retained at all, since all claims are effectively settled by insurance.[91] Whereas, in the past, sceptics such as Atiyah looked to the welfare state to assume the functions of tort law, they now look to private insurance.[92] Others maintain that tort retains an important role 'for the vindication of an individual plaintiff's rights against an individual defendant', but this requires judges to exercise restraint in imposing liability, so that tort is not simply used as a means to find someone who can pay compensation.[93]

Those theorists who continue to see a role for tort have yet to provide a workable theory that defines what should constitute a wrong. Judges, uncertain how far to resolve duty questions on 'corrective' principles, and how far to invoke 'distributive' ones, have tended to muddle along without

[88] *Frost* v. *Chief Constable of South Yorkshire Police* [1999] 2 AC 455, 502.

[89] *Stovin* v. *Wise* [1996] AC 923, 949 (Lord Hoffmann).

[90] See the comments of Brooke LJ in *Parkinson* v. *St James and Seacroft University Hospital NHS Trust* [2002] QB 266 (CA) at 26. See also R. Oppenheim, 'The "mosaic" of tort law: the duty of care question' (2003) *Journal of Personal Injury Law* 151 ff.

[91] J. Morgan, 'Tort, insurance and incoherence' (2004) 67 *Modern Law Review* 384 ff.

[92] P. S. Atiyah, *The Damages Lottery* (Oxford: Hart, 1997).

[93] Stapleton, 'In restraint of tort', 90; see also J. Stapleton, 'Tort, insurance and ideology' (1995) 58 *Modern Law Review* 820 ff.

theory, social or political. Rather than using the tools of social science to weigh the potential effect of their decisions, for instance on the insurance market,[94] they root their decisions in 'legal policy' as opposed to public policy, drawing on their ideas of 'what justice demands'.[95] Although, in recent years, some members of the judiciary have sought to invoke the vocabulary of corrective justice and distributive justice, in resolving these issues,[96] their interest has not been to explore the deeper theoretical issues discussed by legal philosophers. Rather, judges invoking the concept of distributive justice have in mind 'a moral theory' based on the 'judges' sense of the moral answer to a question'. This answer is to be found by asking what the 'traveller on the underground' would instinctively feel was right,[97] or what would offend the ordinary person's notion of distributive justice.[98] In many ways, Sir Frederick Pollock's common-sense approach to tort remains at the heart of common law tort practice.

[94] See R. Lewis, 'Insurance and the tort system' (2005) 25 *Legal Studies* 85 ff.

[95] *McFarlane* v. *Tayside Health Board* [2000] 2 AC 59, 108 (per Lord Millett).

[96] For example, *Frost* v. *Chief Constable of South Yorkshire Police and Others* [1999] 2 AC 455, 503–510 (Lord Hoffmann); *McFarlane* v. *Tayside Health Board* [2000] 2 AC 59, 82 (Lord Steyn); and *Parkinson* v. *St James and Seacroft University Hospital NHS Trust* [2002] QB 266 (CA) (Brooke LJ). See also J. [Lord] Steyn, 'Perspectives of corrective and distributive justice in tort law' (2002) 37 *Irish Jurist* 1 ff.

[97] *McFarlane* v. *Tayside Health Board* [2000] 2 AC 59, 82 (per Lord Steyn).

[98] *Frost* v. *Chief Constable of South Yorkshire Police* [1999] 2 AC 455, 510 (Lord Hoffmann).

7

The left and wrongs: Marxism, law and torts

CHRISTINE SYPNOWICH*

Why do we need law? David Hume answered this question by reference to the 'circumstances of justice'. By this he meant that human beings live under circumstances that require the institutions of law and politics. These circumstances consist of objective factors – that is, moderate scarcity in resources and goods – and subjective factors – that is, our propensity to be selfish, ignorant or weak-willed. Because the human condition is a defective one, law is necessary to adjudicate conflict. Hume did not intend an extremely pessimistic view of human nature: law and justice would be unnecessary if we were saints, but if we were fiends the effort to organise human affairs by means of law and justice would be impossible.[1] Therefore, we need institutions of justice because we, and our condition, are flawed but remediable. This argument remains central to political philosophy, and has been invoked by prominent liberals such as H. L. A. Hart and John Rawls.[2]

The Marxist tradition has tended to accept the Humean analysis of legal institutions, such as rights, as the trappings of a society in which we are partial to ourselves and our friends but capable of engaging in cooperative conduct to further our self-interest. Marxists seek a society beyond these circumstances of justice, however. They thus agree with the communitarian argument made by Michael Sandel that justice is a 'remedial' virtue, 'whose moral advantages consist in the repair it works on fallen conditions'.[3] To live in a society in which law is necessary is to live without fraternity, fellow feeling, solidarity and altruism. The Marxist argument

* Department of Philosophy, Queen's University, Kingston, Ontario.

[1] D. Hume, 'Enquiry concerning the principles of morals' [1751], in *Enquiries Concerning Human Understanding and Concerning the Principles of Morals*, ed. P. H. Nidditch (Oxford: Clarendon Press, 1978), pp. 169 ff., p. 184.

[2] H. L. A. Hart, *The Concept of Law*, 2nd edn (Oxford: Clarendon Press, 1972), pp. 189–95; J. Rawls, *A Theory of Justice* (Cambridge, MA: Harvard University Press, 1972), p. 128.

[3] M. Sandel, *Liberalism and the Limits of Justice* (Cambridge University Press, 1982), pp. 31–3; see also R. Flatham, *The Practice of Rights* (Cambridge University Press, 1976), pp. 182–5.

offers a particular explanation for the need for law, however, that distinguishes it from other communitarian views. Marxists derive the circumstances of justice from economic relations. Institutions of justice are historically specific to societies based on private property. Legal forms such as rights are not the inevitable outcome of the inherently limited nature of human beings and their environment; rather, it is our flawed social arrangements that create the need for law. Any society in which the potential for interpersonal conflict is serious enough to warrant such institutions must be deeply defective and in need of more radical remedy than the apparatus of law can provide.

In this chapter I trace the Marxist critique of law and recent revisionist efforts to conceive of a socialist theory of law. I argue that the experience of Soviet-style socialist societies has caused the left to be more sympathetic to the idea that law may play a role in an ideal egalitarian society. The idea of torts remains impugned, however, by the classical Marxist antipathy to the idea of giving institutional expression to selfish interests. For many Marxists, the nature of tort law, which encourages individual right-holders to claim compensation for their own particular misfortunes, embodies an anti-communitarian form of selfishness. The opportunities it offers for economically powerful actors to shift costs onto others also makes it a paradigmatic example of the inherently capitalistic nature of law. Although this view might seem naive in its inability to recognise the problem of providing remedies for harm, it provides a salutary counterpoint to what many have decried as the heightened litigious nature of contemporary legal culture in Western capitalist societies and the arbitrariness of remedying disadvantage by means of tort.

7.1 Marxist concepts of law

Marxism's view of the relation between law and capitalism is complex, but can be grouped into three themes: law is a vehicle of egoism; law is an instrument of class rule; and law is a form of ideology.[4] Common to all three themes is the idea that law is to be found in a defective society, and that, in an ideal socialist society, law will no longer be necessary – and, indeed, as Friedrich Engels put it, will 'wither away'.[5]

[4] This section is drawn from C. Sypnowich, *The Concept of Socialist Law* (Oxford: Clarendon Press, 1990), ch. 1.

[5] F. Engels, 'Socialism: utopian and scientific' [1880], in K. Marx and F. Engels, *Selected Works*, trans. S. Moore (3 vols.), vol. III (Moscow: Progress, 1970), pp. 95 ff., p. 147.

7.1.1 Law and egoism

Karl Marx defined law as a means of expressing the distorted, selfish interests of capitalist agents in 'A critique of Hegel's *Philosophy of Right*' and 'On the Jewish question'. In these works, Marx argues that law arose with the division of society into the spheres of state and civil society. With the political revolutions that attended the rise of capitalism, the traditional relation between public and private was reversed, so that the state became the instrument of civil society, and the interests of the bourgeois took precedence over that of the citizen. The state in capitalist society assures 'the reduction of man, on the one hand, to a member of civil society, to an *egoistic*, *independent* individual, and, on the other hand, to a *citoyen*, a juridical person'.[6]

Law distinguishes between the rights of citizens and the rights of man, but the latter are no more than 'the rights of a *member of civil society*, i.e. the rights of egoistic man, of man separated from other men and from the community'.[7] Whereas G. W. F. Hegel argued that human beings' role as market actors was merely instrumental and subservient to self-realisation as citizens, Marx regarded this view as wishful thinking. For Marx, under capitalism it is the public domain that is a mere means to the self-interest of the bourgeois, not the other way around.

This understanding of law as a vehicle for egoism was developed into a systematic jurisprudence by the Soviet legal theorist Evgeny Pashukanis, who went beyond the content of law, its policies and prohibitions to the legal form itself, in order to argue that law is inherently capitalistic. His commodity theory of law contends that the legal subject is based on the abstract commodity owner 'raised to the heavens'; the relationship between self-interested parties in a market contract is the model for legality generally. Law's essential function is to mediate the relations between market egoists; liberty and equality are thus tied to their function as facilitating capitalist exchanges between property owners.[8]

Tort is an excellent example of the egoism view of capitalist law. First, individuals seek remedies for injuries from responsible others on the understanding that we are all self-interested agents who will put our

6 K. Marx, 'On the Jewish question' [1844], in K. Marx and F. Engels, *Collected Works*, trans. M. Milligan and D J. Struik (50 vols.), vol. III (London: Lawrence & Wishart, 1975), p. 99 ff., p. 168.

7 Marx, 'On the Jewish question', p. 162.

8 E. Pashukanis, *Selected Writings on Marxism and Law*, eds. P. Beirne and R. Sharlet (London: Academic Press, 1970), pp. 76–81.

interests before others unless we face some kind of sanction. Second, it follows from the assumption of selfishness that, when harm does occur, the harmed individual will expect compensation from the person who inflicted the harm, and will seek the greatest award possible. Society is enlisted to ascribe blame to particular persons, who must pay for the injury incurred. These assumptions are so deep-seated that they may seem uncontroversial, but they reflect what might be dubbed an 'elbows-up society' in which mistrust and avarice abound, and in which the principal assumption is that law exists to ward off and remedy violations of property.

The legal concept of 'duty of care', even though Lord Atkin claimed it derived from the biblical principle of 'Love thy neighbour' in *Donoghue* v. *Stevenson*,[9] is premised on the idea of competing self-interests that make negligence likely. Taking care raises the cost of producing goods for market. The socialist unease with tort arises with the idea that self-seeking behaviour is rational and inevitable, and thus that the cost of avoiding harm must be built into one's market calculations. This is supported by those arguments of theorists in the law and economics movement who have seen tort as an efficient way of distributing the risk of market activity.[10] Socialists, in contrast, seek a society in which social relations presuppose the duty to take care not to harm others, rather than seeing taking care as a mere factor of production.

Legal commentators outside the socialist tradition are also uneasy about current trends in tort law, though they target the claimants, not the defendants, for selfish behaviour. We hear of complaints about the 'blame culture', whereby individuals seek to enrich themselves by exploiting the flimsiest of grounds for harm. In *John Munroe (Acrylics)* v. *London Fire and Civil Defence Authority*, Rougier J complained that 'after every mishap, every tragedy, the cupped palms are outstretched for the solace of monetary compensation' – a result of 'a growing belief that every misfortune must…be laid at someone else's door'.[11]

7.1.2 Law and ideology

The idea that law is a form of ideology is related to the egoism view, since ideology provides a cultural representation of legal institutions such as

9 *Donoghue* v. *Stevenson* [1932] AC 562.

10 R. H. Coase, 'The problem of social cost' (1960) 3 *Journal of Law and Economics* 1 ff.

11 *John Munroe (Acrylics)* v. *London Fire and Civil Defence Authority* [1997] QB 983, 999, quoted by R. Mullender in 'Negligence law and blame culture: a critical approach to a possible problem' (2006) 22 *Professional Negligence* 1 ff., 5.

rights and contracts. Marx and Pashukanis both referred to the ideological aspect of law in their discussion of law's embodiment of market egoism, but the ideological conception is worth analysing separately. It refers to law's role in mediating self-interested persons by means of a legal culture that masks injustice. On the understanding of law as ideology, law is a set of rules that, in their claim to provide a measure of impartiality, equality and freedom, serve in fact to mystify the substantive unfairness, inequality and alienation inherent in capitalist relations. Law resembles religion as a source of false promises, rendering the dehumanising market relations more palatable by depicting them as natural, fair and inevitable.

In order to function as ideology, law's guarantees cannot be total fiction. Marx's metaphor for ideology in 'The German ideology' is illuminating. Ideology should be understood as akin to a *camera obscura*, whereby the image within the camera is an accurate reflection of the object being photographed, with one important difference: it is upside down.[12] Ideology wins compliance through deception, but in order to do so it must not merely falsify reality, but also reflect and regulate it. The role of law in regulating economic relations is expressed by Antonio Gramsci's notion of 'hegemony', by which law serves capitalist society by *expressing* a certain 'type of civilisation' that claims to act on behalf of society as a whole.[13]

Indeed, Marx noted that, in order for legal institutions to sustain their ideological function, they had to have some autonomy from dominant economic forces, and could even come to 'dominate their creator' (i.e. the bourgeois class). This understanding of law's complex role as ideology is in keeping with the view of law and state as the 'superstructure', determined and shaped by the 'real foundation' of economic relations.[14] Ideology is functional to capitalism, and part of that function is to ensure the longevity of the capitalist order by occasionally 'taming' it and compelling it to live up to its ideological claims. As Engels put it: '[R]arely it happens that a code of law is the blunt, unmitigated, unadulterated expression of the domination of a class – this in itself would offend the "conception of right".'[15]

Tort participates in the ideological aspect of law by appearing to regulate harmful acts but in reality doing this in a rather limited way. First of

[12] K. Marx and F. Engels, 'The German ideology' [1846], in Marx and Engels, *Selected Works*, vol. I, pp. 21 ff., p. 25.

[13] A. Gramsci, *Selections from the Prison Notebooks*, eds. and trans. Q. Hoare and G. Nowell Smith (New York: International, 1971), p. 246.

[14] K. Marx, 'Preface to a contribution to the critique of political economy' [1859], in Marx and Engels, *Selected Works*, vol. I, pp. 502 ff., p. 503. See G. A. Cohen, *Marx's Theory of History: A Defence* (New York: Oxford University Press, 1978), pp. 226–34.

[15] F. Engels, 'Letter to C. Schmidt, October 27, 1890', in Marx and Engels, *Selected Works*, vol. III, p. 492.

all, the remedy involves reducing harms to monetary terms. Tort appears to discipline wrongful action when in fact, as Duncan Kennedy notes, 'the moral objective is a limited one, implying no judgment about the qualities of tort or breach of contract in themselves. The wrong involved is the failure to compensate, not the infliction of damage.'[16] Moreover, financial compensation is hardly systematic; only those who successfully bring their case to court will receive it.

Thus, we should put into perspective the common worry that negligence law is too easily marshalled for personal gain. Patrick Atiyah has ventured the idea of a 'damages lottery', contending that negligence law has been 'stretched' so that the requirements of duty of care, proof of causation and proof of harm are easily met; post-traumatic stress disorder is an example of the easy grounds for making a claim.[17] Judges have taken on a 'social insurance principle' that favours the plaintiff and makes it highly likely that compensation will be awarded.[18] Tony Weir bemoans the 'wondrously unstoical and whinging society' brought on by easy victories in negligence cases.[19]

That ordinary citizens are finding it easier to win negligence cases does not mean, however, that tort is necessarily effective in remedying disadvantage. The grounds for negligence have expanded without critical scrutiny because of the assumption that a legal order is progressive if it acts on the complaints of its citizens. Inevitably, though, complaints and their successful resolution are sporadic and unsystematic. As Atiyah argues, some in fact lose in the damages lottery. Tort leaves the economic order more or less intact, despite the ideological representation of victims who are able to punish wrongdoers.

7.1.3 Law and class rule

If legal ideology provides an embellished story about the fairness of capitalism by mitigating the 'harsher effects of class structures',[20] this raises

16 D. Kennedy, 'Form and substance in private law adjudication' (1976) 89 *Harvard Law Review* 1685 ff., 1694.

17 P. S. Atiyah, *The Damages Lottery* (Oxford: Hart, 1997).

18 P. S. Atiyah, 'American tort law in crisis' (1987) 7 *Oxford Journal of Legal Studies* 287 ff.

19 T. Weir, 'Governmental liability' (1989) *Public Law* 40 ff., 55. Weir also refers to the 'staggering march of negligence' in his chapter of that title in P. Cane and J. Stapleton (eds.), *The Law of Obligations: Essays in Celebration of John Fleming* (Oxford: Clarendon, 1998), pp. 97 ff.

20 C. Sumner, *Reading Ideologies: An Investigation into the Marxist Theory of Ideology and Law* (London: Academic Press, 1979), pp. 274–5.

the theme of law's relation to social class. The view of law as ideology considers the mystifying role performed by law to be functional to, as well as the egoistic relations of market actors, the political domination of the economically most powerful social class. The definition of law as class rule, unlike the egoism view, stresses the brute hierarchical relations at work in capitalist social forces, however. Marx's claim that law embodies the interests of individual bourgeois exchangers of commodities is extended in this approach, so that it is the bourgeois as a member of a hegemonic class whose interests are represented by law.

The thought of Marx and Engels gives evidence of a shift in emphasis from the early writings, which centred on the legal form and market relations, to later writings, which focused on the content of law and the class interests that are manifest in particular pieces of legislation. Accordingly, they analysed statutes in nineteenth-century England, such as the Poor Laws, factory legislation and the Corn Laws, in terms of how they consolidated the power of the capitalist class. At his most polemical, Marx proclaimed that law is but 'the will of your [the bourgeois] class made into a law for all', nicely capturing the ideological means deployed by law to achieve rule by the capitalist class.[21]

Nineteenth-century conceptions of tort exemplified the role of law in cementing the interests of the capitalist class. In contrast to contemporary trends, in which tort is interpreted expansively, judges were then reluctant to deploy the law of torts in cases of unintentional human injury, especially on a mass scale. Tort was deemed not applicable to two independent agents who freely entered into consensual, contractual relations. Costs were reflected in the price of labour, and, as a self-determining individual, the worker had the freedom to quit if he objected to the conditions or risks of the job. Thus, despite the rising number of industrial accidents, late nineteenth-century legal doctrine minimised employers' responsibility for work accidents in the name of free contract, and in so doing directly served the interests of property owners.[22]

The depiction of law and state as instruments of the ruling class is particularly characteristic of Vladimir Lenin's *State and Revolution*, a work that considers the dynamics of class in the violent overthrow of capitalism.

[21] K. Marx and F. Engels, 'Manifesto of the Communist Party' [1848], in Marx and Engels, *Selected Works*, vol. I, pp. 98 ff., p. 123; see also G. Lukács, 'Legality and illegality' [1920], in *History and Class Consciousness*, trans. R. Livingstone (London: Merlin, 1971), pp. 256 ff., pp. 264–5.

[22] J. F. Witt, *The Accidental Republic: Crippled Workingmen, Destitute Widows, and the Remaking of American Law* (Cambridge, MA: Harvard University Press, 2004), p. 31.

In the Soviet Union, after Lenin's death, theorists in the Moscow academies rejected Pashukanis's commodity theory of law in favour of a class interpretation.

It might seem surprising that the least attractive Marxist conception of law, which reduces legal institutions to the expression of brute power on the part of the dominant class, would be the one that prevailed in a socialist society. The view of law as a club wielded by the dominant class to subdue other classes suited the Stalinist order, however. Law was used as an instrument of tyranny, but with the rationale that it was a regrettable necessity in the transitional period between capitalism and full-fledged communism, when classes, and class conflict, will have disappeared. The notorious Andrei Vyshinksy, Soviet Procurator General, dismissed Pashukanis's more subtle views (and got rid of Pashukanis himself) for the idea that law is 'an expression of the will of classes dominant in society'.[23]

The class rule view of law persisted in the Soviet Union until the glasnost era under Mikhail Gorbachev. The approach was taken up by many British Marxists in the 1970s, most famously by Ralph Miliband, who expanded the argument to consider how the class make-up of state actors reinforced the role of law and state as instruments of the capitalist class.[24] The debates and fractures in social democratic parties in the second half of the twentieth century over the question of the efficacy of democratic means to achieve socialist ends were certainly affected by the radical view that governmental institutions were inherently instrumental to dominant class interests.

7.2 The withering away of law

All three conceptions of law take legal institutions to be necessary in a defective society. Selfish interests in private property; injustice camouflaged in order to exact compliance; and class conflict whereby the dominant class rules by force – all are reasons for law that socialists abhor. On the egoism view, a socialist revolution would eliminate private property and bring society's resources under social control. Without private

[23] A. Vyshinsky, 'Fundamental tasks of the science of Soviet law', in J. Hazard (ed.), *Soviet Legal Philosophy* (Cambridge, MA: Harvard University Press, 1951), pp. 303 ff., p. 337.

[24] R. Miliband, 'State and revolution', in P. Sweezy and H. Magdoff (eds.), *Lenin Today* (New York: Monthly Review, 1970), pp. 77 ff. See also E. Mandel, *On Bureaucracy: A Marxist Analysis* (London: IMG Publications, 1973); and L. Colletti, 'Power and democracy in a socialist society', in *Leninism or Stalinism? Two Essays* (Lahore: People's Publishing House, 1972), pp. 1 ff.

property, there would not be the egoism and narrow self-interest that render legal institutions such as rights necessary. On the ideology view, remove capitalism and its characteristics of subordination, alienation and inequality, and one removes the need for the camouflage and obfuscation provided by ideological forms such as law. Finally, in the ideal society, in which goods are produced and distributed under conditions of equality and fairness, there will be no class divisions, no class conflict and no need for the institutions of class rule. Thus, Marxists took the view that law and state would not even need to be abolished; they would simply lose their purpose under socialism and, under conditions inhospitable to it, law would – like the dinosaur – become extinct.

By the 1970s and 1980s, however, the left had begun to reconsider the legal nihilism that had been intrinsic to the Marxist tradition since its origins. There were a number of factors at work. First was the rise of the new right in the United States and, especially, Britain, where calls for the protection of individual liberty against the intrusions of the 'nanny state' found support from working-class voters who hitherto had identified their interests with socialist or social democratic parties. The libertarian ideologies prominent during the era when Margaret Thatcher was prime minister, with their emphasis on the intrinsic value of the individual, prompted some soul-searching among intellectuals on the left. In economics, philosophy and sociology, but also in the progressive press and popular pamphlets such as those issued by the Fabian Society, there emerged discussions that entertained a number of previously discredited ideas, such as 'market socialism' and socialist theories of law.[25] The dismissive attitude to liberal institutions under capitalism that distinguished some leftist arguments of the early 1960s, such as Herbert Marcuse's likening of liberal institutions to fascism, seemed an indulgence that could no longer be sustained.[26]

A second important factor contributing to the re-evaluation of Marxist orthodoxy on law was events in eastern Europe. The short-lived glasnost era under Gorbachev in the Soviet Union raised hopes for a revival of socialist ideals, and the possibility that they might be imbued with a new spirit of liberty and democracy. These hopes were dashed with the

[25] See I. Forbes, 'Market socialism: whose choice?', Fabian Pamphlet no. 516 (1986). In the late 1960s a couple of now classic Fabian Society pamphlets probed the question of a left-wing approach to rights. See A. Lester, 'Democracy and individual rights', Fabian Pamphlet no. 390 (1968); and A. Lynes, 'Welfare rights', Fabian Pamphlet no. 395 (1969).

[26] See H. Marcuse, *One-Dimensional Man: Studies in the Ideology of Advanced Industrial Society* (Boston: Beacon Press, 1964).

collapse of communism, but that cataclysmic event also posed the necessity for Marxist revisionism. That is, it seemed imperative to reconceive socialist values once the example, and burden, of 'really existing socialism' had gone.[27] With the collapse of communism came greater exposure of the injustice, tyranny and unfreedom of Stalinist societies. In turn, this prompted greater appreciation for the value of such institutions as individual rights, legal procedures and the rule of law.

Was there any hope of a more positive attitude to law emanating from Marxism itself? E. P. Thompson had paved the way in 1975 when he, controversially, applauded the rule of law as an 'unqualified human good'.[28] For Thompson, intrinsic to the ideological force of law is its capacity to impose inhibitions on economic power: 'The rhetoric and rules of a society are something a great deal more than sham. In the same moment they may modify, in profound ways, the behaviour of the powerful, and mystify the powerless. They may disguise the true realities of power, but, at the same time, they may curb that power and check its intrusions.'[29] This argument finds value in law out of the very ideological function ascribed to legal institutions by the Marxist critique of law. Of course, no one will be attracted to a social institution whose function is to deceive and manipulate people in order to cement injustice. Ideology per se is not being rehabilitated here. What is being defended, however, are those features of a legal system that are of genuine value, that can serve as a palliative for the inequity that otherwise exists. Just as cruelty might be masked by good manners, so too might legal ideology mask injustice; but this does not show that law, or good manners, are of no value. As Thompson puts it, 'If the law is evidently partial and unjust, it will mask nothing, legitimise nothing, contribute nothing to any class's hegemony.'[30]

What, then, are the kernels of morality that lurk beneath their ideological expression in capitalist law? The two other themes, of egoism and class rule, are apposite here. Interestingly, of the three, it is only the view of law as class rule that had any influence as a basis for socialist law. This involved interpreting law in bourgeois society in the worst possible light, however, and then mobilising it for purportedly socialist purposes. Justified by the long-term objective of a socialist utopia, capitalist legal

[27] See C. Sypnowich, 'The future of socialist legality: a reply to Hunt' (1992) 193 *New Left Review* 16 (my response to a critical notice of *The Concept of Socialist Law* that appeared in (1992), 192 *NLR*).

[28] E. P. Thompson, *Whigs and Hunters: The Origins of the Black Act* (New York: Pantheon, 1975), p. 265.

[29] Thompson, *Whigs and Hunters*, p. 265.

[30] Thompson, *Whigs and Hunters*, p. 263.

forms were adapted to intensify their coercive potential. The idea of law as a vehicle of bourgeois egoism, in contrast, is a mine for socialist conceptions of law. This view had a brief heyday in the fledgling socialist republic, when Pashukanis's theory was deployed to develop legal institutions appropriate for the market institutions of the New Economic Policy. It was thought that Russia, still largely feudal in its economic relations, required a 'capitalist stage' before it could become fully socialist, and thus markets were in play in order to enable the capital accumulation for a socialist transition. This policy was controversial and brief, though, and, moreover, orthodox in its view that law was irredeemably capitalistic. The idea that law mediates conflict among individuals is a more general interpretation of the egoism view, however, which raises the possibility that legal institutions could play a valuable role in a society without bourgeois egoists.

On the orthodox view, upon the achievement of socialism, insofar as individuals lose their character as egoistic monads and owners of commodities, law is denied the kind of subject that requires legal regulation. The Marxist rejection of the possibility of socialist law rests on two assumptions derived from Hume's argument about the circumstances of justice: first, that there would be material abundance under socialism, so legal rules governing scarce resources would be superfluous; and, second, that socialism accordingly would be devoid of interpersonal conflict, so that there would be no need for the mediating role performed by law. Both suppositions are problematic, however.

First, since Marx the left has become increasingly aware that the question of who owns the means of production does not automatically settle the question of whether the human exploitation of our natural environment will jeopardise the supply of resources for present and future generations. The 'greening' of the left is in part a recognition of the problems of the productivist and anthropocentric preoccupations of classical Marxism. No longer could it be assumed that, while capitalism's social relations were to be jettisoned, its economic productivity would be harnessed and even heightened.[31]

Second, the claim about interpersonal conflict overlooks the possibility that, even on the assumptions of a transformed set of human relations, of 'communist man' who is imbued with fellow feeling, empathy and a spirit of cooperation, law might be necessary to mediate disagreement. The

[31] See G. A. Cohen, *If You're an Egalitarian, How Come You're so Rich?* (Cambridge, MA: Harvard University Press, 2000), ch. 6.

'withering away' thesis deems interpersonal disputes a contingent aspect of social life; like illiteracy or discourtesy, conflict is a result of ignorance and insensitivity. Once fully educated to live by socialist norms of behaviour, we would live in harmony with our fellows, cooperating in collective projects almost instinctively, without external compulsion. The orthodox view meant that, in the Soviet Union, it was possible to deem instances of antisocial behaviour as qualitatively distinct from the criminal activity of capitalism, and, indeed, to relegate them to a form of mental illness in need not of judicial regulation but of medical treatment. Without calling into question a society's egalitarian and fraternal premises, however, it is possible that socialist citizens could disagree about, for example, the best way to mobilise and distribute resources. If such non-egoistic differences between individuals are possible, then conflict would outlive capitalism, and law would continue to be necessary to mediate socially useful conflicts about how best to achieve socialist ideals.

7.3 Socialist utopia and utopianism about law

What would a socialist concept of law look like? The Soviet example of arbitrary authority certainly underlines the importance of procedural standards. Soviet violations of the ideal of the rule of law were manifest in such pseudo-legal phenomena as the show trials, at which dissenters were prosecuted in sham proceedings; parasite laws, whereby citizens were prosecuted for the non-crimes of laziness, poor reputation or social stigma; and comrades' courts, tribunals notorious for their lack of procedure. The rule of law refers to the principle that law is legitimate only if it governs citizens by reference to known, prospective, clear and precise rules. This was a theme in Thompson's celebration of legality that certainly had resonance at the end of the Soviet era.

Moreover, an emphasis on legal proceduralism promises to offer a distinctively Marxist approach to the problem of the sources of law and the debate between legal positivists and natural lawyers.[32] Pashukanis's view of the normativity of the legal form had made for a kind of legal nihilism on the left, in which law is bound up with individualistic values. Exponents of socialist law therefore tend to be positivists. For example, the Austrian Marxist Karl Renner took the view that law could be dissociated from the normative functions of capitalism, thus permitting the deployment of law

[32] I expound on the idea of a socialist conception of legal proceduralism in chapters 2 and 3 of *The Concept of Socialist Law*.

for socialist purposes. Renner's positivism, which understood the legal norm as a mere 'vessel without content', gave legal institutions an open-endedness that permits a socialist legal system.[33] The positivist view fails to see any intrinsic moral value in law, however, and therefore is limited in its ability to provide any motivation for socialist revisionism.

Instead, a socialist concept of law can forge a rapprochement between natural law and positivist accounts with the idea of law as a normative social practice. By this, I mean that law is inherently moral, but that the moral dimension is imparted to law by human activity, just as Marx argued that human beings endow nature with meaning by objectifying their personalities in the things they fashion with labour. Law is thus a moral legacy that is forged and reforged by successive social orders. The morality in play is not the supra-human moral commands of a deity or natural law. Rather, as a human artefact, law's morality is inherent in the nature of its practice. In order for law to be law, it must live up to a morality of procedure that makes law an authoritative guide to human conduct; this involves stipulating individuals' rights, but also their obligations and responsibilities in cases of wrongdoing, injury or harm.

Legal institutions thus emerge as the indispensable means of mediating conflict between individuals' interests that are not necessarily capitalistic in nature. Many of the contributions to the idea of socialist law take for granted, however, a certain utopianism about socialism itself. By this, I mean that law is considered compatible with socialist ideals so long as the ideals themselves do not undergo too radical a revision. This approach is exemplified by Tom Campbell, who argues that law would be needed in an ideal society to express the interests of socialist altruists. But even those who emphasise the self-regarding interests of socialist citizens are reluctant to see these interests as potentially pernicious for the social order.[34] Socialists may therefore continue to harbour the ideal that the duty of care would be built into an alternative social order to such an extent that it would be unthinkable to sue for damages for unintentional injury. This may seem to retain the naivety of the original 'withering away' thesis, and it might be objected that selfishness is not unique to capitalism, and even the most ideal society will need to protect the victims of carelessness.

[33] K. Renner, *The Institutions of Private Law and Their Social Functions*, ed. O. Kahn Freund, trans. A. Schwarzschild (London: Routledge & Kegan Paul, 1976).

[34] See T. Campbell, *The Left and Rights* (London: Routledge & Kegan Paul, 1983); and Sypnowich, *The Concept of Socialist Law*, ch. 5.

7.4 Righting wrongs

The wrongs targeted by tort law in our society arise in a context in which the means of production is owned privately, in which there are disparities of wealth and power and in which there are cultural and social relations of inequality. Would tort have a role to play in societies with more equal social arrangements? Could tort, like law in general, respond to the 'circumstances of justice' in the traditional Humean sense – that is, circumstances that are inherent in social life, no matter what the social and political order?

Tort centres on the self-interested pursuit of remedy for injuries caused by self-gain; nevertheless, tort's function is, after all, to compensate for the damages inflicted by expressions of self-interest. Tort mitigates bourgeois egoism as much as it expresses it. As such, tort has sometimes figured as an instrument for social change. Certainly, tort jurisprudence has evolved, from the nineteenth-century ideology of free contract indifferent to dangerous conditions of work, to the more sophisticated conception of care and negligence that emerged and developed after *Donoghue*. Tort law offered some recourse in situations of employer-caused harm. Remedy was a hit-and-miss affair, however, and therefore alternative, public law methods, such as special labour legislation and the protections of the welfare state, were sought to ensure more consistent and fair ways of attending to the risks faced by disadvantaged persons in their workplaces, homes and social settings. But the beginnings of labour law in the modern welfare state can be traced to tort as a means of resolving the conflict between unions and employers. A whole host of social harms, be they dangerous working conditions, racism, sexual exploitation or environmental damage, have been addressed through tort cases, and various campaigns for social justice have had significant success finding remedy through private suits seeking the recovery of damages. Thus, those who experience prejudice and disadvantage resist the easy dismissal of individualistic legal institutions by the Critical Legal Studies movement and others on the left.[35] Richard Mullender points out that even tenuous claims can have a positive effect, since they raise issues of public concern 'where judicial scrutiny of the defendant's conduct is valuable'.[36]

[35] See Patricia Williams' discussion of Peter Gabel's rights nihilism in *The Alchemy of Race and Rights* (Cambridge, MA: Harvard University Press, 1992).

[36] 'Evidence submitted by Richard Mullender, lecturer, Newcastle Law School, to the Constitutional Affairs Committee, House of Commons, UK, February 2006' (www.publications.parliament.uk/pa/cm200505/cmselect/cmconst/754/754we55.htm; accessed 8

Moreover, given the extraordinary speed with which technology changes and develops, it is helpful to have 'judge-made common law' track the shifts in our understanding of what counts as reasonably foreseeable harm. Negligence law offers a means by which we can gather and organise knowledge about risk; new negligence claims enable the courts to provide a forum to consider previously unavailable information that may reveal a hitherto unknown threat to individuals in society. In awarding damages, the judge may establish a new liability rule in light of a new danger, or, if the claim is rejected, the judge can inform the public how to manage the ever-changing context of risk. Tort is thus able not only to mitigate the disadvantage suffered by vulnerable persons such as workers, but also to raise awareness of that disadvantage.

There is certainly a precedent for the reappraisal of key legal institutions in market societies in terms of their liberatory potential. I have discussed the role of proceduralism and the rule of law. Human rights are another example: they are now so commonly supposed to be a measure of the justice of a legal order that we might call them a source of law; they are a historical product, yet we say they exist regardless of whether a legal order recognises them. This view has been elaborated by Marxist social theory. Human rights protect human dignity and the constituents of human well-being; they have been central to socialist revisionism about law and socialist jurisprudence. Ernst Bloch's idea of the 'upright carriage' as the foundation for human rights extended Marx's notion of human beings as unique among the species in their capacity to be self-developing and self-realising.[37] Rights have been an important lever for socialist progress. Accordingly, thinkers such as T. H. Marshall argue that human rights should be understood as evolving, to include not just civil or political rights but also socio-economic rights, requiring socialist policies for the redistribution of wealth.[38]

Nonetheless, although thinkers on the left may be prepared to grant a role for some institutions of law in an ideal society, tort may seem to be too bound up with the pursuit of profit and relations of class conflict to be a candidate for a socialist concept of law. It offers a remedy for the

July 2010). Mullender notes that his idea of a 'discovery procedure' comes from F. A. Hayek, who coined the phrase to describe the knowledge-gathering process of the market. See also R. Mullender, 'Tort, human rights, and common law culture' (2003) 23 *Oxford Journal of Legal Studies* 301 ff.

[37] E. Bloch, *Natural Law and Human Dignity*, trans. D. J. Schmidt (Cambridge, MA: MIT Press. 1986).

[38] T. H. Marshall, *Sociology at the Crossroads* (London: Heinemann, 1963).

ill effects of capitalist behaviour, but this behaviour is its precondition. Working people might play the 'rules of the game', and act as self-interested actors who seek enrichment in order to achieve some measure of justice under capitalism, but this is not a model for social life in general. Socialism might have law, but it will not have tort law.

The socialist suspicion of tort can be read, paradoxically, as the expression of a commitment to the procedural ideals of the rule of law: to consistency and universality, treating like cases alike and applying rules to all relevant cases. After all, the benefits of tort law are peculiarly arbitrary. Tort can address and repair serious injustice in certain cases of negligence, and the judiciary is often sympathetic to those who are harmed by the selfish actions of market actors. Indeed, even those who have shaky cases but are willing to 'have a go' can find themselves rewarded.[39] Very often, however, victims of negligence walk away from court empty-handed. Of all the individuals who are harmed by negligence, furthermore, only some are in a position to find success in the courts, depending not just on whether they have the wherewithal to pursue the case but also on whether they can find solvent defendants from which to recover damages. Atiyah's lottery metaphor, and the worry that tort jurisprudence can be unprincipled and unethical, if not unjust, is thus apt indeed.

Moreover, as the culture of litigation grows apace, with nursery playgrounds denuded of potentially dangerous equipment, or hot coffee served in cups with warning labels, the suspicion that lawsuits lurk everywhere is shared by many citizens, socialists or not. Fear of litigation can skew social policy in ways that underline the important Marxist insight that self-interested actors in the market can produce social conditions that undermine the genuine interests of individuals. At the same time, the perception of omnipresent litigation can be ideological, masking the reality of many unpunished and still not righted wrongs. The real risks associated with conducting one's life in a global market economy, in which much of what we consume increasingly comes from unregulated parts of the world, seem only haphazardly addressed.

7.5 Conclusion

The Marxist critique of capitalist law, despite its diminished lustre in the post-Soviet age, remains illuminating in this context. Marxists point to how economic disadvantage accrues from fundamental, structural

[39] Mullender, 'Evidence submitted'.

features of the social order, and thus individual efforts to find compensation for injury, though not unimportant, are of limited efficacy in eliminating disadvantage and inequality. At the same time, the Marxist theory of ideology offers a perspective that can mine the emancipatory potential of tort, calling upon the law to deliver on its promise to attend to injury and harm in a more systematic and even-handed way.

The socialist ideal of an equal society whose legal order protects the interests of all individuals is therefore an important antidote to the litigious and arbitrary, sink-or-swim world of tort. Socialists have joined forces with liberals and social democrats in calling for a radically different approach to accidents so that society as a whole is responsible for the risks sustained by individuals in a variety of contexts, be it workplaces, homes or public places. The proposal that Western legal systems move to 'no-fault' systems of state compensation for accidents is an effort to see the subject of tort as more properly a social obligation. Such views are not exclusively Marxist, since a number of radical perspectives that focus on the interests of the vulnerable, whether women, racial minorities or workers, will amplify this theme. The idea that the state should devise public policy to protect citizens from a variety of risky environments has broad appeal. But I think that Marxism is uniquely placed to analyse the dynamics of capital and labour, profit and wages, class interests and community, morality and ideology, which are so crucial to diagnosing the strengths and weaknesses of tort.

What is needed is a policy that takes human well-being as its starting point, rather than the idea of competition for gain that is assumed by the defendants and claimants alike in tort cases. The idea of a social responsibility for the safety of citizens can reinforce the idea of a social responsibility for the welfare of citizens more generally. As such, the debate about tort has prompted a more general discussion of the need to qualify the operations of the free market so as to ensure that all citizens enjoy a minimum level of human well-being. In sum, the question of tort suggests that perhaps the Marxist critique of law should not yet be consigned to the 'dustbin of history'.

8

The process of codification applied to the law of delicts

JEAN-LOUIS HALPÉRIN*

Prima facie, delictual liability is not treated in completely different ways in civil and common law systems. In both systems, the decisive power in determining whether or not compensation is to be given lies with the judge. This is why the subject has generated a wide body of case law, even in countries with a civil code. In France, the case law on article 1382 of the Napoleonic Code, which has developed since the beginning of the nineteenth century, displays perfectly the influence of what we call 'jurisprudence': the 'jurisprudence' of the Court of Cassation has nearly overwhelmed the text of article 1382. In Austria, Franz von Zeiller (one of the drafters of the 1811 *Allgemeines Bürgerliches Gesetzbuch* (ABGB)) considered that, in the end, it was for the judge to evaluate questions of fault.[1] Similarly, in Germany, the bare bones of the text of the *Bürgerliches Gesetzbuch* (BGB) have been fleshed out by the decisions of the Reichsgericht (the German Imperial Court) before 1945, and thereafter by those of the Bundesgerichtshof (the Federal Court of Justice).[2] There remain some genuine differences, however, between delictual liability in the codified systems and in the common law of tort. The very expression 'tort law' shows us that common lawyers continue to reason about the division of torts – that is, about a multiplicity of cases and of actions – whereas civil lawyers use the general clauses of the code. These clauses are more or less general, but they exist as written guidelines for all delicts and for the principles of liability.

* École Normale Supérieure (Paris).

[1] F. von Zeiller, *Abhandlung über die Principien des allgemeinen bürgelichen Gesetzbuches*, ed. W. Brauneder (Vienna: Manz, 1986), p. 1816.

[2] B. M. Markesinis and H. Unberath, *The German Law of Torts: A Comparative Treatise*, 4th edn (Oxford: Hart, 2002); R. Zimmermann and D. A. Verse, 'Die Reaktion des Reichsgerichts auf die Kodifikation des deutschen Deliktsrechts (1900–1914)', in U. Falk and H. Mohnhaupt (eds.), *Das Bürgerliche Gesetzbuch und seine Richter* (Frankfurt: Klostermann, 2000), pp. 319 ff.; E. von Caemmerer, 'Wandlungen des Deliktrechts', in *Gesammelte Schriften* (2 vols.), vol. I (Tübingen: Mohr, 1968), pp. 460 ff.

In comparing the systems, we need to consider more than just the matter of judicial lawmaking; after all, we know that judges everywhere are prone to decide on whether to compensate or not before they choose the reasons for their decisions. More basically, we need to look at the role of various actors in the legal system. In common law systems, the judge is practically the sole agent: legislative intervention is rare, and academic influence rather small (this was especially so during the nineteenth century). Reference to academic writers is relatively uncommon in judgments, while there is no tradition of reference to preparatory works. By contrast, in codified systems, the domain of delictual liability is shared between three actors: the judge, the legislator and the academic developing doctrine. The last word (to use the expression of Oskar Bülow, in *Gesetz und Richteramt*, 1885) belongs – or seems to belong – to the judge; but the first word is that of the legislator, in deciding whether or not to recognise a delictual liability. Meanwhile, law professors can use their voice, often in rather conservative but sometimes in innovative ways, to restrain the judge by warning against a misinterpretation of the law. It is a game involving three players, which begins with the drawing up of the code, when the legislator, influenced by doctrine, can try to anticipate the reaction of the judge. Nor should one forget that one of the aims of a code is to clarify the law and to give a frame to the judges. The codification movement – especially in penal law, which is not very far from the law of delicts – has been influenced by legalistic feelings of distrust towards the judges.

How far this desire to bind judges can be implemented depends on the circumstances of codification in each country and, in some cases, on the particular context (in political, social and economic life) of the reform of the law of delict. In this chapter, I explore whether it is possible to infer something about the relation between the law of delict, codification and judge-made law, by examining both the history of the drafting of the Napoleonic Code, with its famous *clausula generalis* of article 1382[3] (in section I), and the drafting of codes in the later nineteenth century, in particular the BGB, with its multiple provisions about liability, especially paragraphs 823 and 826.

[3] 'Everyone is obliged to make reparation of the damage caused by his fault.'

8.1 Judicial power, delictual liability and the making of the French *Code civil*

Paradoxically, the drafting of the Napoleonic Code coincided with a rehabilitation of 'jurisprudence' in France. At the beginning of the French Revolution, the members of the Constituent Assembly clearly wanted to curtail the powers of judges. The new representatives of the nation were fearful of so-called 'judicial despotism',[4] remembering the powerful *parlements* of the *ancien régime* – high courts that claimed a share in legislative power and that acted as the principal opponents of the absolute monarchy during the eighteenth century. In contrast to American interpretations of Montesquieu's chapter about the English constitution, the French revolutionaries were sensitive to the idea – expressed in the same text – of a 'terrible power', which had to be reduced to an invisible and void department of justice. Influenced by Cesare Beccaria, especially in penal matters, they felt that the judge should be considered as an automaton, all of whose decisions were predetermined by statute law.[5] According to this restrictive view of the judicial function, judges were forbidden to give a general interpretation of the law and were directed, under the system of the *référé legislatif*, to refer any case in which a gap existed in the statute law to the legislature (Law of 16–24 August 1790). When a Court of Cassation (first named *Tribunal de cassation* by the Law of 27 November–1 December 1790) was created, its mission was to maintain the subordination of the judges to statute law. Some of the members of the Constituent Assembly, such as Isaac Le Chapelier and Maximilien Robespierre, refused expressly to imagine that such a court could create a case law (*jurisprudence*) instead of simply making literal applications of the statute law.[6] Ten years later things looked very different. Although the Tribunal de Cassation was submitted to the yoke, first of the 1792–5 Convention (the national assembly that quashed some of its judgments), then of the 1795–9 Directory (the executive power that fired some of the

[4] 'Relation of Bergasse to the Constituent Assembly, 17 August 1789', in M. J. Mavidal and E. Laurent (eds.), *Archives parlementaires de 1787 à 1860* (47 vols.), vol. VIII (Paris: Dupont, 1867–96), p. 440.

[5] 'Relation of Clermont Tonnerre to the Constituent Assembly, 7 May 1790'; J.-L. Halpérin, '1789–1815: un quart de siècle décisif pour les relations entre la Justice et le Pouvoir en France' (1996) 3 *Justices* 13 ff.

[6] J.-L. Halpérin, *Le Tribunal de cassation et les pouvoirs sous la Révolution 1789–1799* (Paris: LGDJ, 1987), pp. 71–3.

judges in 1797), it managed to survive, to be active (with more than 20,000 decisions in these ten years) and to develop a genuine case law – albeit not on the law of delicts – without being dependent on the *référé legislatif*. No interpretative body of statute law developed in this era.

Attitudes had changed by the beginning of the Consulate (1799), with the decline of parliamentary assemblies and the reinstatement of professional lawyers. When Jean-Étienne-Marie Portalis said that '[c]odes are made only with time – but, properly speaking, they are not made', he was speaking of the judges' power of interpretation and of the place of lawyers.[7] Many pages of the 'preliminary discourse', written by Portalis for the project of the civil code in 1801, were devoted to the importance of 'jurisprudence' – that is, both case law and works of doctrine. Portalis could even claim to uphold the revolutionary line of Jean-Jacques-Régis de Cambacérès, who had said during the Convention that a code could not foresee all legal problems. According to Portalis, many legal questions were to be left to the wisdom of learned men and to the arbitrary power of judges. Of course, this did not apply to criminal matters, for which the principle of a strict interpretation of statute law was based on the maxim *Nullum crimen, nulla poena sine lege*. But for private suits between individuals, Portalis considered the apparent arbitrariness of equity (*équité*) to be preferable to the tumult of passions. Moreover, judges were compelled to decide between the plaintiff and the defendant; for, as the future article 4 of the *Code civil* put it, '[t]he judge who refuses to judge, under pretext of the silence, obscurity or insufficiency of the law, will be subject to prosecution for denial of justice'. Portalis praised the 'equity' of the judge, considered as a return to natural law, albeit without quoting any particular subject, whether the law of delict or contract. In any event, it did not seem hazardous to apply this method in the field of delicts. After all, the writers of the *ancien régime* had thought that compensation and negligence were naturally matters of equity, requiring not a strict application of texts but the free evaluation of facts with standards of conduct (such as that of the 'reasonable man').

Of course, Portalis's discourse was softened by a proclaimed respect towards legality: the judges and legal writers were under the supervision of the legislative power. Even so, there was a real debate between the defenders of the revolutionary idea of legislative supremacy[8] – what we French call *légicentrisme* – and the drafters of the *Code civil*. Significantly,

[7] F. Ewald (ed.), *Naissance du Code civil* (Paris: Flammarion, 1989), p. 48.

[8] For example, Mailla-Garat, in the Tribunate Assembly.

when the Conseil d'État discussed article 4 of the code, François Tronchet (one of the most important drafters of the code) said that it was necessary to leave the judges free to interpret the law. Taking a very modern approach, Tronchet said that civil suits were provoked by the different meanings given to statute law by the litigants; it was for the judge – and not for a new statute – to settle this dispute. Portalis concluded that only a few suits could be decided according a precise text, whereas many of them needed the use of legal science. The *Code civil* did not remove the need for legal knowledge; on the contrary, it presupposed this knowledge.[9] The articles of the Napoleonic Code, especially a *clausula generalis* such as article 1382, were conceived as guidelines for the judges, and created a large field for an innovative case law.

The history of the preparatory works of the Napoleonic Code tells us little about the links between conceptions about delict and a codified law. The subject of delict was not one of the great controversies between 1800 and 1804, unlike family law or even some aspects of the law of property or contracts. There was no real debate, particularly in the Conseil d'État, about the guidelines of the new law of delict. The same seems true in Austria,[10] although preoccupations with economic policy were not absent from the discourse of Zeiller.[11] From the first drafts of a civil code that were drawn up during the French Revolution (called the Cambacérès drafts of 1793, 1794, 1796),[12] there was no doubt that the new codified law had to contain a general clause about compensation for harm, based upon the ideas of the school of natural law and upon the works of Jean Domat and Robert-Joseph Pothier.[13] The formula of article 1382 of the Napoleonic Code was already present in the three Cambacérès drafts, though, for reasons that are hard to determine, it omitted mention of fault. Even at a time when the triumph of the legislature was reaching its apogee – the so-called worship of the law – it was clear to revolutionary lawyers that it was the task of the judge to set compensation.

[9] Ewald, *Naissance du Code civil*, pp. 118–19.

[10] J. Ofner, *Der Ur-Entwurf und die Berathungs-Protokolle der Osterreichischer ABGB* (2 vols.), vol. II (Vienna, Hölder, 1888), p. 196 (meeting of 2 June 1806).

[11] R. Ogorek, *Untersuchungen zur Entwicklung der Gefährdungshaftung im 19. Jahrhundert* (Cologne: Böhlau, 1975), p. 33, notes that Zeiller was aware, in his 'Commentary of the Austrian Civil Code' (1812), of the relation between the law of delict and the development of industry.

[12] J.-L. Halpérin, *L'impossible Code civil* (Paris: Presses universitaires de France, 1992).

[13] O. Descamps, *Les Origines de la responsabilité pour faute personnelle dans le Code civil de 1804* (Paris: LGDJ, 2005), p. 450.

Later, during the Consulate of Napoleon Bonaparte, when the project of the Governmental Commission (1801) was discussed, there was no objection either to a general clause or to the judges being given discretionary power over whether to compensate or not. On the contrary, the project of the Governmental Commission, which already included the principles of liability for fault and the vicarious liability of parents, employers or teachers, was amended with the collaboration of the courts. The courts succeeded in obtaining the joining together of delicts and quasi-delicts and the reinforcement of the vicarious liability of employers. The text submitted to the Conseil d'État provoked no discussion, except with regard to the suppressed reference to the tradition of the *actio de effusis vel deiectis*.[14] It is significant that none of the speeches given in front of the Tribunate or the legislative body referred to the power of judges in the law of delict. The official discourse stressed the enlargement of fault liability, and tried to reassure potential opponents of the general clause by talking about the protection given by the clause to owners, traders and artists, as well as talking about the need for parents and employers to supervise children and employees. The drafters of the Napoleonic Code do not seem, prima facie, to have been aware of any considerations of public policy (protection of things for the wealthy versus protection of poor victims for bodily injury) or of the risks of a developing case law.

The drafters of the Napoleonic Codes were reproached many times during the nineteenth and twentieth centuries for their apparent ignorance of economics, and for ignoring the early forms of industrialisation. For a long time, the legal advisers of Bonaparte were considered to be defenders of an agrarian society, concerned only with the interests of landowners. There can be no doubt about the codifiers' solicitude for ownership in general, and real property in particular: one must always remember the crucial question of the *biens nationaux*, the ecclesiastical estates that were nationalised and then sold to individuals during the French Revolution. However, we must not exaggerate the codifiers' ignorance of commercial, if not industrial, fortunes. Portalis and Jean-Baptiste Treilhard (a member of the Conseil d'État) were persuaded that the more considerable fortunes were already made up by movable property. Article 534 of the *Code civil* deals with shares in joint-stock companies for commerce, finance and industry. When discussing immovable property, ironworks and paper mills are quoted with 'other factories'. If there was prejudice against 'capitalists' – which meant (in the language of Jacques de Maleville) idle holders

[14] Descamps, *Les Origines de la responsabilité*, p. 461.

of assets – attention was also given to the concerns of manufacturers, for example about the rate of interest or the adoption of children by childless wealthy men. One can see traces of this entrepreneurial mentality in the main speech on the fault principle, given by Bertrand de Greuille, a member of the Tribunate, on 6 February 1804.[15] Besides making mention of reason, equity (which could evoke the role of the judge) and morals to justify article 1382, he made some allusions to economics. The duty to compensate was explained as a pecuniary sacrifice by the tortfeasor to repair an economic loss suffered by the victim. Consider, for example, attacks against assets (such as by fire) rather than personal injuries. In such cases, the unjustified diminution of the patrimony of the 'suffering' victim has to be compensated, because it is an illicit disturbance of the natural competition between men. Economic considerations also provide a reason for strict vicarious liability, which may be onerous for parents, teachers and employers, but which is necessary to help the well-off to develop their activities (imagine the consequences of a fire caused by a child in a big factory). It is worthy of note that Bertrand de Greuille used the word 'workmen' when referring to apprentices working under the direction of craftsmen. Is this evidence of an older vision of economics based only on agriculture (there is an allusion to the rural code) and handicrafts? It is not clear. When Bertrand de Greuille discussed those who made a profit from a 'service' causing prejudice to a third person, he might have been referring to an old relation of 'master and servant' or to the new labour contracts in factories. This could explain why French judges, as early as 1841, rejected the theory of common employment to recognise the liability of employers (in cases of proven fault) in labour accidents.[16]

One can also infer how the drafters of the Napoleonic Code saw the relation between penal and civil liability. It should be borne in mind that, beginning with the penal laws enacted during the French Revolution, the word *délit* in French has been applied to intermediary offences, between the more serious crimes and the lighter offences or *contraventions*, as well to delictual liability. According to Bertrand de Greuille, the *clausula generalis* of article 1382 – the first article of the chapter 'Des délits et des quasi-délits' in the code – embraced all forfeitures and misdemeanours. It is clear that civil law goes beyond penal law, however, since it takes into account all the facts of negligence and recklessness. Bertrand de Greuille made a distinction between personal punishment

[15] Ewald, *Naissance du Code civil*, pp. 345–9.

[16] F. Ewald, 'Formation de la notion d'accident du travail' (1981) 1 *Sociologie du travail* 3 ff.

(with all the consequences they entailed for personal honour) and pecuniary compensation. French penal procedure, inherited from the *ancien régime* and embedded in article 3 of the 1808 *Code d'instruction criminelle*, permits the victim, unusually, to obtain compensation – by a 'civil action' – from the penal courts competent to judge the offence. This is the reason for what we in France call the principle of the unity of penal and civil fault.

It was well known, however, from the beginning of the nineteenth century (and probably from the drafters of the Napoleonic Code), that there were some exceptions. There are some penal faults without civil liability, as in cases in which there is no victim (e.g. the prohibition of use of some weapons). More often, there are civil faults (such as negligence), without penal offence. Let us now glance at the articles of the 1810 penal codes dealing with economic offences:[17] infringement of the rules about products of French manufacture (article 413), combinations of employers or employees to obtain the lowering or increase of wages (article 415), enticing offers from foreigners to French workmen 'with a view to harm French industry' (article 417), false statements or combinations of producers to obtain the increase or lowering of prices outside the 'natural competition of commerce' (article 419) and the counterfeiting of books (article 425). The victims of all these offences, which involve restraint of trade, were made up of manufacturers, and probably consumers as well. In such cases, it was permissible to use article 1382 of the civil code to obtain compensation. Here again, the tendency of French case law in the nineteenth century to use article 1382 in competition cases had its source in this 'liberal conception' of a free market with penalties against troublemakers. The *clausula generalis* of article 1382 can be also analysed as a limit to the right to grow rich to the prejudice of others. It rooted out illegal profits that the legislative power (by the penal code) and the judges (by using article 1382) had to punish.

8.2 Judicial power, the law of delict and the drafting of codes in nineteenth-century Europe

Looking back, French writers later in the nineteenth century contrasted the Prussian code (with its 138 articles devoted to fault liability) and the

[17] J.-L. Halpérin, 'Liberalismo e disposizioni di ordine economico nel codice penale del 1810', in S. Vinciguerra (ed.), *Codice dei delitti e delle pene per regno d'Italia* (Padua: Cedam, 2002), pp. clxxxv ff.

Austrian code (with its thirty-seven articles on the same subject) with the French civil code. Whereas former codes 'feared the discretion of judges', the latter wanted courts to be free to judge the facts.[18] This explanation of the difference between codes with casuistic articles and those with general clauses may be persuasive, but it is not clear that it corresponds to the historical intention of the codifiers. It may also be noted that the fact that French doctrinal writers had (with the exception of some, such as Charles Toullier) for so long ignored article 1382 of the Napoleonic Code expanded the field in which judges could develop a new case law. It is remarkable that the first great treatises on civil liability are found in the work of a judge (Auguste Sourdat, first edition in 1852) and in the *Répertoire Dalloz* (1858), which was conceived for practitioners. No protests were raised by nineteenth-century French doctrinal writers about judges abusing their power with respect to civil liability. Such protests began to appear only in the twentieth century, in response to the no-fault liability developed by the Court of Cassation after 1896 (by an extensive interpretation of article 1384 of the Napoleonic Code). For example, the law of 7 November 1922 – one of the rare reforms of article 1384 – was provoked by fears concerning the extension of the liability of lessees for damage caused by fires involving movable property, in the aftermath of a 1920 decision of the Court of Cassation.[19] The legislature intervened, but without any apparent intention seriously to curtail the development of the case law of the Court of Cassation. A codified law is conceived to last. Even if in some cases this forecast turns out to be untrue, and the legislature resumes its power to correct the case law, in general the possibility of reforming the provisions of the code some years after its drafting seems rather small. This raises the question of why legislators intervene in such a limited manner to correct a case law threatening the balanced rules of a code.

To understand the relationship between the law of delict and codification, we need also to consider both the conceptions of judicial power held by different systems and the social and political contexts particular to the law of tort. We must follow a chronological order from the first codes (the Napoleonic Code of 1804 and the ABGB of 1811) that broke up the system of the *lex Aquilia* and opened the way to more judicial activism. The first eighteenth-century codifications, which were heavily influenced by the *lex Aquilia* – such as the Bavarian (1756, Cod. Bav. Liv. 4, ch. 16)

[18] V. A. D. Dalloz, *Répertoire méthodique et alphabétique de législation, de doctrine et de jurisprudence*, vol. XXXIX (Paris: Dalloz, 1858), p. 297.

[19] D.P. 1923.1.89.

and Prussian codes (1794 ALR I, 6) – were far more suspicious about the development of judge-made law than were the Napoleonic and the Austrian codes. A similar attitude can be found in Louis XIV's French Ordinance of Civil Procedure of 1667, which prohibited the interpretation of laws by judges and obliged the courts to refer to the sovereign in cases in which there was a gap in the law, and in the 1723 laws and constitution of the king of Sardinia (the first consolidation of laws in Piedmont), which prevented judges from using any other reason than the authority of royal statutes. This legalistic spirit can also be seen in the 1794 *Allgemeines Landrecht*, the General Code of Prussian Laws: articles 50 to 53 of the introduction of this code (initiated by Frederick the Great for combating the abuses of judges) forced Prussian judges to give a literal interpretation of the words of the statute (with their accustomed signification) and to refer to a Royal Commission (which functioned until 1803) in cases of doubt about the law. Article 8 of this introduction forbade the use of precedents as authoritative texts. It was consistent for such a binding system to provide the judges with no fewer than 138 articles about fault, harms and compensation, which was done in the sixth book of the first part of the code, which dealt with the obligations of those who had committed an act of fault.

Following in many cases the *lex Aquilia*, these articles tried to develop a casuistic method to distinguish between different kinds of fault (gross fault, ordinary fault, light faults of negligence), different kinds of harm (physical, patrimonial or moral, direct or indirect) and different classes of tortfeasors (insane persons and infants were exempt from liability, except for immediate damage and if they were wealthy). The judges were normally obliged to follow very strict guidelines for admitting and calculating compensation; for instance, article 87 of this sixth book said that, in determining the price of a lost object, the judicial decision had to apply the evaluation made by experts. What might have seemed a *clausula generalis* in article 10 of this code – 'whoever has caused damage, with intention or a gross fault, has to repair the offence' – was drowned among these pointillist prescriptions. It is far from clear, however, whether, in practice, the situation was very different for the Prussian judge from what it was for the French one, though the technique of codification was obviously different. By the same token, the politics of the codifiers diverged on the question of vicarious liability: the Prussian code did not recognise in principle the liability of masters or employers for the wrongful acts of their servants (ALR I, 6, § 60). This contrasts with the comparative severity of the Napoleonic Code on this question ten years later.

At the beginning of the nineteenth century delictual liability was not perceived to be an important political question for codifiers, who did not foresee the future development of industrial accidents. The drafters of the *Badisches Landrecht* (1809) – a free translation of the Napoleonic Code with some adjustments – and of the *Codice civile Albertino* (1837) – the civil code of the Kingdom of Sardinia-Piedmont – probably did not want to give a new definition of the relation between judges and tort law when they copied the *clausula generalis* of article 1382. It is noteworthy, however, that the *Badisches Landrecht* did not mention fault, decreeing simply that 'whoever has caused the damage must compensate it'. It should also be noted that the *Codice civile Albertino* said that judges (whose decisions were not binding laws, according to article 17) had to refer to the 'general principles of law' when there was a gap in the statute.[20] In these two cases, the choice of the *clausula generalis* gave judges considerable power in deciding what the causes of liability and the calculations of compensation were. It seems that there was no more discussion of the issue when the French civil code was imitated in other Italian codifications, such as the 1819 Neapolitan code (article 1366), the 1837 *Codice civile Albertino* in Piedmont (article 1500 – a literal translation of article 1382 of the Napoleonic Code, like the following articles: 1501 about negligence and 1502 about vicarious liability) or the 1865 Italian civil code (articles 1151 to 1153).[21] The French general clauses were regarded as natural rules coming from Domat and Pothier,[22] and the powers of the judges were not submitted to a new examination when they were imitated.

The situation was not the same after the first effects of the Industrial Revolution had been felt in continental Europe, when laws were drafted about issues such as railway accidents and workmen's compensation. By now, not only were the consequences of the new economic relations well known, but codifiers could also profit from their knowledge of the case law that had developed in France on article 1382 of the Napoleonic Code. In 1838 the Kingdom of Prussia enacted a law about the liability of railway companies for harms to persons (passengers or workmen) or property.

[20] Article 15; nevertheless, article 14 obliged the judge to follow the clear signification of the legal text and the intention of the legislator.

[21] See D. Ibbetson, 'Harmonisation of the law of tort and delict: a comparative and historical perspective', in R. Zimmermann (ed.), *Grundstrukturen des Europäischen Deliktsrechts* (Baden-Baden: Nomos, 2003), pp. 83 ff., pp. 84–5, with the distinction of the literal translation of article 1382 in Italian codes and the 'reworking' of the formula (with more insistence upon the fault) in the Spanish code of 1889.

[22] S. Solimano, *Il letto di Procuste: diritto e politica nella formazione del Codice civile unitario: i progetti Cassinis (1860–1861)* (Milan: Giuffrè, 2003), pp. 350–1.

The Prussian Council of State chose strict liability for this kind of accident, probably thanks to Savigny, who had argued that the case law of the French courts, which was rather severe when it came to negligence committed by transport companies, was a good thing.[23]

In Germany, the French code continued to be applied in Rhineland and was well known from the handbook on the civil code by Karl Salomo Zachariae, the first edition of which appeared in 1808 during the period of French domination, and many more editions of which were published in the first half of the nineteenth century. Zachariae thought that codification did not spell the end of problems of legal interpretation; even in a codified law there were gaps, obscurities and contradictions (§§ 38 and 39), and the task of the judge was to decide every case that came before him. In tort law in particular – for there was a distinction between civil and penal faults – judges had to say what were wrongful acts (those that violated the rights of another person) and to determine how to calculate the compensation (§§ 624 to 626). It may be noted that Savigny was also in favour of a more extended judicial interpretation and did not hide his admiration for the French Court of Cassation.[24]

When the question of the codification of Swiss law was raised in the second half of the nineteenth century, many Swiss cantons already had their own civil codes, following the Austrian or French models. For instance, the civil code of Zurich (which was drafted in 1854, mainly by Savigny's disciple Johann Caspar Bluntschli) had a complex arrangement of seventy articles on tort law, containing an original combination of the fault principle of the Napoleonic Code and the legacy of Aquilian liability.[25] Swiss codifiers faced the problem of how to unify these texts. They also had to take account both of the specificity of Swiss judges (often elected without legal qualifications) and of the new federal legislation about strict liability in railway accidents (under the law of 1875). The work of the commissions that sat between 1869 and 1872 and 1877 and 1879, in which Bluntschli participated,[26] concluded in favour of a *clausula*

[23] T. Baums, 'Die Einführung der Gefährdungshaftung durch F. C. von Savigny' (1987) 104 *Zeitschrift der Savigny Stiftung* 277.

[24] F. C. von Savigny, *System des heutigen Römischen Rechts*, vol. I (Berlin: Veit, 1840), para. 33, para. 51.

[25] P. Tercier, 'Cent ans de responsabilité civile en droit Suisse', in H. Peter, E. W. Starck and P. Tercier (eds.), *Le Centenaire du Code des Obligations* (Fribourg: Éditions universitaires de Fribourg, 1982), pp. 203 ff., p. 205.

[26] H. Merz, 'Das Schweizerische Obligationenrecht von 1881', in Peter, Starck and Tercier, *Le Centenaire du Code des Obligations*, pp. 3 ff., p. 6.

generalis very like the French model,[27] but with the addition of a specific provision allowing the judge to evaluate compensation in proportion to the gravity of the fault (article 51).[28] The clear intention of the codifiers was to choose a French principle (probably a combination of the code of Berne on the model of the Austrian code)[29] – a principle supposed to be wholly different from the notions of the Germanic tradition.[30]

The drafters of the 1881 Swiss code felt that fault liability had to be extended beyond the cases foreseen in the code of Zurich: corporal damage or deterioration of property. They also tended to favour a severe vicarious liability, following the French example (articles 62 and 63). At the same time, they kept in mind the old solution of the Prussian code about proportionality between compensation and fault. Consequently, the power of the judge to calculate compensation freely was officially recognised. The French system, although it took account of equity, was different, because the compensation awarded had to be complete, whatever the gravity of the fault. There was a conscious policy to extend the freedom of the judge 'contrary to the general practice observed before by courts of German-speaking' systems. It was left to the judges to resolve all the refined questions (*question fort subtile*) about direct and indirect damage, positive damage and pure economic loss (*perte d'un gain*). The intention of the codifiers was clearly to compensate for new kinds of harm, such as moral damages for false statements or the counterfeiting of intellectual property. They also wanted to leave a place for equity (as in the Prussian and Austrian codes, under which the judge could award damages against a person who lacked legal capacity but had large assets) and to separate penal and civil liability completely (article 59). A modern codified 'tort law', based on a new social equity (more contemporary than the natural law of the eighteenth century), was linked to the system of the *clausula generalis*.

Twenty years before Eugen Huber's work on drafting the Swiss civil code (1907) and a new edition of the Code of Obligations (1911), the question of the 'free interpretation' of law by judges had already begun to be

[27] Article 50: *Quiconque cause sans droit un dommage à autrui, soit à dessein, soit par négligence ou imprudence, est tenu de le réparer.*

[28] V. Rossel, *Manuel du Droit fédéral des Obligations* (Paris: F. Payot, 1892), p. 97.

[29] E. Bucher, 'Der Einfluss des französischen Code auf das Obligationenrecht', in P. Caroni (ed.), *Das Obligationenrecht 1883–1983* (Bern: Haupt, 1984), pp. 139 ff., pp. 162–3. It is noteworthy that the remainder of the Swiss Code of Obligations was not very much influenced by French law.

[30] Message of the Federal Council (27 November 1879), *Feuille fédérale suisse*, 1880, I, 148–152.

discussed. Indeed, in 1844 Bluntschli wrote that a legal rule was a kind of guideline, which the judge had to find and to adapt with exceptions.[31] In 1880 Emil Vogt also recognised that the interpretation of statute law was in the hands of judges. Some years later, the reflections of Huber and his correspondence with François Gény – the French jurist who argued for 'free scientific research' (*Méthodes d'interprétation et sources en droit privé positif*, 1899) – led to the famous article 1 of the Swiss civil code, which gave the judge the power, in cases in which there was a gap in the statute law, to act as if he were legislator.

The links between the question of judge-made law in codified systems and the evolution of the law of delict appear – in a European context – in a book by Giovanni Brunetti, law professor in Florence (1906). Brunetti considered that the role of the judge was very important when it came to delictual liability and that he could create law somewhat like the Roman *praetor*, but that this also generated a risk of uncertainty in law. Quoting Gény, Rudolf Stammler, Ernst Zitelmann and Carl Bergbohm – all legal theorists who considered the problem of the relationship between law and judge – Brunetti referred to the French Declaration of the Rights of Man to say that litigants had to know what a wrongful act was in order to be liable.[32]

At the end of the nineteenth century the preparation of the German civil code was accompanied by arguments seeking to recognise or to reinforce the power of judges; the book by Bülow (quoted above) is the best known in a series of texts about filling up the gaps in law (others include those by Eugen Ehrlich[33] and Zitelmann).[34] One of the motives of these writers was to support conservative judges against a possible movement by the legislature towards more radical ideas, notably (as the more fearful spirits of the time thought) socialism.[35]

The process of drafting the German civil code began in 1873. A first project was written by a commission of jurists and published in 1888, and then a second commission, open to non-jurists, sat between 1890

[31] Merz, 'Das Schweizerische Obligationenrecht', p. 21.

[32] G. Brunetti, *Il Delitto civile* (Firenze: B. Seeber, 1906), pp. 119–27.

[33] E. Ehrlich, 'Über Lücken in Rechte' (*Juristische Blätter*, 1888), reprinted in M. Rehbinder (ed.), *Recht und Leben* (Berlin: Duncker & Humblot, 1967), pp. 80 ff.; there is no example in this text taken from delict law, but Ehrlich could not ignore the French case law of the Court of Cassation, which he admired and compared to the English case law.

[34] E. Zitelmann, *Lücken im Recht* (Leipzig: Duncker & Humblot, 1903).

[35] Bülow was much more conservative than Zitelmann and Ehrlich; Windscheid and Jhering were not in favour of judges having too great an amount of power: U. Falk, *Ein Gelehrter wie Windscheid* (Frankfurt: Klostermann, 1989), p. 150.

and 1895.[36] In considering the development of this code, many contextual elements have to be taken in account beyond the legal technique of the debates.[37] The codifiers unifying German civil law had to consider the rules of delictual law that had been applied beforehand in the different territories amalgamated in the empire. Of these, the Prussian code was not regarded as the major source of inspiration. This code, which suffered from Savigny's contempt, appeared as the confirmation of the German common law – that is, of the Roman law reinterpreted.[38] There were mixed views regarding the Napoleonic Code, which applied in the Rhineland from 1814 to 1900. On the one hand, even Savigny felt some admiration for the general clause of article 1382 (especially its well-qualified style) and acknowledged the jurisprudence of the Court of Cassation, more or less precisely. On the other hand, however, German judges (both in the Rhineland and then in the Reichsgericht) wholly rejected the extensive jurisprudence of the Court of Cassation on article 1382, particularly its decisions on unfair competition and moral damage.[39] The model of the *lex Aquilia*, with its casuistic approach, was followed by the civil code of Saxony (1863) and in the projects for the German civil code that came from Dresden and Hesse. The codifiers knew that the Roman rules of the *lex Aquilia* had been approved in case law – for example by rejecting the old German principle of proportion between the compensation and the fault – with some modifications – for instance about compensation for contracts in favour of third parties.[40] Indeed, one can say that, in general, nineteenth-century German case law already constituted a rejection of the general clauses of the 'modern codes'.

36 F. Wieacker, *A History of Private Law in Europe with Particular Reference to Germany*, trans. T. Weir (Oxford: Clarendon Press, 1995), pp. 371–7.

37 H.-P. Benöhr, 'Die Redaktion der Paragraphen 823 und 826 BGB', in R. Zimmermann, R. Knutel and J. P. Meicke (eds.), *Rechtsgeschichte und Privatrechtsdogmatik* (Heidelberg: Müller, 1999), pp. 499 ff.

38 B. Mugdan, *Die Gesammten Materialen zum Bürgerlichen Gesetzbuch für das Deutsche Recht* (5 vols.), vol. II (Berlin: Decker, 1899), p. 404.

39 D. Schumacher, *Das Rheinische Recht in der Gerichtspraxis des 19. Jahrhunderts* (Stuttgart: Kohlhammer, 1969), pp. 94–6, p. 118, pp. 124–5; E. Wadle, 'Das Rheinisch-Französische Delikrecht und die Judikatur des Reichsgerichte zum unlauteren Wettbewerb', in R. Schulze (ed.), *Rheinisches Recht und Europäische Rechtsgeschichte* (Berlin: Duncker & Humblot, 1998), pp. 79 ff.

40 H. H. Seiler, 'Römisches deliktisches Schadensersatzrecht in der obergerichtlichen Rechtsprechung des 19. Jahrhunderts', in D. Medicus, H.-J. Mertens and K. W. Nörr (eds.), *Festschrift für Hermann Lange, zum 70. Geburtstag am 24. Januar 1992* (Stuttgart: Kohlhammer, 1992), pp. 245 ff.

In a parallel direction, the German doctrine of the Pandectists developed a theory of fault (*culpa*) with the clear intention to restrict the field of civil liability.[41] The famous text of Rudolf von Jhering about the 'Schuldmoment' (1867) was the apex of this fault theory. Although the German term *Verschulden* was comparable to the French word *faute*, used in article 1382 of the Napoleonic Code, the outcome was quite different. In 1804 the French codifiers had wanted to extend liability through *faute*, whereas in the second half of the nineteenth century *Verschulden* was the flag used by German jurists to prevent the development of strict liability, which had been extended to railways and all industries by the imperial law of 1871 (the *ReichsHaftpflichtGesetz*, or RHG).

The writers of the first draft, who dealt with the liability articles,[42] presented their project as a compromise between the general clauses of the modern codes (found in the Saxon code and the different projects addressed by the German states) and the desire to limit the scope of fault by defining the illicit acts against absolute rights or the violation of morals (*Gutte Sitten* of § 705 of the first draft).[43] There was no intention to restrain the powers of the judges,[44] but there was a clear distrust of the extensive character of French law, for instance about vicarious liability.[45] When the question came before the second commission, which sat from 1890 and produced the second draft in 1894, there was much tough discourse about the excesses of the French case law. The drafters of the new project hesitated over how much freedom to leave to the judges, seeking to strike a balance between the advantages of a loose formula (to open the way for later scientific developments and not to tie the law down to the intentions of the legislator) and the risks of an excess of case law (as had been found in Prussian and French law).[46] The majority of the commission was in favour of a clearer solution. The German conception of the judicial

[41] See Ogorek, *Untersuchungen zur Entwicklung*, p. 30, about the contribution of Hasse at the beginning of the nineteenth century (1815), then at p. 42 about Jhering.

[42] 1882–8, paras. 704–21 of the first draft. The main drafter, Kübel, was himself a judge from Wurttemberg. He died in 1884, and his text was resumed with the Dresden project about the law of obligations.

[43] Benöhr, 'Die Redaktion der Paragraphen 823 und 826 BGB', p. 538. The Saxon code combined a general clause with a casuistic approach.

[44] See Mugdan, *Die Gesammten Materialen*, vol. II, p. 406; and Markesinis and Unberath, *The German Law of Torts*, p. 13, about encouraging the courts to fill the gaps.

[45] Mugdan, *Die Gesammten Materialen*, vol. II, p. 411.

[46] See Benöhr, 'Die Redaktion der Paragraphen 823 und 826 BGB', p. 542, quoting a sentence in which it is said that the statute law has its own importance, independent of the intentions of the legislator.

office was expressly invoked to determine the frontier between statute law (which defined the protected interests) and case law (in which the judge evaluated fault).[47] It is difficult to say how far the outcome was shaped by nationalist feelings, which presented the German solution as unique, as neither completely Roman nor French, and how far it was influenced either by fears about the development of an overly audacious case law or by a real preoccupation with economic interests.[48] In other matters, such as 'boni mores' (§ 138) and good faith (§ 242), the drafters of the German civil code did not hesitate to use blanket clauses,[49] and one can suppose that the desire to differentiate the German solutions from the French ones was predominant.

The parliamentary discussion[50] was the last chance to take account of the arguments made by economic interest groups against any extension of fault, for example in respect of non-material interests[51] or vicarious liability.[52] Here, tort law was conceived as a means to ensure economic prosperity and to maintain the social hierarchy. Obviously there was a fear that the 'worst elements' of society might take advantage of such a law, for example by making false claims. At the same time, though, many speeches concentrated upon liability questions arising from games and domestic animals, which were very remote from the interests of the whole society.[53]

This apparently technical debate cannot be separated from the political context of the great debate about the 'social' critics of the draft code between 1880 and 1896.[54] Among the most well known texts of these critics (amounting to more than 400, according to one estimate) are those

[47] Mugdan, *Die Gesammten Materialen*, vol. II, p. 1075.

[48] See Mugdan, *Die Gesammten Materialen*, vol. II, p. 1267, with an allusion to the needs of commerce just after the link between statute law and judicial decisions.

[49] Later, in 1933, the flight of judges into these clauses was denounced by Hedemann: J. W. Hedemann, *Die Flucht in die Generalklauseln: Eine Gefahr für Recht und Staat* (Tübingen: Mohr, 1933).

[50] The German rules about liability were the first really discussed in a parliament, but the government was concerned not to allow them to develop into forms of strict liability. The amendments of the Socialist Party were rejected, and just one amendment succeeded, about the inclusion of the abuse of rights in paragraph 826. See H. Schulte-Nölke, *Das Reichjustizamt und die Entstehung des BGBs* (Frankfurt: Klostermann, 1995), pp. 326–9.

[51] Markesinis and Unberath, *The German Law of Torts*, p. 74.

[52] Ogorek, *Untersuchungen zur Entwicklung*, p. 135.

[53] I. S. Forrester, S. L. Goren and H. M. Ilgen, *The German Civil Code* (South Hackensack, NJ: North-Holland Publishing, 1975), p. xiv.

[54] M. John, *Politics and the Law in Late Nineteenth-Century Germany: The Origins of the Civil Code* (Oxford: Clarendon Press, 1989), pp. 105–14.

of the leader of the German school of law, Otto von Gierke, and of the socialist thinker Anton Menger. Both considered the delictual parts of the project to be bad from a social point of view. Although Gierke was not completely against the idea of using the 'fault' criterion, he considered the project to be too restrictive when it came to the exemption of liability of infants or insane persons, remarking that they could be wealthier than the victims and able to compensate. He was also critical of the proposals relating to the liability of employers for damage done by their employees, which made for a less severe rule than in French and Swiss law.[55] Quoting the work of Victor Mataja in 1888 on the links between tort law and economics, Gierke concluded that the draft code was too Roman (even more Roman than Roman law), and that it was too individualistic and was not consistent with the spirit of his age. It is noteworthy that Gierke also defended giving more powers to the judge to evaluate the gravity of the fault (on the model of the Swiss Code of Obligations), noting the contradiction with the tendency to allow the judge easily to admit the fault of the victim. Here the 'social conservative' Gierke – who wanted more drops of 'social oil' in the code – seemed to trust sympathetic judges to give more compensation to the victims. With his socialist principles, Menger also considered that the draft code favoured the well off and did not take account of the interests of women and workmen in tort law.[56]

It is known that the drafters of the German civil code made a pretence of neutrality but with a social model – based on a 'stylisation' of Roman law – that favoured the upper and middle classes.[57] At the same time, a few little 'general clauses' (such as § 826) opened up a great field for further case law and doctrine, ensuring the future success of the civil code. The result was a compromise: general clauses (less general than in the Napoleonic Code) with guidelines and a desire to defend the fault principle against too great a development of strict liability. Whereas the drafters of the Napoleonic Code were not completely aware of the consequences of the new tort law contained in article 1382, the German codifiers were cautious because they knew of the interactions between statute law and judges, fault liability and strict liability.

[55] O. von Gierke, *Der Entwurf eines bürgerlichen Gesetzbuchs und das deutsche Recht* (Leipzig: Duncker & Humblot, 1889), pp. 260–1.

[56] A. Menger, *Das bürgerliche Recht und die besitzlosen Volksklassen: Eine Kritik des Entwurfs eines bürgerlichen Gesetzbuch für das deutsche Reich* (Tübingen: Laupp, 1890), pp. 129–31.

[57] F. Wieacker, *Industriegesellschaft und Privatrechtsordnung* (Frankfurt: Fischer Athenäum Taschenbücher, 1974).

The preparatory works for articles of the European codes dealing with delicts seem to confirm the thesis of continuity between the previous rules, the codified articles and the case law. This does not mean that the decisions of the codifiers – or those of legislators who passed special laws about strict liability – were of no importance. They determined a departure line from which case law can develop. In this sense, French judges were granted a greater degree of latitude than German judges by the codified rules. The codes also determined a possible (but rather virtual) borderline that judges could not pass. Concerning the difference with common law, there is no doubt that the codification process favoured general clauses rather than a collection of special torts. The German example shows that it was, however, possible to resist this tendency towards abstraction and generality. Equivocal feelings regarding judges – a mixture of trust in their sense of responsibility and fear of their scope for interpretation – can also be found in nineteenth-century England. The greater difference between civil law and common law lay elsewhere, in the place taken by legal writing. In continental Europe, the codified rules were destined to be taught by law professors and to induce an intellectual outlook for all civil lawyers. It is why the texts of the codes have produced cultural structures for thinking about the law of delicts that have lasted till the present day, whereas English lawyers and judges have been free to use and transform looser standards.

9

Codifications, commentators and courts in tort law: the perception and application of the civil code and the constitution by the German legal profession

NILS JANSEN*

9.1 The legal profession and the codes

By the time the German civil code (*Bürgerliches Gesetzbuch*, BGB) was enacted in 1896, codification was not a new phenomenon for the legal profession. Indeed, many German states had codified their civil law: Bavaria had had its *Codex Maximilianeus Bavaricus Civilis* since 1756; the Prussian government had laid down its *Allgemeines Landrecht für die Preussischen Staaten* (ALR) in 1794; and, in the Rhine area, lawyers continued to apply the *Code civil* or slightly modified translations of this codification.[1]

These early codes had never really determined the development of private law, however. In fact, the codes never succeeded in becoming the basic reference texts for private law. The German historical school had long been hostile to codifications, which were regarded as unscientific and disruptive for organic legal development.[2] Indeed, during much of the nineteenth century, private law had been understood as largely autonomous from states' political sphere.[3] Instead of becoming a main subject within the academic curriculum, the German territorial codes were therefore

* University of Münster.

[1] R. Zimmermann, 'Das Bürgerliche Gesetzbuch und die Entwicklung des Bürgerlichen Rechts', in M. Schmoeckel, J. Rückert and R. Zimmermann (eds.), *Historisch-kritischer Kommentar zum BGB* [*HKK*], vol. I (Tübingen: Mohr Siebeck, 2003), pp. 1 ff.

[2] Zimmermann, 'Das Bürgerliche Gesetzbuch', pp. 8–10. Indeed, Savigny's powerful attack on Thibaut's codification proposal (F. C. von Savigny, *Vom Beruf unserer Zeit für Gesetzgebung und Rechtswissenschaft* (Heidelberg: Mohr und Zimmer, 1814)) became a programme for the historical school. In the second half of the century, however, the leading members of the historical school began to support the idea of a codification.

[3] H.-P. Haferkamp, 'The science of private law and the state in nineteenth-century Germany', in N. Jansen and R. Michaels (eds.), *Beyond the State: Rethinking Private Law* (Tübingen: Mohr Siebeck, 2008), pp. 245 ff, pp. 246–9, p. 251, pp. 253–5.

relegated to the practical, non-academic part of legal education, and they received little attention in legal literature.[4] Even the ALR was increasingly taught and interpreted from the perspective of the Roman *ius commune*,[5] although the purpose of its detailed provisions had been to control the judiciary.

Much of this had changed after the 'turning point of 1871', with the unification of the German Empire.[6] Now the 'social question' was raised; public values increasingly found their way into private law, and the legal profession identified with the new German Reich. This changing attitude towards the state manifested itself in a remarkable shift of perspective away from Roman sources to the new codification. In 1896 the German academic profession decided, after controversial discussion, to replace the *Corpus iuris* with the BGB as the textual basis of academic teaching and doctrinal research.[7] In retrospect, the importance of this decision may be underestimated; yet it was this decision alone that made the BGB the foundation of positive German law. It had already found expression in an extraordinary amount of exegetical literature on the BGB before 1900, when the BGB went into effect.[8]

Nonetheless, it would be wrong to infer that the BGB was accepted as a means of political domination. True, the BGB was perceived as a 'cathedral of national splendour',[9] but this did not mean that the government would arbitrarily determine private law by means of this codification.

[4] E. Friedberg, *Die künftige Gestaltung des deutschen Rechtsstudiums nach den Beschlüssen der Eisenacher Konferenz* (Leipzig: Veit, 1896), pp. 7 ff.

[5] See, for the ALR, F. C. von Savigny, *Landrechtsvorlesung 1824: Drei Nachschriften*, ed. C. Wollschläger (2 vols.), vol. I (Frankfurt: Klostermann, 1994), pp. 6 f. For a detailed analysis regarding delictual liability, see T. Kiefer, *Die Aquilische Haftung im 'Allgemeinen Landrecht für die Preussischen Staaten' von 1784* (Freiburg: Centaurus-Verlagsgesellschaft, 1989), pp. 191 ff., pp. 225 ff., further references within. In fact, Prussian judges even decided cases on the basis of *Justinian's Corpus iuris civilis* instead of simply applying the ALR.

[6] Haferkamp, 'The science of private law', pp. 258–9; see also S. Lepsius, 'Taking the institutional context seriously', in Jansen and Michaels, *Beyond the State*, pp. 233 ff.

[7] Friedberg, *Die künftige Gestaltung*, pp. 5 ff., pp. 16 ff.; see also Zimmermann, 'Das Bürgerliche Gesetzbuch', p. 15.

[8] See Zimmermann, 'Das Bürgerliche Gesetzbuch', p. 14, further references within. In 1899 a bibliography contained about 4,000 titles of this kind; this was probably more than the literature that had ever been published on the ALR. Even more remarkably, whereas the literature on the ALR had normally contained references to the *Corpus iuris*, this was less the case for the new literature: the BGB was, from an early stage, understood as an autonomous source of the law.

[9] B. Windscheid, 'Das römische Recht in Deutschland' [1858], in P. Oertmann (ed.), *Bernhard Windscheid: Gesammelte Reden und Abhandlungen* (Leipzig: Duncker & Humblot, 1904), pp. 25 ff., p. 48: 'Dom nationaler Herrlichkeit'.

On the contrary: politically disputed issues were left outside the codification. This approach corresponds well with the English Law Commission's perception that a codification should be preceded by legal reform.[10] Thus, statutory legislation addressing the 'social question', such as the *Abzahlungsgesetz* on instalment payments, had been enacted in a special statute before the code came into being.[11] Likewise, the strict liability (*Gefährdungshaftung*) for damages caused by railway accidents, which had already been introduced in Prussia in 1838,[12] never found its way into the nineteenth-century academic systems of private law[13] and therefore had to remain outside the BGB as well.[14]

All in all, the BGB was meant to become a kind of governmental restatement of the law. Of course, the code was now based, constitutionally, on the sovereign's will, and it was taken as replacing all former sources of the law with a new textual basis. The BGB was not meant or understood to be a fundamental change in the law, however. For Bernhard Windscheid, Germany's leading legal scholar at the end of the nineteenth century and an influential member of the First Commission drafting the BGB, the code was not meant to be more than a 'point in the law's development'.[15]

[10] See Alexandra Braun, 'The English codification debate and the role of jurists in the development of legal doctrines', Chapter 10 in this volume.

[11] *HKK*, vol. I/Duve, paras. 1–14 [69] ff., [71].

[12] Paragraph 25 *Eisenbahngesetz* of 1838. On this piece of reform legislation, see T. Baums, 'Die Einführung der Gefährdungshaftung durch F. C. von Savigny' (1987) 104 *Zeitschrift der Savigny Stiftung* (germ. Abt.) 277 ff.; and L. Lenz, *Haftung ohne Verschulden in deutscher Gesetzgebung und Rechtswissenschaft des 19. Jahrhunderts* (Berlin: Lit Verlag, 1995), pp. 57 ff., with further references. See also R. Zimmermann, *The Law of Obligations: Roman Foundations of the Civilian Tradition*, paperback edn (Oxford University Press, 1996), p. 1131.

[13] This can be seen very clearly in the writings of Savigny, who was – in his political capacity as a state secretary – a leading figure behind the Prussian *Gefährdungshaftung* for railways (see Baums, 'Die Einführung'; Lenz, *Haftung ohne Verschulden*, p. 64, p. 72; and, more generally, H.-P. Benöhr, 'Zur ausservertraglichen Haftung im gemeinen Recht', in D. Medicus and H. H. Seiler (eds.), *Festschrift für Max Kaser zum 70. Geburtstag* (Munich: Beck, 1976), pp. 689 ff., pp. 706–10). Nevertheless, Savigny mentioned the *Gefährdungshaftung* neither in his *Obligationenrecht* nor in his *System des heutigen römischen Rechts*: N. Jansen, *Die Struktur des Haftungsrechts: Geschichte, Theorie und Dogmatik außervertraglicher Ansprüche auf Schadensersatz* (Tübingen: Mohr Siebeck, 2003), p. 370; but see also A. Bürge, 'Die Entstehung und Begründung der Gefährdungshaftung im 19. Jahrhundert und ihr Verhältnis zur Verschuldenshaftung: Eine Skizze', in A. Heldrich, J. Prölss and I. Koller (eds.), *Festschrift für Claus-Wilhelm Canaris zum 70. Geburtstag* (2 vols.), vol. I (Munich: Beck, 2007), pp. 59 ff., pp. 64–5.

[14] In the *Reichshaftpflichtgesetz* of 1871; see Jansen, *Die Struktur des Haftungsrechts*, pp. 369 ff.

[15] B. Windscheid, 'Die geschichtliche Schule in der Rechtswissenschaft' [1878], in P. Oertmann, *Bernhard Windscheid: Gesammelte Reden*, pp. 66 ff., 75: 'Punkt in der Entwicklung'.

The same view was held by Gottlieb Planck,[16] a member of the First Commission, the leading figure in the Second Commission and, later, the editor of the first, highly influential, commentary on the BGB.[17] This attitude was not exceptional. A similar understanding had prevailed among the men behind the *Code civil*,[18] and it would be observed, again, in the context of the Dutch civil code.[19]

As a result, what was changed by the codifications was not so much the substance of the law but, rather, the form of legal scholarship: from now on, legal knowledge was increasingly collected and developed in commentaries to the civil code, rather than in learned textbooks systematising Roman sources.[20] Indeed, as the basic system of private law could now be found in the codification, scholars were less concerned with questions of system-building than with internal doctrinal problems within the code's system.[21] In terms of substance, though, there was much more continuity than discontinuity with the former law;[22] and, again, this finding corresponds with French developments after 1804.[23]

9.2 Developing the BGB

Like its French counterpart, the BGB was (and continues to be) rather brief on matters of delictual liability. True, the BGB replaced the wide general clauses of liability for fault, which could be found in the ALR (§§ 1 ff.,

[16] G. Planck, 'Zur Kritik des Entwurfs eines bürgerlichen Gesetzbuches für das Deutsche Reich' (1889) 75 *Archiv für die civilistische Praxis* [*AcP*] 327 ff., 331–3.

[17] G. Planck (ed.), *Bürgerliches Gesetzbuch nebst Einführungsgesetz* (5 vols.) (Berlin: Guttentag, 1897–1902).

[18] See Jean-Louis Halpérin, 'The process of codification applied to the law of delicts', Chapter 8 in this volume.

[19] E. Hondius, 'Das neue Niederländische Gesetzbuch: Allgemeiner Teil' (1991) 191 *AcP* 378 ff., 378, 381, 386.

[20] An overview of the literature on the BGB is found in the *HKK*, vol. I, pp. xxiv ff.

[21] N. Jansen and R. Michaels, 'Private law and the state: comparative perceptions and historical observations' (2007) 71 *RabelsZ* 345 ff., 395.

[22] See the contributions to U. Falk and H. Mohnhaupt (eds.), *Das Bürgerliche Gesetzbuch und seine Richter* (Frankfurt: Klostermann, 2000); for an overview, see Zimmermann, 'Das Bürgerliche Gesetzbuch', p. 17.

[23] K. Zweigert and H. Kötz, *Einführung in die Rechtsvergleichung*, 3rd edn (Tübingen: Mohr Siebeck, 1996), pp. 78 ff., pp. 84 ff.; J. Gordley, 'Myths of the French civil code' (1994) 42 *Am. J. Comp. L.* 459 ff.; see also D. R. Kelley, 'Ancient verses on new ideas: legal tradition and the French historical school' (1987) 26 *History and Theory* 319 ff. For a more detailed analysis of the law of delict, see J.-L. Halpérin, 'French doctrinal writing', in N. Jansen (ed.), *The Development and Making of Legal Doctrine* (Cambridge University Press, 2010), pp. 73 ff.

10 ff. I 6), in the Austrian *Allgemeines Bürgerliches Gesetzbuch* (§ 1295) and in the French *Code civil* (art. 1382), with three more specific 'small general clauses'.[24] Thus, paragraph 823 I BGB is based on the violation of a subjective right or comparable interest; paragraph 823 II BGB attaches liability for the infringement of statutory provisions 'intended for the protection of others' (rather than the general public); and paragraph 826 BGB, the former *actio doli*, makes intentional wrongdoers acting *contra bonos mores* liable for all resulting loss. None of these clauses, however, ultimately determined the matters in question here; the BGB has left it to judges to determine which interests are protected under paragraph 823 I BGB, which statutes should be regarded as protective under paragraph 823 II BGB, what the normative standards leading to liability are under paragraph 826 BGB and what behaviour amounted to negligence.

There was much leeway left for commentators and courts to develop the law in a highly constructive way, on the one hand, and in continuity with the nineteenth century's achievements, on the other. This could be done within the framework of the code, besides its doctrinal structures, or even against its express provisions.[25] As will be seen, it was usually, though not always, the judiciary that took the lead in such developments. In fact, for a commentary to become influential, it had, first of all, to be useful; and that meant, from a practical lawyer's perspective, that it had to give an easily accessible, comprehensive description of the law as it was applied by the courts.[26] Commentaries had to be conservative in their approach.

9.2.1 Rights

The scope of liability had been a major policy issue at the end of the nineteenth century. The question was whether liability could be triggered

[24] K. Larenz and C.-W. Canaris, *Lehrbuch des Schuldrechts*, 13th edn (2 vols.), vol. II (Munich: Beck, 1994), pp. 354 ff. These 'small general clauses' are surrounded by a couple of minor torts without real practical significance. On the discussions during the codification process, see H.-P. Benöhr, 'Die Redaktion der Paragraphen 823 und 826 BGB', in R. Zimmermann, R. Knütel and J. P. Meincke (eds.), *Rechtsgeschichte und Privatrechtsdogmatik* (Heidelberg: Müller, 1999), pp. 499 ff.; and C. Katzenmeier, 'Zur neueren dogmengeschichtlichen Entwicklung der Deliktsrechtstatbestände' (2002) 202 *AcP* 79 ff., 84–5, 106.

[25] See, for what follows, in more detail, N. Jansen, 'Developing legal doctrine: fault in the German law of delict', in *The Development and Making of Legal Doctrine*, pp. 96 ff.; and R. Zimmermann and D. Verse, 'Die Reaktion des Reichsgerichts auf die Kodifikation des deutschen Deliktsrechts (1900–1914)', in Falk and Mohnhaupt, *Das Bürgerliche Gesetzbuch*, pp. 319 ff.

[26] See K. W. Slapnicar, 'Der Wilke, der später Palandt hieß' (2000) *NJW* 1692 ff.

by violations of purely economic interests or by negligent violations of a general right to one's personality, such as a right to privacy or honour. Here, the authors of the BGB had taken a fairly restrictive point of view, at least with regard to purely financial interests, which were clearly excluded under paragraph 823 I BGB. The position was less clear with regard to personality rights, however.[27] Such rights had not been included explicitly in the list of interests protected under paragraph 823 I BGB. The sources reporting the discussions in the drafting commissions are ambiguous, however, as to whether the legislator regarded protection under paragraph 823 I BGB as a matter of course or whether the protection of honour under criminal law and some special provisions in the code were seen as sufficient.[28] Nevertheless, Planck's influential commentary argued that the legislator had not wished to extend the protection of personality; and this contention settled the debate.[29] The prevailing opinion in the literature[30] and also among the judiciary[31] immediately followed suit. All the same, the courts granted some protection of personality under the heading of paragraph 826 BGB,[32] which presupposed intention on the defendant's side. It was not until 1954 that a general 'right to one's personality' (*allgemeines Persönlichkeitsrecht*) was acknowledged in the context of paragraph 823 I BGB.[33]

The judiciary proved more active in the protection of purely financial interests. The code's restrictive position soon appeared too harsh, and

[27] For an overview on the early discussion, see in Planck, *Bürgerliches Gesetzbuch*, vol. I: F. André, para. 823 [2.a].

[28] See D. Klippel and G. Lies-Benachib, 'Der Schutz von Persönlichkeitsrechten um 1900', in Falk and Mohnhaupt, *Das Bürgerliche Gesetzbuch*, pp. 343 ff., pp. 352–4; and Jansen, *Die Struktur des Haftungsrechts*, pp. 466 ff., further references within.

[29] Planck, *Bürgerliches Gesetzbuch*, vol. I (André, para. 823 [2.a]).

[30] P. Oertmann, *Recht der Schuldverhältnisse*, 3rd/4th edns (Berlin: Heymann, 1910), para. 823 [1]; T. Engelmann, para. 823 [II.A.2.e.γ], in J. Staudinger, *J. Staudingers Kommentar zum Bürgerlichen Gesetzbuch*, 7th/8th edns (Munich: Schweitzer, 1912); F. Flad, para. 823 [B.II.1.f.β], in G. Planck, *Planck's Kommentar zum Bürgerlichen Gesetzbuch*, 4th edn (Berlin: de Gruyter, 1928); L. Enneccerus, *Das Bürgerliche Recht: Eine Einführung in das Recht des Bürgerlichen Gesetzbuchs* (2 vols.), vol. I (Marburg: Elwert, 1900), pp. 762 ff. (para. 359).

[31] *Entscheidungen des Reichsgerichts in Zivilsachen* (*RGZ*) 51, 369, 372 ff. (1902), relying on Planck's commentary. See also R. Zimmermann, *Roman Law, Contemporary Law, European Law: The Civilian Tradition Today* (Oxford University Press, 2001), pp. 66 ff.

[32] K. Kastl, *Das allgemeine Persönlichkeitsrecht: Der Prozess seiner Anerkennung als 'sonstiges Recht' im Sinne von § 823 Abs. 1 BGB* (Ebelsbach: Aktiv-Druck und Verlag, 2004), p. 62, pp. 120 ff., pp. 217 ff.; see also Zimmermann and Verse, 'Die Reaktion des Reichsgerichts', pp. 331–2, describing this as a process of cautious extension.

[33] See section 9.3 below.

it was not exactly in tune with the former practice of the Reichsgericht (the German Imperial Court).[34] Thus, in 1904 the court decided, against the legislators' intentions,[35] that possession could under specific circumstances be regarded as 'another right'.[36] Even more important was the court's decision to acknowledge a 'right to an established and operating business' (*Recht am eingerichteten und ausgeübten Gewerbebetrieb*).[37] In cases of unfair competition, this right gave protection to interests that are understood as purely financial in other legal systems. Clearly, this right was difficult to establish on the basis of prevailing doctrine.[38] Nonetheless, the Reichsgericht apparently regarded businesses as insufficiently protected by competition law and therefore wished to provide for an additional legal remedy (the right has lost much of its significance, accordingly, as a result of subsequent statutory regulation of competition).[39] Commentators have always raised critiques,[40] but the majority accepted this step of judicial lawmaking.[41]

Another device for protecting financial interests was contract law. The Reichsgericht had already addressed the issue of negligent misstatements during the last decades of the nineteenth century,[42] and it continued this line of judgments under the BGB. Thus, as early as 1902 the court made a solicitor contractually liable for a misstatement towards a bank, even though there had been no prior contractual relation between the parties.[43] This decision initiated a development towards far-reaching contractual, or quasi-contractual, remedies for negligent misstatements.[44] Even if it

[34] See Zimmermann, *Roman Law*, pp. 57 ff., pp. 63 ff.

[35] Zimmermann and Verse, 'Die Reaktion des Reichsgerichts', pp. 325–6.

[36] *RGZ* 59, 326, 327–8 (1904). [37] *RGZ* 58, 24, 28 ff. (1904).

[38] G. Planck, para. 823 [II.1.f], in *Bürgerliches Gesetzbuch nebst Einführungsgesetz*, 3rd edn (Berlin: Guttentag, 1907).

[39] Larenz and Canaris, *Lehrbuch des Schuldrechts*, vol. II, pp. 543–4.

[40] Planck, para. 823 [II.1.f.γ], in *Bürgerliches Gesetzbuch*, vol. III; Larenz and Canaris, *Lehrbuch des Schuldrechts*, vol. II, pp. 543–4.

[41] Oertmann, *Recht der Schuldverhältnisse*, para. 823 [3.b]; Engelmann, para. 823 [II.A.2.e.β]; Flad, para. 823 [B.II.1.f.γ]; E. Pinzger, para. 823 [6], in O. Palandt (ed.), *Bürgerliches Gesetzbuch*, 2nd edn (Munich: Beck, 1939); K. Schäfer, para. 823 [121]–[169], in J. Staudinger, *J. v. Staudingers Kommentar zum Bürgerlichen Gesetzbuch*, 10th/11th edns (Berlin: Sellier, 1975).

[42] *RGZ* 19, 97, 100–1 (1887); 27, 118, 121 ff. (1891); 42, 125, 131–2 (1898).

[43] *RGZ* 52, 365, 366 f. (1902).

[44] See K. Huber, 'Verkehrspflichten zum Schutz fremden Vermögens', in H. C. Ficker and D. König (eds.), *Festschrift für Ernst von Caemmerer zum 70. Geburtstag* (Tübingen: Mohr Siebeck, 1978), pp. 359 ff.; C. von Bar, 'Unentgeltliche Investitionsempfehlungen im Wandel der Wirtschaftsverfassungen Deutschlands und Englands' (1980) 44 *RabelsZ* 455 ff., 463.

has proved difficult to explain such decisions in a doctrinally convincing way, these remedies have mostly been welcomed by commentators;[45] and, in the course of a reform of the law of obligations in 2002, they were even legislatively restated (§§ 241 II, 311 II, III BGB).

A contrary development, though, can be observed with regard to liability under paragraph 823 II BGB. Here, the 'purpose of protecting another' had originally been understood broadly; even norms that primarily protected the general public were regarded as protecting individuals as members of the general public.[46] As a consequence of the rapid growth of public law during the twentieth century, however, this approach would have led to an explosion of liability, undermining the legislative policy against compensation for purely economic losses. A more restrictive test therefore had to be developed. Here the learned literature took the lead, arguing that the violated norm had to aim explicitly at protecting the individual victim's specific interest that had actually been violated.[47] This test remained good law, even if such formulae could never be watertight. Commentaries therefore supplemented the test with long lists of judgments qualifying norms as protective or not.[48] Again, the normative decisions were made by the courts.

9.2.2 *Verkehrspflichten*

Liability for omissions has always been discussed as a question of fault, because it presupposes positive duties to act in the interest of another person. Today the existence of such duties is a matter of course, and the same was apparently true at the end of the eighteenth century.[49]

[45] For a comprehensive picture of these discussions and the specific requirements of this liability, see Jansen, *Die Struktur des Haftungsrechts*, pp. 524 ff.

[46] Planck, *Bürgerliches Gesetzbuch*, vol. I (André, para. 823[3.b]). This became the prevailing opinion; see Oertmann, *Recht der Schuldverhältnisse*, para. 823 [4.a]; and O. Warneyer, *Kommentar zum Bürgerlichen Gesetzbuch*, vol. I (Tübingen: Mohr Siebeck, 1923), para. 823 [IV].

[47] Planck, *Bürgerliches Gesetzbuch*, vol. I (André, para. 823 [III.2]); Oertmann, *Recht der Schuldverhältnisse*, para. 823 [4]; F. Endemann, *Lehrbuch des Bürgerlichen Rechts*, 5th/6th edns (Berlin: Heymann, 1899), pp. 909 f. (para. 200 a 3). Details on the development and further references in *HKK*, vol. II/Jansen, paras. 249–53, para. 255 [70].

[48] See Engelmann, in *Staudingers Kommentar*, 7th/8th edns, para. 823 [III.A.2.c]; H. Sprau, in Palandt, *Bürgerliches Gesetzbuch*, 67th edn (Munich: Beck, 2008), para. 823 [61] ff. Today, further distinctions are made as to the specific groups of victims or specific interests protected by the relevant statutes.

[49] Jansen, *Die Struktur des Haftungsrechts*, pp. 292 ff.; Zimmermann, *The Law of Obligations*, pp. 1032–3.

Nineteenth-century writers, however, followed by the courts (reluctantly),[50] severely restricted the law in this respect.[51] Omissions could lead to liability only if they could be equated with a positive act,[52] or if a positive duty resulted from 'an earlier or accompanying positive act'.[53] At the same time, responsibility for indirect consequences of one's actions was often conceived of in terms of omissions: the tortfeasor did *not* take precautions against an imminent danger; he had *not* controlled his dangerous property. Thus, the owner of a duly erected industrial plant or another building was not held to be under an obligation to keep it secure.[54]

During the second half of the nineteenth century, however, such duties were increasingly acknowledged by the courts, first in cases of extraordinary danger,[55] and then on the basis of the expanding public and criminal law.[56] From 1890 onwards it could be enough for a positive duty to arise that the defendant had created a danger (e.g. by opening his premises to the general public). Accordingly, owners of residential buildings were made responsible for the safety of the staircases[57] and public authorities had to ensure that streets were safe.[58]

This extended responsibility for omissions had been accepted by leading scholars,[59] and it was clearly the state of the law when the BGB was enacted. There was no explicit provision in the BGB for the question of omissions,

[50] R. Bilstein, *Das deliktische Schadensersatzrecht der Lex Aquilia in der Rechtsprechung des Reichsgerichts* (Münster: Lit, 1994), pp. 39–40; D. Kleindiek, *Deliktshaftung und juristische Person* (Tübingen: Mohr, 1997), pp. 57–8.

[51] J. C. Hasse, *Die Culpa des Römischen Rechts*, 2nd edn (Bonn: Marcus, 1838), pp. 13 ff., pp. 105 ff.; G. F. Puchta, *Pandekten*, 9th edn (Leipzig: Barth, 1863), p. 571 (para. 388).

[52] Hasse, *Die Culpa*, pp. 13 ff., pp. 105 ff.; see Puchta, *Pandekten*, p. 571; and further references in G. Beermann, *Findet die lex Aquilia bei Unterlassungen Anwendung?* (Berlin: Mayer & Müller, 1896), pp. 3–4.

[53] Hasse, *Die Culpa*, pp. 23–4, p. 106; B. Windscheid, *Lehrbuch des Pandektenrechts*, 7th edn, vol. II (Frankfurt: Rütten & Loening, 1891), p. 641 (para. 455).

[54] See Windscheid, *Lehrbuch des Pandektenrechts*, vol. II, pp. 651 ff. (paras. 458–9); A. Brinz, *Lehrbuch der Pandekten*, 2nd edn (4 vols.), vol. II (Erlangen: A. Deichert, 1879), p. 673 (para. 172); H. Dernburg, *Pandekten*, 6th edn (2 vols.), vol. I (Berlin: Müller, 1900), pp. 153 ff. (paras. 230–1).

[55] Obergericht Braunschweig, 10 *Seufferts Archiv für die Entscheidungen der obersten deutschen Staaten* [*SeuffA*] 223 f., n. 165 (1856), for the duty to close gates correctly before the arrival of a train; Oberappellationsgericht Dresden, 4 *SeuffA* 170 f., n. 96 (1850); Oberappellationsgericht München, 4 *SeuffA* 197 f., n. 119 (1851), for the duty to take measures against a possible flood when interfering with the natural flow of rivers; Reichsgericht, 42 *SeuffA* 299 f., n. 210 (1887), for the duty to supervise hazardous activities.

[56] Bilstein, *Das deliktische Schadensersatzrecht*, pp. 40 ff.

[57] *RGZ* 33, 225, 228 f., further references within (1894).

[58] Reichsgericht, 49 *SeuffA* 1, n. 1 (1893) (for waterways); *RGZ* 38, 220 (1897).

[59] Dernburg, *Pandekten*, vol. II, p. 361 (para. 131).

however. Supported by some leading scholars,[60] the Reichsgericht took this as permission to continue with the earlier expansive approach and thus created the instrument of a *Verkehrs(sicherungs)pflicht*:[61] whoever created a danger for the general public was held to be under a positive duty to take suitable precautionary measures. Critical voices[62] never impressed the judges, who steadily extended the range of duties to act, thereby establishing a far-reaching system of liability for omissions that was probably never thought of by the BGB's authors.[63] During the twentieth century the law of delict thus developed into a complex system of duties to take precautionary measures, to control sources of danger and to warn against dangers.[64]

Despite its complexity, this state of the case law is generally accepted today. Early on, commentators had seen their task in collecting[65] and systematising[66] these lines of the jurisprudence. Clearly, the law was made

60 K. Linckelmann, *Die Schadensersatzpflicht aus unerlaubten Handlungen nach dem Bürgerlichen Gesetzbuche für das Deutsche Reich* (Berlin: Heymann, 1898), pp. 34 ff., pp. 39–40, p. 90; F. von Liszt, *Die Deliktsobligationen im System des Bürgerlichen Gesetzbuchs* (Berlin: Guttentag, 1898), pp. 72 ff.; B. Windscheid and T. Kipp, *Lehrbuch des Pandektenrechts*, 9th edn (3 vols.), vol. II (Frankfurt: Rütten & Loening, 1906), p. 974 (para. 455); A. von Tuhr, *Der Allgemeine Teil des Deutschen Bürgerlichen Rechts* (2 vols.), vol. II (Leipzig: Duncker & Humblot, 1918), pp. 465–6.

61 *RGZ* 52, 373, 376 ff. (1902); 54, 53, 55 ff. (1903), emphasising the continuity with the earlier law.

62 'Auf wildem Holz gewachsen': J. Esser, 'Die Zweispurigkeit unseres Haftpflichtrechts', 1953 *JZ* 129 ff., 132; before E. Brodmann, 'Über die Haftung für Fahrlässigkeit, insbesondere über die Haftung des Schiffers' (1906) 99 *AcP* 327 ff., 344; W. Hofacker, 'Über Verkehrssicherungspflicht' (1931) 79 *Bayerische Verwaltungsblätter* 365 ff., 366; later M. Fraenkel, *Tatbestand und Zurechnung bei § 823 Abs. 1 BGB* (Berlin: Duncker & Humblot, 1979), pp. 20 ff.

63 A. Zeuner, 'Historische Linien in der Entwicklung des Rechts am Gewerbebetrieb, des allgemeinen Persönlichkeitsrechts und der Verkehrssicherungspflichten', in F. Hauß (ed.), *25 Jahre Karlsruher Forum* (Karlsruhe: Verl. Versicherungswirtschaft, 1983), pp. 196 ff., p. 199; Kleindiek, *Deliktshaftung*, pp. 105 ff.; for all, see Jansen, *Die Struktur des Haftungsrechts*, pp. 401 ff.

64 E. von Caemmerer, 'Wandlungen des Deliktsrechts', in E. von Caemmerer, E. Friesenhahn and R. Lange (eds.), *Festschrift zum hundertjährigen Bestehen des deutschen Juristentages* (Karlsruhe: C. F. Müller, 1960), pp. 49 ff., pp. 71–4; C. von Bar, *Verkehrspflichten* (Cologne: Heymann, 1980), pp. 83 ff., pp. 102–4, pp. 239–40.

65 Engelmann, para. 823 [II.C.1]; Pinzger, para. 823 [8], [14].

66 See Planck, para. 823 [II.2], describing collecting judgments, which had established a *Verkehrspflicht*, under classificatory headings; similarly, later, Schäfer, para. 823 [264]–[375]; J. Hager, para. 823 [E 12]–[E 406], in J. Staudinger, *J. v. Staudingers Kommentar zum Bürgerlichen Gesetzbuch*, 13th edn (4 vols.) (Berlin: Sellier–de Gruyter, 1993–2007); today G. Wagner, para. 823 [50]–[65], [220]–[295], [407]–[607], in *Münchener Kommentar zum BGB*, 4th edn (11 vols.) (Munich: Beck, 2001–10).

by the courts, not only in substance but also in terms of doctrinal terminology.[67] The commentators' question was usually not whether a particular *Verkehrspflicht*, having been established by a court, was substantially justified but where to place the new duty into the doctrinal system of delictual liability.

German courts have never intervened in the legal system as actively and forcefully as the French Cour de Cassation did when it introduced the far-reaching system of strict *gardien* liability for *faits des choses*[68] on the basis of article 1384 of the *Code civil* – a norm that had evidently not been drafted for this purpose.[69] Unlike their French colleagues, German judges were confronted with a legislature that had created instances of strict liability and continued to do so when this appeared politically appropriate.[70] Hence, strict liability was regarded – as in England[71] – as a highly political matter that should be decided by parliament, rather than by judges. Accordingly, the Reichsgericht and then the Bundesgerichtshof (the Federal Court of Justice) made it clear that they would not apply the exceptional cases of a statutory *Gefährdungshaftung* (strict liability) by way of analogy.[72] The courts could well have taken a less restrictive view – as did the Austrian courts;[73] their reluctance was probably not due to judicial restraint, however.

In the eyes of the German judiciary, there were more subtle and flexible means of introducing quasi-strict liability. *Verkehrspflichten* determine the standards of care; and, by imposing strict standards of care, the

[67] *RGZ* 54, 53, 57, 58 (1903): 'Eröffnung eines Verkehrs', 'Anforderungen der Verkehrssicherheit'.

[68] D.P. 1897.1.433 (*arrêt Teffaine*); D.P. 1930.1.57. (*arrêts Jand'heur*); see C. von Bar, *The Common European Law of Torts* (2 vols.) (Oxford: Clarendon Press, 1998–2000), vol. I, pp. 106 ff., vol. II, pp. 315 ff.; and N. Jansen, *Binnenmarkt, Privatrecht und europäische Identität* (Tübingen: Mohr Siebeck, 2004), pp. 36 ff., with further references on the historical development.

[69] U. Hübner, *Die Haftung des Gardien im französischen Zivilrecht* (Karlsruhe: Verlag Versicherungswirtschaft, 1972), pp. 3 ff.; von Bar, *The Common European Law of Torts*, vol. I, n. 68, [107].

[70] Namely the *Reichshaftpflichtgesetz*; later, strict liability was introduced for cars (para. 7 I *Straßenverkehrsgesetz*, 1908) and for aeroplanes (para. 33 *Luftverkehrsgesetz*, 1922); for the details, see Jansen, *Die Struktur des Haftungsrechts*, pp. 371–2.

[71] See Michael Lobban, 'English jurisprudence and tort theory', Chapter 6 in this volume; from a more doctrinal perspective, see J. Fleming, *The Law of Torts*, 9th edn (Sydney: LBC Information Services, 1998), pp. 377–8.

[72] *RGZ* 78, 171, 172 (1912); *BGHZ* 55, 229, 232 ff. (1971).

[73] H. Koziol, 'Bewegliches System und Gefährdungshaftung', in F. Bydlinski, H. Krejci, B. Schilcher and V. Steininger (eds.), *Das Bewegliche System im geltenden und künftigen Recht* (Vienna: Springer, 1986), pp. 51 ff., pp. 59–60; E. Deutsch, *Allgemeines Haftungsrecht*, 2nd edn (Cologne: Carl Heymanns Verlag, 1995), [653].

judges in effect established liability for 'negligence without fault'. Thus, when damage was caused by a virus or bacterium, this was neither a case of strict liability for damage caused by animals nor of strict liability for a genetically transformed organism. Rather than applying one of these instances of strict liability analogously, however, judges imposed strict duties of care under paragraph 823 I BGB.[74] It is not exceptional to find *Verkehrspflichten* that cannot seriously be understood as standards of reasonable conduct. Thus, a washing machine 'must' be supervised 'acoustically and visually' every five minutes,[75] and it has been firmly established that security standards under statutory law do not limit delictual duties of care. As a matter of fact, judicially imposed delictual 'duties' are often stricter.[76] Moreover, leading judges have made it clear, outside court, that they used *Verkehrspflichten* for justly distributing the risks of accidents.[77] As a result, there is no strict separation between strict liability and liability for fault.

None of these judgments has been radically new; they may be seen as a revival of the earlier concept of *culpa levissima*.[78] Such standards of care are difficult to explain within the prevailing doctrinal system, however, because it conceives of delicts as *unerlaubte Handlungen* (unlawful conduct). Commentators therefore normally ignored such discussions and, instead, collected the relevant judgments. In academic monographs, though, the sliding scale between strict liability and liability for fault, and the equivalence of both regimes resulting from it, have recently been emphasised.[79] Moreover, scholars increasingly acknowledge arguments that have nothing to do with standards of reasonable behaviour, namely the better insurability of risks.[80] Nevertheless, it is fair to say that, in this respect too, commentators have been more descriptive than innovative in their approach.

[74] Bundesgerichtshof [BGH] 1989 *NJW* 2947 f.; see also Larenz and Canaris, *Lehrbuch des Schuldrechts*, vol. II, pp. 613–14.

[75] Oberlandesgericht [OLG] Hamm (1984) *Monatsschrift für deutsches Recht* 668; see also OLG Düsseldorf (1975) *Versicherungsrecht* 159 f.

[76] *BGHZ* 99, 167, 176 (1986); BGH, 1987 *NJW* 372, 373; BGH, 1985 *NJW* 620, 621; Larenz and Canaris, *Lehrbuch des Schuldrechts*, vol. II, p. 416.

[77] E. Steffen, 'Verkehrspflichten im Spannungsfeld von Bestandsschutz und Handlungsfreiheit' (1980) *Versicherungsrecht* 409 ff., 410.

[78] Jansen, *Die Struktur des Haftungsrechts*, pp. 304 ff., pp. 402 ff., pp. 433 ff.

[79] Koziol, 'Bewegliches System', pp. 51 ff.; Jansen, *Die Struktur des Haftungsrechts*, pp. 14 ff., pp. 552 ff.

[80] H. J. Mertens, before paras. 823–5 [48], in *Münchener Kommentar zum BGB*, 3rd edn (Munich: Beck, 1993–9); H. Kötz and G. Wagner, *Deliktsrecht*, 9th edn (Neuwied: Luchterhand, 2001), [228] ff., [300], [523]. *Contra*: Larenz and Canaris, *Lehrbuch des Schuldrechts*, vol. II, pp. 416 f.

9.2.3 *Liability for third parties*

Although all these developments could be described as fleshing out or complementing the rather thin legislative framework of the BGB, the courts have taken a more critical approach with regard to liability for third persons. Here, the code took an extremely conservative position, which was already outdated even at the end of the nineteenth century.[81] Whereas parties are vicariously liable for third persons within a contractual relation (§ 278 BGB), delictual liability for the wrongs of one's employees presupposes fault in selecting or supervising them (§ 831 BGB). Of course, as such fault is normally difficult to find, claimants were in a very bad position, especially in cases in which they were confronted with a large business. In response, the Reichsgericht from an early stage relied on contractual remedies, arguing that there were contractual obligations not to endanger the interests of one's contract partner. Thus, businesses became vicariously responsible for their employees (§ 278 BGB), irrespective of the restrictive approach of paragraph 831 BGB.[82] On the doctrinal basis of an implied term, the courts soon extended the 'protective effect' of the duty beyond the contract partner. They also extended it to those persons for whose well-being the other party could be said to be responsible (*Vertrag mit Schutzwirkung zugunsten Dritter*).[83] Here, again, commentators never really guided or criticised such developments but, rather, saw their task in finding convincing doctrinal explanations for the courts' decisions. They observed and described the judicial developments as opposed to constructively taking part in them.[84]

9.3 Constitutionalising private law

When the German *Grundgesetz* (GG) became the constitutional foundation of the German legal system in 1949, it was axiomatic, in accordance

[81] Zimmermann and Verse, 'Die Reaktion des Reichsgerichts', pp. 335–6.

[82] *RGZ* 78, 239 ff. (1911); see also Zimmermann, *Roman Law*, pp. 72 ff., on other devices for circumventing the restrictions of para. 831 BGB. Other instruments are *Organisationspflichten*, under which businesses are obliged to put members of the board (for whom the business is vicariously liable) in charge of its supervision duties: see Kleindiek, *Deliktshaftung*, pp. 314 ff.; and, critically, A. Matusche-Beckmann, *Das Organisationsverschulden* (Tübingen: Mohr Siebeck, 2001), pp. 49 ff., pp. 89 ff., pp. 134 ff. and passim.

[83] Zimmermann, *Roman Law*, pp. 95–6; *HKK*, vol. II/S. Vogenauer, paras. 328–35 [121] ff.

[84] *HKK*, vol. II/Vogenauer, paras. 328–35 [124], describing doctrine as *nur beobachtend und registrierend tätig*.

with the commonly held view under the constitution of Weimar,[85] that fundamental constitutional rights protected the citizens (only) against the state.[86] In the new German constitution's first article, it was laid down that these rights 'are binding upon the legislator, the administration and the judiciary as immediately applicable law' (art. 1 III GG); hence, they were not binding, normally, between fellow citizens. There are only a few exceptions in which the opposite had explicitly been laid down, most of them outside the classic catalogue of human rights.[87] Accordingly, in the first edition of one of the leading commentaries on the *Grundgesetz*, Hermann von Mangoldt, who had taken a leading role in its formulation,[88] did not even address the question of an indirect effect on human rights. He instead emphasised that the intention of article 1 III of the *Grundgesetz* was to make constitutional rights binding not only on the administration but also on parliament.[89] As a result of this understanding, constitutional rights appeared to be without relevance in the context of the BGB, which remained the unchanged textual foundation of private law.

Within a few years, though, the question of an 'indirect horizontal effect' became a central topic of the postwar discussion of private and constitutional law. Leading scholars, most notably Carl Friedrich Nipperdey, argued that these rights should be effective also within private law relations, especially in labour law.[90] When Nipperdey became

[85] See. G. Anschütz, *Die Verfassung des Deutschen Reiches vom 11. August 1919: Ein Kommentar für Wissenschaft und Praxis*, 14th edn (Berlin: Stilke, 1933), art. 117 [1], art. 118 [556].

[86] H. von Mangoldt, 'Schriftlicher Bericht des Abgeordneten Dr. von Mangoldt über den Abschnitt I: Die Grundrechte', in Parlamentarischer Rat Bonn 1948/9 (1949) *Schriftlicher Bericht zum Entwurf des Grundgesetzes für die Bundesrepublik Deutschland* (= Anlage zum stenographischen Bericht der Sitzung des Parlamentarischen Rates am 6. Mai 1949) 5: *In den Grundrechten sollte also das Verhältnis des Einzelnen zum Staate geregelt werden, damit der Mensch in seiner Würde wieder anerkannt werde.*

[87] See articles 9 III 2, 20 IV, 48 II GG.

[88] Mangoldt, 'Schriftlicher Bericht des Abgeordneten'.

[89] H. von Mangoldt, *Das Bonner Grundgesetz* (Berlin: Vahlen, 1953), art. 1 [4]; see Mangoldt, 'Schriftlicher Bericht des Abgeordneten', p. 7. The problem of an (indirect) effect of constitutional rights between private citizens can be found only in the later edition by Friedrich Klein responding to the discussions after 1948: see H. von Mangoldt and F. Klein, *Das Bonner Grundgesetz*, 2nd edn (Berlin: Vahlen, 1957), pp. 61 ff., and further references within.

[90] H. C. Nipperdey, 'Gleicher Lohn der Frau für gleiche Leistung' (1950), in *Recht der Arbeit*, pp. 121 ff.; H. C. Nipperdey, *Grundrechte und Privatrecht* (Krefeld: Scherpe, 1961), pp. 12 ff.; L. Enneccerus and H. C. Nipperdey, *Allgemeiner Teil des Bürgerlichen Rechts*, 15th edn (2 vols.), vol. I (Tübingen: Mohr Siebeck, 1959), pp. 91 ff.; G. Dürig, 'Grundrechte und Zivilrechtsprechung', in T. Maunz (ed.), *Vom Bonner Grundgesetz zur gesamtdeutschen*

the first president of the Bundesarbeitsgericht (the Federal Supreme Court in matters of labour law), this view was immediately adopted by this court.[91] Only a few years later, the Bundesverfassungsgericht (the Federal Constitutional Court) embraced this position as well,[92] arguing that the constitution's fundamental rights constituted an objective normative order (*objektive Wertordnung*) and that they therefore also bound the courts deciding in matters of private law.[93] Thus, the constitutionalisation of private law rested on the conviction of academic lawyers and judges that the constitution's fundamental rights expressed values that, under the social and economic conditions of the twentieth century, should also become relevant within the private law relations of citizens.[94] Accordingly, most authors and courts explained the indirect horizontal effect of constitutional rights as a 'new doctrine',[95] which reflected a change of the meaning and function of constitutional rights.[96]

The indirect horizontal effect of constitutional rights soon proved to be a useful device for overcoming the restricted state of the protection of personality rights.[97] Now, the young Bundesgerichtshof, the successor of the Reichsgericht, took the chance to change the law and soon acknowledged the 'right to one's personality' (*allgemeines Persönlichkeitsrecht*).[98] In article 1 of the *Grundgesetz*, human dignity (*Menschenwürde*) had been declared 'inviolable'; within the new constitution, it was obviously of the highest value. Likewise, the *Grundgesetz* had given strong protection to individual liberty (art. 2 I GG). This, so the judges argued, had to be 'translated' into a corresponding private law right under § 823 I BGB. Clearly, innovative arguments of this kind were motivated by the judges'

Verfassung: Festschrift zum 75. Geburtstag von Hans Nawiasky (Munich: Isar Verlag, 1956), pp. 157 ff., p. 175, pp. 176 ff.

[91] See *Entscheidungen des Bundesarbeitsgerichts* [*BAGE*] 1, 185, 191 ff., 193 (1954).

[92] *Bundesverfassungsgerichtsentscheidungen* [*BVerfGE*] 7, 198, 203 ff. (*Lüth*, 1958).

[93] On the later development of the relevant case law, see C. D. Classen, 'Die Drittwirkung der Grundrechte in der Rechtsprechung des Bundesverfassungsgerichts' (1997) 122 *Archiv für öffentliches Recht* 65 ff.

[94] On the debate, see K. Stern, *Das Staatsrecht der Bundesrepublik Deutschland* (3 vols.), vol. I (Munich: Beck, 1988), pp. 1515 ff.; see also M. Ruffert, *Vorrang der Verfassung und Eigenständigkeit des Privatrechts* (Tübingen: Mohr Siebeck, 2001), pp. 8 ff.; H.-J. Papier, 'Drittwirkung der Grundrechte', in D. Mertens and H.-J. Papier (eds.), *Handbuch der Grundrechte in Deutschland und Europa* (7 vols.), vol. II (Heidelberg: C. F. Müller, 2006), pp. 1331 ff. [2] ff.

[95] Nipperdey, *Grundrechte*, p. 15: 'neue Lehre'.

[96] Nipperdey, *Grundrechte*, pp. 15 ff.; *BVerfGE* 7, 198, 205 (*Lüth*, 1958).

[97] See section 9.2.1 above, at notes 28 ff. [98] *BGHZ* 13, 334 ff. (*Leserbrief*, 1954).

experience of the National Socialist regime's contempt of the person and personality rights. Constructing the constitution in a way that required the protection of personality rights within private law as well was a means of introducing moral values into the law.

At first, claimants were granted injunctions only against actual violations of their rights. Compensatory claims for non-pecuniary damages were soon added,[99] however, although prevailing opinion regarded these as contrary to the explicit provisions of paragraphs 253 I, 847 BGB.[100] Here, the argument was that such damages were necessary for deterring misbehaviour and therefore obligatory from a constitutional perspective.[101] Even if the Bundesverfassungsgericht was reluctant to embrace fully this bold proposition on the constitutionalisation of private law, it nevertheless accepted the Bundesgerichtshof's constructive and rather self-assured development of the law.[102] Indeed, in more recent times this court even allowed for a disgorgement of profits resulting from an infringement of the personality right, again for constitutional reasons relating to effective deterrence.[103]

All these decisions were difficult to explain on convincing doctrinal terms, yet commentators mainly accepted the new law. They searched for better doctrinal justifications for the claims in question and tried to describe the personality's protection in a rational way. They did not so much see their task in developing the law as in doctrinally describing the law's development.

9.4 Concluding observations

Today, the German law of delict presents itself as a body of judge-made law. During the twentieth century delictual responsibility was transformed by thick layers of praetorian law specifying, fleshing out and even correcting

[99] *BGHZ* 26, 349, 352 ff. (*Herrenreiter*, 1958).

[100] W. Dunz, in *Reichsgerichtsräte-Kommentar BGB*, 12th edn (Berlin: De Gruyter, 1976) para. 823 annex I [141] ff.; H. Lange, *Schadensersatz*, 2nd edn (Tübingen: Mohr, 1990), pp. 448 ff. Later, doctrinal writers rather suggested the original approach of an analogy to paragraph 847 (see footnote 101): Larenz and Canaris, *Lehrbuch des Schuldrechts*, vol. II, pp. 494–5.

[101] *BGHZ* 35, 363, 367 ff. (*Ginseng*, 1961). This reasoning was not fully developed in the *Herrenreiter* decision, though, in which the court justified an analogy to paragraph 847 BGB (claim for pain and suffering) with a reference to the constitutional protection of the personality.

[102] *BVerfGE* 34, 269, 292 (*Soraya*, 1973).

[103] *BGHZ* 128, 1, 14 ff. (*Caroline* I, 1994); 143, 214, 218 f. (*Marlene Dietrich*, 1999); for the doctrinal discussion, *HKK*, vol. II: Jansen, paras. 249–53, para. 255 [122] ff.

the BGB's thin provisions and adding meaning to the new constitution.[104] In substance, this process, which mirrored parallel developments in other European countries,[105] amounted to a steady expansion of delictual protection. At the same time, the law of delict, a body of rules that penalises wrongful behaviour, developed into a system of non-contractual liability (*Haftungsrecht*) that distributes the risks of accidents in society.[106] Of course, these developments were strongly informed by actual legislation, but they were never determined by the legislator. Rather, they were the legal system's response to changes in society and public morality.

Commentators, even if occasionally influential, never really determined these developments. Instead, they saw their role in observing and doctrinally reconnecting the praetorian law with the BGB's legislative framework. What is more, the judicial developments were accompanied, from time to time, by controversial discussions as to the foundations of delictual liability.[107] Scholars emphasised the interdependence of insurance and the law of delict,[108] and they proposed complementing, or even replacing, the general clauses of liability for fault with a general clause of strict liability (*Gefährdungshaftung*).[109] Yet these discussions, which were often based on a common European or Western legal discourse,[110] were *de lege ferenda*: they remained outside the doctrinal commentaries to the BGB; and they did not usually get an explicit response from the judiciary. Indeed, the reader usually looks in vain for explicit statements on the part of judges explaining their change of approach with regard to delictual liability. German judges present their decisions as an interpretation and application of the existing legislation. Usually, they neither acknowledge that they are making the law nor openly address politically contested questions of policy. Nevertheless, it is not unlikely that the discussion of the foundations of delictual responsibility contributed to the judges' development of the law. These authors were the academic voices

[104] These developments have already been described, famously, by von Caemmerer, 'Wandlungen des Deliktsrechts'.

[105] N. Jansen, 'The development of legal doctrine in Europe: extracontractual liability for fault', in N. Jansen (ed.), *The Development and Making of Legal Doctrine*, pp. 1 ff.

[106] Jansen, *Die Struktur des Haftungsrechts*, pp. 385 ff.

[107] For references, see Jansen, *Die Struktur des Haftungsrechts*, pp. 377–85.

[108] See, especially, H.-L. Weyers, *Unfallschäden* (Frankfurt: Athenäum Verlag, 1971); and J. Fleming, J. Hellner and E. von Hippel, *Haftungsersetzung durch Versicherungsschutz* (Frankfurt: Metzner, 1980).

[109] On these debates, see Jansen, *Die Struktur des Haftungsrechts*, pp. 383 ff., pp. 558 ff.

[110] Jansen, 'The development of legal doctrine in Europe'.

of the changes in public morality that ultimately resulted in the judicial activity described above; and these voices were heard by the judges.[111]

[111] Indeed, all these issues have been discussed at the Karlsruher Forum, where the participants were leading judges of the Bundesgerichtshof, especially of the 6th Senat, which is in charge of non-contractual liability. These judges meet annually with leading academic tort and insurance lawyers and with leading representatives of the insurance industry.

10

The English codification debate and the role of jurists in the development of legal doctrines

ALEXANDRA BRAUN*

The complex debate surrounding codification in nineteenth- and twentieth-century Britain represents a fascinating aspect of English legal history, the appreciation of which would require a more thorough treatment than this chapter allows. Even though England never introduced a complete and comprehensive code, several attempts were undertaken over the centuries to introduce codifying measures in certain areas of the law. Although the idea of reducing English law to a systematic legal order is much older, a real codification movement developed only with Jeremy Bentham. His proposal for a complete legislative statement of the whole body of English law met, however, with little success. Nevertheless, the debate over codification did not come to an end with the failure of his efforts, nonetheless, and to some extent it still goes on. The need to improve the form of the law became apparent to many and eventually led to the adoption of a variety of measures, such as consolidating and codifying Acts of Parliament. Though never resulting in an English code, these instruments contributed to the reduction of the law into a more orderly and systematic shape. In addition to these acts, England developed a type of legal literature that contributed to the simplification and systematisation of the law, and, ultimately, probably functioned as a substitute for a code.

This chapter analyses the history of the nineteenth- and twentieth-century codification movement in England and attempts to understand why England never introduced a code such as the one Bentham envisaged. It asks what role legal scholars played in the debate and how they contributed to the development of the law through what Sir Henry Maine defined as the 'tacit codification' of English law.

* Fellow and Tutor in Law, Lady Margaret Hall, University of Oxford. CUF Lecturer, University of Oxford.

10.1 The nineteenth-century codification debate

Although, at least since the reign of Henry VIII, attempts had been undertaken to reduce parts of English law to a systematic legal order,[1] Bentham was the first to introduce the use of the expression 'codification'.[2] For him, existing law was terribly cumbersome and illogical and advanced only the interests of lawyers. In his opinion, the rules of common law were often based on historical accident rather than rational design and were simply obstacles in the way of major social reform. In fact, in the eighteenth and early nineteenth centuries, the state of the law was perceived by many as bulky, incomprehensive, contradictory and unwieldy. Statute law was vast, overgrown and incongruous and the common law obscure and lacking in clear principles.[3] Furthermore, much of English legal literature consisted of collections and abridgments of cases and did not therefore make the law more accessible or systematic.[4]

According to Bentham, the only answer to this state was the complete replacement of all law with a complete code of laws. Historians are divided over the sort of code Bentham ultimately envisaged, and over the degree of lawmaking power that his code would have granted to the judiciary.[5] It appears, however, that in the eyes of Bentham the complete code was meant to play a central role among the sources of law and that, as a consequence, everything that was outside the code was not to be considered law.[6] What he had in mind, therefore, implied a different understanding of the sources of English law. Even if Bentham did not completely rule

1 See, in particular, B. Shapiro, 'Codification of the laws in seventeenth-century England' (1974) *Wisconsin Law Review* 428 ff.; and B. Shapiro, 'Law reform in seventeenth-century England' (1975) 19 *Am. J. Legal Hist.* 280 ff.

2 J. H. Baker, *An Introduction to English Legal History* (London: Butterworths, 2002), p. 217, n. 127; W. Holdsworth, 'Bentham's place in English legal history' (1940) 28 *California Law Review* 568 ff., 583.

3 See T. Wood, *An Institute of the Laws of England*, 5th edn (London: B. Lintot and R. Williamson, 1734), pp. i–iii.

4 J. C. Gray, *The Nature and Sources of the Law* (New York: Columbia University Press, 1909), p. 247; A. W. B Simpson, 'The rise and fall of the legal treatise: legal principles and the form of legal literature' (1981) 48 *U. Chi. L. Rev.* 632 ff., 663–6; F. Pollock, *A Digest of the Law of Partnership*, 4th edn (London: Stevens & Sons, 1888), p. xviii: 'We have a number of treatises overlapping one another in all directions, and yet letting many things entirely or almost entirely fall through.'

5 See M. Lobban, *The Common Law and English Jurisprudence 1760–1850* (Oxford: Clarendon Press, 1991), chs. 5–7, esp. p. 117.

6 J. Bentham, 'General view of a complete code of laws' [1782], in J. Bowring (ed.), *The Works of Jeremy Bentham* (11 vols.), vol. III (Edinburgh: W. Tait, 1859), p. 205.

out a judicial contribution to the process of legislation, there is no doubt that the function of the judges would have significantly changed under the presence of such a code. Their power would have been limited by the legal propositions expressed in the code. In other words, judges would have been dethroned from their role as principal lawmakers and forced to become interpreters of the law as expressed in the code.

As is well known, Bentham never really managed to produce a complete and detailed code as he had himself envisaged,[7] and, for reasons that I explore later, his proposals did not find many supporters. His attacks on the common law had a strong influence on the way nineteenth-century lawyers perceived the law, however, and, indeed, paved the way for attempts to render English law more systematic and accessible to practitioners and laymen. Nevertheless, although it was evident that both statute and common law were in need of systematisation, clarification and simplification, many doubted whether this goal would be best achieved by means of a code. The result was that much energy went into the consolidation of statute law rather than codification. This was not only because consolidation left the common law untouched, but also because consolidating acts became law with virtually no debate. However, what consolidation actually meant was not always entirely clear, and it does not therefore come as a surprise to find that the terms 'codification' and 'consolidation' were used in a somewhat loose fashion.

Attempts at formulating consolidating statutes aside, the 'code' was occasionally invoked again as a potentially useful measure for improving the state of English law. Following Henry Brougham's famous speech to the House of Commons in 1828,[8] two Royal Commissions were appointed, one on real property and one on criminal law, with the function of producing a 'digest' that could replace the existing common law and statute law. Though Brougham, who would soon become Lord Chancellor, sympathised with Bentham, he preferred the idea of a digest to a code, intending only to 'consolidate, arrange and systematize' the law without essentially altering it.[9] Moreover, although it is undoubtedly true that the terms 'digest' and 'code' were often used interchangeably, the kind of final product these two commissions envisaged was a good deal removed

[7] Lobban, *The Common Law*, p. 119.

[8] HC Deb. vol. 28 (NS) cols. 241, 244, 245 (1828).

[9] H. Brougham, 'Letter from Lord Brougham to Sir James Graham, on the making and digesting of the law (London, 1849)', in *The Making of the Modern World* (Gale, 2010, http://galenet.galegroup.com/servlet/MOME?af=RN&ae=U3606888672&srchtp=a&ste=14;, last accessed 5 October 2010), pp. 11 ff.

from what Bentham had hoped for.[10] In any case, in the end, both Royal Commissions fell short of codification.

The Real Property Commission was strongly influenced by James Humphrey's *Outline of a Code of the Laws of Real Property*,[11] but ended up opposing the project and expressing a number of recommendations that were informed by an attempt to preserve the spirit and language of the common law. At the same time, the Royal Commission on the Criminal Law, set up in 1831, did considerable work and produced eight substantial reports, published between 1833 and 1845. The reports appeared at a time when the climate had changed significantly, however, and the opposition to codification had once again grown. As a result, Brougham's efforts remained unsuccessful. Nevertheless, the call for a codification became strong again during the second half of the nineteenth century,[12] when several substantial attempts to codify parts of different areas of English law were undertaken. The idea of a 'code' found new support, both in Britain and in the colonial territories. In England this support was concerned especially with two areas: criminal law and commercial law.

10.1.1 Criminal law

As with the attempts to codify criminal law that were undertaken during the first half of the nineteenth century, later efforts were equally unsuccessful.[13] In 1853 Lord Cranworth, the Lord Chancellor, submitted to English judges a draft bill to 'codify' the criminal law, which he hoped would result in a 'Code Victoria'.[14] The judges replied unanimously in

[10] M. Lobban, 'How Benthamic was the Criminal Law Commission?' (2000) 18 *Law and History Review* 427 ff.; contra L. Farmer, 'Reconstructing the English codification debate' (2000) 18 *Law and History Review* 403 ff.

[11] B. Rudden, 'A code too soon: the 1828 Property Code of James Humphreys: English rejection, American reception, English acceptance', in P. Wallington and R. M. Merkin (eds.), *Essays in Memory of Professor F. H. Lawson* (London: Butterworths, 1986), p. 101 ff.

[12] Codification became a topic of discussion in newspapers and law journals such as, for instance, the *Law Times*, the *Edinburgh Review*, the *Papers of the Juridical Society*, the *New Century Review*, the *Law Magazine* and the *Quarterly Review of Jurisprudence*. See M. Graziadei, 'Changing images of the law in XIX century English legal thought', in M. Reimann (ed.), *The Reception of Continental Ideas in the Common Law World, 1820–1920* (Berlin: Duncker & Humblot, 1993), p. 115 ff., p. 132.

[13] For an outline of the history of the codification of English commercial law, see [Dame] M. Arden, 'Time for an English commercial code?' (1997) 56 *CLJ* 516 ff.

[14] HL Deb. 3rd series, vol. 124 col. 41 ff. 58–66 (14 February 1853).

unfavourable terms, however.[15] Unlike Lord Brougham, Lord Cranworth was mainly concerned with the reform of statute law. In fact, he created an informal statutes revision board (which he eventually replaced with a Statute Law Commission) with the goal of beginning the process of revision and consolidation. Although Cranworth was unable to achieve the consolidation of any legislation during his chancellorship, the statutes were eventually consolidated and became part of the Criminal Law Consolidation Acts of 1861.

Only two years later, in 1863, Lord Westbury LC raised the matter of 'codification' and reform in Parliament,[16] and in 1866 a Royal Commission was established under the chairmanship of Lord Cranworth 'to enquire into the expediency of a digest of law'. The commission recommended the preparation of *digests*, not *codes*, of particular branches of the law, excluding criminal law. The commission determined instead to perform its experiments in particular in three areas of private law: bills of exchange, mortgages and easements. Several barristers took over the task, but ultimately the digests were judged unsatisfactory and no further steps were taken.

Some ten years later Stephen Martin Leake produced draft digests of contract and property law in the hope that they would be conducive to the advancement of the law in the direction of a public code or digest, but they never led to legislation.[17] In 1876 Sir James Fitzjames Stephen published a *Digest of the Law of Evidence*, and, in the following year, a *Digest of the Criminal Law*. Most notably, the *Digest of the Criminal Law* aroused new interest and led to the appointment of another Royal Commission, which in 1879 produced a draft criminal code. The time for codification seemed ripe. The Criminal Code Bill was introduced by the government and then referred to a Royal Commission composed of eminent judges, such as Lord Blackburn (the chairman), Lord Justice Lush, Mr Justice Barry and Stephen himself, who were clearly in favour of the measure. When the bill was reintroduced into Parliament, however, it never passed into law. Those who hoped that it would be possible to codify an entire branch of English law were soon disillusioned.

[15] *Copies of the Lord Chancellor's Letters to the Judges and of their Answers respecting the Criminal Law Bills of the last session* no. 303 (1854). *Parliamentary Papers* 1854 (389) LII.

[16] HL Deb. 3rd series, vol. 171, col. 775 (12 June 1863); J. F. Macqueen, *Speech of the Lord Chancellor on the Revision of the Law* (London: W. Maxwell, 1863).

[17] S. M. Leake, *An Elementary Digest of the Law of Property in Land* (London: Stevens & Sons, 1874); S. M. Leake, *An Elementary Digest of the Law of Contracts* (London: Stevens & Sons, 1878).

10.1.2 Commercial law

The attempts at a codification of English commercial law were similarly difficult and laborious. As early as 1853 a Royal Commission had been set up to analyse the differences between the mercantile laws of England and Scotland and to show how they could be overcome.[18] After 1856 attention turned away from the particular matter of commercial law, however, and focused more on criminal law. Things changed towards the end of the 1870s, following the success German lawyers had in producing a common commercial code in 1862.[19] The idea of a 'code of commercial law' was then advanced, but, because of the failure of the proposed criminal law code, Lord Chancellor Selborne was unreceptive. Selborne suggested that, instead of a complete code of commercial law, suitable branches of commercial law should be codified. As a result, albeit after several unsuccessful attempts, towards the end of the nineteenth century three codifying acts were passed: the Bills of Exchange Act 1882, the Partnership Act 1890 and the Sale of Goods Act 1893.

The first codifying enactment which found its way into the English statute book was the Bills of Exchange Act 1882. Based upon the *Digest of the Law of Bills of Exchange*, produced by Mackenzie Chalmers and drafted following the experience of the working of the Indian codes,[20] the purpose of the act was to reproduce as exactly as possible the present law rather than to codify it. Chalmers knew that a project aimed at more profound reforms would encounter opposition, and he was therefore in favour of a more cautious approach.[21] The Partnership Act 1890, drafted by Sir Frederick Pollock (based upon his *Digest of the Law of Partnership*, which was inspired by Stephen's *Digest of the Law of Evidence* and *Digest of the Criminal Law* mentioned earlier), proposed considerable changes to the law, and did indeed take longer to be approved.[22] Although it was finalised before the Bills of Exchange Act, it was 1890 before it became law. Three years later, in 1893, the Sale of Goods Act was enacted. Like the earlier Bills of Exchange Act, it was drafted by Mackenzie Chalmers and

[18] J. Kirkpatrick, 'On the codification of mercantile law' (1880) 24 *Journal of Jurisprudence* 638 ff., 640. See also M. D. Chalmers, 'Codification of mercantile law' (1903) 20 *LQR* 10 ff.

[19] A. [Lord] Rodger, 'The codification of commercial law in Victorian Britain' (1992) 109 *LQR* 570 ff., 575 ff.

[20] M. D. Chalmers, 'An experiment in codification' (1886) 2 *LQR* 125 ff., 128.

[21] Chalmers, 'An experiment in codification'.

[22] Interestingly, although Pollock preferred to employ the term 'digest', Chalmers himself spoke of 'codifying enactments'.

was not an attempt to reform or revise the law, only to reproduce the law as it was.

Thus, instead of a complete codification in the field of commercial law, England introduced three 'codifying acts', which were soon followed by others, such as the Arbitration Act 1889,[23] the Marine Insurance Act 1906 and the Companies (Consolidation) Act 1908.[24] Unlike consolidating acts, these codifying acts not only gathered together and harmonised statutory enactments but also embodied the common law. At the same time, however, they did not represent codes in the sense that Bentham had envisaged, and this was probably the reason why they could be passed in the first place. None of the three acts abrogated the old law; they only restated in legislative form existing case and statute law. Courts were therefore still able to make reference to cases decided before these acts.[25] Hence, the rules of the common law continued to be in force except insofar as they were inconsistent with the express provisions of the act.[26] In other words, what these codifying acts achieved was the systematisation of the law in the respective areas.

In the course of the second half of the nineteenth century the debate thus shifted its focus from the project of a complete and comprehensive codification of entire branches of English law towards a systematic revision of limited areas through piecemeal codifying measures. Perhaps not surprisingly, much of the stimulus for these codification attempts derived from the success of the codes that had meanwhile been adopted in India.

[23] This act was preceded by Lord Bramwell's arbitration code of 1884–9, which was never adopted, however. See V. V. Veeder and B. Dye, 'Lord Bramwell's arbitration code 1884–1889' (1992) 8 *Arbitration International* 329 ff.

[24] In the course of the twentieth century similar codifying acts were introduced also in the field of criminal law, such as the Perjury Act 1911, the Forger Act 1913 and the Larceny Act 1916.

[25] The courts were called upon to decide whether previous case law could still be referred to. Favourable to this solution was Cave J in *Re Gillespie, ex p. Robarts* (1885) 16 QBD 702 and the Court of Appeal in *Vagliano Brothers* v. *Bank of England* (1889) 23 QBD 243 (CA). In the House of Lords, however, Lord Herschell expressed the view that previous cases ought not to be taken into consideration unless for some special reason (*Bank of England* v. *Vagliano Brothers* [1891] AC 107, 144–145 (HL)). The view was shared by Cozens-Hardy MR in *Bristol Tramways* v. *Fiat Co.* [1891] AC 144. In practice, however, judges and practitioners continued to refer to previous case law.

[26] See the so-called 'saving clauses' contained in the various acts: Bills of Exchange Act 1882, sect. 97; Partnership Act 1890, sect. 46; Sale of Goods Act 1893, sect. 61(2) (Sale of Goods Act 1979, sect. 62(2)); Marine Insurance Act 1906, sect. 91(2).

10.1.3 The Indian codes

Although the idea of a code was opposed in England, it was acknowledged as a valid tool for the colonial territories. Aside from representing an effective way of imposing English law on the colonies, codes were a useful measure in providing India with a complete and defined system of law, which was much needed in the absence of an educated legal profession and with no body of legal literature at its disposal.

Work on the codes started when the Indian Charter of 1833 provided for the appointment of a London-based Law Commission, which, within two years, published a first draft of the Indian Penal Code. These efforts did not become law until 1860, however, by which time a new Commission had been at work for some years. Its recommendations resulted in important legislation. Apart from the Penal Code, in 1859 a Code of Civil Procedure was passed, followed by a Code of Criminal Procedure in 1861, all of which adopted a particular style, incorporating hypothetical factual examples.[27]

In 1861 a third commission was nominated, which went on to present seven reports altogether, but the friction that had arisen between the Law Commissioners and the government of India prevented many of their proposals from being implemented. Thanks to Stephen, the beginning of the 1870s was a period of great legislative activity, with the introduction of the Contract Act.[28] This activity soon came to an end, however, as a result of the uneasiness that the rapidity and amount of legislation passed had caused, both in India and in England.

At the end of that decade the government of India proposed the appointment of a new commission, with the task of completing the codification of substantive law. This was to be based in India, not in England. The commission was set up in 1879 and started reporting at the end of that same year. For the first time tort law came under consideration. Maine had been consulted, and he submitted memoranda that stressed the importance of codifying the law of torts. The commission agreed that the law of wrongs should be codified, and the government of India instructed Pollock to prepare a draft bill on the subject of torts or civil wrongs, which

[27] W. Stokes (ed.), *The Anglo-Indian Codes* (2 vols), vol. I (Oxford: Clarendon Press, 1887), pp. xxiii–xxvii. See also B. C. Acharyya, *Codification in British India* (Calcutta: S. K. Banerji, 1914). For a history of the codification in India, see C. P. Ilbert, *Legislative Methods and Forms* (Oxford: Clarendon Press, 1901), pp. 129 ff.

[28] C. P. Ilbert, 'Sir James Stephen as a legislator' (1894) 10 *LQR* 222 ff.

he completed in 1886.[29] In the end, though, no attempt was made to proceed with it. With the exception of the law of torts, however, all the most important branches of English law applicable to India were codified.[30] India therefore turned out to be the most successful field of application of English codification.

10.2 Why no 'legislative' code for England?

Although several codes had been introduced in Continental legal systems, and even in India, by the end of the nineteenth century England was still without a code, leaving aside the codifying acts. There are several reasons why English law never came to complete codification. First, the political and legal conditions in England were different from those leading to the Continental codifications. In Germany and Italy, the code was a tool for the creation of territorial and legal unity.[31] More generally, on the Continent the plurality of legal sources rendered the law highly insecure and arbitrary and required a unified legislative foundation.[32] In England, on the other hand, political and legal unity had already been achieved long beforehand.

Moreover, in France the code represented a way not only to unify the law but also to subordinate the judges to the legislator, and so to limit their lawmaking powers.[33] The complexity of the sources of law and the profusion of the law was giving judges too much discretion, and the code was thus seen as a means through which their power could be weakened.[34] A similar worry does not seem to have existed in England. In addition, the Continental codes were the expression of a desire to manage the overwhelming doctrinal material and to keep the proliferation of literature under control.[35] No such problem emerged in English

[29] The draft is contained in the thirteenth edition of Sir Frederick Pollock's *The Law of Torts*, 13th edn (London: Steven & Sons, 1929), pp. 618 ff.

[30] Pollock, *The Law of Torts*, pp. 618 ff. According to Pollock, a considerable majority of the opinions from judicial and other officers were unfavourable to the code.

[31] In the United States, a certain degree of legal unity was achieved through the Restatements.

[32] N. Jansen, *The Making of Legal Authority: Non-Legislative Codifications in Historical and Comparative Perspective* (Oxford University Press, 2010), p. 16.

[33] See the contribution in this volume by Jean-Louis Halpérin, Chapter 8.

[34] P. Stein, *The Character and Influence of the Roman Civil Law: Historical Essays* (London: Hambledon Press, 1988), p. 142.

[35] D. Ibbetson, 'English law and the European *ius commune* 1450–1650', in J. Bell and C. Kilpatrick (eds.), *The Cambridge Yearbook of European Legal Studies*, vol. 8 (Oxford: Hart, 2006), pp. 115 ff., pp. 131–2.

law, with the production of legal literature growing only somewhat later. Hence, some of the forces behind the Continental codifications were missing.

Furthermore, in England the debate over codification was initiated mostly by the enthusiasm and drive of individuals rather than by a political agenda or by identifiable powerful interest groups. In fact, although by the middle of the nineteenth century codification was on the agenda of the government, in England the code never became an instrument of political power. In addition to the lack of strong governmental support, there was in general little public interest in codification.[36] The only real pressure seemed to come from within the commercial world.[37]

To this one has to add the lack of interest, and at times resistance, of a fairly conservative legal profession.[38] Although it admitted a need to reform the law, it remained suspicious of codification. At all times, solicitors, barristers and judges were involved in the different stages of the codification and consolidation attempts, but the type of 'code' they envisaged was not going to affect the substance or the content of English law, nor would it have affected the lawmaking power of the judiciary. The idea of a code that would become the central source of the legal system was indeed foreign to them. Statute law had always been seen as merely correcting the common law or as a gap-filling measure, and Parliament had left the development of the law to the judges. The introduction of a complete and comprehensive code would have involved a legislative formulation of a series of general rules in particular areas of the law, thus implying a rejection of the common law as the ultimate repository of legal principle in the area of law to be codified.

This would obviously have changed the status and role of judges, who would no longer have been able to 'make' law. Law would have been made by the legislature, and brought under popular control through

[36] In this sense, see Pollock, *A Digest of the Law of Partnership*, p. xxviii.

[37] The Bills of Exchange Act 1882, for instance, was promoted by the Banker's Institute and the Associated Chambers of Commerce. See R. B. Ferguson, 'Legal ideology and commercial interests: the social origins of the commercial law codes' (1977) 4 *B.J.L.S.* 8 ff.; and Rodger, 'The codification of commercial law', 586. On the other hand, the Sale of Goods Act 1893 seems to have been mainly the result of a move for legal rationality from certain members of the profession. In this sense, see J. H. Farrar and A. M. Dugdale, *Introduction to Legal Method*, 2nd edn (London: Sweet & Maxwell, 1984), p. 178.

[38] Not all judges were against the idea of a code. The Criminal Law Code was mostly defeated by the opposition coming from Cockburn LCJ, but among the judges in favour of it was, for instance, Blackburn J. Equally in favour of a codification was Sir James Fitzjames Stephen.

democratic procedures. It does not come as a surprise, therefore, that the legal profession was rather lukewarm about the idea of a complete and comprehensive code. Furthermore, since the common law was an oral tradition, English lawyers were not accustomed to working around a developed body of written law. They may also have been afraid that a code would inhibit the gradual development of the law.[39] In addition, unlike on the Continent, in England the legal profession was somewhat suspicious of generalisations and seemed to believe that general propositions of law had to be misleading.[40] Finally, as Max Weber put it, 'In England the reason for the failure of all efforts at a rational codification of law...was due to the successful resistance against such rationalisation offered by the great and centrally organized lawyers' guilds... [T]hey successfully fought all moves towards rational law that threatened their social material position.'[41]

This conservatism on the part of the profession is perhaps explicable given the poor state of English legal education at the time. In other words, the legal profession was not acquainted with the scientific study of law and therefore took little interest in the question.[42] Indeed, the codification proposals and the underlying attacks on the state of the law gave rise to defences of common law reasoning.[43] In France, the legal profession too had opposed the idea of a code, but in this case the codification movement was backed not just by a strong political agenda but also by a strong academic profession, which was absent in England. Until the end of the nineteenth century England had not developed a community of legal scholars able to prepare the ground for a code or to be involved in its drafting, such as was, for instance, the case in Germany and France. In a certain sense, there was a lack of intellectual context.

In addition, the introduction of a code would have required changes to the style of parliamentary acts. Since codifying statutes sought to cover

[39] That, in reality, codes are never a suitable device for controlling the law's further development, is suggested by Jansen, *The Making of Legal Authority*, p. 18.

[40] In this sense, see J. F. Stephen, *A Digest of the Law of Evidence* (London: Macmillan, 1876), p. xvi.

[41] H. H. Gerth and C. Wright Mills (eds.), *From Max Weber: Essays in Sociology* (London: Routledge, 1948), pp. 217–18.

[42] Among the practitioners in favour of a codification were W. Blake Odgers and Vaughn Hawkins. See V. Hawkins, 'Digests and codes, with reference to law reform' (1870) 3 *Papers Read before the Juridical Society* 110. Among the opponents one could count W. M. Best (1858) 1 *Papers Read before the Juridical Society* 209; and J. P. Wilde (1864) 38 *Law Times* 518 ff.

[43] Lobban, *The Common Law*, pp. 219–22.

every foreseeable situation and had always been conceived of as derogations from the common law, new methods of drafting and different rules of interpretation would have been necessary. It is not therefore surprising to find that resistance also came from within Parliament, which, jealous of its power, scrutinised very closely any reforming instruments.[44] The lack of a special parliamentary procedure for codification measures allowed parliamentary control to slow down the reform process. Conservatism on the part of the legal profession as well as the inaction (if not resistance) of the legislature thus played a significant role in preventing the introduction of a code.[45]

Finally, because of dissatisfaction with procedural law, much energy went into this area. It might well be that both these problems – civil procedure and the rise of social legislation – diverted attention from issues of substantive law, which was probably thought of as sufficiently developed.[46]

10.3 'Codification' through private academic enterprise

Those who were in favour of a code saw it as a tool that could bring the common law into order by setting it forth in a systematic and comprehensible way. In other words, the code was perceived as a promising response to the need for certainty and predictability in the law, which could render English law more compact and accessible to lawyers and laymen alike, and which would favour a logical and coherent development of the law. The concern was thus to improve the form of the common law rather than to change its substance.

As mentioned earlier, in some areas of the law these objectives were achieved partly by means of codifying acts, which were based on digests written by legal writers so as to facilitate a codification of a specific

[44] A. H. Manchester, *A Modern Legal History of England and Wales 1750–1950* (London: Butterworths, 1980), p. 47. According to Stephen, *Digest of the Law of Evidence*, p. xv, the reluctance of Parliament was attributable to a lack of confidence: 'I am now convinced by experience that the unwillingness of the legislature to undertake such an operation proceeds from a want of confidence in its power to deal with such subjects, which is neither unnatural nor unfounded. It would be as impossible to get in Parliament a really satisfactory discussion of a Bill codifying the law of evidence as to get a committee of the whole House to paint a picture.'

[45] For a discussion of the possible difficulties of a codification, see A. L. Diamond, 'Codification of the law of contract' (1968) 31 *MLR* 361 ff.

[46] See, in this sense, R. Pound, *Jurisprudence* (5 vols.), vol. III (St Paul, MN: West, 1959), p. 676.

area of the law.[47] Alongside these texts, other legal textbooks and treatises were produced that took the form of codes. Examples of such texts include Albert Venn Dicey's *Rules for the Selection of the Parties to an Action* (1870), his *Law of Domicil as a Branch of the Law of England stated in the Form of Rules* (1879) and his *Digest of the Law of England with Reference to the Conflict of Laws* (1896); Spencer Bower's *Code of Actionable Defamation with a Continuous Commentary* (1908) and his *Law of Actionable Misrepresentation Stated in the Form of a Code, followed by a Commentary* (1911); William Bowstead's *Digest of the Law of Agency* (1896); and Sir Arthur Underhill's *The Law Relating to Trusts and Trustees* (1878).

These were not, however, the only genres of legal literature produced at that time. With the development of the academic study of the law, towards the end of the nineteenth century a new type of book emerged, the 'modern textbook', which contributed significantly to the development of the law. In fact, the late nineteenth-century academics published textbooks that, unlike practitioner textbooks, consisted of an analysis of existing case law aimed at identifying the underlying principles of law and linking them to a systematic and coherent doctrine.[48] These books were meant to fill the gaps left by the disappearance of the forms of action and, in the absence of a code, to promote a more systematic development of the law.[49] Most nineteenth-century legal academics, such as Sheldon Amos,[50]

[47] J. F. Stephen, *A Digest of the Criminal Law* (London: Macmillan, 1877), p. vi: 'I felt, however, that the course taken by the Committee was a reason, not for laying aside the subject, but for attempting to exemplify the possibility and convenience of codifying the Criminal Law by performing, as a private enterprise, the work of making a Digest of it which might serve as a first step towards a Code.'

[48] A. W. B. Simpson, 'The rise and fall of the legal treatise: legal principles and the forms of legal literature', in *Legal Theory and Legal History: Essays on the Common Law* (London: Hambledon Press, 1987), pp. 273 ff., p. 305; T. F. T. Plucknett, *Early English Legal Literature* (Cambridge University Press, 1958), p. 19; C. H. S. Fifoot, *Judge and Jurist in the Reign of Victoria* (London: Stevens & Sons, 1959), p. 27.

[49] F. H. Lawson, 'Doctrinal writing: a foreign element in English law?', in E. Caemmerer, S. Mentschikoff and K. Zweigert (eds.), *Ius Privatum Gentium: Festschrift für Max Rheinstein zum 70. Geburtstag am 5. July 1969*, vol. I (Tübingen: Mohr Siebeck, 1969), pp. 191 ff.

[50] S. Amos, *Science of Law* (London: Stevens & Sons, 1874), ch. 13, p. 360; S. Amos, *A Systematic View of the Science of Jurisprudence* (London: Longmans, Green, 1872), p. 471; S. Amos, *An English Code: Its Difficulties and the Modes of Overcoming Them* (London: Strahan, 1873).

John Austin,[51] Dicey,[52] Sir Thomas Erskine Holland,[53] Maine and Pollock, believed that codification was highly desirable. In fact, Pollock and Maine were even involved in the codification process in India. They saw codification as a tool to improve not only the state of the law, but also the quality of legal education and the character of the legal profession.[54] However, some legal writers sensed that codification by authority would be a difficult endeavour, and therefore suggested codification by private enterprise.[55] In other words, in the absence of a code, 'indirect legislation' through legal writings was seen as a valuable alternative.[56] As Sir Courtney Ilbert put it: 'A good text-book...has often been the foundation of a code, and in the meantime is not a bad substitute.'[57]

Legal writers could not, of course, enact general principles in authoritative form, nor could they make the law more certain,[58] but they could produce private texts that reduced the mass of contradictory case law into an ordered and rational set of principles, and hence facilitate the work of the legal practitioner by rendering the law more accessible. To a certain

[51] J. Austin, *Lectures on Jurisprudence*, 5th edn (2 vols.), vol. II (London: John Murray, 1885), lecture 39; J. Austin, 'Notes on codification', in *Lectures on Jurisprudence*, vol. II, p. 1021.

[52] A. V. Dicey, *Can English Law Be Taught at the Universities?* (London: Macmillan, 1883), pp. 26–7.

[53] See T. E. Holland, 'Codification', *Edinburgh Review*, October 1867; T. E. Holland, 'A plan for the formal amendment of the law of England', *Edinburgh Review*, March 1867. Both papers are republished in T. E. Holland, *Essays upon the Form of the Law* (London: Butterworths, 1870).

[54] At the same time, they believed that the improvement of the teaching would have an impact on the development of treatises and codes: Dicey, *Can English Law*, p. 27.

[55] Pollock, *A Digest of the Law of Partnership*, p. iii, p. xxvii.

[56] This view was shared also by some practitioners, such as Stephen and the Parliamentary Counsel to the Treasury, Sir Courtney Ilbert. Ilbert, *Legislative Methods and Forms*, p. 161: 'What is needed to supply the motive power and the material for codification in England is the improvement of legal education, and the concomitant improvement of legal textbooks.' Stephen shared the same view: *A Digest of the Law of Evidence*, p. xvi: 'Hence, if anything considerable is to be done towards the reduction of the law to a system, it must, at present at least, be done by private writers.'

[57] C. P. Ilbert, 'A plea for the codification of English law' (1897) 6 *New Century Review* 475 ff., 490.

[58] In contrast to the Continent, where the need to ensure the certainty and predictability of the law was furthered by the introduction of codes, in England protection against arbitrarily administered justice was met by the binding character of precedent: A. Tunc, 'The grand outlines of the code', in B. Schartz (ed.), *The Code Napoleon and the Common-Law World* (New York University Press, 1956) pp. 19 ff., p. 19; S. Vogenauer, 'Zur Geschichte des Präjudizienrechts in England' (2006) 28 *ZNR* 48 ff.

extent, their works were functionally equivalent to the type of code envisaged at that time. In the absence of a compact body of law that is self-sufficient and establishes authoritatively what the law is, legal scholars developed doctrines or theories of law and contributed to the shaping of the common law. However, these textbooks were not published just to fill the gaps left by the absence of a code or to make the law more accessible. They were also meant to improve the state of legal education, and thus to be used as introductory books for students. Furthermore, by producing a type of legal literature that could be valuable to students and practitioners alike, legal academics also sought to find a way to legitimate their function and their role in the eyes of a sceptical legal profession.[59]

Through these works, academics set off an intellectual transformation of the common law that did not encounter the direct opposition of the legal profession. This is not altogether surprising. Textbooks can be consulted, but they are not authority. Thus, judges can depart from them at any time. They do not call into question the position of the judiciary as lawmaker and do not interfere with or alter the law in a direct manner. Furthermore, since they do not carry legislative force, their presentation of the law has the advantage of being more flexible. In fact, they can be changed without difficulty. Lastly, they leave the control of the lawmaking process in the hands of lawyers, of technocrats, and not in the hands of laymen. In all, textbooks fulfilled an important function, and, ironically, one of the arguments invoked later against the codification of English law was that, with the presence of textbooks, codes were no longer needed.[60]

These modern textbooks covered most areas of the common law, including tort law. Although tort law developed rather late and mainly through the initiative of judges, jurists also contributed to shaping the English law of torts in various ways.[61] On the one hand, academics became members of various reform committees,[62] and had an impact on the development of statute law that way. On the other hand, through their writings they also influenced the development of the common law. As Michael Lobban

[59] A. Braun, *Giudici e Accademia nell'esperienza inglese: Storia di un dialogo* (Bologna: Mulino, 2006), pp. 120–8.

[60] In this sense, see Lord Goff, 'Judge, jurist and legislature' (1987) *Denning Law Journal* 79 ff., 92.

[61] For an examination of the contribution made by academic writers, see P. S. Atiyah, *Pragmatism and Theory in English Law* (London: Stevens & Sons, 1987), pp. 174 ff. See also Fifoot, *Judge and Jurist*, pp. 52 ff.

[62] An example is the Law Revision Committee, appointed by Lord Sankey in 1934. Several reports relate to fault liability.

has shown,[63] among the legal academics who played a major role in tort law are Pollock and Sir John Salmond, who, at the end of the nineteenth century, attempted to develop a theory of tort law distinguished from the law of contract.[64] By applying the method of analytical jurisprudence (but also by borrowing ideas from Continental writers),[65] they tried to identify the principles underlying the law generated by the history of the common law, thereby fixing the contents and boundaries of this area of law. As mentioned above, the object of writing treatises was to make the common law more systematic and coherent. In the field of tort law, this meant explaining the law in terms of underlying interests and identifying the traditional forms of action with the protection of distinct types of interest or the prevention of distinct types of harm, damage or injury. Further, in the attempt to find an underlying unifying principle, legal writers focused on the grounds for liability, be that intent, negligence or strict liability. Whether and to what extent they succeeded is another issue,[66] which is not treated in this chapter. Nevertheless, these efforts seem to have been particularly important in the absence of any attempt to codify or consolidate the law in this area.

10.4 A debate that has not come to an end

The closure of the nineteenth century did not bring the codification debate to an end. Interest in a code revived in the first half of the twentieth century, but soon faded at the outbreak of the First World War. With the establishment of the Law Commission in 1965, however, the idea of codifying English law once again became popular in Britain.[67] Indeed, one of the tasks of the Law Commission consists in reviewing the law with a view to its systematic development and reform, including, inter alia, its codification.[68] The Law Commissions Act 1965 thus contemplates codification

[63] See the contribution by Michael Lobban in this volume, Chapter 6. See, further, M. Lobban, 'Common law reasoning and the foundations of modern private law' (2007) 32 *Australian Journal of Legal Philosophy* 39 ff.

[64] For an analysis of their contribution, see J. Gordley, *Foundations of Private Law: Property, Tort, Contract, Unjust Enrichment* (Oxford University Press, 2006), p. 159.

[65] M. Graziadei, 'Stili dottrinali nell'area anglo-americana e modelli di civil law' (1989) *Quadrimestre* 537 ff.; Gordley, *Foundations of Private Law*, p. 159.

[66] Quite critical is Atiyah, *Pragmatism and Theory in English Law*, p. 179.

[67] Lord Chorley and G. Dworkin, 'The Law Commission Act, 1965' (1965) 28 *MLR* 675 ff.

[68] According to North, a former law commissioner, '[T]he whole purpose and ethos of the Law Commission at the time of its creation was directed towards codification of some areas at least of the common law.' P. M. North, 'Problems of codification in a common law system' (1982) 46 *RabelsZ* 490 ff., 491.

but does not require it.[69] It is therefore left up to the Law Commission to decide whether it would regard a code as a useful tool towards achieving the simplification and modernisation of English law.

Quite surprisingly, the Law Commissions Act 1965 provides no definition of what is intended by a code. From the debates preceding the enactment of the act, it would appear that Parliament was referring to the codifying acts that had been introduced at the end of the nineteenth century.[70] It would seem, however, that, during a joint meeting of the English and Scottish Law Commissions in February 1968, the assumption was made that the commissions' proposed codes should contain provisions of greater generality than those contained in the United Kingdom or English codifying statutes, though of less generality than those in the codes of the civilian legal systems.[71] On the other hand, Sir Leslie Scarman, the first chairman of the English Law Commission, appears to have favoured a definition of 'code' more in line with Bentham's idea. Scarman described the code as a species of enacted law that purports to formulate the law so that it becomes, within the 'field of its application, the primary source of the law'.[72] Thus, it is not clear what type of code the Law Commission envisaged. Be that as it may, the wording of section 3(1)[73] of the 1965 act reveals that only areas of law in need of specific reform can be codified, not the entire law.[74]

In light of this provision, the Law Commission started working on a progressive and gradual codification of single areas considered to be in need of modernisation and systematisation, such as contract law, the law of landlord and tenant, criminal law and family law.[75] The first attempt at codification made by the commission was in the area of contract law. Harvey McGregor QC was appointed to draft a code of contract law for the English and Scottish Law Commissions as a joint project. The preparation

69 L. Scarman, *A Code of English Law? A Lecture Given in the University of Hull on 25 February 1966* (University of Hull, 1966), p. 3.

70 See A. E. Anton, 'Obstacles to codification' (1982) *Juridical Review* 15 ff., 19.

71 Anton, 'Obstacles to codification', 20.

72 Scarman, *A Code of English Law?*, p. 3.

73 Section 3(1) states: 'It shall be the duty of each of the Commissions to take and keep under review all the law with which they are respectively concerned with a view to its systematic development and reform, including in particular the codification of such law, the elimination of anomalies, the repeal of obsolete and unnecessary enactments, the reduction of the number of separate enactments and generally the simplification and modernisation of the law.'

74 L. Scarman, *Codification and Judge-Made Law: A Problem of Co-Existence* (University of Birmingham, 1966).

75 Law Commission, 'First programme of law reform', Law Com. no. 1 (1965); Law Commission, 'Second programme of law reform', Law Com. no. 14 (1968).

of drafts started in 1966 and lasted for over six years. The outcome was a draft that attempted to reform, as well as to harmonise, the law in this field.[76] However, a lack of resources – as well as interest – in the project outside the commission, and difficulties in finding agreement between England and Scotland as to what the unified rules of contract for the whole of the United Kingdom should be, brought the project to a halt. As a consequence, in 1971 the Scottish Law Commission withdrew from the project, and a year later the English Law Commission suspended work on the code and decided to adopt a topic-by-topic approach.[77] Although the project has not been officially abandoned, it is now moribund.

Equally unsuccessful (though not a joint project of the two commissions) was the attempt to codify the law of landlord and tenant.[78] The person in charge of preparing the code was L. A. Blundell QC, who had been asked to draft a set of propositions that would constitute the framework of the code. The commission focused mostly on a few areas that were perceived as particularly controversial, among which were the obligations of landlords and tenants. Although the Law Commission published a 'Report and draft bill on obligations of landlords and tenants' in 1975,[79] resistance at governmental level soon made it clear that the project had no realistic prospects of success. The commission therefore concentrated on a statutory restatement of a number of aspects of the law in which reform appeared particularly desirable, and no code was ever enacted.

Although some substantial progress had been made, difficulties were also faced in the field of criminal law. A draft criminal code was first presented in 1985,[80] but, after having been revised, expanded and republished in 1989,[81] it met with a mixed response.[82] As was the case in other areas, it

[76] H. McGregor, *Contract Code: Drawn Up on Behalf of the English Law Commission* (London: Sweet & Maxwell, 1994).

[77] Law Commission, 'Eighth Annual Report, 1972–1973', Law Com. no. 58 (1973), paras. 3–5.

[78] M. Kerr, 'Law reform in changing times' (1980) 96 *LQR* 527 ff.

[79] Law Commission, 'Report and draft bill on obligations of landlords and tenants', Law Com. no. 67 (1975).

[80] 'Codification of the criminal law: a report to the Law Commission', Law. Com. no. 143 (1985).

[81] 'A criminal code for England and Wales', Law Com. no. 177 (1989). Although the codification project in relation to criminal law has now been removed from the programme of the Law Commission, it is currently revising part 1 of the draft criminal code, especially the part on 'conspiracy and attempts' and 'intoxication'. See Law Commission, 'Tenth programme of law reform', Law Com. no. 311 (2008).

[82] For a critical view of the draft, see G. De Búrca and S. Gardner, 'The codification of the criminal law' (1990) 10 *OJLS* 559 ff.

soon became apparent that there was no real chance of Parliament finding time to deal with such a major measure,[83] and the commission decided not to press for a complete code but, rather, to proceed to work on specific offences.

In the field of family law, the commission has focused mainly on reforming statutory provisions and consolidating them so as to allow for a future codification. A gradual reform has been carried out, for instance, on matters such as the status of children, time limits for divorce and custody. Although much seems to have been achieved, whether real progress towards codification has been made in this field of law is doubtful.[84] In fact, so far no draft code has been presented.

Despite its various efforts, and after more than forty years of work, the Law Commission has not succeeded in its attempt to introduce a code. Why is this?[85] It may be partly due to the fact that, despite the initial announcement, codification has never actually been a priority for the Law Commission. In fact, the commission has adopted the view that a codification had to be preceded by a reform of the relevant areas of law.[86] Moreover, legal resources continue to be scarce, and the Law Commission cannot invest its energy in codification alone.

Apart from that, there are other reasons that explain the lack of a code, some of which reflect those preventing codification in the nineteenth century. Although things have changed (e.g. legal education and the legal literature have significantly improved), many of the problems discussed earlier remain the same, such as the lack of parliamentary support. Once the commission presents its report, the decision whether to adopt it or not is out of its control.[87] Nevertheless, although consolidation is speedy, passing a code would clearly engender long parliamentary debates, especially since Parliament is concerned that no outside body should usurp its sovereignty over the detail of legislation. Parliament may sense that

[83] Lord Justice Bingham, 'A criminal code: must we wait forever?' (1998) *Criminal Law Review* 694 ff.

[84] S. M. Cretney, 'The codification of family law' (1981) 44 *MLR* 1 ff.

[85] For a recent account of possible obstacles to a codification in England, see Anton, 'Obstacles to codification'; and North, 'Problems of codification', 504–8. For a critical approach to codification, see H. R. Hahlo, 'Here lies the common law: rest in peace' (1967) 30 *MLR* 241 ff.

[86] G. Gardiner and A. Martin (eds.), *Law Reform NOW* (London: Victor Gollancz, 1963), p. 12. For the field of family law, see Cretney, 'The codification of family law'. See also Law Commission, 'Tenth programme of law reform', 5–6.

[87] For further discussions, see Cretney, 'The codification of family law', 8–9.

provisions expressed in the general language of a code might alter the balance of power between itself and the judiciary. Furthermore, there are problems with implementing the proposals by legislation that stem from parliamentary procedures and the difficulty of securing time in legislative programmes.[88] In addition, a radical reform of the drafting of parliamentary bills would be needed.[89]

The lack of support from the legal profession plays a role too.[90] Moreover, as in the nineteenth century, there is little political motivation today for the introduction of a code. In addition, the need for an improvement of the state of the law has been met through the intervention of legislation and the proliferation of legal literature, supplemented by the constant reform and modernisation of the law facilitated by the presence of the government-backed Law Commission.

10.5 Conclusion

The English codification debate stretches across two centuries and is still not exhausted. Several codification attempts were made, but, apart from India, no code was ever introduced in England, at least not in the sense that Bentham envisaged. Bentham contemplated a code that was a complete legislative statement of the whole body of the law, self-sufficient, and not to be developed, supplemented or modified except by legislative enactment. He imagined a type of code that would have assumed a central place and therefore provoked a change not only of the content of the law but also of the hierarchy of the sources of law.

The concept of 'code' that emerges from the codification debate of the last 150 years or so is a rather different one. The type of code discussed is principally that of a piece of legislation that has the function of restating and consolidating in clear language single branches of the law, but that is coexistent with the common law. Hence, the history of the English codification debate is the history of a debate that has moved away from the vision of a complete code of the laws towards a narrower concept of codification. Further, it is the history of a series of compromises. When the idea of a complete code turned out to be a difficult enterprise, it was

88 Kerr, 'Law reform in changing times', 515.

89 For further details, see North, 'Problems of codification', 507–8; and Veeder and Dye, 'Lord Bramwell's arbitration code', 349.

90 North, 'Problems of codification', 505. See, however, Bingham, 'A criminal code'.

abandoned in favour of piecemeal codification measures. Similarly, when it was clear that any attempt at reform of the substance would meet with resistance and opposition, attention was placed on merely reproducing the existing law, albeit in a more systematic manner.

Most interestingly, however, it was the desire to improve the form, rather than the desire to change the substance and the content of the law, that seems to have inspired the English codification movement.[91] It is therefore perhaps not surprising that the term 'code' has often been used interchangeably with 'digest', and 'codification' with 'consolidation'. Moreover, since the code was seen primarily as a way to improve systematically the form of the law, alternative measures could be explored that, in the absence of a code, could meet some of those needs. In other words, the necessity of rendering English law more systematic and simple could be achieved by other means. Statute law was thus reformed through consolidating acts, while common law was systematised, partly through codifying acts and partly through textbooks and treatises, which have proliferated since the second half of the nineteenth century. The function of systematising the law and of defining legal concepts was, in fact, largely taken over by academics, who through their writing gave rise to a phenomenon that Maine defined as 'tacit codification'.[92] Instead of one complete code of laws, England ended up with several codifying acts and a number of 'private codes',[93] which have probably rendered the need for a legislative codification less urgent.

As far as tort law is concerned, apart from the draft bill of the law of tort for India by Pollock, which was never enacted, however, no codification attempts have been made in this field. This is perhaps not surprising given that tort law developed only late and that for a long time it did not have sufficiently defined boundaries. At the same time, however, precisely because tort law was such an unsettled area, a code might have improved the development of the law, especially since academic lawyers were never able to rationalise the law in this area in the same way they did in the area of contract law.[94] Interestingly, tort law is not among the areas of the law

[91] This is not too dissimilar to what happened in Germany, where the *Bürgerliches Gesetzbuch* was not meant or understood to be fundamentally changing the law. See the contribution by Nils Jansen in this volume, Chapter 9.

[92] Baker, *An Introduction to English Legal History*, p. 220; H. S. Maine, *Village-Communities in the East and West: Six Lectures Delivered at Oxford* (London: John Murray, 1871), p. 368.

[93] Pound, *Jurisprudence*, p. 722.

[94] Atiyah, *Pragmatism and Theory in English Law*, p. 175.

in which the Law Commission expressed an intention to codify. Indeed, although the Law Commission has exerted considerable efforts in order to reform the law in other areas, not much work seems to have been done in the field of tort law.[95]

[95] See P. Mitchell 'The impact of institutions and professions on fault liability in England', in P. Mitchell (ed.), *The Impact of Institutions and Professions on Legal Development* (Cambridge University Press, forthcoming).

11

Regulating workplace hazards: the role of medical, scientific and technical experts in legal change

P. W. J. BARTRIP*

This chapter evaluates the importance of specialist knowledge in the regulation of occupational health hazards in Britain (not purely England and Wales) between the mid-nineteenth and late twentieth centuries. Although it considers the much-debated influence of theorists, notably Jeremy Bentham, its main focus is on the evolving role of advisers, both civil servants and others, who were medically, scientifically or technically qualified. The role of these experts is subjected to particular scrutiny in the context of asbestos regulation, especially in the periods 1928 to 1931 and 1965 to 1970. The chapter plays down the influence of bureaucratic expertise in health and safety regulation during much of the Victorian period. It goes on to argue that specialist knowledge became more influential from the 1890s onwards and that it was critical in determining the terms of the Asbestos Industry Regulations 1931. The retention of these regulations for nearly forty years and their replacement by the Asbestos Regulations 1969 also owed much to expert appraisal. The chapter begins by considering the meaning of the words 'experts' and 'expertise'.

11.1 Experts, advisers and inspectors

An 'expert' may be defined as a specialist, someone who has gained skill through experience, or acquired authority by reason of special knowledge. The *Oxford English Dictionary* records no printed use of the noun before 1825 (in an Act of Parliament), with the next earliest recorded use occurring as late as 1858.[1] The dictionary traces printed use of the word

* Centre for Socio-Legal Studies, University of Oxford.

[1] *Oxford English Dictionary* (http://dictionary.oed.com, last accessed 5 October 2010). As an adjective in the sense of 'having experience', usage can be traced back to Chaucer.

'expertise,' in the sense of expert opinion or the quality or state of being an expert, to 1868. Roy MacLeod offers a slightly different chronology; he maintains that both terms were in colloquial use from around 1860 and that by the 1880s an expert was generally regarded as someone with special skills or knowledge.[2]

MacLeod, drawing on a wide range of sources, sees the emergence of bureaucratic expertise in the service of the British government as a Victorian phenomenon. He and contributors to his book *Government and Expertise* were mainly concerned to explore the relationship between specialist knowledge and the so-called 'nineteenth-century revolution in government'. For MacLeod and many others (most notably, perhaps, Oliver MacDonagh), demographic, industrial and urban growth, combined with bouts of economic depression and social unrest, created conditions that were both 'intolerable' and beyond the ability of the traditional machinery of government to handle. Many reformers saw the need for government action to address crises in the poor law, the workplace, public health and public order, however: 'central government had need to act' but needed 'to find help from new quarters…and into the breach came new officials and new boards of different kinds, with statutory powers to act in the name of the State'.[3]

This analysis suggests not only that experts were key figures as midwives for the regulatory state that burgeoned from the middle of the nineteenth century, but also that the regulations and the officials who implemented them both came into existence through force of circumstances rather than any ideological commitment. Each of these suggestions has been contested within the historiography, however. There is not even consensus about the degree to which the state impinged on the lives of nineteenth- and early twentieth-century Britons or the point at which laissez-faire gave way to collectivism. Albert Venn Dicey dated the 'age of collectivism' from 1865 or perhaps 1870.[4] W. L. Burn wrote about state coercion in the 1850s, however, albeit coercion applied 'quietly and decorously'. For his part, A. J. P. Taylor maintained that as late as '1914 a sensible, law-abiding Englishman could pass through life and hardly notice

[2] R. MacLeod (ed.), *Government and Expertise: Specialists, Administrators and Professionals, 1860–1919* (Cambridge University Press, 1988), p. 256, n. 11.

[3] R. MacLeod, 'Introduction', in *Government and Expertise*, pp. 1 ff., p. 2; O. MacDonagh, 'The nineteenth-century revolution in government: a reappraisal' (1958) 1 *Historical Journal* 52 ff.

[4] A. V. Dicey, *Lectures on the Relation between Law and Public Opinion in England during the Nineteenth Century* (London: Macmillan, 1905), pp. 63–9.

the existence of the state, beyond the post office and the policemen'.[5] Pat Thane judges that 'Victorian central government involved itself in the lives of its citizens in many ways', but also that 'by the 1880s the only agent of the central state whom the provincial citizen could regularly expect to encounter was the benign post office clerk'. If this observation implies that things changed in the 1880s rather than in 1914, it receives support from Philip Harling, who maintains that '[a]s late as 1880 the British state was chiefly notable for its virtual absence from broad areas of social and economic life'.[6]

Detailed review of these assessments is beyond the scope of this chapter. It is noteworthy, however, that there has been vigorous discussion about the roles of ideology, especially Benthamite, as an influence on government.[7] Lack of consensus about the meaning of Benthamism has clouded the debate. Dicey equated Benthamism with individualism but also 'above all things' with 'reform of the law'. He viewed the years 1825 to 1870 as a period when Parliament was constantly eliminating 'restraints on individual liberty' and checks on 'individual freedom'.[8] As Henry Parris has observed, though, 'Anyone who knows anything of British history in the nineteenth century can think of things that do not fit Dicey's interpretation.' Moreover, the contradictions are 'too numerous to be dismissed as exceptions'.[9] The key principle of Benthamism was, of course the 'greatest happiness for the greatest number'. The pursuit of this objective could justify state intervention, non-intervention or, in the case of the new poor law, intervention aimed at inducing the populace to rely less on public intervention. Benthamites and Benthamism could therefore support a wide range of policies and enactments.

[5] W. L. Burn, *The Age of Equipoise: A Study of the Mid-Victorian Generation* (London: George Allen & Unwin, 1964), p. 136; A. J. P. Taylor, *English History, 1914–1945* (Harmondsworth: Pelican Books, 1970), p. 25.

[6] P. Thane, 'Government and society in England and Wales, 1750–1914', in F. M. L. Thompson (ed.), *The Cambridge Social History of Britain*, vol. III, *Social Agencies and Institutions* (Cambridge University Press, 1990), pp. 1 ff., pp. 1–2; P. Harling, *The Modern British State: An Historical Introduction* (Cambridge: Polity Press, 2001), p. 112.

[7] See, for example, L. J. Hume, 'Jeremy Bentham and the nineteenth-century government' (1967) 10 *Historical Journal* 361 ff.; U. R. Q. Henriques, 'Jeremy Bentham and the machinery of social reform', in H. Hearder and H. Loyn (eds.), *British Government and Administration: Studies Presented to S. B. Chrimes* (Cardiff: University of Wales Press, 1974), pp. 177 ff.; H. Parris, 'The nineteenth-century revolution in government: a revolution re-appraised' (1960) 3 *Historical Journal* 17 ff.; J. Hart, 'Nineteenth-century social reform: a Tory interpretation of history' (1965) 31 *Past and Present* 39 ff.

[8] Dicey, *Lectures on the Relation*, pp. 63–4.

[9] H. Parris, *Constitutional Bureaucracy* (London: George Allen & Unwin, 1969), p. 17.

Some of the key administrators in the early Victorian period have been identified as Benthamites. Harling, for example, mentions Edwin Chadwick, James Kay Shuttleworth, Southwood Smith, Leonard Horner, Hugh Tremenheere and William Farr.[10] Whether all these men were experts is another matter. Two of those on Harling's list, Horner and Tremenheere, were industrial inspectors, of factories and mines, respectively, and MacDonagh judged that inspectors played important roles in lawmaking and in extending the reach of government.[11] Were Horner, Tremenheere and other inspectors experts, though, and did they approach their tasks as ideologues or as practical men in search of workable solutions to challenging problems? Did inspectors appointed in later years hold different qualifications or approach their duties differently? It is hard to answer these questions without noting that, from the first, the law invested different inspectorates with different powers and responsibilities. Mines inspectors, for example, were essentially advisers to the mining industry with minimal powers of law enforcement. Factory inspectors, on the other hand, at least in their earliest incarnation, were effectively industrial policemen, prosecutors, jurors and judges. Though their powers were soon diluted, factory inspectors retained the power to prosecute offenders throughout the nineteenth and twentieth centuries.[12]

The early inspectorates also possessed contrasting backgrounds, experience and qualifications. In the aftermath of the Haswell Colliery disaster of 1844, when ninety-five men died in an underground explosion at a Durham pit, an editorial in *The Times* called for investigations by 'scientific men'. The government apparently agreed, for it dispatched Professor Michael Faraday, the 'noted scientist', and Charles Lyell, the 'famous geologist', to the north-east.[13] *The Times* editorial made no mention of the need for state inspection of subterranean operations but when, in 1846, Tremenheere urged the government to appoint underground mining inspectors he recommended the selection of 'men of scientific and other superior qualifications'.[14] Tremenheere, who, since 1842, had been the one and only inspector of mines, 'had neither technical knowledge

[10] Harling, *The Modern British State*, p. 104.

[11] MacDonagh, 'The nineteenth-century revolution', 59–60.

[12] P. W. J. Bartrip, 'British government inspection, 1832–1875: some observations' (1982) 25 *Historical Journal* 605 ff.

[13] *The Times*, 11 October 1844. See also *The Times*, 14 October 1844; *The Times*, 14 March 1845; and A. Bryan, *The Evolution of Health and Safety in Mines* (Letchworth: Ashire, 1975), p. 43.

[14] National Archives [NA] HO 45/1490. H. Tremenheere to Sir G. Grey, 31 December 1846.

of mining nor any technical function to discharge'. He had no responsibility for safety and his official duties did not take him below ground. He was entirely concerned with enforcing the law relating to the employment of women and children and the payment of wages.[15] Following a succession of serious mining accidents in the late 1840s the government again responded by appointing renowned scientists, such as the geologist Sir Henry de la Beche and the chemist Dr Lyon Playfair, to investigate and report. Experienced mining engineers such as Warington Smith, of the Geological Survey, Professor John Philips FRS, of King's College London, and J. Kenyon Blackwell were also employed. For all the involvement of such famous names, however, Sir Andrew Bryan maintains that British scientists 'at that time were much too ignorant of mining dangers and the ways of safeguarding against them to be able quickly to raise the standards of mine safety'.[16]

The Coal Mines Inspection Act 1850 was concerned with mine safety. It provided for the appointment of underground mine inspectors but did not stipulate any qualifications, merely that appointees should have no business connection with mines or collieries.[17] In practice, however, all post-1850 inspectors had pre-appointment experience as mining engineers.[18] Railway inspectors were in much the same position. The Railway Regulation Act 1840 (3 & 4 Vict. c.97) prohibited the appointment of anyone who was or had recently been a director or employee of a railway company. It said nothing about inspectors' credentials, however. Like their mines counterparts, they had few powers to sanction errant railway companies; also like the mine inspectors, they were required to be knowledgeable about their field of inspection. In the absence of a numerous body of men who were knowledgeable about railways and unconnected

[15] R. K. Webb, 'A Whig inspector' (1955) 27 *Journal of Modern History* 352 ff.; E. L. Edmonds and O. P. Edmonds, *I Was There: The Memoirs of H. S. Tremenheere* (Eton: Shakespeare Head Press, 1965), p. xi. See also E. L. Edmonds and O. P. Edmonds, 'An account of the founding of HM Inspectorate of Mines and the work of the first inspector, Hugh Seymour Tremenheere' (1963) 10 *British Journal of Industrial Medicine* 210 ff.

[16] See, for example, *Parliamentary Papers* [*PP*] 1847 xvi, Reports on the Gases and explosions in Collieries by Sir Henry de la Beche, Dr Lyon Playfair and Warington Smith, pp. 159–236; *PP* 1850 xxiii, Report on Ventilation of Mines by J. Kenyon Blackwell, pp. 443–73; *PP* 1850 xxiii, Report on the Ventilation of Mines and Collieries by John Phillips Esq. FRS, pp. 475–569; and Bryan, *The Evolution of Health and Safety in Mines*, pp. 43–4, p. 57 (all pagination for parliamentary papers is taken from the set housed in the Bodleian Library). On de la Beche and Playfair, see *Oxford Dictionary of National Biography* [*ODNB*] (www.oxforddnb.com).

[17] Act for the Inspection of Coal Mines, 1850 (13 & 14 Vict. c.100).

[18] Bartrip, 'British government inspection', 620.

with railway companies, they were always recruited from the ranks of the Royal Engineers.[19] Similarly, when explosives inspectors were appointed in 1875 under the terms of the Explosives Act, the Home Office appointed Royal Artillery officers (supported by a scientific adviser).[20]

Whether all or any of the appointees to the Mines, Railways, Alkali or Explosives Inspectorates were 'experts' is questionable. They brought some practical knowledge and experience to their duties, and Bryan dates the existence of a 'technical and well qualified Mines Inspectorate' to 1850, but with few exceptions, such as Robert Angus Smith FRS of the Alkali Inspectorate, 'perhaps the most celebrated sanitary chemist in the country', Victorian inspectorates contained few genuine scientific, medical or technical experts. The first truly expert mine inspector was appointed in 1908, when Professor Richard Redmayne, chair of mining at Birmingham University, became chief inspector; there was no permanent medical inspector of mines until 1927.[21]

As for their commitment to reform, Burn argued that inspectors 'did not interest themselves in certain things simply because they were servants of the State, they were servants of the State because they were interested in those things, because they had formed opinions which an official position allowed them to translate into action'.[22] Several historians have quoted these words with approval; furthermore, Parris has identified the 'great majority' of early inspectors as 'zealots'. In contrast, David Roberts has stated that inspectors' 'basic beliefs' were little different from 'other members of the Victorian middle class'.[23]

In many ways, factory inspectors were in the vanguard of Victorian industrial regulation. Not only were they the first in the field, they were more numerous, more powerful, better paid and more esteemed within government than their counterparts in other areas. The Treasury, for example, deemed them 'the highest class of inspectors'.[24] Unlike their railway, mines,

19 H. Parris, *Government and the Railways in Nineteenth-Century Britain* (London: Routledge & Kegan Paul), p. 32.

20 J. Pellew, 'The Home Office and the Explosives Act of 1875' (1974) 18 *Victorian Studies* 175 ff., 189 ff.

21 R. MacLeod, 'The Alkali Acts Administration, 1863–84: the emergence of the civil scientist' (1965) 9 *Victorian Studies* 85 ff., 90 ff.; Bryan, *The Evolution of Health and Safety in Mines*, p. 54, pp. 91–2. On Redmayne, see *ODNB*.

22 Burn, *The Age of Equipoise*, pp. 223–4.

23 Pellew, 'The Home Office', 177; Parris, *Constitutional Bureaucracy*, p. 202; D. Roberts, *Victorian Origins of the British Welfare State* (New Haven, CT: Yale University Press, 1960), p. 168; Bartrip, 'British government inspection', 619.

24 MacLeod, 'The Alkali Acts', pp. 90–1.

alkali and explosives counterparts, however, factory inspectors were, for decades, not required to possess any specialist knowledge. The 1833 act that allowed for their appointment did not even require their independence from the textile industry they inspected. Some historians have accused them of being rather too sympathetic to manufacturers.[25] Among the first appointees (in 1833), two, Leonard Horner and Robert Rickards, possessed business backgrounds in textiles (the only branch of industry covered by factory legislation until the 1860s). Neither they nor any of their colleagues possessed much medical, scientific or technological expertise, though.[26]

The one exception was Robert Baker, who spent forty-four years in the Factory Inspectorate. He was medically qualified and, before becoming a bureaucrat, had practised medicine in Leeds and held a medical appointment at a Leeds woollen mill.[27] Baker showed little interest in occupational disease, however. His apparent indifference may have reflected the undeveloped state of British occupational medicine in the middle of the nineteenth century. This cannot provide a complete explanation, though, for Charles Turner Thackrah, also of Leeds, wrote about occupational hazards in 1831 and produced an enlarged second edition of his path-breaking book in 1832. Furthermore, at much the same time the potential hazards to health of textile employment were being raised by other medical men, such as Peter Gaskell and Andrew Ure, and by lay authors such as Edward Baines and W. Cooke Taylor.[28] Baker apart, none of the early factory inspectors displayed an interest in the improvement of working conditions before being appointed to the inspectorate. None, Baker included, deserves to be called a zealot.

[25] See, for example, U. R. Q. Henriques, 'An early factory inspector: James Stuart of Dunearn' (1971) 50 *Scottish Historical Review* 17 ff.

[26] Horner was an accomplished amateur geologist but this branch of science was hardly relevant in the context of textile regulation. See *ODNB*.

[27] W. R. Lee, 'Robert Baker: the first doctor in the Factory Department' (1964) 21 *British Journal of Industrial Medicine* 85 ff., 167; *ODNB*.

[28] C. T. Thackrah, *The Effect of Arts, Trades and Professions and of Civic States and Habits of Living on Health and Longevity: With Suggestions for the Removal of Many of the Agents which Produce Disease and Shorten the Duration of Life*, 2nd edn (London: Longman, Rees, Orme, Brown, Green & Longman, 1832); A. Ure, *The Philosophy of Manufactures: Or an Exposition of the Social, Moral and Commercial Economy of the Factory System of Great Britain* (London: Charles Knight, 1835); P. Gaskell (ed.), *Artisans and Machinery: The Moral and Physical Condition of the Manufacturing Population Considered with Reference to Mechanical Substitutes for Human Labour* (London: Frank Cass, 1968); E. Baines (ed.), *History of the Cotton Manufacture of Great Britain* (London: Frank Cass, 1968); W. C. Taylor (ed.), *Notes on a Tour in the Manufacturing Districts of Lancashire* (London: Frank Cass, 1968).

The dominant figure within the nineteenth-century Factory Inspectorate, if only because of his length of service, was Alexander Redgrave (of *Redgrave's Factories Acts* fame). Born in 1819, he joined the Home Office criminal registry department in 1834 before becoming clerk to the factory inspectors from 1837 to 1847 and sub-inspector of factories from 1847 to 1852. He then served as a full inspector for a further thirty-nine years; he was chief inspector of factories between 1878 and 1891. Redgrave's credentials for such an extended and distinguished career were almost non-existent.[29] In line with most of his colleagues, he obtained any expertise he possessed entirely through experience acquired in the post. Not surprisingly, factory inspectors were criticised in some quarters for their lack of practical knowledge and expertise.[30]

In view of the brevity of his formal education, it may seem unlikely that Redgrave approached his inspectorial duties imbued with the ideas of Bentham, John Stuart Mill, Herbert Spencer or any other political theorists. As Jonathan Rose has demonstrated, however, it is unwise to underestimate the extent of self-instruction among nineteenth- and twentieth-century Britons who received little or no schooling.[31] The fact is, however, that we know too little about Redgrave, except in his official capacity, to evaluate the role of ideas in influencing his approach to his duties. As a factory inspector, he compiled many annual reports and other official documents; in the absence of other sources, his views on laissez-faire and state intervention must be derived from these writings. They show an inspector who, though responsible for enforcing the will of Parliament, was at best ambivalent about government involvement in business activity. To paraphrase Roberts, this ambivalence probably did not make Redgrave very different from most other men of his age and class.[32]

The practice of recruiting generalists to the Factory Inspectorate did not change until the last years of the nineteenth century. Redgrave was in post for so long that his immediate successors as chief inspector, Sprague Oram and F. H. Whymper, had only short periods in charge.[33] In 1896,

[29] *ODNB*.

[30] Bartrip, 'Expertise and the dangerous trades, 1875–1900', in MacLeod, *Government and Expertise*, pp. 90 ff.

[31] J. Rose, *The Intellectual Life of the British Working Classes* (New Haven, CT: Yale University Press, 2001).

[32] *ODNB*; Bartrip, 'British government inspection', 605–26.

[33] Frederick Whymper (1828–93), Redgrave's immediate successor, was an old Etonian who graduated from Cambridge University in 1851 with a first class degree in classics. Although he was admitted to Lincoln's Inn in 1851, it is not clear what Whymper did

though, B. A. Whitelegge commenced a term of office that lasted until 1917. With BSc and MD degrees from University College London, a Diploma in Public Health from Cambridge and a Fellowship of the Royal College of Physicians (FRCP) to his name, Whitelegge's academic credentials for appointment to the Factory Inspectorate were far superior to those of any of his predecessors. At the time of his appointment, his voluminous book *Hygiene and Public Health* (1890) had already gone through several editions. Though new to the Factory Inspectorate when installed as its head, he had previously served as medical officer of health for the industrial areas of Nottingham and the West Riding of Yorkshire. He had also been a member of the Factory Statistics Committee from 1893 to 1895. Whitelegge's appointment was a case of 'introducing an outside expert to run the factory department rather than following the tradition of promoting internally on the basis of strict seniority'.[34]

The process of appointing specialists, initially women inspectors (who focused on female employment) and 'inspectors of textile particulars', had begun before Whitelegge took office.[35] It continued under his leadership, most notably with the appointment of the first medical inspector of factories, Thomas Legge MD (Oxon), DPH (Cantab), in 1898. When he took up his post, Legge's background in occupational medicine was modest (he was more a public health specialist), but he soon became an acknowledged expert on the subject. When he received a knighthood in 1925 a colleague termed him 'the greatest living authority on industrial disease'.[36] Thus, following the departure of the elderly and conservative Redgrave, the Factory Inspectorate was reorganised – so much so that it is fair to talk about the start of a new era in the 1890s, one feature of

professionally before his appointment as superintending inspector of factories in 1872. He appears, however, to have had no technical or scientific training. See F. Boase, *Modern English Biography*, 2nd edn (6 vols.), vol. VI [1921] (London: Cass, 1965), p. 863; and J. A. Venn (compiler), *Alumni Cantabrigienses*, part 2, vol. VI (Cambridge University Press, 1954), p. 456. Richard Edward Sprague Oram (1830–1909) was chief inspector of factories between 1893 and 1896. Little is known about his credentials for office. An important change introduced during Oram's term of office concerned the obligation on factory occupiers to notify government of cases of certain industrial diseases (initially lead, arsenic and phosphorus poisoning and anthrax). *Who Was Who 1897–1915* (London: A & C Black, 1920), p. 395.

[34] Bartrip, 'Expertise and the dangerous trades', p. 104.

[35] On women inspectors, see M. D. McFeely, *Lady Inspectors: The Campaign for a Better Workplace, 1893–1921* (Oxford: Basil Blackwell, 1988); and H. Jones, 'Women health workers: the case of the first women factory inspectors in Britain' (1988) 1 *Social History of Medicine* 165 ff.

[36] *ODNB*.

which was an injection of expertise. Before assessing the impact of these changes, it is worth considering the achievements of the pre-1890s Factory Inspectorate in terms of legal change relating to occupational safety and health and compensation.

Notwithstanding their general lack of pre-appointment expertise and experience, Victorian factory inspectors occasionally played a substantial part in reforming the law on occupational health and safety. This was particularly the case with industrial lead poisoning. Charles Dickens' periodical *All the Year Round* raised the problem of illness among white lead workers in 1869. The issue came to Redgrave's attention in 1875 and he requested junior inspectors to investigate. Their findings prompted Redgrave to raise the subject in a half-yearly report and in evidence to the Royal Commission on the Factory and Workshop Acts (1876). The Factory and Workshop Act 1878 excluded children and young persons from employment in white lead works. The Factory Inspectorate, particularly Redgrave, also played a significant part in creating the White Lead Act 1883, a measure that required manufacturers to take precautions to protect the health of employees if they were to obtain and retain the Home Office certificate that would enable them to stay in production. During Whymper's brief spell as chief inspector the law relating to health precautions in white lead works was revised, largely on the basis of Whymper's recommendations.[37]

Other, scattered, examples could be cited, but on the whole the generalist Victorian Factory Inspectorate did not play a major role in developing the law on industrial health and safety. Neither is there much evidence to indicate that it ever had an ideological interest in effecting such change. Politicians, pressure groups, 'moral entrepreneurs' and, on occasion, the press exerted greater influence.[38] There is evidence that, with experts on staff, the inspectorate became much more influential in the twentieth century. It is often stated, however, that long into the twentieth century the leading civil servants were usually generalists who had attended a public school before proceeding to an ancient university, often Oxford, from where they graduated in an arts subject. Furthermore, although the expert was recognised as having a part to play, he was usually permitted to play only a supporting role.[39]

[37] Bartrip, 'Expertise and the dangerous trades', p. 94

[38] P. W. J. Bartrip, *The Home Office and the Dangerous Trades: Regulating Occupational Disease in Victorian and Edwardian Britain* (Amsterdam: Rodopi, 2002).

[39] See, for example, G. K. Fry, *Statesmen in Disguise: The Changing Role of the Administrative Class of the British Home Civil Service, 1853–1966* (London: Macmillan, 1969), p. 57;

The rest of this chapter explores the exercise of expert influence in relation to the regulation of asbestos-related disease. It is argued that, in this case, scientific and medical expertise determined the nature and timing of this regulation.[40]

11.2 The Asbestos Industry Regulations 1931

Asbestos is the generic name for a group of naturally occurring fibrous minerals that have many applications, especially in connection with fireproofing and heat insulation. Although its remarkable properties had been known for centuries, the industrial and commercial potential of asbestos was little exploited until the last quarter of the nineteenth century. The possible health hazards of breathing asbestos dust were first noted by Britain's lady inspectors of factories in the 1890s. Legge was consulted at an early stage and a deputy medical inspector, Edgar Collis, commented on the issue in 1910. A Factory Inspectorate inquiry in 1917 found 'no further evidence incriminating asbestos…either at home or abroad', however. Accordingly, no action to address the health hazards of asbestos was taken. Legge later rued this failure to act.[41]

From 1924 onwards medical articles began to indicate a possible link between lung fibrosis and employment in an asbestos factory. Previously, the leading figures in British occupational medicine, notably Thomas Arlidge and Thomas Oliver, had ignored asbestos dust as a possible cause of illness.[42] In 1931, following further inquiry by specialist factory

and W. H. Greenleaf, *The British Political Tradition*, vol. III, *A Much-Governed Nation* (London: Methuen, 1987), part 1, pp. 199–201.

40 The following section, based on research conducted for my book *The Way from Dusty Death: Turner & Newall and the Regulation of Occupational Health in the British Asbestos Industry, 1890s–1970* (London: Athlone Press, 2001), was partially funded by T&N/Federal Mogul in the period from 1996 to 2001.

41 E. R. A. Merewether, 'A memorandum on asbestosis' (1933) 15 *Tubercle* 72 ff.; T. Legge, *Industrial Maladies* (London: Oxford University Press, 1934), pp. 190–1. See also Bartrip, *The Way from Dusty Death*, p. 14.

42 T. Arlidge, *The Hygiene, Diseases and Mortality of Occupations* (London: Percival, 1892); T. Oliver (ed.), *Dangerous Trades: The Historical Social and Legal Aspect of Industrial Occupations as Affecting Health, by a Number of Experts* (London: John Murray, 1902); T. Oliver (ed.), *Diseases of Occupation: From the Legislative, Social and Medical Points of View* (London: Methuen, 1908); T. Oliver, *Occupations from the Social, Hygienic and Medical Points of View* (Cambridge University Press, 1916); E. L. Collis, *Industrial Pneumoconioses, with Special Reference to Dust Phthisis (Milroy Lectures)* (London: HMSO, 1919). See also E. L. Collis and M. Greenwood, *The Health of the Industrial Worker* (London: J. A. Churchill, 1921). For biographies of Arlidge and Oliver, see *ODNB*.

inspectors, regulations to control asbestosis, the one disease then known to be causally associated with the inhalation of asbestos dust, were enacted. In the same year asbestosis become a compensable disease under the terms of the Asbestos Industry (Asbestosis) Scheme.[43]

The Workmen's Compensation Act 1897 applied only to accidents; initially, it offered no prospect of redress to victims of occupational disease. In 1902, however, the House of Lords ruled that a workman infected by anthrax was entitled to recover compensation on the grounds that the entry of anthrax bacillus into the body constituted an accident.[44] Four years later the Workmen's Compensation Act 1906 allowed for the compensation of workers suffering from occupationally induced lead, phosphorus, arsenic and mercury poisoning or ankylostomiasis (though apparently not as a consequence of any suggestion from the inspectorate).[45] While the bill was under consideration the home secretary appointed a departmental committee to consider the inclusion of further disease.[46]

This four-member committee consisted of Herbert Samuel MP (under-secretary at the Home Office), a senior Home Office official and two experts: Legge and Thomas Allbutt, the Regius Professor of Physic at Cambridge University (though Allbutt, for all his eminence as a physician, had little background or active interest in occupational medicine, notwithstanding his twenty-eight years as a consulting physician in the industrial city of Leeds).[47] In the course of its investigation the committee took 350 pages of oral evidence from 159 witnesses, ninety-two of whom were doctors (the others were employers and workers). They visited factories, advertised for witnesses in the press and contacted organisations such as the Trades Union Congress (TUC). They also consulted factory inspectors' reports and Thomas Oliver's monumental book *Dangerous Trades* (1902). In addition, Legge and Allbutt clinically examined workers.[48] The committee recommended making a further eighteen diseases compensable under the

[43] Statutory Instruments [SI] 1931 no. 344; N. J. Wikeley, *Compensation for Industrial Disease* (Aldershot: Dartmouth, 1993).

[44] *Brintons Ltd* v. *Turvey* [1905] AC 230; 74 LJKB 474; 92 LT 578; 21 TLR 444. See P. W. J. Bartrip, *Workmen's Compensation in Twentieth Century Britain: Law, History and Social Policy* (Aldershot: Avebury, 1987), p. 26, p. 135.

[45] 6 Edw. 7 c.58 s.8 and schedule 3. Ankylostomiasis is caused by a parasitic worm; it could affect miners because of the lack of underground sanitary facilities.

[46] Bartrip, *Workmen's Compensation in Twentieth Century Britain*, p. 53.

[47] *ODNB*; H. D. Rolleston, *The Right Honorable Sir Thomas Clifford Allbutt KCB: A Memoir* (London: Macmillan, 1929).

[48] *PP* 1907 xxxiv: *Report of the Departmental Committee on Compensation for Industrial Diseases*, pp. 1045–74; *PP* 1907 lxviii: *List of Scheduled Diseases under the Workmen's Compensation Acts, Order of 22 May 1907*, pp. 767–70.

terms of the Workmen's Compensation Act. Every recommendation was accepted. This list was refined and extended over the years in response to expert recommendation. For example, the departmental committee's second report, dated 12 October 1908, proposed compensating for glass-workers' cataract and telegraphists' cramp and clarifying the eligibility of eczema sufferers. Again, each recommendation was swiftly accepted.[49] The departmental committee was accordingly instrumental in decisions as to which industrial diseases were compensable. Although the committee included non-experts, its recommendations were based on medical criteria. Its key criterion for recommending a disease as compensable was as follows: 'Is it so specific that the causation of the disease or injury by the employment can be established in individual cases?' Such a question could be answered only by the application of medical expertise.[50]

In 1907 the departmental committee declined to recommend that fibroid phthisis caused by asbestos (or any other dust) should be a compensable disease. This decision reflected the difficulty of distinguishing between occupationally induced chest disease and the pulmonary tuberculosis that was then widespread among workers and others. Another factor was the difficulty of determining which employer should be responsible for paying compensation for a disease that could develop over a long period when a worker might have had numerous employers. The committee also feared that lung-impaired workers would become unemployable once an obligation to pay compensation was established.[51]

When the question of whether asbestos dust was a health hazard resurfaced in 1924 it was raised not by a doyen of occupational medicine but by an otherwise obscure figure in the history of occupational medicine, William Cooke, honorary pathologist and bacteriologist at Wigan Infirmary.[52] Other investigators, including Oliver, then took up

49 *PP* 1908 xxxv: *Second Report of the Departmental Committee on Compensation for Industrial Diseases*, pp. 1–8; *PP* 1908 xcviii: *List of Scheduled Diseases under the Workmen's Compensation Acts, Order of 2 December 1908*, pp. 995–8. See also *PP* 1913 xviii: *Report of the Departmental Committee on Compensation for Industrial Diseases*, pp. 649–58. Legge and Allbutt also served on this committee.

50 *PP* 1907 xxxiv: *Report of the Departmental Committee on Compensation for Industrial Diseases*, p. 1051.

51 *Report of the Departmental Committee on Compensation for Industrial Diseases*, pp. 1066–7.

52 W. E. Cooke, 'Fibrosis of the lungs due to the inhalation of asbestos dust' (26 July 1924) *BMJ* 147 ff. Cooke was a well-qualified and experienced doctor who had already published papers in the *BMJ*, *The Lancet* and other journals. See *Medical Directory 1924* (London: Churchill, 1924).

the matter.[53] Official interest was aroused less by the appearance of articles in medical periodicals, however, and more by knowledge of a case of pulmonary fibrosis affecting a Glasgow asbestos worker. In 1928 the Factory Inspectorate launched an inquiry.[54] A medical inspector of factories, Edward Merewether, undertook the inquiry. Merewether had joined the inspectorate only in 1927, at which point he had little experience of industrial medicine. He 'quickly made a brilliant reputation' as a medical inspector of factories, though, and enjoyed a 'long and illustrious career', latterly as senior medical inspector of factories. He published a number of important papers on pulmonary disease and occupational health, and collected a string of honours and appointments.[55] It is clear, therefore, that Merewether was an expert in occupational medicine, albeit, in 1928, an emergent one.

Merewether's brief in undertaking his inquiry was to determine whether working with asbestos created a risk of pulmonary fibrosis. He concluded that 'the inhalation of asbestos dust over a period of years results in the development of a serious type of fibrosis of the lungs'. In short, 'fibrosis of the lungs is a definite occupational risk among asbestos workers as a class'. The disease could lead to complete disablement or death, and the risk of such outcomes was greatest for those who experienced prolonged and heavy exposure.[56] Merewether's findings were not entirely gloomy, as he concluded that even after several years of exposure the amount of disablement was 'surprisingly slight', that light exposure was not dangerous and that dust control measures could control the hazard even to the point of 'the almost total disappearance of the disease'.[57] Dust control raised technical issues of ventilation that were beyond Merewether's competence. The inspectorate's recruitment of specialists over the previous thirty years or so meant that it had in-house expertise to hand in the form of engineering inspectors, however. So it was that Charles Price, engineering inspector of factories, proceeded to investigate dust-producing

[53] See, for example, T. Oliver, 'Some dusty occupations and their effects upon the lungs' (1925) 46 *Journal of the Royal Sanitary Institute* 224 ff.; T. Oliver, 'Clinical aspects of pulmonary asbestosis' (3 December 1927) *BMJ* 1026 ff.; T. Oliver, 'Pulmonary asbestosis in its clinical aspects' (1927) 9 *Journal of Industrial Hygiene* 483 ff.

[54] *PP* 1929–30 xiii (Cmd. 3360): *Annual Report of the Chief Inspector of Factories and Workshops for 1928*, p. 559.

[55] (28 February 1970) *BMJ* 571; (28 February 1970) *Lancet* 477–8; *ODNB*.

[56] E. R. A. Merewether and C. Price, *Report on Effects of Asbestos Dust on the Lungs and Dust Suppression in the Asbestos Industry* (London: HMSO, 1930), p. 9, p. 13.

[57] Merewether and Price, *Report on Effects of Asbestos Dust*, pp. 11–18.

processes and methods of dust suppression with a view to recommending dust control methods.[58]

The Merewether–Price Report (as it came to be known) has been widely praised as a 'classic' and a 'comprehensive' study 'of great scientific value'.[59] When Merewether's superior, J. C. Bridge, saw a draft he immediately recognised that 'regulations…will inevitably have to be introduced'. Draft regulations were swiftly compiled, and, in line with long-established practice, representatives of the asbestos industry and organised labour were then consulted. These consultations brought additional expertise into the regulatory process, for in 1930 Legge, who had by then resigned from the Factory Inspectorate, was part-time medical adviser to the TUC. Industry representatives in these discussions were businessmen with little or no scientific, medical or technical expertise; the government was represented by six factory inspectors, five of whom were either engineering or medical specialists. These consultations led to some modification of the Home Office's proposals but, essentially, the Asbestos Industry Regulations that were agreed in 1931, and phased in from 1 March 1932, were based on the Merewether–Price Report. The regulations applied to all factories and workshops in which asbestos was handled and covered six processes deemed to generate dust in harmful concentrations. They sought to prevent the creation of dust and, when it was generated, to safeguard the workforce from hazardous exposure, either by the use of ventilation equipment or through the provision of breathing apparatus.[60] Although the regulations referred to the elimination of dust, the whole thrust of the discussions that preceded their enactment was the achievement of safe dust levels – the borderline between safety and danger being known as the 'dust datum'.

11.3 Revising the regulations

The Asbestos Industry Regulations 1931 remained in force until 1970. Some observers have argued that they should have been revised earlier as new information demonstrated their inadequacy. Nick Wikeley, for example, points out that the dust datum established in 1931 was provisional

[58] Merewether and Price, *Report on Effects of Asbestos Dust*, pp. 31–3.

[59] (28 February 1970) *BMJ* 571; (28 February 1970) *Lancet* 477–8; G. Wolstenholme (ed.), *Lives of the Fellows of the Royal College of Physicians of London* (6 vols.), vol. VI (Oxford: IRL Press, 1982), pp. 335–6; Bartrip, *The Way from Dusty Death*, p. 13.

[60] SI 1931 no. 1140. For the process by which the regulations were agreed, see Bartrip, *The Way from Dusty Death*, ch. 1; and, from a rather different perspective, see N. J. Wikeley, 'The Asbestos Regulations 1931: a licence to kill' (1992) 19 *Journal of Law and Society* 365 ff.

pending the emergence of further knowledge about the hazards of asbestos. He maintains that no reassessment of the datum took place for forty years. The chief inspector of factories did state at the outset that the dust datum was 'provisional and...subject to alteration in the light of further medical experience'.[61] Any claim that the regulations were not reviewed for nearly four decades is misleading. Between the 1930s and 1960s medical specialists who assessed the evidence repeatedly observed that the 1931 regulations had effectively addressed the problem of asbestos-related disease in the United Kingdom. Thus, in 1955 Georgiana Bonser *et al.* of Leeds University wrote: 'Since the introduction of the regulations for the control of asbestos dust in 1931, the amount of exposure of the workers to dust has been enormously reduced and we shall therefore expect to see a disappearance of those severe degrees of pulmonary fibrosis that have been described heretofore and possibly a disappearance of associated cancer.'[62] A year later Andrew Meiklejohn, then a senior lecturer in industrial health at Glasgow University, observed:[63]

> the dictum...that 'For practical purposes the conditions arising from flyer spinning carried on without exhaust under good conditions may... be taken as the dust datum' was agreed, and this level of dust production was accepted as the basis on which to assess the dustiness (and hence the necessary protective measures) of other processes. Nothing has emerged to suggest departure from this practical standard.

Even in 1968, when the process of replacing the 1931 regulations was well under way, as eminent a figure as Richard Doll judged that there had been a 'significant decrease' in hazard since the implementation of the 1931 regulations. The fact is that, until the 1960s, there was neither a scientific case nor a demand from any quarter for their revision. In other words, expert opinion was instrumental not only in the establishment of the regulations but also in their long retention.[64]

[61] N. J. Wikeley, 'Measurement of asbestos dust levels in British asbestos factories in the 1930s' (1993) 24 *American Journal of Industrial Medicine* 509 ff.; National Archives: Ministry of Labour [NA LAB] 14/70, G. Bellhouse to J. Clynes, undated.

[62] G. M. Bonser, J. S. Faulds and M. J.Stewart, 'Occupational cancer of the urinary bladder in dyestuffs operatives and of the lung in asbestos textile workers and iron-ore miners' (1955) 25 *American Journal of Clinical Pathology* 126 ff.

[63] A. Meiklejohn, 'Silicosis and other fibrotic pneumoconioses', in E. R. A. Merewether (ed.) *Industrial Medicine and Hygiene* (3 vols.), vol. III (London: Butterworth, 1956), pp. 117 ff.

[64] J. F. Knox, S. Holmes, R. Doll and I. D. Hill, 'Mortality from lung cancer and other causes among workers in an asbestos textile factory' (1968) 25 *British Journal of Industrial Medicine* 293 ff.

The first steps towards the revision of the 1931 regulations, which culminated in the establishment of the Asbestos Regulations 1969, were taken in 1965. Although there is insufficient space here to track the revision process, it is clear that it was not initiated by the demands of politicians, organised labour or the media. Neither in Parliament, within the TUC nor the pages of national newspapers was concern about asbestos-related disease aired until after consultations on revising the regulations had begun.[65] In reality, the process was started by the growth of medical knowledge about asbestos-related disease. As the chief inspector of factories noted in the mid-1960s: 'Medical knowledge about the hazards of asbestos has been developing in recent years... In view of this knowledge it was thought wise to review the effectiveness of the Asbestos Industry Regulations 1931.'[66]

In what ways did medical knowledge grow in the 1960s? A key discovery, made chiefly by American and British scientists, was the recognition that asbestos hazards were not confined to workers in the dustiest parts of asbestos factories but could affect non-factory workers, especially insulators. Around the same time, J. C. Wagner and others, initially in South Africa, discovered a 'new' asbestos-related disease, mesothelioma, that could be caused by light and brief dust exposure.[67] A scientific conference on asbestos held in New York in October 1964, which brought together specialists on asbestos-related disease from Europe, North America and South Africa, provided another important stimulus for change.[68] In the United States there was a direct relationship between these scientific

[65] Bartrip, *The Way from Dusty Death*, p. 216.

[66] *PP* 1966–7 xxxi: *Annual Report of the Chief Inspector of Factories*, pp. 451–2. See NA LAB 14/1590, A. F. Hatfull to K. G. Reeve, 3 March 1967.

[67] See, for example, I. J. Selikoff, J. Churg and E. C. Hammond, 'Asbestos exposure and neoplasia' (1964) 188 *JAMA* 22 ff.; I. J. Selikoff, J. Churg and E. C. Hammond, 'Relation between exposure to asbestos and mesothelioma' (1965) 272 *New England Journal of Medicine* 560 ff.; M. Newhouse and H. Thompson, 'Mesothelioma of pleura and peritoneum following exposure to asbestos in the London area' (1965) 22 *British Journal of Industrial Medicine* 261 ff.; D. O'B. Hourihane, 'The pathology of mesotheliomata and an analysis of their association with asbestos exposure' (1964) 19 *Thorax* 268 ff.; and C. A. Sleggs, P. Marchand and J. C. Wagner, 'Diffuse pleural mesotheliomas in South Africa' (1961) 35 *South African Medical Journal* 28 ff. Mesothelioma is a cancer of the pleura or peritoneum. It is an extremely painful disease that develops quickly in its later stages; there is no known cure.

[68] See (1965) 132 *Annals of the New York Academy of Sciences* 765 ff.; M. Greenberg, 'Biological effects of asbestos: New York Academy of Sciences 1964' (2003) 43 *American Journal of Industrial Medicine* 543 ff.; and P. W. J. Bartrip, *Beyond the Factory Gates: Asbestos and Health in Twentieth-Century America* (London: Continuum, 2006), pp. 85–94.

developments and the enactment of the Occupational Safety and Health Act 1970, which made health and safety at work a federal responsibility. In Britain the expansion of knowledge led directly to the Asbestos Regulations 1969. These regulations, developed over a period of some five years with input from industry, organised labour, scientists at the London School of Hygiene and Tropical Medicine and others, came into operation in May 1970 and provided the basis for asbestos control until the 1980s.[69]

11.4 Conclusion

In the space available it has been possible to document only some aspects of the relationship between scientific, medical and technical expertise and legal change between the middle of the nineteenth century and late in the twentieth century. In the areas reviewed, medical, scientific and technical experts were able to have a substantial, even decisive, influence on the law relating to occupational health and safety. At the same time, it appears that expert opinion became considerably more influential from the 1890s. In the case of occupational health, a few pioneering individuals, such as Sir John Simon, were active in the early and mid-Victorian years, but no major study of the subject was published in the period between Charles Turner Thackrah's pioneering study in the 1830s and Thomas Arlidge's *Diseases of Occupations* some sixty years later. Only after Arlidge had revitalised the subject and Legge had assumed office as medical inspector of factories did medical expertise become a force in changing the law. Neither before the 1890s nor since then has it been possible to discern much influence from theorists on the regulatory process. Rather, this process deserves to be characterised, in Sidney Webb's words, as an 'example of English practical empiricism' in action.[70]

[69] See Bartrip, *Beyond the Factory Gates*, chs. 8–11; Bartrip, *The Way from Dusty Death*, esp. ch. 6.

[70] See B. L. Hutchins and A. Harrison, *A History of Factory Legislation* (London: P. S. King & Son, 1926), p. ix.

12

Expertise and the evolution of private law: the case of occupational illness in twentieth-century France

PAUL-ANDRÉ ROSENTAL*

The court cases about asbestos in the last two decades, and the media attention devoted to them, create the impression that there has been a decisive turning point recently in the recognition and compensation of occupational diseases in France.[1] Only in the last several years has public opinion grown sensitive to the issue of occupational health. Previously, public indifference to the matter contrasted sharply with the media coverage of the related theme 'suffering at work' (*souffrance au travail*).[2] The expression, coined by Christophe Dejours,[3] does not connote occupational health in the traditional sense; instead, it draws attention to all forms of stress and harassment created by the intensification of work in contemporary economies. The concept has proved influential because of the unique way in which it relates everyday psychological knowledge to the ideological critique of neoliberalism, which is particularly strong in France. By contrast, during the course of the twentieth century the increasingly specialised field of industrial medicine came to be seen as a body of antiquated professionals of uncertain functions and usefulness, which not only undermined expert opinion about asbestos-related illness but also limited public interest in occupational health more generally. These developments have had enormous implications for the legal treatment of occupational illness under French civil law.

The heightening drama around asbestos did more than contrast with the relative indifference in twentieth-century France to questions of occupational health. It also marked the arrival of the judiciary in a sphere hitherto dominated by a political-administrative approach. The struggle

* Sciences-Po and INED, Paris.

[1] E. Henry, *Amiante: Un scandale improbable: Sociologie d'un problème public* (Presses universitaires de Rennes, 2007).

[2] D. Fassin, 'Et la Souffrance devint sociale' (2004) 680 *Critique* 16 ff.

[3] C. Dejours, *Souffrance en France: La banalisation de l'injustice sociale* (Paris: Seuil, 1988).

for the recognition of occupational diseases, one of the key stakes in the history of occupational medicine, had previously been played out almost entirely in commissions. From the Commission of Industrial Hygiene (CIH), created in 1900, to the Commission of Occupational Diseases today, such bodies brought together state representatives, trade unionists, employers' delegates and medical experts. By contrast, the multiplication of court cases involving asbestos allowed new voices to be heard. Trials not only provided a platform for isolated individuals presenting their cases or unions speaking as natural defenders of workers' rights, but, above all, they endowed victims' associations with a means to call for change. In this context, the cause of asbestos-related illnesses was taken out of the exclusive field of workplace issues and became a crusade of public health.

The politicisation of asbestos was aided in particular by developments outside the field of work. The new legal obligation to search for asbestos prior to every property transaction is just one example here. Similarities with the history of AIDS a decade earlier[4] contributed further to this development, by making the fight for the recognition of asbestos an emblem of the struggle of civil society and its representatives. In particular, a variety of associations lobbied against the utilitarianism of private companies and against the indifference or complicity of the state. Beyond these dimensions, which are the most significant in the case of France, the mobilisation against the ill effects of asbestos reveals the growing importance of the European Union for the legal recognition of occupational disease. For example, the European Union has imposed strict thresholds for exposure to asbestos for workers in France and has regularly applied financial sanctions since the 1980s for the violation of these measures of minimal precautions.

Finally, the transformation of expertise played an important role in shaping public opinion about occupational diseases. Until asbestos became recognised as a large-scale and potentially lethal problem for French workers, specialists were called to a kind of 'dialogue of the deaf' for cases of occupational illness: they served more or less as explicit speakers for the different groups present in public commissions – that is, employers and trade unions. Above all, their arguments served to legitimate administrative decisions ex post, reflecting pre-existing tests of strength.[5] By contrast, the case of asbestos led to the advent of a new mode

[4] N. Dodier, *Leçons politiques de l'épidémie de sida* (Paris: Éditions de l'EHESS, 2003).

[5] E. Henry, 'Quand l'action publique devient nécessaire: qu'a signifié "résoudre" la crise de l'Amiante?' (2004) 54 *Revue Française de Science Politique* 289 ff.

of hygiene-related intelligence, mobilising bodies that were neutral by vocation, beginning with institutes of public research. Over time, expert activity became characterised by uncertainty, just as French society grew increasingly haunted by the principle of precaution.[6] The transformation of expertise in the case of asbestos points to a broader development in the relationship between expert opinion and private law; and this development has certainly not been unique to France.[7]

12.1 The relevance and necessity of a historical perspective

If examined more closely, this portrayal of an irrepressible march towards the public recognition of occupational health hazards appears too straightforward. In fact, the case of asbestos fits into a longer history that goes back to the late nineteenth century, when occupational health first became a major public issue.[8] Over time, white lead, white phosphorous, silicosis, asbestosis, musculoskeletal disorders and, more recently, glycol ethers and occupational cancers have been the milestones of the history of occupational health in France and of its successive 'failures'.

Examining the case of asbestos historically enables us to explain how it relates to the legal treatment of occupational illness in general. Since the 1940s occupational medicine in France has maintained the same institutional framework,[9] which has consistently encouraged a test of strength between employers, workers, doctors and the state. In particular, practitioners of occupational medicine have been mostly limited to the evaluation of workers' fitness for particular jobs.[10] They have therefore been hindered from moving towards the broader and more preventative role

[6] P. Lascoumes, 'La Précaution comme anticipation des risques résiduels et hybridation de la responsabilité' (1996) *L'Année sociologique* 359 ff.; P. Lascoumes, 'L'Expertise, de la recherche d'une action rationnelle à la démocratisation des connaissances et des choix' (2002) 103 *Revue française d'administration publique* 369 ff.

[7] T. M. Porter, *Trust in Numbers: The Pursuit of Objectivity in Science and Public Life* (Princeton University Press, 1996).

[8] L. Bonneff and M. Bonneff, *Les Métiers qui tuent: Enquête auprès des syndicats ouvriers sur les maladies professionnelles* (Paris: Bibliographie sociale, 1905); J.-C. Devinck, *La Création de la médecine du travail en France, 1914–1946* (Paris: Unsa Education, 2002); C. Moriceau, *Les Douleurs de l'industrie: L'Hygiénisme industriel en France, 1860–1914* (Paris: Éditions de l'EHESS, 2010).

[9] The 1946 law, which still sets the overall framework for the practice of industrial medicine, broadly reproduces the terms of a 1942 Vichy law, which itself relays the arrangements of an official recommendation formulated on 1 June 1940 by the Third Republic.

[10] C. Omnès and A.-S. Bruno (eds.), *Les Mains inutiles: Inaptitude au travail et emploi en Europe* (Paris: Belin, 2004).

to which they aspire.[11] In fact, since their appearance in the first half of the twentieth century, occupational physicians have been suspected of promoting companies' productivity – 'smelling savings'[12] – and even of betraying the confidentiality of workers. They have not been able to gain full legitimacy in the eyes of workers, which has made it difficult for occupational physicians to stand as neutral mediators.

Industrial medicine has literally found itself 'stuck'. Employers see in it either a financial burden of somewhat doubtful use or a simple tool for managing personnel and improving productivity. Unions still tend to turn the problem of unsanitary working conditions into an argument for pay rises, rather than an issue for medical expertise. Public opinion is generally indifferent to occupational medicine and occupational illness more generally; the state therefore ratifies new policies agreed between these groups – when necessary – rather than arbitrating between them. Moreover, the Conseil de l'Ordre des Médecins, the powerful corporatist body that has ruled French medicine since its creation in 1940 under the Vichy regime, has always worried about the potential and 'unfair' competition of company doctors against free practitioners. Ultimately, the test of strength for these various interests is whether the state will shift some of the cost of occupational diseases towards health insurance – and away from the sphere of court cases and liability claims.

The picture painted here is no doubt too general, but it does shed some light on the legal difficulties involved in addressing occupational illness by outlining the conflicts involved. To what extent has the relationship between expertise and liability actually changed with the case of asbestos-related disease and similar occupational illnesses? The following sections examine the general tendencies of the French model, evaluating its potential for the legal treatment of occupational illness in the longer term.

12.2 The difficult recognition of occupational diseases

12.2.1 Dynamics of the struggle for recognition: recording a long history

The recognition of occupational diseases has been a prominent area of conflict between unions and employers. Tensions between the two groups

[11] S. Buzzi, J.-C. Devinck and P.-A. Rosental, *La Santé au travail (1880–2006)* (Paris: La Découverte, 2006).

[12] L. Ranc, 'Les ouvriers et la médecine d'usine', in M. Eck (ed.), *La Médecine sociale: Bilan et perspectives d'avenir* (Paris: Librairie sociale et économique, 1944), pp. 10 ff.

go back to the end of the nineteenth century, when working-class movements began to mobilise around the issue.[13] This struggle with the unions, which was particularly strong in the period running up to the Second World War,[14] played an important role in the broader movement for social legislation at the time. It was carried along, from the last decade of the nineteenth century, by a group of international associations such as the International Association for the Legal Protection of Workers and the more specialised Permanent International Committee for the Study of Occupational Diseases (today the International Commission for Occupational Health).

The International Labour Organization (ILO), created in 1919, extended and officialised the action of this international 'reformers' nebula'.[15] In order to address – in its own words – the 'French delay', the ILO promoted the 1929 Lyons Congress, which marked the birth of occupational medicine both as a notion and as an institution.[16] *Mutatis mutandis*, and not having the space necessary to nuance this comparison, it can be said that the growing importance of the European Union over the last twenty years only repeats the importance of this earlier transnational framework in the matter of occupational health.

Supported by the ILO and well organised at the international level, union leaders have committed themselves to a struggle for the recognition of occupational diseases with the broadest possible definition: every disease contracted in the framework of occupational activity is an occupational illness. In response, employers' experts have tended, ever since the 1920s, to deny the occupational origin of diseases, usually by calling on the seemingly objective reasoning of probabilities: that it is impossible to assert with statistical certainty that there is always a causal link between exposure to a product and the contraction of a disease at work. This sort of epistemological argument, which is obviously inspired by financial considerations, has taken centre stage in medical explanations since the interwar period.[17] Only its modalities have differed, reflecting the terms of medical science employed in any given period of time.

[13] Moriceau, *Les Douleurs de l'industrie*, esp. ch. 4, pp. 141 ff.

[14] It has been much overlooked, however: see Devinck, *La Création de la médecine du travail en France*.

[15] C. Topalov (ed.), *Laboratoires du nouveau siècle* (Paris: Éditions de l'EHESS, 1999); P.-A. Rosental, 'Géopolitique et état-providence: le BIT et la politique mondiale des migrations dans l'entre-deux-guerres' (2006) 61 *Annales: Histoire, Sciences Sociales* 99 ff.; P. Weindling (ed.), *International Health Organisations and Movements, 1918–1939* (Cambridge University Press, 1995).

[16] Buzzi, Devinck and Rosental, *La Santé au travail*, pp. 31–4.

[17] P. Vineis, *Nel Crepuscolo della Probabilità: La Medicina tra Scienza ed Etica* (Turin: Einaudi, 1999); N. Dodier, *L'Expertise médicale: Essai de sociologie sur l'exercice du jugement* (Paris: Métailié, 1993).

A similar line of argument can be found in the reasoning evoked to free employers from their responsibility and shift it onto workers.[18] For example, when Decree number 2001–97 of 1 February 2001, on carcinogenic, mutagenic and reproductive risks, was promulgated in France, an intense debate erupted around the idea that some individuals are more prone than others to catch occupational illnesses, especially if those diseases can be linked to heredity.[19] In their fight against the growing use of genetic, so to speak eugenic tests in firms,[20] industrial physicians, supported by the Conseil de l'Ordre, did not realise that they were continuing a struggle that has gone on for over a hundred years, and even has its roots in medieval scholastic thought.[21] In the same way, the attribution of occupational disorders to harmful behaviours outside work (alcoholism, dirtiness) or to poor living conditions due to insufficient wages (unsanitary lodgings, bad nutrition) harks back not only to the nineteenth century[22] but also to the entire *ancien régime*.[23]

Employers have also looked to the organisation of work in order to deflect claims for compensation; in the nineteenth century, as today, employers sought to shake off responsibility for the development of occupational illnesses by pointing to the high level of turnover at the workplace. On the one hand, employers could cite internal mobility between jobs that entailed a greater degree of danger and those that were less dangerous within an establishment. Whether in Lille's white lead factories

[18] The same tendency can be observed in the material aimed at increasing workers' sensitivity to work hazards: N. Blétry, 'Ceci n'est pas un risque: les affiches de prévention des risques professionnels et sanitaires en France au XXe siècle', in C. Omnès and L. Pitti (eds.), *Cultures du risque au travail et pratiques de prévention au XXe siècle* (Presses universitaires de Rennes, 2009), pp. 155 ff. Throughout the twentieth century posters displayed within companies played on workers' guilt and unawareness, implicitly saying that occupational injuries and diseases were due to employees' carelessness rather than deficient work organisation.

[19] The decree states that 'workers cannot be given work exposing them to a carcinogenic, mutagenic or toxic agent for reproduction, unless they have been subjected to a preliminary examination by the occupational doctor and if the file of aptitude attests that they do not present any medical counter-indication to these works'.

[20] S. Douay, 'Tests génétiques en entreprise: une irruption à contre-courant de la législation sociale' (2003) 2 *Revue Internationale de Droit Économique* 233 ff.

[21] M. van der Lugt, 'Les maladies héréditaires dans la pensée scolastique (XIIe–XVIe siècles)', in M. van der Lugt and C. de Miramon (eds.), *L'Hérédité entre moyen âge et époque moderne: Perspectives historiques* (Florence: Sismel, 2008), pp. 273 ff.

[22] J.-P. Barrière, 'Perception du risque au travail et préhistoire d'une maladie professionnelle: l'industrie de la céruse dans le nord de la France (1800–1950)', in D. Varaschin (ed.), *Risques et prises de risques dans les sociétés industrielles* (Piertelen: Peter Lang, 2007), pp. 87 ff.; A. Cottereau, 'La tuberculose: maladie urbaine ou maladie de "l'usure au travail"?' (1978) 2 *Sociologie du Travail* 192 ff.

[23] A. Farge, 'Les artisans malades de leur travail' (1977) 32 *Annales ESC* 993 ff.

in the nineteenth century, or in those that polished pebbles a hundred years later,[24] the rotation of personnel in the most exposed jobs was both a means of preventing occupational diseases at the least cost and of complicating eventual demands for financial compensation. On the other hand, employers could cite the movement of workers from firm to firm. Especially in the case of diseases that become evident after a period of time has elapsed, it could prove almost impossible to link the contraction of an occupational illness to a particular workplace. Moreover, the poor quality of statistical records can make it very difficult to follow careers and reconstruct exposure to risk.

These problems are at their most acute in the case of migrant workers. In France, as in most industrialised countries, there has been a natural link between immigration and occupational health: in many sectors, the jobs most exposed to health risks have been given to foreign workers. No doubt, some members of the unions have been complicit in this arrangement. However this complicity is quite difficult for the historian to record: immigrant labourers are the workers least able to obtain the acknowledgement of legal breaches regarding occupational health and to obtain financial compensation for them. This dynamic has been cumulative. By allowing prevention costs to be minimised, the employment of migrant workers for these kinds of jobs has not only perpetuated difficult working conditions. It has also reduced the appeal of certain jobs for domestic workers and encouraged employers to recruit a continuing flow of foreigners. As a result, migrants often become limited to working in the most precarious sector of the economy (that is, the temporary or 'informal sector'), in which working contracts, in law or in practice, effectively reduce the forms of legal protection against risks at work. Thus, for example, the collieries in France have successively recruited Polish, Italian and Moroccan miners.[25]

With the exception of the militant period at the beginning of the 1970s, France has hardly benefited from the role played by foreign workers, who, with the help of their country of origin, have lobbied for improvements in the treatment of occupational health. By contrast, migrant workers based in other states have seen more progress in their attempts to improve conditions at work. As early as the end of the nineteenth century, for example,

24 Barrière, 'Perception du risque au travail'; A. Thébaud-Mony (ed.), *La Reconnaissance des maladies professionnelles* (Paris: La Documentation française, 1991).

25 P.-A. Rosental and J.-C. Devinck, 'Statistique et mort industrielle: la fabrication du nombre de victimes de la silicose dans les houillères en France de 1946 à nos jours' (2007) 95 *Vingtième Siècle* 75 ff.

the British government sought to protect Cornish miners by encouraging South Africa to develop a law for the compensation of silicosis, a pulmonary illness that is similar to asbestosis due to its protracted development. The British experience with South Africa provided an international model, but not one that had a great impact on developments in France.

In France, as elsewhere, workers have often been required to justify their lifestyle, character and sometimes even heredity, placing them in a weak and paradoxical position. They must argue both on a personal level, shaking off a long list of suspicions, and on a collective level. Moreover, they are able to put forward only general links between their jobs and occupational illness when they are expected to prove without a doubt a clear correlation between the two. This long-term configuration sheds light on the significance, the contribution and the limits of the 1919 law on occupational illness, which extended the 1898 law on work injuries and remains the foundational text of current French legislation. As the cautious wording of a founding father of occupational medicine suggests,[26] the legacy of the law was ambiguous: by not requiring workers to provide proof of the occupational origin of certain specified, legally recognised illnesses, 'this legislation no doubt suppresses interminable discussions concerning such or such a case, but it leads to [some] diseases being considered as occupational diseases when they are perhaps not, and it rejects others which probably are'. The result of this ambiguity has been the mutually antagonistic positions between trade unionists and employers' delegates within the successive commissions that, since the creation of the CIH in 1900, have been in charge of establishing a list of occupational diseases. As Marc-Olivier Déplaude writes,[27] even today – and in contrast to the alliances that often take place in other branches of the social security system – the Commission of Occupational Diseases never sees unions divided when dealing with employers.

This conflict has made it difficult for industrial physicians to take up the role of arbiters, to which they have aspired since the interwar period. Nonetheless, to a certain extent, it has been inherent in the very structure of the CIH. Created by the reformist minister Alexandre Millerand and limited to a consultative role, the committee was reorganised in 1931 and became an intermediary body between unions, employers, medical experts and the state. Contrary to what some sociologists and political

[26] H. Desoille, *La Médecine du travail*, 3rd edn (Paris: Presses universitaires de France, 1979), p. 17.

[27] M.-O. Déplaude, 'Les maladies professionnelles: les usages conflictuels de l'expertise médicale' (2003) 53 *Revue Française de Science Politique* 707 ff.

scientists suggest, the use of expertise that it applied was not radically different from that which prevails today. It called upon the work of 'independent' experts, many of whom held positions within public bodies. The difference from today resides less in the process itself than in the institutional framework.

Certainly, institutes of public research did not exist in the early twentieth century in the sense that one sees in contemporary France, for example, with INSERM (the National Institute for Health and Medical Research). They did not truly flourish until the period of intensive statism that began at the end of the Third Republic and continued under Vichy and with the Liberation. But other institutions, such as the CNAM (the National Centre for Industrial Knowledge) or the Institute of Industrial Hygiene, founded in 1908, offered their members sufficient independence to carry out the work of expertise and claim scientific legitimacy. The creation of specialised university institutes in the 1930s that focused on occupational health further expanded the available expertise in the country.

In the background, there were a number of further institutions in which the scientific debate on occupational illness took place. In the case of the struggle for the recognition of silicosis, which was the major issue concerning occupational medicine in the 1930s, expertise played a crucial role. In this case, experts provided 'intelligence', directly articulating the latest medical research and applied knowledge.[28] Having objective, scientific information on the issue of silicosis became so critical that every proposal for legal reform faltered in parliament over the issue of insufficient data. The situation in the 1930s resembled that of today: parliamentarians sensitive to the employers' lobby could rely on uncertainty about the pathology of the illness, whose very existence divided the medical profession.

In other respects, too, the conflict about expertise in the 1930s followed a pattern that will be familiar to twenty-first century readers. For example, Jean Magnin, an occupational medical doctor close to Christian unions and sensitive to the question of silicosis, proposed taking X-rays of affected lungs as part of the long crusade for the recognition of the disease in France. In part, he was inspired by the 1929 Lyons Congress, which had been supported by the ILO. In fact, France was seen internationally as a latecomer country in the matter of occupational health, and was therefore subjected to pressure from the ILO. The head of its hygiene service, Luigi

[28] P.-A. Rosental, *L'Intelligence démographique: Sciences et politiques des populations en France (1930–1960)* (Paris: Odile Jacob, 2003); F. Buton, 'De l'expertise scientifique à l'intelligence épidémiologique: l'activité de veille sanitaire' (2006) 65 *Genèses* 71 ff.

Carozzi, made silicosis his pet cause and heeded the lobbying of South Africa, which already had compensation laws for the disease and wished to forge an international medico-legal standard in order to legitimate and optimise its use of migrant black labour.

In the mining sector, as in so many others,[29] the efforts of the ILO structured the French debate. To counter ILO pressure on the issue of silicosis, French collieries began, from 1930 onwards, appointing four leading medical professors who argued against the existence of silicosis – or, at least, its occurrence in France.[30] In this context, the struggle over compensation for silicosis, which was finally granted in 1945, took place in academic arenas as well as in the major political bodies (parliament, ministries and institutions representing the interests of employers, such as the General Council of Mines). In this respect, the case of silicosis resembles conflicts over occupational health in France today. As far as expertise was concerned in the interwar period,[31] the relevant places were the Academy of Medicine and the academic societies that focused on various aspects of occupational illnesses involving the lungs: the Society of Scientific Studies on Tuberculosis, the French Society of Forensic Medicine and the French Society of Radiology. In this struggle, the CIH played a critical role, because it set research agendas and shaped scientific findings. Moreover, the experts in charge of preparing its reports were attributed a quasi-official status. Just as in France today, or as in international bodies, disputes within the CIH were therefore resolved by the choice of experts invoked.[32]

12.2.2 The difficult promotion of occupational diseases

The first major conflicts over the recognition of occupational diseases or the abolition of toxic products, e.g. white lead and white phosphorous, were covered extensively in the press around 1900. In particular,

[29] Metallurgy provides a good example: D. Fraboulet, 'Le patronat de la métallurgie et l'(in)aptitude durant la première partie du XXᵉ siècle', in Omnès and Bruno, *Les Mains inutiles*, pp. 287 ff.

[30] J.-C. Devinck and P.-A. Rosental, '"Une maladie sociale avec des aspects médicaux": la difficile reconnaissance de la silicose comme maladie professionnelle dans la France du premier XXe siècle' (2009) 56 *Revue d'histoire moderne et contemporaine* 99 ff.

[31] This was a time when public research and organisation in laboratories were little developed in themselves: J.-F. Picard, *La République des savants: La recherche française et le CNRS* (Paris: Flammarion, 1990).

[32] T. Cayet, P.-A. Rosental and M. Thébaud-Sorger, 'How international organisations compete: occupational safety and health at the ILO, a diplomacy of expertise' (2009) 2 *Journal of Modern European History* 173 ff.

journalists reported on the struggle of female workers in the match industry.[33] It is difficult to find such enthusiasm subsequently. A disease such as silicosis never received similar public interest in France, except during a brief period in the 1970s when occupational health in general became a major social issue. In this respect, the French experience with silicosis differed from that elsewhere. In the United States, for example, silicosis became the subject of a media campaign in the 1930s, with an abundance of press articles and information films, and even a movie.[34]

In part, the fact that there were only a small number of court cases in France over the issue of occupational illness accounts for this contrast. During the interwar period it seems that one disease above all was the object of French court cases: dermatosis linked to the exposure to potassium bichromate. Moreover, recourse to boards of arbitration (including employers and workers in industrial disputes) for any occupational illnesses seems to have been rare at this time.[35] After the war there is no evidence that a massive recourse to tribunals for occupational diseases took place. Here, too, the case of silicosis is exemplary. Immediately following the war it became the subject of a number of complaints and court cases, but this was a transitory phase, linked to the coming into force of the ordinance of 2 August 1945.[36] In general, the condition, like other occupational illnesses, did not receive much legal attention.

A number of factors account for the lack of judicial attention to silicosis in France. On the one hand, French law does not permit class-action law suits, and, for individual employees, the complexity and the cost of a judicial action are not inconsiderable. Furthermore, the potential costs for individuals are doubled in light of possible reprisals by employers.[37] In addition, before 1993 workers could not receive compensation for diseases contracted at work but not officially recognised as 'occupational',

[33] B. Gordon, 'Ouvrières et maladies professionnelles sous la IIIe République: la victoire des allumettiers français sur la nécrose phosphorée de la mâchoire' (1993) 3 *Le Mouvement Social* 77 ff.

[34] D. Rosner and G. Markowitz, *Deadly Dust: Silicosis and the Politics of Occupational Disease in Twentieth-Century America* (Ann Arbor: University of Michigan Press, 1991).

[35] L. Machu, 'Entre prévention et réparation: les syndicats ouvriers français face à la question du risque pendant l'entre-deux-guerres', in Omnès and Pitti, *Cultures du Risque*, pp. 189 ff.

[36] I. Metge, 'Les problèmes juridiques posés par la législation relative à la silicose des mineurs' (1951), thèse de droit, University of Paris.

[37] This fear is no doubt even stronger today. According to the report of the committee instituted by article 30 of Law no. 96–1160 of 27 January 1996 for financing social security for 1997, more than 50 per cent of sick people had to leave the firm after having declared their pathology, especially following a dismissal for medical incapacity.

meaning that it would have been futile for many workers to take their claims to court.[38]

On the other hand, trade unions in France have discouraged actions of this kind. They have preferred mass action to individual initiative, as, for example, through court cases. This scenario, of course, differs entirely from that in a country such as the United States, where, in the 1930s, court trials played a major role in sensitising public opinion to silicosis. The French case can also be compared to other national examples, though. In Fascist Italy, for instance, the recognition of silicosis in 1943 instead resulted in a series of court cases that were encouraged by the unions, which collected part of the indemnities when they were successful.[39]

By contrast, in France union action focused above all on law suits of general interest. In 1941 French unions succeeded in gaining compensation for workers by invoking the legal notion of an 'employer's inexcusable mistake' – that is, negligence under the *Code civil*. This jurisprudential notion was important because it undermined the principles of the 1919 law on occupational health as well as the 1898 law on work injuries. Both laws had been compromises based on the idea of an employer's liability without mistake. In other words, under both laws, employers were liable to compensate workers in case of workplace injuries or officially recognised occupational diseases, but they could not be held personally responsible for damage in general. The idea of an 'employer's inexcusable mistake' was at the root of a series of judicial decisions in 2002 related to asbestos. The rulings both reactivated and extended this 1941 notion, with the result that employers have subsequently been held liable for safety – that is, held to an *obligation de résultats*. Significantly, under French law, any case of occupational disease or injury can now be considered an 'inexcusable mistake' if the employer was aware or should have been aware of a work-related risk and took no measure to prevent it.

In most cases during the course of the twentieth century, however, union action focused more on addressing problems directly associated with occupational health than on seeking the intervention of the courts. In the 1930s it was epitomised by Dr Guy Hausser, from the Confédération

[38] N. Hatzfeld, 'Les maladies périarticulaires au temps de la clandestinité: une longue bataille administrative (1919–1972)' (2009) 56 *Revue d'histoire moderne et contemporaine* 177 ff.

[39] F. Carnevale, 'La silicosi nell'industria Italiana tra '800 e '900' (1978) 15 *Classe* 67 ff.

Générale du Travail (CGT).[40] Occupational medicine was on the rise at the time, as employers were beginning to realise that it could provide results not only in terms of productivity but in terms of social peace as well.[41] Hausser endeavoured to capitalise on this growing field. He aimed to rally employees and factory doctors alike, the former to push for legislation on occupational diseases and the latter to privilege workers' health over industrial productivity. To this purpose, besides publishing numerous information pamphlets,[42] he promoted national congresses on occupational health and campaigns against the use of certain products, such as benzene derivatives. He also lobbied against cheap methods of disease prevention, such as the distribution of milk in factories, which was meant to protect workers against industrial poisons. Although many workers believed in the effectiveness of such measures, Hausser denounced them as pretences for genuine prevention. Moreover, he pushed for the creation of an institute for the study and prevention of occupational diseases, which was indeed set up and run by the CGT with the support of the Popular Front government, in which worker delegates from the Committee of Industrial Hygiene came to prepare their cases and employees found assistance that was both medical and juridical. Hausser's strategy in the struggle against occupational diseases suited the French system because it took a political-administrative approach. As discussed earlier, though, this approach ran into an intractable obstacle: powerful forces of inertia on the side of employers and even liberal medicine, and, on the other side, the suspicion of employees and the indifference of public opinion.

One of the features of this enduring test of strength was essentially medical. The only diseases that were legally recognised were those with an obvious link between exposure to a product and certain characteristic symptoms. For example, as mentioned earlier, the use of phosphorous in manufacturing matches was outlawed in France at the turn of the twentieth century, when it became clear that workers in match factories were faced with phosphorous poisoning in the form of unequivocal oral

40 This trade union is close to the French Communist Party. Guy Hausser, the most prominent militant figure in occupational health in twentieth-century France, was assassinated during deportation.

41 Y. Cohen, 'L'invention des techniciens sociaux: du commandement social après juin 1936 chez Peugeot' (1996) 114 *Actes de la recherche en sciences sociales* 30 ff.; L. L. Downs, 'Les surintendantes d'usine et la rationalisation du travail en France' (1993) 164 *Le mouvement social* 53 ff.

42 Practical handbooks by Hausser include *Les Maladies professionnelles, conseils pratiques, législation* (Paris: Librairie syndicale, undated); and *Le Code du travail et l'hygiène* (Paris: Centre confédéral d'éducation ouvrière, undated).

problems. In contrast, at the same time, tobacco workers failed to win recognition for the occupational origins of their illnesses, which, linked to nicotinism, were manifested by more commonplace symptoms (nervous irritability, nausea, diarrhoea, problems with reproductive functions). In many respects, one can say that the criterion of a distinctive and more or less specific manifestation of a disease remained consistent throughout the century.

During the twentieth century other features of the struggle for the recognition of occupational diseases were, instead, of a sociological, technical or economic nature. For the historian, the asymmetry between occupational health and public health, which has had much greater potential to mobilise societies, is noteworthy.[43] Jean-Paul Barrière has demonstrated this dichotomy in the case of white lead in the nineteenth century:[44] in contrast to painters in the building industry, who were consumers of paint containing white lead, workers involved in manufacturing the paint were less well placed to get its dangerous nature legally recognised. Nonetheless, builders did not obtain a durable solution to the problem; although a 1919 law explicitly targeted lead poisoning, it was only in the 1990s that information on the risks of lead poisoning led to protective measures for workers – at a time when the risks to residents of buildings with lead paint were being recognised.

An additional feature characterised the legal treatment of occupational illness in twentieth-century France. It was all the more difficult to prohibit exposure to a product when that product was hard to substitute and when substituting it was expensive. The case of silicosis again exemplifies this pattern, which was to be repeated later with asbestos. In the specific case of collieries, which were responsible for numerous cases of silicosis, coal was a strategic source of energy as much for industries as for homes until the 1960s. Until this time the cost of and compensation for silicosis were directly incorporated in the balance of the French economy, especially because the extraction of coal was so labour-intensive. In this context, it is noteworthy that the ordinance of 2 August 1945 began with a discussion of the reasons behind the law that concluded with an explicit appeal to the collieries' physicians to arbitrate between the health of workers and economic imperatives.

This preponderance of economic factors cannot, as we have noted, be understood without referring to the relationship between the different

[43] See Henry, *Amiante: Un scandale improbable*.

[44] Barrière, 'Perception du risque au travail'.

groups concerned with occupational health. From both comparative and historical perspectives, one can see that the relative weakness of the social security system in France has played a major role in determining the distinction between occupational diseases and 'private' diseases. In fact, these terms have become widespread in the last several years. All official reports, whether from government or parliament, indicate an under-declaration of occupational illnesses.[45] Therefore, since the mid-1990s, parliament has voted annually for the transfer of funds from the work injuries and occupational diseases branch of the social security system, which is exclusively funded by employers, to the health branch, which is jointly funded by employers and employees (and, de facto, the state). In a way, the transfer of funds between these two branches of social security stands as an official acknowledgement that a significant part of the cost of occupational diseases has been unfairly placed on employees and taxpayers when it should be provided by employers alone. Beyond the problems associated with compensation for occupational illnesses within this system, one can foresee the consequences for prevention: it is not encouraged by such a relatively lax regime of compensation.[46]

This imbalance between the branches of social insurance, which has recently diminished under the effect of the increasing indemnities linked to asbestos, has more historical roots. Having opposed social insurance in principle at the beginning of the twentieth century, employers, especially after major reforms to the system in 1928, sought to take advantage of it as far as possible. The sector of occupational health is an ideal exemplar of this process. To the extent that social insurance expanded in the latter postwar period into an ambitious system of social security, employers tried to allocate the largest possible part of expenses linked to work injuries and occupational diseases risks to other components of the social security system: disease, disability, retirement or, later, early retirement.

The mutual insurance funds that participated in the social security system obviously had an inkling of this danger right from the beginning. In the 1930s they created services that permitted the diagnosis of occupational diseases that employees suffered from and attempted to allocate their costs to the employers. One of the numerous reasons why Vichy was the first regime to make occupational medicine compulsory is that the 'strongman' of the profession at the time, André Gros, was an

[45] S. Volkoff (ed.), *L'Ergonomie et les chiffres de la santé au travail: ressources, tensions et pièges* (Toulouse: Octarès Éditions, 2005).

[46] V. Viet and M. Ruffat, *Le Choix de la prévention* (Paris: Economica, 1999).

occupational physician who had made his career in the Mutuality of the Seine. He sought to minimise costs that unduly affected the mutual funds and transfer them to employers.

To a great extent, this attempt by employers to have the cost of occupational diseases taken up by social institutions had deeper roots. Barrière has demonstrated how, at the end of the nineteenth century, the struggle against white lead diseases was first observed in the Hospices de Lille. This municipal institution needed to collect information on the issue and bring employers before the courts in order to recover the costs of caring for these illnesses.[47] The role of the Hospices de Lille here was hardly clear-cut, however: with the introduction of social insurance, municipalities, like the central state, have been influenced by industrialists and have been passive in dealing with occupational illnesses.

12.3 The weaknesses of the French system for the recognition of occupational diseases in comparative historical perspective

In many cases, the social insurance system has struggled in its attempts to shift responsibility onto employers. In order to understand this, one must place the French case in a comparative and historical perspective. In effect, two types of institutional arrangement for the treatment of occupational diseases have emerged since the late nineteenth century. Their respective features can be traced broadly, along with the advantages and inconveniences of each when it comes to treating occupational diseases. Again, the case of silicosis provides a useful example for comparing the two systems.[48]

Several common points unite countries that have had to deal extensively with silicosis. The complex aetiology and nosology of the disease, as in the case of asbestos, slowed research on the matter and prevented agreement within the medical community. The weight of old medical models must be considered, too. At the end of the nineteenth century the old Ramazzinian model that separated diseases by occupation[49] lost favour to the microbial model, based on contagions. As a result, pneumoconiosis, a

[47] Barrière, 'Perception du risque au travail'.

[48] The subject is part of an international project led by the author, Étude Transnationale d'une Maladie Professionnelle Exemplaire: La Silicose et la Santé au Travail en France et dans les Pays Industrialisés, in response to the call for research projects in 2006 by the programme Santé–Environnement et Santé–Travail (SEST) of the Agence Nationale de la Recherche.

[49] B. Ramazzini, *Diseases of Workers* [1713] (New York: Hafner, 1964).

generic term for lung diseases such as silicosis, came to be 'deprofessionalised'. Pneumoconiosis became dissociated from the workplace, and was instead seen as the outcome of workers' housing and general living conditions rather than the work environment. Moreover, it was increasingly viewed as a form of tuberculosis, the great plague of the century,[50] which was seen as a disease of the 'private sphere'. The new diagnosis of the illness came to obscure the perception of the problem throughout the first third of the twentieth century, and even beyond. The question of complications and post-infection illnesses contributed greatly to obscuring the problem, while it fixed silicosis, on the one hand, and asbestosis, on the other, in a common history.

A combination of two factors – institutional structures and modes of compensation – led to the development of two very different models for dealing with the disease. The first, well described by Gerald Markowitz and David Rosner for the American case,[51] was characterised by private insurance, court cases and 'experimental' statistical models.[52] Ultimately, it was statistical rather than medical factors that were used to identify silicosis in the observations of actuaries in the United States in the first decades of the twentieth century. They found that the diagnosis of 'tuberculosis' did not apply in all cases and noted a marked overrepresentation of fields associated with particular trades, such as mining, when considering cases that could be considered silicosis. This unexpected finding pushed actuaries to rally behind the idea of an occupational disease that was distinct from tuberculosis in terms of its causes. As Philippe Askenazy has noted, this close link between the importance of private insurance and the relative quality of statistical data was a landmark in the long history of dealing with occupational illness in the United States.[53]

The second type of system for dealing with occupational illnesses has emerged in countries such as France, Belgium, Luxembourg and the Netherlands. This 'front of refusal', decried by ILO experts, differed markedly from the United States in its treatment of silicosis. These states possessed a well-developed social security system (especially in the case of

[50] J.-P. Bardet, P. Bourdelais, P. Guillaume, F. Lebrun and C. Quétel (eds.), *Peurs et terreurs face à la contagion: Choléra, tuberculose, syphilis, XIXe – XXe siècles* (Paris: Fayard, 1988), pp. 155 ff.

[51] Rosner and Markowitz, *Deadly Dust*.

[52] These are models that try to test the respective 'pure' impact of the supposedly explanatory variable on the phenomenon to be explained.

[53] P. Askenazy, *Les Désordres du travail: Enquête sur le nouveau productivisme* (Paris: Le Seuil, 2004).

illness or disability); a powerful trade union movement allied to progressive parties, privileging, as we have seen, collective struggle at the expense of individual recourse to tribunals; an essentially descriptive form of statistics; and an absence of reliable data. Reflecting the lack of statisticians, the struggle for the recognition of silicosis was fought in an essentially medical field, and it was relatively easy for employers to try and become dominant, by circumventing specialists in the relevant medical fields.

A distinct 'solution' to the problem of silicosis corresponded to each of these two models. In the United States, legislation enacted at the state level sought to dissuade financially, rather than prohibit, and its degree of application strongly depended on the economic and political context. If silicosis, as we have seen, became a national cause in the 1930s, it was with the help of large numbers of unemployed, as the contaminated employees had nothing to lose by turning against their former employers for compensation. In France and in its neighbouring countries to the north-east, two approaches to compensating for silicosis emerged. The first, practised in Belgium, consisted of entirely shifting the financial compensation for silicosis to the disability branch of social insurance. Disregarding the medical recognition of silicosis, which was well advanced in the kingdom in the 1930s, the policy focused on the social and economic treatment rather than the epidemiological treatment of the disease. This approach made Belgium the last major industrialised country to recognise the existence of silicosis, which it did only in 1963, under pressure from miners who had migrated from Italy.[54]

In France, political forces linked to the temporary government of the Liberation tried to present the recognition of silicosis in 1945 as a victory for the workers: in contrast to Belgium, the burden of compensating salaries fell on collieries. Although the new measure appeared a coup for workers in light of their treatment under Vichy, it nonetheless granted only a minimal, conditional and restrictive recognition of the disease. In practice, whether one received compensation at all, and the quality of compensation that one might receive, was left to a test of strength between various social forces. Compared to Belgium, compensation for silicosis existed in France, but in the form of a compromise. The balance, a priori precarious for employees, broke down when the 1948 Lacoste decrees in effect handed over responsibility for the medical evaluation of silicosis claims to

[54] É. Geerkens, 'Quand la silicose n'était pas une maladie professionnelle: genèse du premier régime de réparation des pathologies respiratoires des ouvriers mineurs en Belgique (c.1927–1940)' (2009) 56 *Revue d'histoire moderne et contemporaine* 127 ff.

the collieries. Since then, there has been a disparity between silicotics and 'silicotics'. The former have 'simply' contracted the disease while the latter have a legal status – verified by the collieries – that acknowledges it. Those workers who have been granted status as a 'silicotic' then embark on a 'paper career',[55] which begins most modestly with a disability rate recognised at a rate of 0 per cent and financial indemnities that are equally null. If, despite everything, it makes sense for miners to pursue the status of a 'silicotic', it is because this status allows them, through annual re-evaluations of their rate of disability, to benefit from increasing bonuses, but, above all, to hope for a form of protection for their dependants: the higher the rate they reach (a rate that, because of the complexity of the illness, is somewhat arbitrary from a medical standpoint), the higher the chance for their dependants to establish that their father's or husband's death was indeed due to silicosis and to get a pension.

12.4 Conclusion

At the end of the twentieth century the appearance of a new class of actors, asbestos victims' organisations, gave some observers the feeling that compensation for occupational diseases was entering a new era. Relying on the diffusion of 'civic epistemology',[56] they were increasingly successful in court. The ambiguities of the 1898 and 1919 laws, which made employers financially responsible for work injuries and occupational diseases but wiped out their general liability, were to be removed by recourse to the 1941 jurisprudential notion of an 'employer's inexcusable mistake'.

Recent events tend to invalidate, or at least relativise, this scenario. After a few years of popularity in the media, asbestos cases are being replaced by a new issue: 'occupational suicides'.[57] Occupational suicides are a way to focus again, as in the 1980s and 1990s, on stress at work. Moreover, they have directed public attention towards the suffering of clerks and executives that has resulted from the reorganisation and 'casualisation' of labour in the global economy.[58] Even though this new problem echoes

[55] A. Spire, *Étrangers à la carte: L'Administration de l'immigration en France, 1945–1975* (Paris: Grasset, 2005).

[56] S. Jasanoff, *Designs on Nature: Science and Democracy in Europe and the United States* (Princeton University Press, 2005).

[57] At the time of writing there had been more than thirty cases involving France Télécom alone during the previous twelve months. The company has thus become the symbol for 'psychological mismanagement'.

[58] M. Benquet, P. Marichalar and E. Martin, 'Responsabilités en souffrance: les conflits autour de la souffrance psychique des salariés d'EDF-GDF (1985–2008)' (2010) 79 *Sociétés*

many of the observations made concerning the intensification of labour,[59] it far from captures the whole issue of workplace hazards. Indeed, the exposure of hundreds of thousands of workers to significant risks of cancer[60] does not attract comparable attention, which confirms the hierarchical division between white- and blue-collar professions in terms of public opinion.

Moreover, the impossibility of organising class-action law suits in France and the reluctance of trade unions to go to court have limited the amount of media coverage surrounding the issue of occupational health. The French system for compensating occupational illnesses relies mainly on commissions that bring together civil servants, trade unionists, employers' representatives and experts. The 'tripartite' combination (state, labour, capital) illustrates the functioning of the French welfare state model, which, to some extent, started to develop at the very beginning of the twentieth century around the issue of workplace injuries.[61] In the case of occupational illnesses, however, reference to the social dialogue and principle of equality that stand at the core of French political culture is deceptive. In fact, it is an issue for the most complex expertise, combining medicine, law and engineering. In effect, only the national organising body for employers, Medef (Movement for companies in France), can afford to hire and coordinate top-rank experts in all the specialised fields involved.

From a comparative perspective, and despite the diversity of social security systems in industrialised countries, occupational health has provided the most fragile link between sanitary and social protection.[62] As a result, each system has developed cautiously, only gradually questioning and reforming the relative efficiency of the various channels (administrative, political, judicial, insurance, parliamentary, media or trade union) involved in recognising and compensating occupational diseases. In the case of France, though, a variety of factors make the law on occupational

contemporaines 121 ff.; P.-A. Rosental, 'Le modèle de la "souffrance au travail" aide-t-il à réduire la souffrance au travail?' (2010) 1 *Revue de droit du travail* 11 ff.

59 M. Gollac and S. Volkoff, *Les conditions de travail* (Paris: La Découverte, 2000).

60 This is according to epidemiological studies: N. Sandret and N. Guignon, 'Les expositions aux produits cancérogènes, mutagènes et reprotoxiques' (2005) 104 *Documents pour le médecin du travail* 471 ff.

61 F. Ewald, *L'État-providence* (Paris: Grasset, 1986).

62 M.-C. Blandin, C. Kieffer and C. Lecoanet, *Survey on Under-Reporting of Occupational Diseases in Europe* (Paris: Eurogip, 2002); G. Pransky, T. Snyder, A. Dembe and J. Himmelstein, 'Under-reporting of work-related disorders in the workplace: a case study and review of the literature' (1999) 42 *Ergonomics* 171 ff.

health especially problematic: the lack of unity among and the structural weakness of trade unions; the absence of class-action law suits; and employers' ability to dominate expert knowledge and manipulate the social security system in order to offload part of their costs. Ultimately, for businesses, the law on occupational health provides a reference to bypass rather than an active set of regulations. There is no analogous counterweight to employers in the French case, with the exception of a few prominent court trials that attain some publicity in the media.

13

The notion of a European private law and a softer side to harmonisation

LUCINDA MILLER*

The harmonisation of private law in Europe is a rather beguiling notion, particularly when presented as an indispensable solution to the inefficient functioning of markets across EU member states. It is this mode of argumentation that underpins the European Union's[1] programme of private law harmonisation, harnessing it to internal market objectives with remarkable success. Despite the lack of explicit competences in private law,[2] an extensive, and increasingly intrusive, body of EU private law has developed. Nowadays, the *acquis* is no longer simply 'nibbling'[3] at the edge of national contract law but – to continue the borrowed metaphor – is taking substantial bites. The tentacles of European private law have now spread into jealously protected areas of member states' private law, and, whether it be common rules on product liability, unfair consumer contract terms or consumer sales, it is impossible to deny that a

* Faculty of Laws, University College London.

1 Following the successful ratification of the Treaty of Lisbon in December 2009, the three-pillar structure of the European Union, as established by the Maastricht Treaty, has now been abolished. It should be noted, however, that it is under the European *Community* pillar that contract law legislation has been adopted and contract law policies pursued. Although mindful of the historical division between Community and Union, this chapter uses the term 'European Union' throughout.

2 Competence has been found within the general harmonising provision of the treaty, namely article 114 of the Treaty on the Functioning of the European Union (TFEU) (ex article 95 of the European Community Treaty (TEC)).

3 S. Vogenauer and S. Weatherill, 'The EC's competence to pursue harmonisation', in S. Vogenauer and S. Weatherill (eds.), *The Harmonisation of European Contract Law: Implications for European Private Laws, Business and Legal Practice* (Oxford: Hart, 2006), pp. 105 ff., p. 105. EU private law interventions have been depicted as *islands* in a sea of national law: R. Schulze, 'European private law and existing EC law' (2005) 1 *ERPL* 3 ff., 4. As the European private law *acquis* has grown, the metaphoric islands could now be described as creating a European private law continent: C. Schmid, 'The instrumentalist conception of the acquis communautaire in consumer law and its implications on a European contract law code' (2005) 2 *European Review of Contract Law* 211 ff., 212.

significant body of private law rules, common[4] to the member states, has now evolved.[5]

As if this were not enough, the stakes in the harmonisation programme have been raised considerably in more recent years. Dissatisfied with the sector-specific approach to harmonisation,[6] work on a broader initiative known as the Common Frame of Reference (CFR) was set in motion by the European Commission, the first phase of which (the Draft Common Frame of Reference (DCFR)) is now complete.[7] This DCFR, a non-binding

[4] Whether the development of common rules at the EU level of governance ultimately results in the harmonisation of member states' law is, of course, quite a different matter; see, for example, P. Legrand, 'European legal systems are not converging' (1996) 45 *ICLQ* 52 ff.; and L. Miller, 'The Common Frame of Reference and the feasibility of a common contract law in Europe' (2007) 4 *Journal of Business Law* 378 ff.

[5] For a fuller list of EU legislation that affects private law (the consumer contract law *acquis*), see P.-C. Müller-Graff, 'EC directives as a means of private law unification', in A. Hartkamp and M. Hesselink (eds.), *Towards a European Civil Code* (The Hague: Kluwer, 2004), pp. 77 ff., p. 77. Contract law has been the area of private law most susceptible to European attention – unsurprisingly, perhaps, in light of the political objectives of removing barriers to inter-state trade.

[6] The European Union's practice of piecemeal legislation had created problems with internal coherence, and considerable inconsistencies and gaps between directives. One commentator has recently summed up the *acquis* in unsparing terms: the 'odd batch of Directives…are ill-adjusted to each other, prolix, needlessly complex, and questionable in many respects': R. Zimmermann, 'The present state of European private law' (2009) 57 *Am. J. Comp. L.* 479 ff., 484.

[7] The seeds for a broader programme of harmonisation were first planted by the Commission in 2001 with its Communication on European Contract Law (2001), 398 COM. This was quickly followed up by further consultation papers, which fleshed out the future direction of the Commission's programme, including the CFR. See, for example, (2003) 68 COM and (2004) 651 COM. The DCFR was submitted to the Commission at the end of 2007. A draft outline edition was published in 2008, *Principles, Definitions and Model Rules of European Private Law: Draft Common Frame of Reference* (Munich: Sellier, 2008). Approximately a year later this interim outline edition became an outline edition, this latter version modifying the former to take account of criticisms that had been made via public discussion on some aspects of the text, as well as to accommodate the addition of chapters uncompleted at the time of the publication of the previous edition. C. von Bar, E. Clive and H. Schulte-Nölke (eds.), *Principles, Definitions and Model Rules of European Private Law: Draft Common Frame of Reference (DCFR): Outline Edition* (Munich: Sellier, 2009). It is available at http://webh01.ua.ac.be/storme/2009_02_DCFR_OutlineEdition.pdf. Finally, a six-volume opus was produced that incorporated full comments and comparative notes, published by both Oxford University Press and Sellier: C. von Bar and E. Clive, *Principles, Definitions and Model Rules of European Private Law: Draft Common Frame of Reference (DCFR)* (Oxford/Munich: Oxford University Press/Sellier, 2010/2009). Although there is still much ambiguity as to the final outcome of this process, the DCFR is currently being scrutinised by the political institutions of the European Union with the assistance of an 'Expert Group on the CFR' (see note 54). A final, 'political', CFR is likely to emerge. The DCFR is broad, extending beyond contract law to the law of tort,

document providing 'fundamental principles, definitions and model rules' of European private law, reflects a broader, horizontal approach to private law harmonisation. Although its final form and purpose are still shrouded in much ambiguity, it may eventually provide the basis of a future 'optional instrument',[8] fanning the flames of a wider debate on the possibility and (un)desirability of a European Civil Code.

In one respect, the denomination of this body of law as European *private* law raises an interesting aspect concerning terminology. Ever since Roman times, the definition of private law has rested on criteria that distinguish it from its opposing concept, public law.[9] At the national level, the dichotomy between public and private law has been subjected to a range of attacks that now make a strict separation untenable to maintain in its purest form. Nevertheless, the public/private law divide remains meaningful and has not collapsed. The dichotomy becomes particularly fragile at the European level of governance, however, and may make the term 'private' law, if not entirely misleading, at the very least conceptually problematic. The functionalistic, policy-oriented approach of the European Union cuts across the 'pre-European Union' categorisation of public and private categories.[10] EU law is guided by political, social, economic and other regulatory aims and is replete with mandatory, paternalistic and distributive provisions.[11] In this respect, EU 'private' law can never be described as an apolitical body of law. Indeed, from an ordoliberal perspective, the market integrative, policy-driven EU private law, which has supremacy over national law, might be better defined as *constitutional* law.[12]

Interestingly enough, and somewhat disingenuously, perhaps, the public/private law divide has been resurrected by those most closely associated

unjustified enrichment, benevolent intervention in another's affairs, trusts and, ultimately, some movable areas of property law. It is expected that the political version will be far narrower in substantive reach and focus chiefly on contract law.

8 This is a set of contract law rules that parties can choose as the governing law for their contract, the so-called twenty-eighth European contract law system.

9 In the 3rd century AD Ulpian defined private law as the law that concerns private, as opposed to public, interests: Dig. 1.1.1. (Ulpian); Inst. 1.1.4 (Ulpian). Furthermore, private law is said to be concerned with corrective rather than distributive justice and involve horizontal, equal relationships between private parties, rather than vertical relationships that involve the state and include elements of subordination and domination.

10 C. Joerges, 'The impact of European integration on private law: reductionist perceptions, true conflicts and a new constitutional perspective' (1997) 3 *ELJ* 378 ff., 394.

11 More recently, it has been recognised that private law in Europe needs to acknowledge fundamental rights and constitutional values.

12 See C. Joerges, 'European challenges to private law: on false dichotomies, true conflicts and the need for a constitutional perspective' (1998) 18 *Legal Studies* 146 ff., 147.

with the European harmonisation of private law. On the one hand, private law's apolitical legacy has been resurrected by the Commission as an attempt to present its harmonisation ambitions simply as a technical exercise, lacking in any political significance. The discourse of private law, with its supposedly neutral trappings, is thereby manipulated in order to give the project political opacity.[13] Since an EU private law is necessarily internal-market-oriented, and therefore policy-driven, the private law language and identity seem ill-suited. They nevertheless have remarkable endurance. On the other hand, the public/private law divide has been reinvigorated within national circles in an attempt to resist further EU encroachment in the private law systems. This time, however, it is the *public law values* inherent in private law that are highlighted in an effort to force a collective, political reflection on the constitutional implications of the private law harmonisation processes.[14] The more that the values of private law are imbued with political salience, the more that the EU encroachment into such private law arenas will need to be negotiated with member states. Both these examples reveal how 'private' law can be manipulated as a political tool and how the public/private dichotomy refuses to be buried.

An additional conceptual issue arises from the development of a transnational private law. EU private law seems to suggest a fundamental transformation in the role of the state, recalibrating the relationship between the state and its private law.[15] In much the same way as the rise of the new *lex mercatoria*[16] has fostered intense discussion as to the legitimacy and validity of lawmaking practices that are independent of the state,[17] so the thorny debate on an EU private law seems to reflect a similar concern with

[13] '[T]his technical character should not lead to the misapprehension that the issues posed by the construction of a European law of contract are merely technocratic, to be solved in pragmatic ways by experts': Study Group on Social Justice in European Private Law, 'Social justice in European contract law: a manifesto' (2004) 10 *ELJ* 653 ff., 655.

[14] For illustrations drawn from property law: D. Caruso, 'Private law and public stakes in European integration: the case of property' (2004) 10 *ELJ* 751 ff., 751.

[15] More generally, the notion of transnational law is theoretically challenging, since it 'breaks the frames' of the traditional national/international dichotomy that has inhabited the legal landscape for so long: G. Teubner, 'Breaking frames: the global interplay of legal and social systems' (1997) 45 *Am. J. Comp. L.* 149 ff.

[16] A private law created outside, and independently from, the state, based on the customs and rationality of commerce.

[17] See, for example, G. Teubner, 'Global Bukowina: legal pluralism in the world society', in G. Teubner (ed.), *Global Law without a State* (Aldershot: Ashgate, 1996), pp. 3 ff.; and H.-J. Mertens, 'Lex mercatoria: a self-applying system beyond national law?', in Teubner, *Global Law without a State*, pp. 31 ff.

the apparent retreat of the state in the face of transnational developments in private law. An EU private law forces us to consider the extent to which private law can, and should, be denationalised. At first, this is conceptually rather challenging. From the time that the European legislators appeared on the scene in the eighteenth and nineteenth centuries, state sovereignty and national identity have been intimately connected with the state's private law. In continental Europe, the civil code was an ideal instrument for extending sovereignty into private law, since it was a manifestation of the power of the legislator and the state's dominance in shaping and controlling the law.[18] It was the legislator that was to be at the helm of lawmaking, and the legislator that ultimately determined the legal rights of its subjects.[19] Other legal actors, notably the judiciary, were sidestepped,[20] as the code professed to contain a coherent, systematic and predetermined set of principles that could be logically applied to any variety of factual situations.[21] In short, the code spoke of the power of the state in civil matters, thereby entrenching the state's position in relation to its private law.

Moreover, a code was also a mechanism for nation-state-building and a unified national identity, further consolidating the nexus between the state and its private law. This one legal instrument provided the state with a coherent body of law, governing private law relationships within defined geographical borders – features that defined the modern European state. Thus, underlying the enactment of the codes was the aspiration of a common culture, a single language through which to express that culture and a national identity to distinguish one people from another.[22]

The concept of a European private law therefore raises a whole variety of conceptual and systematic questions about the possibilities of private law existing independently from the state. Europeanisation forces us to confront

[18] N. Jansen and R. Michaels, 'Private law and the state: comparative perceptions and historical observations' (2007) 71 *RabelsZ* 345 ff., 378.

[19] H. Collins, 'Governance implications for the changing character of private law', in F. Cafaggi and H. Muir-Watt (eds.), *Making European Private Law: Governance Design* (Cheltenham: Edward Elgar, 2008), pp. 269 ff.

[20] In France, for example, the code provided a governmental bulwark to give protection from a corrupt judiciary.

[21] The code was to be *applied* rather than *interpreted* by the judge. As Montesquieu pithily puts it : '[L]e juge est la bouche de la loi.' Of course, the image of the civilian judge as simply a spokesman for the law is no longer a credible one. In practice, case law has a far more significant role to play than orthodox theory would hold, and the judiciary has played a major part in developing the body of private law as contained within the codes.

[22] The emergent eastern European codifications show the modern-day relevance of this legacy: D. Caruso 'Private law and state-making in the age of globalization' (2006) 39 *N.Y.U. J. Int'l L. & Pol.* 1 ff., 26.

what appears to be a 'state-less' private law and to rethink what seems to be a naturally given relationship between law and the state. It is little wonder that it is a topic that is 'fashionable, important and widely discussed'.[23]

A transnational private law might present fewer problems than first imagined, however.[24] First, EU member states retain significant powers in the development of European private law through their powers in the European Council. In this respect, it is difficult to describe the European lawmaking processes as 'state-less'. Second, legal development has never been fully within the grasp of the legislator. Codes are not static monoliths but, regardless of what constitutional theory might hold, have been subject to the interpretative forces of the judiciary, entrusted with the gradual development of the codes so as to align them with the social and political mores of the time. Meanwhile, a complementary role in lawmaking processes has been occupied by the jurist,[25] through the publication of persuasive commentary and case notes, and in their expert assistance with legislative texts, prior to parliamentary submission. In this way, private law has retained a significant autonomy from the state even when codifications have occurred, making the existence of transnational private lawmaking a far less troublesome phenomenon.[26]

This less visible aspect to national private law development has resonance at the transnational level today. In the same way that national private law owes much to an active judiciary and a community of scholars, so the academic and judicial participation in lawmaking and reform has played a crucial role in laying the groundwork for, and fostering the notion of, a common European private law. The harmonisation headlines might be replete with legislative and other 'top-down' processes, but the development of a European private law is a narrative that has a far softer side.

13.1 European private law and the academic

One of the repercussions of EU activity in private law is the birth of a new generation of scholar: the European private law scholar. For long, the private law academic was content to banish the EU market integration

[23] N. Jansen and R. Michaels, 'Beyond the state? Rethinking private law: introduction to the issue' (2008) 56 *Am. J. Comp. L.* (special symposium issue) 527 ff., 527.

[24] For a historical and comparative account that discredits such a naturally given relationship, see Jansen and Michaels, 'Private law and the state'.

[25] The relationship between law as promulgated by the state and law as understood by the jurist is described as 'symbiotic' by J. Gordley, 'The state's private law and legal academia' (2008) 56 *Am. J. Comp. L.* 639 ff.

[26] Jansen and Michaels, 'Private law and the state', 394.

programme to a world of public international law and the public law institutions that this categorisation denoted.[27] Hiding behind the core areas of national private law, the jurist remained at an intellectual distance from the legal developments within the EU institutions. The European private law programme has dragged the private lawyer out of his national isolation, however, and forced him into the heart of the debate on European integration. With the European Union's ever greater involvement in private law, he has quickly become a fully fledged member of the European legal community.[28]

The transition has not seemed excessively painful. The jurist has quickly warmed to his role, and the notion of European private law has become the topic *du jour*. This new discipline has spawned a whole host of academic journals,[29] university courses, university chairs, text- and casebooks,[30] and has been the subject of a bewildering amount of academic and practitioner conferences. From within these forums has emerged a rich and protean debate on issues such as the constitutional legitimacy of such activity,[31] its feasibility and/or desirability[32] and the most appropriate form that any final instrument should adopt.[33] More recently, attention has turned to assessment of the structure, substantive content and policy choices contained within the DCFR.[34] These arguments have featured

[27] This is paradoxical in light of the economic foundations of the European Union (formerly known as the European Economic Community).

[28] It was the Unfair Contract Terms Directive in 1993 (Directive 13/93/EC) that really brought it home to the private law scholar that the EU integration programme was something to be taken seriously. This directive goes right to heart of the general structures of contract law, challenging the fundamental notion of contractual autonomy and thereby forcing the private lawyer to engage fully with the EU contract law programme.

[29] See, for example, *The European Review of Private Law*; *The European Review of Contract Law*; *Zeitschrift für Europäisches Privatrecht (ZEuP)*; *Europa e Diritto Private*; and the *Revue des Contrats*, which has a special section devoted to European and comparative law.

[30] The '*Ius commune* casebooks' provide one such example. A full overview on the concept, aims and research methods of this project of casebooks, as well as details of the book titles, can be accessed from the project's own website: www.casebooks.eu.

[31] See, for example, S. Weatherill, 'The Commission's options for developing EC consumer protection and contract law: assessing the constitutional basis' (2002) 13 *European Business Law Review* 497 ff.

[32] See, for example, L. Miller, 'The Common Frame of Reference'; P. Legrand, 'Against a European civil code' (1997) 60 *MLR* 44 ff.; and Hartkamp and Hesselink, *Towards a European Civil Code*.

[33] A broad range of the debates can be found in Hartkamp and Hesselink, *Towards a European Civil Code*.

[34] See, for example, H. Eidenmüller, F. Faust, C. Grigoleit, N. Jansen, G. Wagner and R. Zimmermann, 'The Common Frame of Reference for European private law: policy choices and codification processes' (2008) 28 *OJLS* 659 ff.

heavily in the European literature of modern times and do not need further rehearsal here. Bypassing any direct engagement with such prominent issues, this chapter instead examines the various ways in which the scholar has been a powerful ingredient in the many processes associated with private law harmonisation in Europe today.

An initial observation in this respect is how, from the abundant body of scholarship, the concept of European private law materialises as a 'legal term of art' and an established discipline.[35] Although the precise contours of the discipline may not be yet determined[36] or may remain controversial,[37] legal knowledge has started to be uprooted from the national legal system, and a pan-European intellectual network has truly evolved.[38] Academic cooperation has become a key feature of the development of European private law – a fact that allows one to assert confidently that we are witnessing a Europeanisation of legal scholarship.[39]

Much of the academic activity has organised itself into specific intellectual groupings, with identifiable research objectives for each. There now exists a myriad of academic networks involved in the development of European private law. The following observations on a small selection of these academic institutions give a flavour of how the inevitable

[35] A. Wijffels, 'A new software package for an outdated operating system', in M. van Hoecke and F. Ost (eds.), *The Harmonisation of European Private Law* (Oxford: Hart, 2000), pp. 101 ff., p. 102.

[36] As one German professor puts it: 'Europäisches Privatrecht – aber was ist es?' (cited by Wijffels, 'A new software package', p. 102).

[37] If an unambiguous definition for 'private law' is problematic at the national level, it is not difficult to understand why determining the parameters of a European private law proves elusive. For contrasting definitions of private law within Germany and the United States, see the illuminating discussion in R. Michaels and N. Jansen, 'Private law beyond the state? Europeanization, globalization, privatization' (2006) 54 *Am. J. Comp. L.* 843 ff., 846–53.

[38] For the transformations that such a pan-European outlook to private law has brought to national private law thinking, see M. Hesselink, *The New European Private Law: Essays on the Future of Private Law in Europe* (The Hague: Kluwer, 2002), pp. 46–9.

[39] See R. Zimmermann, 'Europeanization of private law', in M. Reimann and R. Zimmermann (eds.), *The Oxford Handbook of Comparative Law* (Oxford University Press, 2007), pp. 539 ff. For some, this truly European legal research is the triumph of private law's Roman heritage and a revival of a pre-1800 *ius commune*, in which 'a common European legal culture, centred around a legal scholarship and legal practice that were informed by the same sources, did once exist': R. Zimmermann, 'Roman law and the harmonisation of private law in Europe', in Hartkamp and Hesselink, *Towards a European Civil Code*, pp. 21 ff., p. 24. We are therefore witnessing a *re*-Europeanisation of private law, or a *novum ius commune Europaeum*: N. Roos, 'NICE dreams and realities of European private law', in M. van Hoecke (ed.), *Epistemology and Methodology of Comparative Law* (Oxford: Hart, 2004), pp. 197 ff.

cooperation and cross-fertilisation between a number of research institutions create synergetic effects. Such effects assist in the gradual construction of 'carefully crafted building blocs of a larger edifice'[40] the groundwork for a truly European private law

Two notable examples of academic collaboration are private initiatives known as the Commission on European Contract Law[41] and the European Group on Tort Law, each consisting of an independent body of self-selecting academics who, in the fashion of the American Restatements, have produced sets of non-binding principles: the *Principles of European Contract Law* (PECL)[42] and the *Principles of European Tort Law* (PETL),[43] respectively. These publications have been received as landmark events for the development of European private law.[44] Not only do they bolster the impression that the creation of common private law principles is a feasible exercise, but they have a more practical aim. These non-binding sets of principles are intended to act as common frameworks for the further unification of European private law, and perhaps even the precursors to a European Civil Code.[45] The creators of these instruments also intend them to act as sources of inspiration for the further development and improvement of national law. As such, the principles are intended to play a key role in more organic, gradual harmonisation processes as differences between legal systems are gradually eroded. Of course, much will depend on the extent to which the principles work their way into

[40] M. Reimann, 'The progress and failure of comparative law in the second half of the twentieth century' (2002) 50 *Am. J. Comp. L.* 671 ff., 695.

[41] This group is also known as the Lando Commission, after its chairman, Professor Ole Lando.

[42] O. Lando and H. Beale (eds.), *The Principles of European Contract Law: Parts 1 and 2* (The Hague: Kluwer, 2000); and O. Lando, E. Clive, A. Prum and R. Zimmermann (eds.), *Principles of European Contract Law: Part 3* (The Hague: Kluwer, 2003).

[43] See European Group on Tort Law, *Principles of European Tort Law: Text and Commentary* (New York: Springer, 2005).

[44] See, for example, M. Hesselink and G. J. P. de Vries, *Principles of European Contract Law* (Deventer: Kluwer, 2001), p. 11.

[45] PECL, Parts I and II, introduction, xxiv. The PECL were intended to have a variety of uses, including providing an alternative, and neutral, set of contractual principles to be incorporated into contracting parties' contracts, thereby going outside much of the national law that would otherwise be applicable. See C. Twigg-Flesner, *The Europeanisation of Contract Law* (London: Routledge-Cavendish, 2008), p. 14; and B. Koch, 'The "European Group on Tort Law" and its "Principles of European Tort Law"' (2005) 53 *Am. J. Comp. L.* 189 ff., 191. The inevitability of such a legislative instrument is still far from settled but, as we see below, a more tangible contribution to the harmonisation process has been through the use of the PECL as a source for the DCFR. This illustrates the very practical use that can be made of these soft law instruments.

the textbooks, journals, legal education and culture of the various jurisdictions in the European Union. The extent of their influence (particularly the PECL) will also largely depend on whether they are superseded by more ambitious harmonisation projects, such as the elaboration of the CFR.

Another group worthy of mention is the Trento Common Core Project, founded in 1994 by Professors Mauro Bussani and Ugo Mattei.[46] This is the largest existing academic network in Europe today, in terms of the huge number of participants involved in its activities. This research initiative is noteworthy for its methodology. Rather than the development of 'Restatements' or codified principles, the project takes a functional approach to comparative law, focusing on hypothetical fact scenarios, with each scholar documenting the legal resolution from the perspective of his own jurisdiction. In reaching their conclusions, the scholars draw on the entirety of 'legal formants'[47] in each system, thus eschewing the rules-based approach to comparative law. The Trento project differs from the groups previously discussed by virtue of its descriptive, rather than normative, position. It is not concerned with creating a blueprint for harmonisation. Instead, the project is more neutral in its objectives: to map the common core of the bulk of European private law as it stands today,[48] and in this way to promote understanding of the various legal systems across Europe. By publishing their research in individual volumes dealing with the pertinent legal problems of the day, members of the project have provided invaluable tools for a transnational private law education, and the groundwork for a convergence of European private law.

Dovetailing its activities with the European Union's harmonisation programme is the Study Group on a European Civil Code,[49] an independent group of European scholars working on the creation of common European private law principles. This Study Group has been working on the development of common principles in the 'core area of patrimonial

[46] M. Bussani and U. Mattei (eds.), *The Common Core of European Private Law* (The Hague: Kluwer, 2003); M. Bussani and U. Mattei (eds.), *Opening Up European Law* (Munich: Sellier, 2007).

[47] The term 'legal formant' is a neologism for the traditional distinction between 'loi', 'jurisprudence' and 'doctrine' (enacted law, case law and scholarly writing): R. Sacco, 'Legal formants: a dynamic approach to comparative law' (1991) 39 *Am. J. Comp. L.* 1 ff.

[48] See www.jus.unitn.it/cardozo/Common.core/Insearch.html.

[49] See www.sgecc.net. This is the successor to the Commission on European Contract Law. The SGECC uses the PECL as a starting point for its work and has assumed the task of reviewing the PECL.

law'[50] – principles that will 'constitute the most suitable private law rules for Europe-wide application'.[51] More recently, the Study Group has played a prominent part in the elaboration of the DCFR. Responding to the European Commission's call for expressions of interest[52] from the research community to produce a draft CFR, academics from the study group joined together with other research institutions[53] to form a Europe-wide network known as the Joint Network on European Private Law (CoPECL). It is this so-called 'network of excellence' that has been at the helm of the broader programme of EU private law harmonisation, as described at the opening of this chapter. In many ways, the dialogue between academic actors in the elaboration of the DCFR, and the final CFR,[54] is one of the most fascinating aspects of the development of this contract law instrument, highlighting the pan-European academic collaboration in private law as well as the prominent position of the scholar in European private lawmaking.[55] Legal scholarship has become the source of European legal thinking[56] as well as the driving force for its future development.

The creation of this remarkable body of research emphasises the 'softer', more organic approach to the harmonisation of private law.[57] Although the principles, or sets of 'model rules', that result from these academic exercises can in no way be denoted as law, in the formal (or 'hard') sense,

[50] Examples of these are the law of obligations and the law of movable property. As the SGECC states, these areas are less likely to present difficulty in finding common principles since they are not as embedded in the nation's social or political values as other areas of law, such as land law, employment law or family law. Moreover, areas such as the law of obligations are related to the European Union's internal market programme.

[51] See www.sgecc.net/pages/en/introduction/100.aims.htm.

[52] *Official Journal of the European Union*, S 148, 31 July 2004.

[53] The chief ones are the European Research Group on the Existing EC Private Law (Acquis Group) (www.acquis-group.org) and the Restatement of European Insurance Contract Law (www2.uibk.ac.at/zivilrecht/restatement), along with other, smaller, groups. For full details of those involved, see H. Beale, 'The future of the Common Frame of Reference' (2007) 3 *ERCL* 257 ff., 258.

[54] Academic members have been appointed to the 'Expert Group on the CFR' to assist with the elaboration of the political CFR.

[55] It should be noted that the academic's prominence in private law development is controversial and has been the subject of much criticism. The central thrust of most of the discussion concerns the illegitimacy of private law development resting in non-political and unaccountable hands. See the text accompanying note 77.

[56] B. Fauvarque-Cosson, 'The contribution of European jurists to contract law', in M. Andenas, S. Diaz Alabart, B. Markesinis, H. Micklitz and N. Pasquini (eds.), *Liber Amicorum Guido Alpa: Private Law beyond the National Systems* (London: British Institute of International and Comparative Law), pp. 363 ff., 376.

[57] This soft law approach is evidence of a shift away from formalism towards substance in the new European private law: Hesselink, *The New European Private Law*, p. 53.

nevertheless, they are invaluable in instilling the notion that a common European private law can thrive and that legal knowledge can be independent from national legal systems. The existence, as well as the substantive quality, of this body of soft law makes it an ideal tool for the development of European private law education and important elements for debate. Often appearing in casebooks or textbooks on European private law,[58] the soft law principles encourage a slow unifying of European legal culture within legal schools and literature.[59] Moreover, in terms of its authority, one should be wary of drawing too sharp a line between hard and soft law. For example, despite its non-binding character, the DCFR is nonetheless likely to prove 'irresistible'[60] and a potent source of authority for answering questions of private law.[61] In its first few months of life the DCFR has already made an appearance in the 'Opinions' of two advocates-general at the European Court of Justice (ECJ).[62] It is likely that domestic and European courts will have repeated recourse to this soft law text owing to its similarities with a formal civil code. Furthermore, the authoritative status (*imperio rationis*) of a legal text derives not only from its treatment as such by the judiciary, but also from its manipulation by the community of private lawyers as part of the recognised legal discourse.[63] Even if a 'political' CFR does eventually emerge, the expected broader scope of the *draft* CFR means that it will undoubtedly remain as a highly persuasive authority. All of which is likely to guarantee that the academic voice will remain a powerful one in the future European private law.

The proliferation of academic research initiatives and the authority of the work that is produced is clear evidence of the prominent role that the academic has cast for himself in the development of a European

[58] The '*Ius commune* casebook' on contract law (see note 30), for example, includes the PECL at the beginning of each subject heading.

[59] D. Clark, 'Nothing new in 2000? Comparative law in 1900 and today' (2000) 75 *Tulane L. R.* 871 ff., 908.

[60] M. Hesselink, 'The Common Frame of Reference as a source of European private law' (2009) 83 *Tulane L. R.* 919 ff., 923.

[61] For a discussion on the authority of non-legislative texts, see N. Jansen, *The Making of Legal Authority: Non-Legislative Codifications in Historical and Comparative Perspective* (Oxford University Press, 2010).

[62] See A.G. Maduro in C-412/06 *Annelore Hamilton* v. *Volksbank Filder eG* (opinion delivered on 21 November 2007); and A.G. Trstenjak in C-227/08 *Eva Martín Martín* v. *EDP Editores SL* (opinion delivered on 7 May 2009). A national court has also made express reference to the DCFR: Supreme Court of Sweden, Case nr. T 3–08, 3 November 2009.

[63] N. Jansen, 'The authority of an academic "DCFR"', in H.-W. Micklitz and F. Cafaggi (eds.), *European Private Law after the Common Frame of Reference* (Cheltenham: Edward Elgar, 2010), pp. 147 ff.

private law. Not since the time of the debate between Friedrich Carl von Savigny and Anton Friedrich Justus Thibaut in nineteenth-century Germany has the scholar asserted his position so emphatically in law-making and reform.[64] We have yet to consider why European private law has proved such a seductive discipline, however. The growth of scholarship that transcends its territorial boundaries and the eagerness with which scholars have begun to think and act transnationally[65] mark a significant evolution. From one perspective, this enthusiasm may seem surprising. Modern legal scholarship has not been as prone to breaching its territorial boundaries as such other university disciplines as, for example, archaeology, medicine or philosophy. Instead, the reach of legal scholarship has seemed synonymous with political borders,[66] the contours of scholarship mirroring the university curricula that emphasise the national perspective on, for instance, contract, family or public law.

Nevertheless, despite this tendency, the discipline of European private law has clearly caught the imagination of academic circles. Much of the scholarship is conducted by the comparatist.[67] Indeed, as Reinhard Zimmermann observes, 'One can sometimes gain the impression that hardly any project, or study, in the field of comparative private law in Europe is launched today without at least a reference to its utility within the process of Europeanization of private law or private law scholarship.'[68] On closer inspection, the comparatist's engagement with European private law might seem self-evident. The comparative lawyer is equipped with the most suitable intellectual tools to tackle research that will inevitably transcend the boundaries of his own jurisdiction,

[64] The prominent academic role in modern-day lawmaking is not limited to the transnational sphere. In France, the recent proposals for a reform of the French law of obligations and prescription has been drafted entirely by university academics. For a discussion, in English, on this reform, see J. Cartwright, S. Vogenauer and S. Whittaker (eds.), *Reforming the French Law of Obligations: Comparative Reflections on the Avant-projet de Réforme du Droit des Obligations et de la Prescription ('the Avant-projet Catala')* (Oxford: Hart, 2009).

[65] P. Glenn, 'A transnational concept of law', in P. Cane and M. Tushnet (eds.), *The Oxford Handbook of Legal Studies* (Oxford University Press, 2003), pp. 839 ff., 844.

[66] Zimmermann, 'Roman law and the harmonisation of private law in Europe', 21.

[67] The legal historian is also a prominent participant in European private law harmonisation, but takes an interdisciplinary approach, linking the study of European legal history with comparative law.

[68] Zimmermann, 'Europeanization of private law', p. 570. Likewise, the emerging European private law has turned most self-respecting private lawyers into comparative lawyers: Hesselink, *The New European Private Law*, p. 46.

and possesses an agility and familiarity with foreign legal concepts and languages.[69]

Regardless of these considerations, however, the harmonisation of private law has provided the discipline of comparative law with a much longed-for opportunity finally to emerge out of the backwaters of legal academia and assert itself in the academy. It is this factor that might best explain the fascination. Comparative law has been beset with ontological difficulties since the time of the Paris congress of 1900, an event widely considered as the 'birth hour' of modern comparative law[70] in the sense that it was the starting point of methodological and scientific comparative law proper.[71] Since then, debates have abounded over comparative law's justification and status as a discipline in its own right. At times, it has been categorised as simply a methodology. All of which has left it at the periphery of mainstream scholarship. Attempts to bolster its status from within its own ranks have at times been cogently made,[72] but, even today, there remains a legacy of its lack of self-confidence and struggle to define its position to the external world.[73] In this way, the practical project of harmonisation bestows on comparative law a *raison d'être* and a central preoccupation in the modern world.[74] European private law throws

[69] On the other hand, comparative law might be deemed to be an unsuitable discipline for the development and commentary on a transnational discipline. After all, is it not the case that comparative law rests on a framework that is structured around the comparison of *national* systems, and thus could be seen as an obstacle to going that one step further forward and becoming a truly European discipline with its own internal logic? See C. von Bar, 'Comparative law of obligations: methodology and epistemology', in M. van Hoecke (ed.), *Epistemology and Methodology of Comparative Law* (Oxford: Hart, 2004), pp. 123 ff.

[70] Reimann, 'The progress and failure of comparative law', 671; but see also W. W. Hug, 'The history of comparative law' (1932) 45 *Harvard Law Review* 1027 ff.; and C. Donahue, 'Comparative law before the Code Napoléon', in Reimann and Zimmermann, *The Oxford Handbook*, pp. 3 ff.

[71] E. Örücü, 'Methodology of comparative law', in J. Smits (ed.), *Elgar Encyclopedia of Comparative Law* (Cheltenham: Edward Elgar, 2006), pp. 442 ff.

[72] O. Kahn-Freund, 'Comparative law as an academic subject' (1966) 82 *Law Quarterly Review* 41 ff.; B. Markesinis, 'Comparative law: a subject in search of an audience' (1990) 53 *MLR* 1 ff.

[73] See the recent provocatively entitled article by M. Siems, 'The end of comparative law' (2007) 2 *Journal of Comparative Law* 133 ff.

[74] A sense of purpose for comparative law did start to emerge from the Paris Congress in 1900, at which comparative law was seen by some as crucial for fostering the international unification of law. Other jurists saw this as utopian, however. See Clark, 'Nothing new in 2000?', 871. As the title of this article suggests, this author believes that the aims and purpose of comparative law are the same today.

comparative law a much-needed lifeline.[75] One might also suggest that the comparatist's enthusiasm for involvement with harmonisation has a hint of what could be termed the 'Napoleon syndrome' – for, as Napoleon Bonaparte himself seemed to perceive, there is nothing for which one might be better remembered than the elaboration of a written code that will appear in the annals of legal history.[76]

Such legal prominence raises vital questions about the legitimacy of legal development resting in non-political hands, however, spurring vehement criticism from some circles. The Social Justice Manifesto, for example, has bemoaned the academic involvement in the drafting of the DCFR owing to the political as opposed to scientific nature of private law creation. Democratic processes are therefore deemed vital for the development of a European private law.[77] Moreover, and in relation to this last point, the programme of lawmaking, such as that involved in the (D)CFR, is aimed at establishing a unified structure of legal thinking; it is part of a process of creating a private law system. As seen above, the reform and construction of private law systems have always had associations with the state. Even in a world in which the nation state is losing power to other forms of institutional configuration, lawmaking should be tied closely to mechanisms of governmental representation through the institutional channels of the European Union, rather than be left in the hands of the jurist.

[75] The engagement and – perhaps one might even deem it – usurpation of the harmonisation project by comparative law could suggest that the discipline has had new life breathed into it. Nevertheless, although harmonisation should have been the catalyst for rethinking the discipline because of the epistemological complexities involved, some commentators contend that, unfortunately, comparative law has remained in an underdeveloped state: see Reimann, 'The progress and failure of comparative law', 694. One might consider that the harmonisation project has obfuscated just how little the discipline has evolved since the time of the Paris Convention. See also G. Samuel, 'English private law in the context of the codes', in Hoecke and Ost, *The Harmonisation of European Private Law*, pp. 47 ff.

[76] Napoleon is said to have enthusiastically proclaimed, from exile in Saint Helena, 'Ma vraie gloire n'est pas d'avoir gagné quarante batailles. Waterloo effacera le souvenir de tant de victoires; ce que rien n'effacera, ce qui vivra éternellement, c'est mon Code civil.'

[77] As this group of scholars states, '[L]egal scholars would frankly admit that many of the more interesting experiments in national contract law were the product of democratic legislatures and that the expertise that is required for the creation of European contract law needs to be able to embrace democratic legislative processes and interventions': Study Group on Social Justice in European Private Law, 'Social justice in European contract law', 663. For recent arguments about the need for democratic legitimacy in private law, see F. Rödl, 'Private law beyond the democratic order? On the legitimatory problem of private law beyond the state' (2008) 56 *Am. J. Comp. L.* 743 ff.

One might have sympathy with these complaints.[78] This 'democratic deficit' objection becomes more fragile, however, when it is remembered that lawmaking is a collaboration between the jurist and the legislator, the former providing the groundwork for any final legislative document enacted by the latter. Any academic contribution is subject to political acceptance, and the final document that emerges may differ substantially from its academic predecessor.[79] Furthermore, one might find persuasive counter-arguments in leaving the task of system-building to academia,[80] particularly if one accepts the contention that democratic principles are unnecessary if law can be found in abstract principles. The formulation of doctrine and systems is something to be developed with criteria 'internal' to the law: technical precision, adequacy and internal coherence. Such criteria are independent of political authority.[81] Lastly, and by way of conclusion to this short account of the academic contribution to European private law, one should remember that the academic has always played an ancillary part in lawmaking and reform in Europe. On the transnational stage, where the complexities of political agreement multiply the difficulties in lawmaking, academic expertise might well be something to embrace rather than lament.

13.2 European private law and the judiciary

In examining the less visible processes in the development of a European private law, brief mention should also be made of another legal actor at work – one to whom a role in the softer side of harmonisation can also be attributed: the judge. Beyond the constitutional functions given to the judge at the ECJ,[82] he is less often perceived as an instrumental player in

[78] For similar concerns about the political legitimacy of such academic involvement in lawmaking, see also Y. Lequette, 'Quelques remarques á propos du projet de code civil europeén de M. von Bar' (2002) 28 *D. chron.* 2202 ff.; and P. Deumier, 'La doctrine collective législatrice: une nouvelle source du droit?' (2006) 4 *RTDC* 63 ff.

[79] This process is clear from the example of the CFR. As mentioned in note 7, the (academic) DCFR is to be followed by a (political) CFR. The political instrument that finally emerges will be a very different document from its academic predecessor.

[80] The SGECC website asserts that 'jurists themselves should venture the construction of a pan-European codification of private law because only those trained in the discipline can pursue the essential task of intensive comparative research free from the constraints of representing national interests and accommodating political expediency' (www.sgecc.net/pages/en/introduction/88.background.htm).

[81] Jansen and Michaels, 'Private law and the state', 396.

[82] This chapter looks beyond the judicial role in harmonisation through mechanisms such as the doctrine of direct effect, the doctrine of interpreting national law in conformity

the processes of harmonisation. Nevertheless, through the increasing practice of dialogue between courts across the world, and with an openness to engage in comparative law,[83] the judge is becoming remarkably willing to look outside his jurisdiction and to borrow ideas from other courts. In addition, the modern judge is a far more mobile and social individual, sacrificing the intellectual and physical comfort of his own jurisdiction to engage actively in external programmes and cooperate with other courts. The prevalence of both these forms of interaction, and the dissemination of the ideas that it fosters, is a further dimension in the convergence of private law. Judges are not usually driven by any desire to build harmonised or global legal systems but, instead, by more prosaic concerns, such as heavy caseloads and increasing transnational litigation. Nonetheless, through dialogue and cooperation, they help to dissipate the natural hostility to the private law of another system. As such, these practices provide an additional element to which this chapter devotes some attention.

Let us first make some brief observations concerning the physical interaction. In much the same way that the academic networks described above have been responsible for private law scholarship being uprooted from its national environment, similar processes of interaction and contact between judicial actors can be seen to be a conduit for the transmission of ideas and, ultimately, have the potential to approximate private law. Although, at first blush, this geographical displacement may appear simply as an opportunity to sample the delights of another European city, it is nonetheless significant that judges are becoming increasingly favourable to the idea of face-to-face contact with their brethren in other jurisdictions. These opportunities to meet, both informal and formal, develop the ideal breeding ground from which intellectual barriers can be penetrated and understanding across jurisdictions can grow.

Such meetings have at times been given institutional form, giving some credence to how valuable the practice is perceived to be. For example, an international non-governmental organisation known as the European Judicial Training Network[84] was established in 2000 with the aim of

with EU law and state liability for incorrect implementation. The ECJ has been a potent force in harmonisation through these strategies: see A. Johnson and H. Unberath, 'Law at, to or from the centre? The European Court of Justice and the harmonisation of private law in the European Union', in F. Cafaggi (ed.), *The Institutional Framework of European Private Law* (Oxford University Press, 2006), pp. 149 ff.

[83] B. Markesinis and J. Fedtke, 'The judge as comparatist' (2005) 80 *Tulane L. R.* 11 ff.

[84] See the website of the EJTN: www.ejtn.net/www/en/html/index.htm.

promoting training programmes and exchanges (physical and virtual alike) for the European judiciary within the borders of the European Union.[85] Its goal is an improvement in understanding between judges and prosecutors – important ingredients for the fracturing of intellectual barriers and the development of a common understanding across jurisdictions. In addition to this initiative there is the Lisbon Network,[86] another example of institutionalised cross-border 'dialogue' between national judicial institutions in Europe, this latter example established under the aegis of the Council of Europe. Again, the aim is to establish an infrastructure for cross-border understanding and the exchange of information. Although neither of these initiatives is directly channelled towards harmonisation, they are both concrete examples of how continuing processes of cross-fertilisation across jurisdictions are likely to engender a platform for mutual understanding and increasingly give rise to a visible consensus on various issues.

The circulation of judicial ideas and personnel operates in spontaneous ways as well, however. Many national judges seek contact with their peers as a way to exchange information and establish 'best practices' in their particular areas of law (for example, the Association of European Competition Law Judges). Often physical meetings are arranged through the conference format, and a process of continual learning is set in motion. Loose networks such as these occur because of a growing awareness of common problems in a globalising world, and because of a responsiveness to the real limitations of national solutions to transnational problems.

Unlike the academic collaboration described above, however, the judicial networks described thus far have little *direct* concern with private law. Much of the judicial interaction, both physical and intellectual, takes place in the sphere of human rights.[87] Private law seems to be a less natural area of convergence on the judicial stage. Explanation for this might be located in the way that human rights tend to be perceived as the protection of citizens against the state. This makes the topic a more attractive candidate for transnational discourse, since it can be readily justified as an autonomous body of law independent from the state.[88] Another reason for the lack of visibility of private law in such forums might be the

[85] In 2008 approximately 550 exchanges took place, either through judges being placed at certain courts or through individually tailored projects.

[86] See the network's website: www.coe.int/lisbon-network.

[87] There are also some notable examples in administrative law, however: see J. Schwarz, *European Administrative Law* (London: Sweet & Maxwell, 1992).

[88] See Jansen and Michaels, 'Private law and the state', 355.

professional identity of the judges who populate the supranational and international courts. Such judges are commonly drawn from the ranks of those specialised in international and public law, or those who have held office in public administrations.[89]

One might therefore expect that the development of a European private law owes little to such collaborations.[90] Judicial networking, in whatever sphere of law that it operates, rides in tandem with an intellectual cross-fertilisation that has a tendency to seep into all legal disciplines, however. This in turn encourages judicial practices, including in the area of private law, that transcend national legal borders. For example, although it might be difficult to gather hard empirical evidence, physical contact between judges is likely to have a corollary psychological impact, making judges feel part of a European (or international) judicial community.[91] These trends are all likely to contribute to an increase in what is known as judicial transplantation, or the borrowing of legal ideas – a practice that can be seen to operate in private law. Going hand in hand with a willingness to engage in comparative law, the practice of judicial borrowing has become a prevalent factor in the legal landscape today. It plays a role, if a subsidiary one, in the harmonisation of private law. This 'free trade in legal ideas'[92] is compounded through more modern forms of technology, making judicial transplants a far more feasible enterprise. Technological advances in communication, such as the internet, make access to, and thus knowledge of, foreign law a far less daunting process. At the touch of a few keys, information that only very recently would necessitate weeks to discover is revealed immediately. With access to foreign law facilitated, resort to it becomes more prevalent.

Judges may be becoming less reticent about looking elsewhere for legal solutions, but the motivations that underpin their enthusiasm are diverse and often difficult to identify. It is certain that much can be attributed to the lack of a solution in their own jurisdiction. Tried and tested ideas from abroad provide a convenient and potentially rich source of ideas to be plundered, particularly when they might provide a remedy to the

[89] See Caruso, 'Private law and state-making'.

[90] It has already been seen how private law might be deemed a far less natural candidate for transnationalisation, or denationalisation, owing to the way that it has been traditionally perceived as embedded in the identity of the state.

[91] It must not be forgotten how joint membership of international organisations such as the Council of Europe and the European Union is prone to decrease psychological barriers to 'foreign' law.

[92] O. Kahn-Freund, 'On uses and misuses of comparative law' (1974) 37 *MLR* 1 ff., 10.

problem of a legal 'black hole'.[93] The use of a foreign solution could also act as a convenient guide for the modernisation of local law. In instances such as these, judicial actors do not possess any broader motivation than the internal workability of the system and the ability to benefit from the authority that an already-tested principle provides. Borrowing therefore often owes as much to pragmatism as to anything else.

Nevertheless, there are indications that the porosity of judicial borders has led to instances in which the judge is mindful of wider law reform and conducts his borrowing with the broader picture of harmonisation as a backdrop. In the House of Lords[94] decision of *Fairchild*,[95] for example, Lord Bingham put the legal issue at hand (the issue of double or multiple causation) in a wider perspective, extensively examining the case law from a whole spread of jurisdictions, including civil law jurisdictions as well as European private law doctrine.[96] The comparative foray enabled his lordship to conclude that, although a convergence in socio-economic cultures has been responsible for similar problems in Europe, a whole range of legal responses nonetheless exist. He found that, in light of his review of other jurisdictions, English law might not present the most acceptable solution. Rather, 'if…a decision is given in this country which offends one's basic sense of justice', then English law could be fine-tuned in light of more acceptable decisions elsewhere. After all, '[i]n a shrinking world…there must be some virtue in uniformity of outcome'.[97]

[93] See, for example, *Alfred McAlpine Construction* v. *Panatown* [2001] 1 AC 518. See also *White* v. *Jones* [1995] 2 AC 207.

[94] The House of Lords does not have a monopoly on this practice of mutual learning across jurisdictions, but it is, rather, that the style of judgment is more able to incorporate arguments and solutions from other jurisdictions. In contrast, the cryptic judgment of the civilian jurisdictions, particularly France, does not permit disclosure of the ownership of an idea. There is no overt use of foreign law. Moreover, citation of any academic or foreign source would be grounds for a legal challenge (*pourvois*) in France. 'En France, la cour de cassation et les autres juridictions sont structurellement contraintes par le style d'écriture traditionnel de l'arrêt à phrase unique et l'impossibilité de l'explication interprétative de la règle, à ne pas se référer expressément aux droits étrangers dans le corps même de l'arrêt': G. Canivet, 'Le juge entre progrès scientifique et mondialisation' (2005) 1 *RTDCiv* 33 (cited by Markesinis and Fedtke, 'The judge as comparatist', 29).

[95] *Fairchild* v. *Glenhaven Funeral Services Ltd and others* [2003] 1 AC 32.

[96] In particular, Lord Bingham referred to C. von Bar, *The Common European Law of Torts*, vol. II (Oxford University Press, 2000); and B. Markesinis and H. Unberath, *The German Law of Torts: A Comparative Treatise* (Oxford: Hart, 2002).

[97] *Fairchild* [2003] 1 AC at 66.

13.3 Conclusion

The harmonisation of private law in Europe is a challenging task. The challenge has both a conceptual dimension and a practical dimension. The emergence of a new site of private lawmaking, with a normative logic (the internal market) that differs from that at the national level, forces us to reconsider the legitimacy, validity and accommodation of private law arrangements beyond the state. Such transnational processes have also unsettled orthodox understandings of the 'private' and the 'public', and in turn should compel us to question the extent to which such concepts remain fitting for the post-national constellation. The development of a common European private law is also a task of daunting practical proportions, however, not least because of the diversity of private law rules that exist as the background to any harmonisation attempt. This chapter has explored the softer side to harmonisation, showing how the academic and judicial contributions to lawmaking and reform have played an enormous part in fostering a climate of cooperation and mutual learning and assisted in breaking through the frames of national private law. If harmonisation is to mean anything more than simply a semantic exercise in the creation of common legislative rules, it is these 'bottom-up' processes that will lay the groundwork on which a truly European private law can rest.

INDEX